The Financial Crisis of Our Time

FINANCIAL MANAGEMENT ASSOCIATION

ROBERT W. KOLB

The Financial Crisis
of Our Time

OXFORD
UNIVERSITY PRESS

2011

OXFORD
UNIVERSITY PRESS

Oxford University Press, Inc., publishes works that further
Oxford University's objective of excellence
in research, scholarship, and education.

Oxford   New York
Auckland   Cape Town   Dar es Salaam   Hong Kong   Karachi
Kuala Lumpur   Madrid   Melbourne   Mexico City   Nairobi
New Delhi   Shanghai   Taipei   Toronto

With offices in
Argentina   Austria   Brazil   Chile   Czech Republic   France   Greece
Guatemala   Hungary   Italy   Japan   Poland   Portugal   Singapore
South Korea   Switzerland   Thailand   Turkey   Ukraine   Vietnam

Published by Oxford University Press, Inc.
198 Madison Avenue, New York, New York 10016

www.oup.com

Library of Congress Cataloging-in-Publication Data
Kolb, Robert W., 1949–
The financial crisis of our time / Robert W. Kolb.
p.   cm.
Includes bibliographical references and index.
ISBN 978-0-19-973055-1 (cloth : alk. paper) 1. Financial crises—United States—History—20th
century. 2. Financial crises—United States—History—21st century. I. Title.
HB3743.K58 2011
330.973—dc22
2010015648

9 8 7 6 5 4 3 2 1

Printed in the United States of America
on acid-free paper

CONTENTS

The economic crisis that began in 2007 has changed the economic lives of Americans and many people around the world. By any measure, this financial crisis of our time is one of the most important economic events of the last century, and compared to all other economic and financial upsets since the Great Depression, it is surely the most significant. Like the Great Depression itself, these current financial problems, already dubbed the Great Recession, are proving to have profound social significance as well.

There are already many signs that the economic and social derangements caused by the crisis have affected the way that people think about their economic lives, their living habits, and their fundamental values. For example, we Americans have been notorious for our high consumption and low savings rate. Yet that behavior seems to have changed in just a few months. Contrary to our former love of conspicuous consumption, newspapers feature the joy of frugality that many of our fellow citizens claim to have discovered. Whether such new habits will persist will be revealed in time, and for the present these accounts may certainly occasion skepticism. However, such uncertainty about the meaning of the interesting times in which we live is characteristic of all evolving social phenomena of any significance. On any understanding, the events through which we are now living are sure to have profound importance.

Millions of individuals have lost very substantial portions of their wealth. With broad U.S. stock market measures having declined a full 50 percent from their recent peaks, the losses have touched almost everyone. While the markets have rebounded considerably from their low in March 2009, they are far from a full recovery. Further, the collapse of stock market values scared many from the markets altogether, so they failed to participate in the partial rebound that has occurred. As a result, many Americans, as well as many abroad, are changing their life plans and postponing their long-anticipated retirements.

Additionally, there is the prospect that these shattering financial events may change attitudes toward risk-taking. The United States has long been a vital source of the world's innovation and entrepreneurship, and increasing fear of risk may cause that source of wealth creation and human betterment to falter. The lives of those who lived through the Great Depression were often transformed by that experience, with a resulting focus on saving and financial conservatism, along with a general fear of risk. By contrast, the children of the Great Depression's generation have generally exhibited a striking confidence and optimism about the future. Presently there are many signs that this positive attitude toward investment and the future may be lost. These signs of vast psychological adjustment may prove to be merely temporary, or they may be profound and enduring.

Today the role of business and commerce in our society is under revision and a renewed attack. Vociferous protests rage against high levels of compensation. Many think that the unbridled pursuit of profit led to the economic crisis with its resulting enormous adverse effects on the real economy. Factory workers who have lost their jobs see a causal connection leading directly from a greedy pursuit of profits, high levels of compensation, and flagrant risk-taking, on the one hand, to their own very real financial difficulties, on the other. Each new round of business distress brings with it an increase in government scrutiny and a new wave of regulation. This was certainly true after the corporate scandals of the early 2000s, and all of the signs today suggest that there will certainly be more vigorous regulation of financial firms, including their compensation of executives. Further, it seems that this crisis may provide an important impetus for global cooperation in regulation, a movement that was already in progress before the present difficulties.

The current financial crisis is a social phenomenon of a kind similar to the Great Depression, the Enclosure Movement in England of the nineteenth century, or the economic awakening of China in our own day. While our financial crisis is unlikely to be of the same magnitude, it is nonetheless a development that alters the lives of millions. Like these and many other social events or movements that change the lives and perceptions of millions of people, the financial crisis of our age will be the subject of study and debate for decades. The public at large, professional economists, policy experts, public intellectuals, and the citizenry are all struggling to understand the crisis that has washed over us. Everyone has an interest in understanding its meaning for our lives, and many efforts have already sprung up to attempt to identify the causes of the crisis.

To some extent, it has become a sport to identify *the cause* of the financial crisis. Various single-cause explanations focus alternatively on personal and corporate greed, global imbalances between suppliers and demanders of investment funds, excessive liquidity in the financial system, low interest rates and weak monetary policy at the Federal Reserve, poor lending practices at financial institutions, predatory lending by rapacious financial institutions, mortgage fraud by housing speculators, too little regulation, too much regulation, or a faulty process of generating new securities. Ultimately, few people believe that any single one of these causes can account for the entire disaster, and many fall back on the metaphor of a "perfect storm" to emphasize that many factors operated together to generate the financial crisis. In contrast to those who seek to emphasize a single cause of the current crisis, this book moves from a broad study of the economic history of our times to focus on several decisive changes. In addition to exploring the causes of the current crisis, the book provides the reader with a comprehensive review of the context within which these events unfolded.

This book argues that no single such cause can be identified. At the same time, however, virtually all analysts agree that housing finance played a central role in the events that have come to dominate our lives. For example, those who focus on excessive liquidity as a primary cause of the crisis typically also note that the resulting loose cash was directed toward housing and helped to inflate the pricing of residential real estate. While realizing that no giant social phenomenon can have a single cause, this book also argues that the events of 2006–2009 cannot be understood without comprehending the mechanism by which the housing industry came into crisis. Those events essentially began in

2006 as residential real estate prices peaked and then started to fall, threatened the world's largest and most respected financial institutions beginning in 2007, and confronted the real economy with serious problems and even disaster in 2008, leading to profound unemployment that persisted through 2009 and well into 2010. In briefest terms, this book offers part of the answer to the big question: "Why would millions of dopes, geniuses, saints, scoundrels, and ordinary people all work together to lose trillions of dollars?"

Whatever one chooses as a favorite candidate for *the cause* of the crisis, this book further argues that any account must consider the housing finance system as it developed throughout the twentieth century, and especially in the period from 1990 to 2006. The account must also examine the participants in the new industrial organization of housing finance. As the book will show, the movement from an originate-to-hold to an originate-to-distribute model of mortgage financing confronted market participants with an entirely new array of incentives that proved to be a "clockwork of perverse incentives." That is, the perverse incentives of all of the participants in the new world of mortgage finance—including borrowers, mortgage brokers, appraisers, loan originators, securitizers, due diligence firms, rating agencies, ultimate investors, legislators, and bureaucrats—fit together in a manner that constituted an intricate mechanism or clockwork. The unique feature of this system was that the various participants, simply by responding individually to the incentives that lay before them and pursuing their narrow personal interests, participated in an elaborate mechanism that led to disaster. Unlike clockwork, however, there was no overall architect or designer for the system of housing finance that led to ruin. Instead, the system was an unhappy organic production of many individuals, groups, and forces.

After briefly discussing the industrial organization of housing finance and the older originate-to-hold model, which will serve as a contrast, the book proceeds to a narrative of the crisis as it developed and continues by analyzing the participants in the originate-to-distribute model, starting with the home buyer and ranging through to the ultimate investors in CDOs—collateralized debt obligations. At each step, and as shown in the table of contents, the book explains in a nontechnical manner the essential relationships among the market participants and zeroes in on the incentives facing each party. Thus, one primary contribution of the text is to analyze the incentives facing all the actors in the originate-to-distribute mortgage cycle, because only by understanding the incentives that various parties confronted can we understand their behavior and its ultimate effect.

The book is organized as follows. Chapter 1, *Introduction*, reviews the structure of U.S. residential real estate markets as it developed in the twentieth century and discusses its economic and regulatory features. In doing so, this chapter provides the necessary background for understanding the financial and regulatory innovations that played such a central role in the current crisis. For example, the chapter examines the growth in the rate of home ownership and the economic changes and government policy that stimulated that growth. As later chapters will reveal, the push for ever more widespread home ownership had its own important role to play in generating the crisis.

Chapter 2, *From Securitization to Subprime*, discusses two models of industrial organization for the mortgage market. Following World War II and lasting until the late twentieth century, the U.S. mortgage market followed an *originate-to-hold* model of mortgage production. In briefest terms, a prospective home buyer applied to a local financial institution, typically a savings and loan association (S&L). If the loan was granted, the S&L then held that mortgage in its own portfolio for the full life of the mortgage, which was typically 30 years. While this model worked quite well in many respects, technical aspects of the model eventually came to be seen as retarding growth in home ownership. With public policy directed toward stimulating home ownership, the originate-to-hold model was eventually supplanted by the *originate-to-distribute* model. Under this approach, the initial lender (such as the S&L in the originate-to-hold model) would initiate a mortgage loan and then immediately sell that loan to another financial institution, and the homeowner's payments on the mortgage would be used as the financial basis for that purchaser to issue new securities. This is the process of *securitization*—using the cash flows from one set of securities as the financial basis to issue a completely new second set of securities with quite different characteristics, a process explained in chapter 2. Chapter 2 also explains the reasons for the transition from the originate-to-hold to the originate-to-distribute model and briefly explains the elements of the more complicated originate-to-distribute model, especially the critical role of securitization.

Chapter 3, *Before the Deluge*, considers the false paradise that preceded the financial crisis. In that apparently happy state, ours was a world of expanding home ownership, low interest rates, readily available credit, and escalating home prices. Much of this comforting illusion was driven by subprime lending, and this chapter chronicles the rise of subprime up to the peak of housing prices that occurred at about the end of 2006. We all now know that this world of illusion was merely the prelude to disaster.

Chapter 4, *From the Subprime Crisis to Financial Disaster: An Overview*, quickly surveys the development of the crisis, starting from the housing peak. The chapter provides a synoptic view of the buildup to the crisis, considers the architecture of the governmental response to the crisis, and takes the narrative up to the point at which the threat to the entire economy began to diminish. All of the themes introduced in this chapter are explored in more detail in the chapters that follow.

Chapters 5 through 8 focus on individual major firms that played prominent roles in the crisis. Chapter 5, *Extinctions*, turns the spotlight on major depository institutions that disappeared from the scene through outright failure or acquisition. Countrywide Financial, perhaps the most notorious of giant subprime lenders, was absorbed by Bank of America. In one of the largest bankruptcies in history, the Federal Deposit Insurance Corporation (FDIC) seized IndyMac, which had been spawned by Countrywide. In a deal brokered by the FDIC, JP Morgan Chase (often referred to in this book and elsewhere as just "JPMorgan") acquired the huge Washington Mutual, another subprime lender that rivaled Countrywide in size and scope. Citigroup, itself among the walking wounded, reached an agreement to take over Wachovia National Bank, based on promised assistance from the FDIC. At the last minute, Wells Fargo entered the scene and wrested Wachovia away from Citigroup, making Citi one of the luckiest losers in the entire financial crisis. (Citi would prove to have its own near-death experience, as chapter 7 explains, and was actually in no position to take on another large firm with a bad mortgage portfolio.)

Chapter 6, *The End of Investment Banking*, chronicles the sudden disappearance of an entire industry. Before the crisis, five firms—Goldman Sachs, Morgan Stanley, Merrill Lynch, Lehman Brothers, and Bear Stearns—dominated the industry. In a period of six months, all five firms either disappeared entirely or suffered a major change in corporate form. The federal government helped JPMorgan acquire Bear Stearns; Lehman declared bankruptcy; and Merrill Lynch collapsed into the arms of Bank of America. Facing the blast of the financial crisis, even august Morgan Stanley and brash Goldman Sachs ran to the Federal Reserve for protection, and they became bank holding companies, swallowing their pride and accepting a more intrusive regulatory regime, all in order to improve their access to additional capital.

There is a twilight between survival and failure occupied by zombies—the undead dead, or alternatively, those who are actually dead, but refuse to acknowledge that fact.

Chapter 7, *When Zombies Walk the Earth*, focuses on firms that refused to die or that did die and refuse to bear witness to their own passing. These are once proud firms with tremendous market capitalizations that almost disappeared. For all of them, their stock prices reached the one dollar range, and most continue to trade at a price near that level. Fannie Mae and Freddie Mac, two *government-sponsored enterprises* (GSEs), continue to hold more than $5 trillion in mortgages, yet they are in conservatorship—a more polite word for bankruptcy that governments like to use when discussing their failures. AIG and Citigroup, two quite disparate firms, are united by both being zombies.

Chapter 8, *Policy Responses and the Beginnings of Recovery*, considers the broad array of governmental responses designed to forestall the crisis and avert another Great Depression. This is a story of a desperate struggle characterized by hasty plans, initial missteps, retrenchments, and ever deeper intrusion of the government into previously private sectors of the economy. But these were desperate times, and the failure to act seemed to offer only certain disaster. As the chapter discusses, this array of policy initiatives, bailouts, and rescues is certainly subject to the most severe criticism. But somehow it does seem that the financial system and the economy have survived, and it may very well be that the governmental response is the only thing that staved off utter disaster. While it is easy to criticize the actions taken, a fair analysis must also acknowledge that the situation was completely unprecedented and that economic theory offered little sure guidance. While the path taken to recovery was almost surely not the ideal one, there is no way to say what that ideal response would have been.

Writing in the first half of 2010, it does now seem that we are beginning to step out of the shadow of financial and economic disaster, and it has become clear that, over the last century, the economic consequences of the financial crisis are second only to the Great Depression. But it is now possible to begin to assess the causes of the crisis. While thankfully not matching the Great Depression in scale and scope, our own financial crisis is a social phenomenon of enormous proportions with many causes. Chapters 9 through 14 are devoted to assessing these causes.

Chapter 9, *Causes of the Financial Crisis: Macroeconomic Developments and Federal Policy*, begins the analysis by considering the broad-scale economic movements and federal policy choices that helped to bring about the crisis. A variety of macroeconomic policies and developments all played a causal role, including: a policy of economic stimulus designed to bring the United States out of the dot-com bubble, persistently low interest rates, a low savings rate in the United States coupled with a high savings rate in developing Asian countries and excessive liquidity in financial markets. On the housing policy front, a decades-long and accelerating policy of efforts to expand home ownership also contributed to causing the crisis by expanding home ownership beyond those individuals and families that were actually financially capable of owning their own home.

Chapter 10, *Causes of the Financial Crisis: The Failure of Prudential Regulation*, evaluates those institutions and policies that were supposed to restrain private economic activity that might lead to financial difficulty. Thus, while chapter 9 considers the federal policies that pushed toward disaster, chapter 10 analyzes the failure of federal policies and institutions meant to prevent financial excesses. The chapter focuses on the failure to successfully regulate depository institutions, securities markets, credit rating agencies, accounting rules, the development of financial innovations, and oversight of the mortgage market.

Chapters 11 and 12 offer a more detailed analysis of the problems inherent in the originate-to-distribute model of mortgage production. Chapter 11, *Causes of the Financial Crisis: From Aspiring Home Owner to Mortgage Lender*, focuses on the initial part of the production chain, while chapter 12, *Causes of the Financial Crisis: From Securitizer to Ultimate Investor*, explores the creation of securities and follows them through to the ultimate investor. For both chapters, the analysis concentrates on the inherent incentive conflicts that pervade virtually all elements of the entire mortgage-production process. Further, the discussion shows that these conflicts were essentially absent from the old originate-to-hold model. For example, in the old model the mortgage lender, typically an S&L, would originate a mortgage and hold it in its own portfolio for 30 years. Consequently, the originator had every incentive to ensure that the borrower could pay as promised and that the property really was worth more than the amount being lent. In the originate-to-distribute model, the initial lender makes the initial loan with the intention of selling it immediately. As a result, the incentives become quite different, with the probity of the borrower and the value of the collateral becoming much less important. Not surprisingly, these new incentives helped lead to the creation of many mortgage loans that lenders never should have made, and these bad loans set up home buyers for default. As the two chapters show, similar transformations of incentives pervade the entire chain of participants in the originate-to-distribute model. In spite of its role in our spectacular financial mess, securitization can bring major benefits to financial markets. In the aftermath of the financial crisis, securitization remains moribund, so the challenge going forward is to revitalize securitization in a way that avoids these pervasive incentive conflicts.

Chapters 13 and 14 turn to an examination of the causal role of financial firms. Chapter 13, *Causes of the Financial Crisis: Financial Innovation, Poor Risk Management, and Excessive Leverage*, shows how new financial instruments served to heighten risk, explains how firms thought they had superb risk management when they did not, and illustrates how an excessive reliance on faulty techniques of risk management led firms to increase their financial leverage—to borrow more money to invest in risky securities. (Financial leverage arises when a firm or investor borrows money, couples those borrowed funds with existing funds, and invests the total. It is called leverage, because this policy increases the effect of both good and bad outcomes, just as a small movement on one end of a lever can cause the other end to move a great distance.) As seems to happen quite frequently with the development of new and more complex financial instruments and strategies, these innovations were not as well understood by their creators as they thought. After initial apparent successes, these elegant mathematical financial innovations ultimately failed to perform as advertised in real-world markets, especially when markets came under stress. These disappointments played a major role in fomenting the crisis.

Chapter 14, *Causes of the Financial Crisis: Executive Compensation and Poor Corporate Governance*, turns the spotlight on failures at the most elevated levels of corporate management, namely the boards of directors of financial institutions. These boards, whose members typically include the titans of the financial industry, are charged with the high-level management of their firms and with putting in place the right top management, giving these managers their marching orders, and ensuring that those managers perform as instructed. The current financial landscape, littered as it is with corpses of large firms and financial zombies stumbling about, bespeaks tremendous managerial failures. This chapter questions the incentives that boards put in place for CEOs, other top managers, and financial traders, and shows how those incentives played into creating the crisis. Finally, the chapter takes the actual financial results that lie before us as conclusive evidence of massive managerial failure that pervaded the largest and supposedly most sophisticated financial firms in the world.

Chapter 15, *Consequences of the Financial Crisis and the Future It Leaves Us*, concludes the book. This chapter assesses the likely lasting economic consequences of the financial crisis. At present, there is an inchoate movement to change the regulatory system of the financial industry, as if fine-tuning the present system could solve our problems. The chapter briefly surveys those incipient efforts and questions whether such regulatory innovations are likely to help prevent the next crisis, particularly in light of the massive policy and regulatory failures that first stimulated the crisis and then failed to prevent its full development. Finally, the chapter offers a brief and preliminary assessment of the role that the financial crisis is playing in the standing of the United States in the world, both in terms of its economic position and geopolitical power.

Acknowledgments

For many of us who work in finance, the development of the financial crisis has consumed our attention for the last many months. I would like to thank three of my colleagues at Loyola for the many discussions we have had of the events as they unfolded: George Kaufman, Tassos Malliaris, and Don Schwartz. George, Tassos, and Don also read the manuscript of this book and offered many useful comments and suggestions. Ron MacDonald read and edited the entire book in page proofs and made valuable corrections.

Because I wanted this book to be useful to both finance specialists and a wider audience, I imposed on a number of friends from many walks of life to read the manuscript as well. These included a health professional, a U.S. bankruptcy judge, a political philosopher and classicist, and business managers. They were all generous with their time and kind with their suggestions and criticisms, so I extend my great appreciation to Wayne Ambler, Tom Bugnitz, Diane Dimeff, and Leslie Tchaikovsky. My wife, Lori, also read the book in manuscript and helped me to improve the presentation of ideas. Several finance colleagues at other universities—Don Chance, Sungiae Kim, and Tung-Hsiao Yang—helped me gain access to difficult-to-obtain data. Also, my graduate assistant, Ejov-wokoghene (Ejus) Biakolo, helped mightily with his rapid fact-checking and data-management skills. To all of you, my great appreciation. The usual disclaimer applies to the present book with full force: While I much appreciate everyone's efforts to help me improve the book, I alone remain responsible for any errors or failures to heed their advice.

Bob Kolb
Chicago
April 2010

ABS	Asset-backed security
AIGFP	AIG's Financial Products Division
ARM	Adjustable-rate mortgage
AUS	Automated underwriting system
CBO	Congressional Budget Office
CDO	Collateralized debt obligation
CDS	Credit default swap
CMO	Collateralized mortgage obligation
CPP	Capital purchase program; part of TARP
CRA	Community Reinvestment Act of 1977
FDIC	Federal Deposit Insurance Corporation
FHFA	Federal Housing Finance Agency
GSE	Government Sponsored Enterprise
HMDA	Home Mortgage Disclosure Act of 1975
HUD	Department of Housing and Urban Development
LIBOR	London Interbank Offered Rate
LTV	Loan-to-value
MBS	Mortgage-backed security
NRSRO	Nationally recognized statistical rating organization

OFHEO	Office of Federal Housing Enterprise Oversight
OTD	Originate-to-distribute
OTH	Originate-to-hold
S&L	Savings and Loan Association
SEC	Securities and Exchange Commission
SIV	Structured-investment vehicle
SPE	Special-purpose entity
SPV	Special-purpose vehicle
TALF	Term Asset-Backed Securities Loan Facility
TARP	Troubled Asset Relief Program
VaR	Value-at-Risk

The Financial Crisis of Our Time

Introduction: The Financial Crisis of Our Time

We can understand the broad arc of housing finance and policy over the last one hundred years as the repetition of a process: stable and slow development, followed by a crisis and regulatory response, with each innovation laying the foundation for an ensuing period of renewed stability, which leads to a new crisis. From this perspective, the current crisis originated in the response to the previous upset, and it is necessary to understand the previous crisis and the response to that event to comprehend our present state. This way of looking at the problem suggests an infinite regress of explanation, so picking a historical starting point for the analysis is somewhat arbitrary. Nonetheless, it seems reasonable to begin with the situation as it stood just before the watershed events of the Great Depression, because that economic disaster and the regulatory response to it set the basic conditions that eventually led to our present difficulties.

For our purposes it is useful to divide this preliminary discussion into four historical periods:

- Before the Great Depression
- From the Great Depression to financial deregulation

- From financial deregulation to the savings and loan crisis
- The development of securitization.

This chapter surveys the first two of these periods, roughly from the pre-1930s until the 1980s. Financial deregulation here refers to the gradual dismantling of the restrictions on financial markets and institutions that were put in place during the Great Depression. Chapter 2 covers the 1980s through the development of securitization, roughly from the 1980s up until 2002. Securitization is a topic that runs throughout the book, but here we offer a very casual definition: *securitization* is a process that uses cash flows promised from one set of financial instruments to provide the financial wherewithal to back a completely new set of financial instruments. Thus, payments from a collection of mortgages provide cash flows, and ownership of those cash flows can be carved up in a variety of ways, and title to these new patterns of cash flows can be sold as new financial instruments with characteristics that differ radically from the original mortgages. Chapter 3 surveys the illusory happy time before the crisis in the subprime market. The remainder of the book focuses exclusively on the subprime crisis, which subsequently became a much broader crisis—the financial crisis of our time.

Before the Great Depression

Early in the twentieth century, banking regulation was much more lax than it is at present. Even though the Office of the Comptroller of the Currency had been established in 1863 as a department of the U.S. Treasury and has overseen all commercial banks holding a national charter since that time, the Federal Reserve System was established only in 1913. In the United States there has long been a parallel system of state-chartered and nationally chartered commercial banks. State governments allow commercial banks to operate by granting a state bank charter, while at the national level, the U.S. Comptroller of the Currency in the Department of the Treasury grants national charters. Mortgages were generally made by insurance companies or savings and loan associations, rather than commercial banks.

For our purposes, the most important feature of this mortgage finance environment was the structure of these mortgages in comparison with what we might call a touchstone mortgage—the most typical mortgage form in the twentieth century. Let us define a *touchstone mortgage* as a mortgage that has a 30-year life, a fixed rate of interest, level payments, requires a significant down payment of about 20 percent, and is self-amortizing. This touchstone mortgage, therefore, has 360 equal-dollar payments. A portion of each payment repays the principal on the loan with the remaining portion paying the interest for the month. Because the payment is the same each month, the early payments consist mainly of an interest payment with a very small portion of each early payment reducing the principal. Over time, these proportions change, such that by the end of the 30 years virtually the entire payment goes toward reducing the principal.

Compared to this touchstone mortgage, mortgages before the Great Depression had extremely unusual features. Most mortgages in this early era had a floating rate of interest and a short term of five to ten years. Further, the payments on these loans typically covered only the interest, so the entire principal balance was due at the maturity of the loan. In addition, the mortgage loan amount relative to the value of the property, the loan-to-value (LTV) ratio, was usually less than 50 percent.[1]

These terms were advantageous for the lender, particularly the requirement that the value of the property had to be large compared to the loan amount. But these features often required borrowers to renegotiate the loan frequently, particularly as few borrowers would be able to save the entire principal balance during the short life of the loan so that they could pay off the entire value of the home at the loan's termination. Thus, this kind of loan was susceptible to the phenomenon known as "crisis at maturity"—an event that occurs when a borrower is able to make the sequence of small early interest payments, but is unable to pay the large balloon amount at the loan's maturity.

In a stable environment, the loan could be renegotiated and continued, but the structure of the loan gave the lending institution the option to terminate the relationship at maturity and demand full repayment. Failing such repayment, the lender could seize the property and expect to recoup its full loan amount, which was, after all, only half the value of the property at the time the loan was initiated.

Designed for the safety, comfort, and convenience of a lender in a stable market, this design set the stage for disastrous defaults in a time of stress, which the Great Crash in October 1929 and the onset of the Great Depression provided in an extreme form, with the bank runs—the sudden widespread customer withdrawals of deposits—of that era. Property values plunged by almost 50 percent from their peak, so lenders were unable or disinclined to refinance the loans at all, and they certainly were unwilling to lend the previous full amount on the same property that now might be worth only the amount of the earlier loan. As a result, lenders refused to renew the loans and demanded full payment of the principal. Borrowers, of course, were also under extreme stress of their own and were often unable to pay as promised. Bank deposits were not insured at this time, so a common experience befell many borrowers with home mortgages: they lost their bank deposits when their bank failed, they lost their income when their employer failed, and they faced a demand for payment of the full principal balance on their home loan.

The consequence was a widespread wave of defaults, property seizures by lenders, and desperate efforts at subsequent resale—a practice that only helped to drive home prices lower. From 1931 to 1935 there were typically 250,000 foreclosures per year, and at its worst time, the Great Depression saw almost 10 percent of homes in foreclosure.[2] This model, which had seemed so safe and conservative from the lender's point of view, proved to have very serious problems for both lenders and borrowers, and this experience led to a federally inspired transformation of the mortgage finance market in the United States.

From the Great Depression to Financial Deregulation

Before the Great Depression, the financial industry in the United States was lightly regulated. During the 1930s the federal government erected an edifice of regulation that remained in place until the late 1970s and early 1980s, at which time a process of financial liberalization, or deregulation, began. Intense federal management of the mortgage and home finance industry dates from the Great Depression. One action taken by the Hoover administration in 1932 was the passage of the Federal Home Loan Bank Act. This act created a system of Federal Home Loan Banks to be supervised by the Federal Home Loan Bank Board (FHLBB). By creating this system, the government hoped to provide liquidity to savings and loan associations (S&Ls), to stimulate mortgage lending and to regulate the conduct of federally chartered S&Ls. The act initiated a policy of restricting deposit rates for commercial banks and S&Ls, allowing them to make only longer-term mortgages at fixed rates, and limiting S&L lending to a 50-mile radius, thereby making them purely local institutions. Subsequent legislation established the Federal Savings and Loan Insurance Corporation (FSLIC) to guarantee deposits in S&Ls and to act as a companion agency to the Federal Deposit Insurance Corporation (FDIC), which guaranteed the safety of deposits in commercial banks.[3]

In 1933, with the accession of the Roosevelt administration, the federal government established the Home Owner's Loan Corporation (HOLC) and financed this new institution with government-issued bonds. The HOLC used these funds to buy mortgages that were in default and to reinstate the mortgages with drastically new terms. In essence, they converted the old-style mortgages into a form very much like our touchstone mortgage, except that the typical maturity was only 20 years, rather than 30. From 1933 to 1936 the HOLC processed one million loans in this manner and was then allowed to pass out of existence.

A potential home mortgage lender in 1933, having just witnessed a massive wave of defaults and foreclosures—a situation similar to, but even worse than the circumstances that prevailed in our present crisis— would certainly exhibit a reluctance to lend. To stimulate home mortgage lending, the federal government created the Federal Housing Administration (FHA) in 1934 to provide protection to lenders in the case of a home owner's default. The borrower pays for this insurance through payments on the mortgage, and the FHA guarantees payments on the mortgage to the lender. All FHA-insured mortgages have the essential features of our touchstone mortgage, and the widespread prevalence of this mortgage form stems from the intervention of the federal government during the Great Depression.[4]

The Federal National Mortgage Association (FNMA), now known as Fannie Mae, was initiated in 1938 to stimulate a secondary market for mortgages. Fannie issued bonds and used the funds to purchase mortgages. This available outlet for lenders to dispose of mortgages made them more willing to lend in the first place. With Fannie Mae in operation, S&Ls could lend, create a mortgage loan, sell the loan to Fannie Mae, and use the funds to make another loan. However, from its inception through 1948, Fannie purchased only 67,000 mortgages in total, and fewer than 7,000 in 1948. This contrasts with housing starts that were always at least close to 100,000 per year and had approached one million in the peak year of 1925. Therefore, these beginnings were quite modest, had little early impact on the housing market, and gave little indication that Fannie would grow to a firm with assets of $882 billion, or mortgage investments of almost 3 trillion dollars—or that it would become a firm that could lose $58 billion in a single year.[5]

These emergency actions emerged from the crucible of the Great Depression, and at the same time, the federal government began to develop a consciously articulated policy to foster home ownership. Within weeks of his inauguration, President Franklin D. Roosevelt asked Congress to pass legislation to relieve the housing markets and to protect home ownership, saying on April 13, 1933: "Implicit in the legislation which I am suggesting to you is a declaration of national policy. This policy is that the broad interests of the Nation require that special safeguards should be thrown around home ownership as a guarantee of social and economic stability, and that to protect home owners from inequitable enforced liquidation, in a time of general distress, is a proper concern of the Government."[6]

While the enactment of specific legislation to promote home ownership initiated a more activist era, Roosevelt was, to some extent, giving voice to an attitude that already prevailed. After all, President Herbert Hoover had already called the owner-occupied home ". . . a more wholesome, healthful, and happy atmosphere in which to raise children." While federal activism in the housing market may stem from the 1930s, it has been sustained for the last 75 years, with broad support from presidents and other politicians of both parties. For example, against the background of the urban blight of the 1960s, President Lyndon Johnson asserted that ". . . owning a home can increase responsibility and stake out a man's place in his community. . . . The man who owns a home has something to be proud of and reason to protect and preserve it." For his part, President Ronald Reagan said that home ownership ". . . supplies stability and rootedness."

In spite of launching explicit support for home ownership in the 1930s, there appeared to be little impact for many years. Figure 1.1 shows the decade-by-decade percentage of Americans living in their own homes and reveals a slight decline from the 46.5 percent of 1900 to the 43.6 percent on the eve of World War II, although this lack of growth was no doubt due to a drop of 4 percentage points in the home ownership rate during the Great Depression. As the figure also shows, home ownership rates never took off until after World War II, and this postwar surge was almost certainly due principally to the rapid formation of families after the war and the great increase in wealth that began at this same time, rather than being caused by federal policies.

However, by the early 1990s, the growth in home ownership stagnated, with almost no growth in the ownership rate for the ten years that preceded the Clinton presidency, which began in 1993. When President

Figure 1.1 Percentage of Americans Living in Homes They Own
Source: U. S. Census Bureau, Housing Vacancies and Homeownership, http://www.census.gov/hhes/www/housing/hvs/historic/index.html

Clinton said that ". . . more Americans should own their own homes, for reasons that are economic and tangible, and reasons that are emotional and intangible, but go to the heart of what it means to harbor, to nourish, to expand the American Dream,"[7] he was merely giving further voice to a long-standing consensus of U.S. policy leaders. Consistent with the tradition of previous thinking on the importance of housing, Clinton advanced the general policy more aggressively with his National Home-ownership Strategy in 1994, which had the explicit purpose of driving home ownership to unprecedented heights. Clinton's Department of Housing and Urban Development put the point this way: "At the request of President Clinton, the U.S. Department of Housing and Urban Development (HUD) is working with dozens of national leaders in govern-ment and the housing industry to implement the National Homeownership Strategy, an unprecedented public-private partnership to increase home ownership to a record-high level over the next 6 years."[8] This specific goal was achieved, but it also led directly to the present economic disas-ter, as we will see in later chapters.

If we think of a household budget, certain proportions must be allo-cated to various categories such as food or housing. To a considerable degree, those proportions are flexible, but they can never be completely arbitrary and so are malleable only to a certain degree. Poor households (and poor societies) spend a higher proportion of income on food and must therefore spend less on other goods and services. One way of understanding the crisis in housing is by considering whether the proportion of incomes devoted to purchasing housing behaved in an erratic or unsustainable way. Viewed from this standpoint the question is: Was the run-up in housing prices in the early 2000s and the subsequent house price collapse due to an unsustainable allocation of an ever higher proportion of income to home purchases? Of course, there is no one "right" proportion of personal income to be devoted to housing, but it is possible to consider trends and departures from previous allocations.

Figure 1.2 shows the historical relationship between disposable income and U.S. median home prices and takes three starting points, 1963, 1988, and 2000 as alternative norms. The longest line of figure 1.2 covers 1963–2008 and takes the ratio of disposable income to the median home price in 1963 as being equal to 1.0. From that starting point, the line reflects how the relationship between incomes and housing prices varies in subsequent years. (This initial starting point of 1963 was chosen because comparable data between income and home prices begin only at that time.) As figure 1.2 shows, that ratio has been above 1.0 ever since, even during the recent years of rapid home price expansion. This means that even during the "bubble" years, Americans, on average, were spending less of their income on housing than they were in 1963. (Also of interest, the quality of housing has improved tremendously over this period, with houses being larger, having more bathrooms, and having a generally higher level of finish than houses built in 1963.)

However, if we take different starting dates as the norm, figure 1.2 shows quite a different picture. The middle line of figure 1.2 takes 1988 as a norm of 1.0 and considers the next 21 years to the end of 2009. Similarly, the bottom line starts from a norm of 1.0 for 2000. For recent years, both lines dip well below 1.0, indicating that median home prices grew compared to incomes.

This graph suggests that the ratio of incomes to median home prices was never completely unsustainable, especially compared to 1963, as incomes relative to median home prices have always been higher than they were in 1963—even at the height of the housing bubble. However, compared to a starting point of 1988, and compared especially to a starting point of 2000, home prices accelerated substantially compared to incomes. This rapid acceleration of home prices relative to incomes in recent years may imply an unsustainable level of housing spending, especially if other portions of household budgets were relatively fixed by long-term commitments.

It is also important to emphasize that figure 1.2 pertains to the United States as a whole and does not consider various income groups or locations. We have already noted that lower income households typically devote a higher percentage of their incomes to essentials such as food, thereby limiting the proportion of income that they can choose to devote to housing. While housing may not have been disproportionate to incomes for the entire population compared to historical experience, it may well be the case that certain demographic groups committed an unsustainable portion of their income to home purchases. As a final point about the line starting in 2000, it shows that housing prices rose very rapidly compared to incomes up to the housing peak in 2005–2006, but since that time the ratio of income to housing expense has rebounded very rapidly. At the end of 2009, the graph shows that incomes were higher than they were in 2000 compared to housing prices.

For most of the post–World War II period, figures 1.1 and 1.2 present a fairly optimistic view of more Americans living in their own homes[9] and of relatively less disposable income being devoted to housing. Most

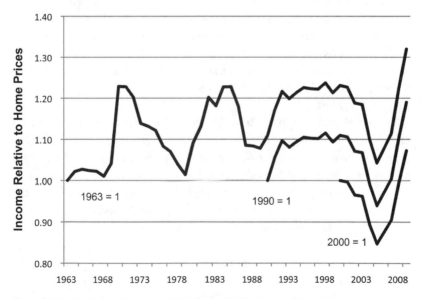

Figure 1.2 U. S. Disposable Income Relative to Median Home Prices
Source: Bureau of Economic Analysis, Personal Income and Its Disposition, Monthly, U.S. Census Bureau, Median and Average Home Prices, and author's calculations.

of this period was dominated by the institutions created during the Great Depression as described above. On the assumption that stability, increasing home ownership, and expanding incomes relative to housing costs were good results, this policy worked remarkably well through the 1950s, 1960s, and most of the 1970s.

From Financial Deregulation to the Savings and Loan Crisis

The process of deregulating financial institutions and markets in the United States began in 1979–1980 and was a response in part to problems that had emerged with the regulatory regime established during the Great Depression. The post–World War II era was a period of remarkable financial stability in the United States, but in the 1970s the financial system started to show new signs of stress, with two major recessions occurring in that decade. Real estate loans came under pressure, and the failure rate of banks increased from their previously very low levels. While the recession of 1973–1975 had been particularly severe, the recession that began in 1978 caused great difficulties for financial institutions. Market interest rates rose a full 10 percent above the regulated deposit rates (about 4–5 percent) that banks and S&Ls were permitted to pay, and deposits flowed away from these institutions into new deposit vehicles, such as money market accounts with interest rates that were not regulated. At the same time, virulent inflation came to the fore in 1979, and interest rates shot upward to unprecedented heights, as figure 1.3 shows.

For a depository institution that could pay only a fixed rate of interest mandated by government fiat and that was restricted to making long-term fixed rate loans, rising interest rates held fatal potential. These trends were particularly problematic for S&Ls, which were trying to attract savers with a government-mandated low rate of interest at a time when rates in other sectors of the market were quite high. Further, S&Ls held most of their assets as long-term fixed-rate mortgages. This situation threatened the S&Ls with an inability to attract enough deposits to fund their existing assets and made it virtually impossible to secure new deposits that they could lend to create new mortgages. Largely in response to this crisis, the early 1980s saw the passage of several laws that were particularly important in rearranging the regulatory landscape for depository institutions.

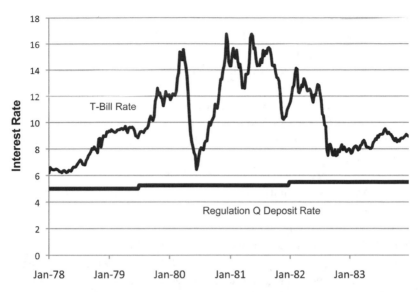

Figure 1.3 The Surge in Interest Rates
Source: http://www.federalreserve.gov/releases/h15/data/Weekly_Friday_/H15_TB_M3.txt

In 1980, the Depository Institutions Deregulation and Monetary Control Act (DIDMCA) became law. This act began the process of eliminating the control of depository interest rates, a deregulation that was phased in over the period of 1981–1986; it allowed S&Ls to make consumer loans for the first time in history; it preempted various state usury laws, so lenders could charge a market rate of interest on commercial and mortgage loans; it authorized credit unions holding a federal charter to start making mortgage loans; and it allowed S&Ls and credit unions to offer checking accounts. At the same time, the law allowed commercial banks to enter the real estate lending market more aggressively, an arena that previously had been a more protected preserve of S&Ls.

The second major piece of legislation in this era was the Garn–St. Germain Depository Institutions Act of 1982 (GSGDI). Its purpose was largely embedded in its full title: "An Act to revitalize the housing industry by strengthening the financial stability of home mortgage lending institutions and ensuring the availability of home mortgage loans." From 1980 to 1982 the situation with S&Ls had worsened, largely due to very high interest rates. But technological change and increasing competition from nonbank financial institutions also contributed to the woes of S&Ls. While the GSGDI Act gave regulators new powers to deal with troubled institutions, it also liberalized the environment in which S&Ls could operate. For the first time, S&Ls were permitted to offer money market demand accounts (MMDA)—basically, checking accounts—so that they could compete with money market funds. The act allowed federal S&Ls to expand their commercial and consumer loan portfolios, and it broadened the range of permitted investments for S&Ls as well.[10]

A third piece of legislation, the Alternative Mortgage Transaction Parity Act of 1982, finally ended the decades-long restriction of mortgage lending's regulated resemblance to the touchstone mortgage described above, with its long-term to maturity, fixed-rate, and self-amortizing features. Key provisions included the overriding of state laws and explicitly allowing mortgages with adjustable rates, mortgages with balloon payments, and interest-only mortgages. These three laws had a major impact in liberalizing the financial landscape, and with their provisions fully implemented, the regulatory landscape for the kind of mortgage loans available today were largely in place.

While external events—high interest rates, high inflation, and rapid technological change in the finance industry—had all brought depository institutions into difficulty, these new laws also increased competitive pressures, particularly for small and less sophisticated financial institutions, such as smaller S&Ls. Renewed recession in 1981 contributed to the stress on all depository institutions, and the S&L industry suffered particularly acutely. While commercial banks remained profitable, return-on-equity for S&Ls was negative across the industry at about -15 percent in 1982. Clearly the industry could not bleed at that rate for very long and continue to exist.

These developments set the stage for a spectacular debacle. Under the aegis of the environment established from the 1930s on, S&Ls had operated within a regulatory cocoon that protected them from competition and external market realities. Now, in the extremely challenging financial circumstances of the early 1980s, they were largely unshackled, but they were also exposed to the blast of competition from larger and more sophisticated financial institutions.

S&Ls still held portfolios that consisted mainly of mortgages that had been issued with the mandated long-term and low fixed rates of the preceding era of more intense regulation. As a result, they were being asked to compete in a new financial age while saddled with underperforming legacy assets from a previous period. Many S&Ls found themselves with a business plan that would imply certain failure in the absence of new, unfamiliar, and risky ventures, such as commercial lending and other new lines of business. Some institutions on a glide path toward bankruptcy grasped at the hope of hitting it big on risky ventures with the potential to change their fates. These included investments in casinos, fast-food franchises, junk bonds, interest rate derivatives, ski resorts, and windmill farms.[11] Perhaps not surprisingly, for the industry as a whole these efforts met with general failure. At the same time, the new more relaxed regulatory landscape encouraged the formation of new S&Ls with the specific intention of making full use of the full range of new S&L powers.

In the next few years, the industry as a whole continued to move toward disaster, with the failure of an increasing number of institutions. At the same time, the implementation of the remaining regulatory structure was reduced, with slashes in the budget for the FHLBB examination function. In spite of its limited resources, the FHLBB was well aware of the brewing problems. In an effort to save the industry, regulators implemented a policy of "regulatory forbearance"—a phrase that means little else than neglecting to enforce existing regulations. In addition, regulators abandoned the imposition of Generally Accepted Accounting Principles (GAAP) and adopted a more lenient regime of Regulatory Accounting Principles (RAP). In essence, institutions that were failing under GAAP could be made to appear alive, or at least comatose, under RAP.[12] These policies allowed the existing problems to mushroom. Table 1.1 gives a clear picture of the crisis of the S&L Industry.

As more and more S&Ls failed, the FSLIC was called upon to redeem ever more deposits, and it became insolvent by the end of 1986. The FSLIC had been funded with assessments on S&Ls, so its payouts had not yet cost taxpayers directly. However, the depletion of FSLIC funds and continuing S&L failures threatened to leave taxpayers on the hook for these new costs, and the government's effort to deal with the crisis had not yet fully accelerated.

In many respects, the real resolution of the crisis began in 1989 with the passage of the Financial Institutions Reform, Recovery and Enforcement Act (FIRREA). This act abolished the previous regulatory structure for S&Ls, so the FHLBB and the FSLIC passed out of existence. The Act created the Office of Thrift Supervision (OTS) to replace the FHLBB, and the FDIC took over the deposit insurance role of the now deceased FSLIC. The act also established the Federal Housing Finance Board

Table 1.1

The Savings and Loan Industry in Crisis

	1981	1983	1985	1987	1989
Number of S&Ls	3,751	3,146	3,246	3,147	2,878
S&L Failures	34	51	54	59	190
S&L Mergers	269	117	57	79	N/A
Insolvent S&Ls	112	55	705	672	516
Industry Profits (billions)	−$4.6	$1.9	$3.7	−$7.8	−$17.6

Source: FDIC, *History of the Eighties: Lessons for the Future, Volume I: An Examination of the Banking Crises of the 1980s and Early 1990s*, 1997, Chapter 4, "The Savings and Loan Crisis and Its Relationship to Banking," 167–188. See specifically pp. 168–169.

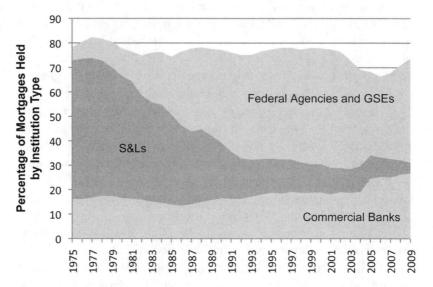

Figure 1.4 Proportion of Outstanding Mortgages Held by Commercial Banks, S&Ls, and Government Agencies
Source: Board of Governors of the Federal Reserve System, "Federal Reserve Statistical Release, Z.1, Flow of Funds Accounts of the United States"; published: March 6, 2008; http://www.federalreserve.gov/releases/z1/20080306/.

(FHFB) to supervise the twelve federal home loan banks, and it established the Resolution Trust Corporation (RTC) to dispose of failed thrifts and their lingering assets and liabilities.[13] In a somewhat unrelated move, FIRREA gave Fannie Mae and Freddie Mac a new mandate to support mortgage lending to lower-income families—an initiative that became an important part of the subprime story, as we will see.

The troubles of depository institutions—particularly the difficulties that beset S&Ls—had already transformed the mortgage lending landscape by 1990. Figure 1.4 shows that in 1975 commercial banks and S&Ls between them held 73 percent of all mortgages in the United States, with S&Ls holding more than 56 percent of all mortgages. Government agencies and government-sponsored enterprises (GSEs), such as the Government National Mortgage Association, Fannie Mae, and Freddie Mac held a 5 percent sliver of the market among them. (The remaining 22 percent was divided among insurance companies, pension funds, finance companies and so on.) By 1990, these four players (banks, S&Ls, federal agencies, and GSEs) still held about 78 percent of all mortgages. During these 15 years the proportion held by banks stayed steady, but the role of S&Ls was cut by more than one-half, down to 22 percent. At the same time, the agencies and GSEs portion grew from 5 to 38 percent.

The cleanup of the S&L crisis took a full decade, from the passage of FIRREA in 1989 to 1999. Estimates of the entire cost of the debacle have varied widely, but perhaps the most representative estimates are in the range of $150–160 billion, including about $130 billion of federal taxpayers' funds.[14] Even though the S&L cleanup was just getting underway in 1990, the depository institutions' industry reached an important milestone. In 60 years, the industry traveled from a lightly regulated industry at the onset of the Great Depression, to a tightly regulated industry operating under quite severe restrictions from 1933 to 1980, to a disaster for the thrift part of the industry from 1979 to 1989, and through a period of deregulation in response to that disaster that largely freed these institutions from many restrictions on the lines of business they could enter and the types of loans they were allowed to make. The new rules of the 1980s instituted a new regulatory structure of supervising and insuring depository institutions, as we have seen. The industry was ready for the next big thing, and that proved to be securitization.

From Securitization to Subprime

The Development of Securitization

Within the living memory of many in the United States—that is, until about 1980—there was no subprime mortgage market and very little securitization of mortgage financing in the contemporary sense. Instead, the creation of mortgages was a fairly simple matter, with few participants and a structure that was easy to understand. The market was dominated by—or even almost entirely constituted by—an originate-to-hold (OTH) model of mortgage production. The principal actors involved in producing mortgages were the prospective mortgagor (the home buyer) and a lending institution that funded the mortgage loan, which was usually a local S&L. The entire process was circumscribed by a somewhat stifling regulatory regime, with S&Ls being tightly regulated at both the state and federal level, as we have seen in chapter 1. The type of mortgage that was available conformed very closely to what we have called a touchstone mortgage—one characterized by a 30-year maturity, level payments, self-amortization, and requiring a hefty down payment.

Acquiring a mortgage typically required a prospective home buyer to visit a financial institution, usually an S&L, to complete an application.

After the applicant completed the mortgage, the S&L would carefully review the application and verify the representations made by the home buyer, especially with regard to the applicant's creditworthiness, sufficiency of assets, adequacy of down payment, and salary and other terms of employment. In addition, the S&L would investigate the property that was to serve as collateral for the loan, typically hiring its own appraiser to report on the condition and value of the property. Once satisfied with the financial probity of the borrower and the value of the collateral, the S&L would issue the mortgage.

If the S&L granted the loan, the property would be in the geographically confined service area of the S&L—the 50-mile radius permitted by regulation. Further, the S&L would typically hold the mortgage in its own portfolio of assets for the life of the loan and would service the loan itself by collecting payments on the loan, including escrow payments for taxes and insurance. The S&L would fulfill this role within a structure of elaborate regulation enforced by both state and local regulatory authorities. Figure 2.1 depicts the structure of this relatively simple institutional arrangement—the originate-to-hold (OTH) model of mortgage production.

This system of mortgage finance grew up in the aftermath of the Great Depression, came into full flower with the growing wealth of the United States in the 1950s–1970s, and reached its full potential before 1975. Nothing if not conservative, this institutional arrangement for

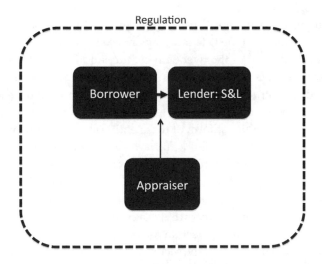

Figure 2.1 The Originate-to-Hold Model of Mortgage Production

housing finance served the public fairly well, but by the mid-1970s some important limitations had become quite obvious, in addition to the critical susceptibilities to high interest rates that we have already considered.

As long as the S&L used the deposits it received from the local community to fund housing purchases and held those mortgages to their maturity, the growth in housing finance was constrained to match the growth in deposits at the S&L, and the deposit growth for each S&L roughly paralleled the growth of the local economy in which it operated. As a consequence, S&L deposits tied up in funding a particular mortgage represented dead money during the life of the loan, in the sense that those deposits could not be used to expand home financing any further.

The federal government has long been concerned with stimulating mortgage lending and in ensuring that potential home buyers have good access to mortgage funding. As we have seen, this activist approach came to prominence with New Deal legislation during the 1930s, as represented by the National Housing Acts of 1934 and 1938. These acts and subsequent legislation created a number of governmental and quasi-governmental entities that will be a continuing part of our story. These include the Federal Housing Administration (FHA), the Federal National Mortgage Association (FNMA, or Fannie Mae), the Federal Home Loan Mortgage Corporation (FHLMC, or Freddie Mac) and the Government National Mortgage Association (GNMA, or Ginnie Mae), all of which played important roles in developing the securitization of mortgages.

In total, these government or governmentally sponsored institutions have dominated the U.S. mortgage market from the Great Depression through the rest of the twentieth century and into the twenty-first. Together they have largely determined the types of mortgages that can be offered, the structure of the market in which those mortgages are traded, and the way in which mortgages have come to be securitized. However, the institutional form of these entities has changed over time, as has their various roles, and a full accounting of their histories and functions would occupy a complete book in itself. Therefore, we will follow the development of securitization, bringing a brief account of these agencies into the analysis as necessary.

A *mortgage-backed security* (MBS) is a security that represents a claim on the cash flows from a collection, or pool, of underlying mortgages, which serves as collateral for the security. A mortgage is *securitized* when it is included in a pool of mortgages that act as collateral for the issuance of a new security based on that pool. The simplest and earliest form of MBS was a mortgage *pass-through* security. Consider a firm that buys many mortgages and forms a portfolio of mortgages by collecting those purchased mortgages into a pool. That firm might then sell a *pass-through* security, or *participation certificate*, to various investors. The purchase of that pass-through represents a fractional interest in the entire pool of mortgages, and the pass-through purchaser receives a proportional share of all of the payments that are made by all the mortgages in the pool. Thus, each month the payments from all the mortgages are collected and then passed through to the owners of the pass-through securities.

The firm that pools the mortgages and issues the pass-through securities acts as the *securitizer* or *arranger*. In many instances, the securitizer may also be the originator, so commercial banks and S&Ls are active as both originators and securitizers. The securitizer must be paid for its services as well, so it collects a fee that is paid before the pass-through certificate holders receive their payments. In addition, the firm that services the mortgages (collects the mortgage payments, handles the escrow account for insurance and taxes, and so on) also receives a fee. Finally, many mortgages that find their way into these pools have mortgage insurance, which guarantees payment of the promised mortgage payments to the purchaser of the pass-through, so there is a guarantee fee as well in such a situation. These fees are relatively small, so it is fairly accurate to think of a pass-through security as giving a fractional ownership right to the mortgage payments that come from all the mortgages in the pool.

These first MBS originated in 1970 with Ginnie Mae, which was created in 1968 when the functions of the already extant Fannie Mae were partitioned by Congress. The essential function of Ginnie Mae is to guarantee the timely payment of all promised cash flows from mortgages. As an agency of the U.S. government, Ginnie Mae's guarantee is backed by the full faith and credit of the U.S. Treasury. Ginnie Mae restricts its guarantees to mortgages that are insured by the Federal Housing Administration (FHA), the Department of Veteran Affairs (VA), the Department of Agriculture's Rural Housing Service, or HUD's Office of Public and Indian Housing. Of these, FHA and VA mortgages represent the overwhelming majority.

Ginnie Mae merely provides guarantees, but it does not buy or sell mortgages, and Ginnie Mae deals with mortgage pools that contain various types of mortgages. While the dominant type is our touchstone mortgage, GNMA pass-throughs also exist on adjustable rate and other types of mortgages as well. Because GNMA merely guarantees mortgage payments, but does not own mortgages, the mortgages that comprise the pool are held by another party. The securitizer initially commits its capital to create the pool and is anxious to sell the pass-through certificates to free its capital for other purposes. Over its life, Ginnie Mae has insured almost $3 trillion of mortgages in total.[1]

The provision of the GNMA guarantee was designed to play an important social role in stimulating the housing market. The guarantee helped to make securitization possible, because it gave pass-through investors confidence that they would receive payments as promised. In effect, the GNMA guarantee substituted the promise of the federal government for the promise of both the mortgagors represented in the pool and the securitizer. Relying on the GNMA pass-through structure, the originator of the mortgage can put the mortgage in a pool and sell pass-throughs based on the pool. This returns the originator's capital, which can then be used to grant other mortgages. Without securitization, the mortgage market remains trapped in the situation we described for the S&L that originates and holds mortgages for the duration of the mortgage.

While the GNMA pass-through structure has been quite successful in terms of meeting a market test, it suffers from two important limitations. First, the GNMA guarantee is available to relatively few mortgages, essentially only to FHA and VA mortgages. Further, GNMA requires that mortgage pools be very homogenous in terms of the mortgages in a given pool, and this too limits the creation of pass-through securities. A second limitation is that of risk. Although the iron-clad, fully backed guarantee of GNMA makes the pass-throughs free of default risk, it does not eliminate one other very important kind of risk—prepayment risk.

Consider a pool of mortgages issued at an interest rate of 10 percent. Pass-throughs based on that pool might be expected to pay 10 percent (less fees) to investors over the life of the mortgage. However, every mortgagor has the right to prepay the mortgage at any time. If interest rates drop below 10 percent, then home owners may elect to refinance at the new lower rates and pay off the 10 percent mortgage. In such a situation, the holder of the pass-through suffers no loss from default, but the prepayment terminates the 10 percent rate of interest that the investor was receiving and returns the principal to the pass-through investor. This return of principal leaves the investor holding cash and facing a lower interest rate environment in which he must invest. As we will see, prepayment risk was instrumental in stimulating more sophisticated types of MBS.

Fannie Mae and Freddie Mac have also been extremely important players in the MBS market in general, as well as in the creation of pass-through certificates. Fannie Mae was created in 1938 as part of the Federal Home Mortgage Association and was given a charter by Congress to provide liquidity and stability to the U.S. housing market. In 1968, its charter was changed to make it a government-sponsored entity (GSE). A GSE is a legal entity created by the U. S. government to undertake business activities with a public purpose, and each GSE has some degree of governmental control, combined with private ownership. Thus, a GSE has a status that is not fully private, yet not fully public. After noting that there is no "fixed meaning" to the term, the Congressional Budget Office (CBO) defined a GSE in the following manner:

> Broadly defined, a GSE is a corporation chartered by the federal government to achieve public purposes that has nongovernmental status, is excluded from the federal budget, and is exempt from most, if not all, laws and regulations applicable to federal agencies, officers and employees. . . . Narrowly defined, a GSE is a privately owned, federally chartered financial institution that has nationwide operations and specialized lending powers and that benefits from an implicit federal guarantee that enhances its ability to borrow.[2]

The status of Fannie and Freddie contrasts with that of Ginnie Mae, which is an agency of the U.S. government, backed by the full faith and credit of the U.S. government. Congress chartered the Federal Home Loan Mortgage Corporation (FHLMC, or Freddie Mac) in 1970 with a charter that was quite similar to that of Fannie Mae.

Historically there has always been some question as to the extent of the government's commitments to Fannie Mae's and Freddie Mac's obligations. In the event of financial difficulty, would the federal government pay Fannie's debts? The markets have always acted as though there was an "implicit guarantee" of Fannie's and Freddie's debts, and this belief allowed them to borrow at very low rates in the capital markets. This is effectively a subsidy from the taxpayer to Fannie and Freddie, an issue that is considered more fully in chapter 7.

Fannie Mae and Freddie Mac operate in the housing market by buying mortgages and issuing debt securities to finance those purchases.

Their activities channel investment from the larger capital markets to the U.S. housing market. As Fannie Mae describes its key business activity: "We make mortgage funding available at all times and under all economic conditions, so our lenders will always have funds available for home buyers."[3] Part of the public mission of Fannie and Freddie has been explicitly to increase home ownership, to expand the supply of "affordable housing," and to expand access to home ownership to minorities and "underserved communities."

Fannie and Freddie historically have bought only certain kinds of mortgages that meet their underwriting standards, and such mortgages are called *conforming* mortgages. To qualify for purchase by Fannie or Freddie, a mortgage must not exceed a certain principal amount, must not have too great a loan-to-value (LTV) ratio, and the mortgage payment must not be too great relative to the homebuyer's income. Mortgages that do not meet these requirements are *nonconforming* mortgages. (For many years, Fannie Mae and Freddie Mac purchased only conforming loans, but they expanded their activities to the subprime market in the second half of the 1990s in a small way, and soon grew to be major players in this area. This expansion into subprime probably contributed to the real estate bubble and certainly increased their losses.)

In essence, Fannie Mae, Freddie Mac, and Ginnie Mae have all been involved in the same kind of activity—channeling funds from the broader capital markets to the U.S. housing market. However, their methods are essentially different. Ginnie Mae guarantees payments on mortgages but does not own mortgages. In contrast, Fannie and Freddie buy mortgages directly. All three organizations have been quite important in creating MBS, but Fannie and Freddie typically own the mortgages that comprise the pools. From 1970 until 1983, Ginnie Mae, Freddie Mac, and Fannie Mae all issued similar pass-through securities.

If we consider an entire pass-through security issuance, the total cash flows received by the pass-through security purchases match the total payments made by the home owners whose mortgages are held in the pool. (This ignores servicing fees.) Further, all of the pass-through investors have exactly the same pattern of receipts, and these are proportional to the amount they invested in the pass-through security issuance. But, in June 1983, Salomon Brothers and First Boston helped Freddie Mac introduce a new kind of MBS that would come to be of tremendous importance. It is called a *collateralized mortgage obligation*, or CMO. Rather than issuing a pass-through security, Freddie issued several different kinds of MBS based on the same pool of mortgages, and these different securities had payment characteristics that were very different from the total stream of cash flows coming from the pool of mortgages. This same idea can be expanded to other assets. So a *collateralized debt obligation* (CDO) is a new security based on a pool of assets, and a CMO is a particular kind of CDO—one that is based on a pool of mortgages.

In this first creation of a CMO, Freddie Mac purchased a pool of mortgages consisting of our touchstone mortgage type. Based on the cash flows from this pool of mortgages, Freddie Mac offered three different kinds of debt securities, or *tranches*. (More exactly, the tranches in a CDO issuance are different securities that have different payment characteristics, but that are related by all being based on a common pool of underlying assets that provide the basic cash flows that fund the CDO issuance.) In this first very simple issuance, each of the classes of bondholders received interest payments each month. However, one tranche received *all* of the principal payments from *all* of the mortgages until that tranche was paid off. The second tranche would start to receive principal payments at this point, and the investors in the second tranche then received all principal prepayments until they were paid off. At that point, investors in the third tranche would receive the remainder of the prepayments.

As we have noted, prepayments were a huge problem for investors in pass-through certificates. They would receive prepayments at the whim of the home owners, so it was impossible to know the life of the investment. Further, prepayments tended to be highest when interest rates were lowest. Therefore, as a pass-through investor, you would likely get your money back when it would have to face reinvestment at a very low rate.

With the issuance of this first CMO, investors could know the maturity of their investment within narrow limits. For example, those in the first tranche described above could expect to be paid off within 5 years, the second tranche would be paid off somewhere between 7 and 15 years, and the third tranche would be paid off sometime between 15 and 30 years.[4] Carving the payouts into these tranches of differing maturities met the needs of potential investors in a way that mere pass-through securities could not.

This CMO model quickly proved extremely attractive and flexible. Soon other firms were assembling pools of mortgages and using them as collateral for much more varied debt issues. For example, securitizers found it possible to issue securities with different levels of default risk, all based on the same underlying pool of mortgages. In addition, for a given CMO issuance, some of the bonds could have fixed yields, while others could have floating rates. The possibilities were limited only by the ingenuity of the issuing firms and the investment tastes of the public. Both proved to be virtually unbounded.

CMOs could be issued with the cash flows from the mortgage pool providing the only source of value for the tranched securities. However, Fannie Mae and Freddie Mac soon started using their high market standing to provide guarantees to back the securities in the CMO. They could promise to make good on all promised payments on the CMO securities if the cash flows from the mortgage pool proved inadequate due to defaults on some of the mortgages in the pool.

In July 1983, just one month after Freddie Mac issued the first CMO, Pulte Homes issued the first private CMO—a private CMO being one that is offered by a private firm rather than a GSE. Most private deals relied on pools of mortgages guaranteed by Ginnie Mae, Fannie Mae, or Freddie Mac, but soon CMOs were being issued based on pools of mortgages guaranteed by private entities such as General Electric and Aetna.[5]

At an earlier time, Fannie and Freddie restricted their purchases of loans quite closely. These conditions specified the requirements necessary to be a conforming loan, that is, one that met the guidelines Fannie and Freddie specified if they were to purchase the loan. Such loans are also know as *prime loans*. To be a conforming loan, the loan had to meet four essential requirements. First, the debt service on the mortgage was restricted such that the monthly mortgage payment for principal and interest, for property taxes, and for insurance on the property (PITI) should not exceed 28 percent of the borrower's before-tax monthly income. In addition, total payments for indebtedness to include the mortgage and all other debt service, such as payments for credit cards and automobiles, should not exceed 36 percent of before-tax income. Second, there was a credit requirement, namely that there should not have been more than one late payment within the previous year, and the prospective borrower was required to have a credit score that met a specific level. Third, the home buyer needed to have his or her own funds for the closing costs and the down payment, plus cash in the bank to cover an additional two months of loan payments. Fourth, as a final requirement, the loan size was limited. This limitation was based on the number of families that the property housed and had special categories for properties in especially expensive areas. As time passed and housing prices became higher, the bound was adjusted. As points of reference, for a single-family home in a normally priced area, the limits were $93,750 in 1980, $187,450 in 1990, $252,700 in 2000, and $417,000 in 2009.

If the loan size exceeds the Fannie and Freddie conforming limit, the loan is regarded as a *jumbo loan*. Such larger loans were traditionally not eligible for purchase by Fannie or Freddie and have historically had a higher interest rate than a conforming loan granted to a home purchaser of the same credit quality. Paperwork demands for conforming loans have typically been rather high. For example, one needs to prove income and assets. Thus the next category of loans is called Alternative-A or Alt-A. An Alt-A mortgage is one granted to a person of generally good credit standing who might not meet all of the requirements necessary to receive a conforming loan. Technically, only an MBS can be an Alt-A, but the terminology is also extended to individual mortgages.

The Federal Reserve Bank of New York provides the following definition of an Alt-A mortgage: "Loans marketed in alt-A securities are typically higher-balance loans made to borrowers who might have past credit problems—but not severe enough to drop them into subprime territory—or who, for some reason (such as a desire not to document income) choose not to obtain a prime mortgage. In addition, many loans with nontraditional amortization schedules such as interest only or option adjustable rate mortgages are sold into securities marketed as alt-A."[6] A number of factors might drop a particular mortgage from prime to Alt-A: reduced borrower income and asset documentation, as was the case with stated-income loans; a debt-to-income ratio that is too high; a credit history that is good, but not good enough for a conforming loan; or a loan-to-value ratio on the property that disqualifies the loan from being a conforming loan.

These specifications are somewhat elastic, and there might well be loans of extremely varying quality all classified as Alt-A. For example, consider a successful small business owner with income from a variety of sources that are difficult to document. Such a person could be quite wealthy and very capable of servicing a loan, but could be unable to document that ability. A *stated-income loan* is a loan made to a borrower who merely states his or her income, rather than proving such income (so there is a reason that a stated-income loan is sometimes derogatorily referred to as a *liar's loan*). A loan to a person who lies about his or her income might be classified as an Alt-A loan, even though the home purchaser has insufficient capacity to meet the financial requirements of the mortgage.

A loan that is not prime (or conforming), jumbo, or Alt-A is a *sub-prime loan*. There is no standard definition of the term, but loans are generally classified based on the credit score of the borrower. Some regard all loans granted to those with a credit score of 660 or below as subprime, while others specify the cutoff as 640 or 620. Still others classify a loan as subprime based on some combination of credit score and the loan-to-value ratio. Thus the world of housing finance consists of a variety of actors and several types of mortgage loans. All of these entities play a role in the process of securitization and their interactions determine the types of mortgage-backed securities that are created and also determine the parties that can create them.

The Process of Securitization: An Overview

Creating an MBS requires a pool of home mortgages.[7] Many mortgages are originated with the lender's specific intention of selling them once they are created. Such mortgages are often destined to find their way into a pool of mortgages that will serve as the collateral for the issuance of other securities. This idea of originating a mortgage with the intention of selling it is known as the originate-to-distribute (OTD) model of mortgage production. Compared to the OTH model of figure 2.1, this process has quite a few steps and is much more complicated. Figure 2.2 diagrams the OTD model of mortgage production, which goes hand in hand with the securitization process.

A financial institution can acquire a portfolio of mortgages by originating the mortgages itself and collecting them into a portfolio. Alternatively, a financial firm that wishes to be in the securitization business can purchase mortgages in the open market from originators to assemble the needed collection of mortgages. The mortgage originator has already performed its due diligence on the individual mortgages, so if the originator chooses to securitize those mortgages it is already knowledgeable about the quality of those mortgages. In contrast, a firm that wishes to buy mortgages needs to perform its own due diligence on the mortgages, and it will typically hire a specialized due diligence firm to inspect the quality of mortgages prior to the purchase.

The mortgages in a pool can be homogenous or extremely diverse. We have seen that Ginnie Mae works with quite homogeneous mortgages, but that need not be the case. Mortgages in a pool can have different loan amounts, different interest rates, different maturities, and

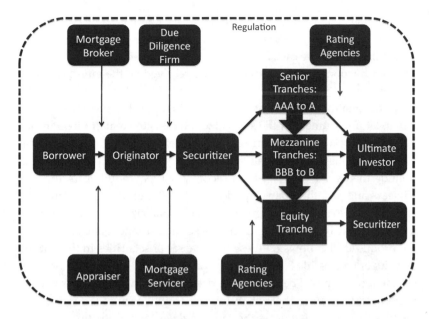

Figure 2.2 The Originate-to-Distribute (OTD) Model of Mortgage Production

different qualities. The mortgages can be geographically dispersed or drawn from a common locale, and the included mortgages can bear fixed or adjustable rates. However the mortgage pool is constituted, the mortgages in the pool collectively promise a sequence of cash flows, and that stream of promised future cash flows provides the raw materials from which the securitizer or arranger constructs its CMO.

As a simple example, consider a pool of identical mortgages that conform to our touchstone mortgage described earlier—one that has a 30-year life, that is self-amortizing, and that bears a fixed rate of interest. Assume that each mortgage has an initial principal balance of $100,000 and that the interest rate is 5.5 percent. Each such mortgage promises a sequence of 360 payments of $567.79 each month. Assume further that the pool consists of 5,000 such mortgages, so the principal balance of the entire mortgage pool will be $500 million and the owner of the pool should receive $2,838,950 (5,000 mortgages x $567.79 for each mortgage payment) each month—assuming that each mortgage pays every payment and that no home owner prepays the mortgage early.

Based on this promised stream of cash inflows of $2,838,950 a month for the next 360 months, the securitizer can issue an MBS or a CMO. The simplest way to do this is with a pass-through structure, as we have seen with Ginnie Mae. A purchaser of an ordinary Ginnie Mae pass-through receives a fraction of the $2,838,950, less the servicing and guarantee fee, each month. Thus the cash flows paid out on a pass-through are merely a constant fraction of the total cash inflows received on the mortgage pool.

However, this need not be the case, as Freddie Mac proved in 1983 with the creation of the first CMO. To illustrate this process in more detail, let us assume that the securitizer chooses to create two securities based on this pool, a short-term and a long-term security. The short-term security will make payments for the first 15 years or 180 payments, and nothing thereafter. The long-term security will pay nothing for the first 15 years and will then pay in periods 181–360. Let us also assume that each of the two securities is given the same total size, with each portion divided into 10,000 securities. Under these circumstances, table 2.1 shows the promised cash flows on these two classes of securities in total. If the securitizer creates 10,000 of each type of security, the promised monthly payment on each will be $283.90. Notice that the total cash flows in each period are the same as the cash throw-offs from the entire mortgage pool because this example ignores the servicing fees for simplicity.

The prospective purchaser of these securities is buying them from the securitizing financial institution and must consider different kinds of risk associated with these promised payments. First, if a home owner defaults on a mortgage payment, funds will not be available to make all the promised payments. This should be particularly worrisome for the purchaser of the long-term security, who might fear that it would never receive a single payment, as the promised payments do not even start for 15 years. A second kind of risk concerns prepayments. Every home owner in the pool has the right to prepay the mortgage at any time. If that happens, the actual inflows to the mortgage pool will not match the

Table 2.1		
A Simple CMO		
	Promised Cash Inflows for Mortgage Pool	
Months 1–360	$2,838,950	
	Promised Cash Outflows for CMOs	
	10,000 Short-Term Securities (Monthly Payment on Each)	**10,000 Long-Term Securities (Monthly Payment on Each)**
Months 1–180	$283.90	0
Months 180–360	0	$283.90

promised outflows. Third, purchasers of the two CMO securities are buying them from the issuer, so the purchaser must be concerned about the financial probity of that issuer. In practice, these risks are addressed through credit enhancement. While a later section in this chapter discusses credit enhancement more thoroughly, credit enhancement essentially involves techniques designed to ensure that the CMOs make the payments they have promised.

A critical element that is not shown in table 2.1 is the profit potential for the securitizer. The table shows every dollar of cash inflow being converted to a cash outflow to the purchasers of the two securities. However, there can still be profit for the securitizing firm. For example, the market may place a higher value on the payment patterns being offered by the CMOs than it does on the underlying mortgages themselves. If the market does value the payment patterns of the two CMOs sufficiently, they will be worth more than the underlying mortgages, and the securitizer may be able to secure a profit from this differential.

To continue the numerical example, assume that the short-term security has an interest rate of 4.8 percent instead of 5.5 percent, and the long-term security has a yield of 5.7 percent. (This difference in yields might reflect the greater perceived risk of the long-term security as well as a market preference for shorter-term securities. Part of the securitizer's job is to know what kinds of securities the market particularly desires.) With these new yields, the total value of the 10,000 short-term securities will be $363,768,259, and the long-term securities will be worth $146,155,793. So together the two sets of newly created securities will have a value of almost $510 million, instead of the original $500 million when all of the mortgages yielded 5.5 percent. Table 2.2 compares the original mortgages with the two securities created from the mortgages in the pool. In the example, the securitization gives a gross profit of almost $10 million, from which the securitizer can pay the cost of the securitization and perhaps still have a profit.

As a second example, let us assume that the underlying mortgages in the pool are of less than prime quality, and that they do not bear a guarantee from Ginnie Mae, Fannie Mae, or Freddie Mac. In this situation, purchasing the mortgages directly may be a quite risky proposition, as it exposes the investor directly to the risk that the home owners will default. If the securitizer is a financially solid firm, it may offer its own guarantee that all the payments will be made as a kind of credit enhancement. Now the prospective investor can look to the cash flows from the pool for its payments, plus the promise of the securitizer to make them whole. In this

Table 2.2

Original Mortgages Compared to Two New Securities

Description	Total Value
Original Mortgages Comprising the Mortgage Pool: 5,000 mortgages promising payments of $567.79 each month for 360 months; Yield: 5.5%	$500 million
The Securitization:	
New Short-Term Securities: 10,000 securities promising payments of $283.90 each month for months 1–180; Yield: 4.8%	$363,768,258.54
New Long-Term Securities: 10,000 securities promising payments of $283.90 each month for months 181–360; Yield: 5.7%	$146,155,793.01
Total Value of Both Classes of New Securities	$509,924,051.55

example, the securitizer bears some of the risk by offering its guarantee, so this helps to make the CMOs more valuable than the underlying mortgages alone. Assuming that all goes reasonably well with the payments, the securitizer's guarantee never comes into play, and the securitizing firm can make a profit on the deal. Of course, if mortgage defaults in the pool become widespread, the securitizer will have to pay off on its guarantee, and fulfilling this obligation can drive the deal into a loss.

Compared to our numerical example, a more sophisticated and more prevalent way of creating CMOs is to choose a sequential, or senior-subordinated, structure. In this type of CMO payment scheme, some security holders have a preemptive claim on the cash flows from the pool. For example, the promised cash flows from our sample mortgage pool might be used to create two classes of otherwise identical securities, except that one is senior to the other. This means that the cash flows in any period promised to holders of the senior security must be paid in full before any payment flows to the junior security holders. With this structure, the senior security has less default risk than the junior security, and with other features being equal, the senior security is more valuable in the marketplace than the junior security.

This structure of senior and junior payments gives rise to the metaphor of the CMO *waterfall*. We may think of the cash flows due on a security as water; the issuer of a security has promised a certain amount of cash, or water, that is sufficient to discharge the promised payment, or to fill the "bucket," of a particular security owner. With the senior-subordinated structure, the bucket of the senior-most security owner must be completely filled before the cash overflows that bucket and starts to fill that of the next senior-most security owner. Figure 2.3 presents a simplified view of this process, with just three tranches of securities.

In practice it is customary to create a number of different types of securities to appeal to investors with different time preferences and risk tolerances, and it is not unusual for a single pool of mortgages to serve as collateral for as many as seven different kinds of securities, or tranches. These various tranches can differ in default risk, maturity, yield, fixed vs. floating rate, and so on.

Differences in default risk are particularly important. Viewed from the securitizer's point of view, an important goal is to create securities that get the highest possible rating from credit rating agencies such as Standard & Poor's, Moody's Investors Service, and Fitch Ratings. These agencies rate securities using a letter grade system to express the probability that the security will default—that is miss or delay a payment. Table 2.3 compares the three rating systems.

These ratings are extremely important in the marketplace for three reasons. First, the rating has a large influence on the price of a security. Other factors being equal, the higher the rating, the higher the price the security can command. Second, many financial institutions operate in a regulatory environment that encourages, or even requires, that they invest only in securities of a sufficiently high rating. The Securities and Exchange Commission (SEC) recognizes particular agencies as nationally recognized statistical rating organizations (NRSRO), and the rating provided by such organizations is used to determine how much capital a financial institution must have to hold a particular security in its portfolio. Further, some financial institutions are compelled by regulations to limit their investment to only *investment grade* securities, those with a BBB- or better rating from Standard & Poor's or Ba3 from Moody's.

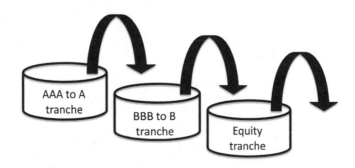

Figure 2.3 The CMO Waterfall

During the heyday of the subprime market, circa 2004, there were only five NRSROs, with Standard & Poor's, Moody's, and Fitch having a 90 percent market share of the ratings business. The formal recognition of NRSROs, coupled with the role that their ratings play in the regulatory process, gives these private firms both power and responsibility in credit markets. They have the power through their ratings to influence the pricing of securities and to determine which securities are actually purchased or sold by many financial institutions and other investors. As these NRSROs are officially recognized, they have a responsibility to conduct their business in a responsible manner and to give ratings that are honest and reasonable. As we will see, these credit rating agencies played a pivotal role in the subprime crisis, because they played such a crucial role in the process of creating MBS and CMOs.

The securitizer wants to issue a security that costs the least to create and sells for the most, and the rating an agency gives to that security is of fundamental importance in determining the price. Therefore, the

---

Table 2.3

Ratings Systems for Debt Obligations

	Standard & Poor's	Moody's	Fitch
Lowest Default Risk/ Best Quality	AAA	Aaa	AAA
	AA	Aa	AA
	A	A	A
	BBB	Baa	BBB
	BB	Ba	BB
	B	B	B
	CCC	Caa	CCC
	CC	Ca	CC
	C	C	C
	D		DDD
			DD
Highest Default Risk/ Worst Quality			D
	Pluses and minuses provide further indication of a security's standing within a rating.	Numbers (1, 2, 3) indicate relative standing within a rating, with 1 being the highest quality.	

Source: Office of the Comptroller of the Currency, *Rating Credit Risk: Comptroller's Handbook,* April 2001, pp. 35–40.

security issuer wants to achieve a given rating at the least possible cost. Because the ratings categories are discreet, there will always be some securities that are at the top end of a given rating, while others just barely qualify for the same rating. To economize on the cost of creating a security, the securitizer wants to hit the bottom end of a given range for a particular rating. There is no one better to advise a securitizer on the way to achieve this goal than a rating agency itself. Therefore, it became customary for a securitizer to hire a rating agency as a consultant to help design the securities that it planned to issue.

Before securities enter the market, the securities must receive a rating. Typically, the securitizer hires the same rating agency that helped to design the securities to provide a rating. Thus the rating agency gets paid as a consultant to design a security and gets paid a second time for providing a rating. Once the securities are rated, they become available for sale. The tranched securities have been created with the tastes and needs of different investors in mind. We have already noted that regulations restrict the credit rating of securities that securitizers can hold in their portfolios. Among MBS generally, and CMOs more particularly, the highest demand is for the top-rated securities. Thus securitizers try to make the proportion of their CMOs that are AAA rated as large as possible. Other investors with less stringent regulatory constraints and greater risk tolerance take the next riskiest investments, the so-called *mezzanine tranches*.

For a given mortgage pool, one of the costs of creating a very high proportion of AAA securities is the corresponding creation of at least some very low-rated or unrated securities. For a given pool, promising a very high proportion of the cash inflows to the securities intended to garner an AAA rating just necessarily means that the securities at the bottom will only receive the residual payments after all more senior claimants have been paid. So these securities have a considerably higher default risk. This class of CMO is known as the equity tranche, or less charitably as the *toxic waste*. For this riskiest class of securities there is relatively little demand, and the securitizer usually retains a considerable portion of the less-desired equity tranche.

Credit Enhancement

In a securitization, the securitizer aims to obtain the best credit ratings possible for the securities it issues and seeks to tailor the credit quality of its issuances to the tastes of the market. Because more highly rated securities are worth more, and because demand for highly rated securities is more robust due to investment policies adopted by or imposed upon investing institutions, securitizers are particularly interested in generating the highest proportion of AAA and AA securities. If a given mortgage pool will not support the desired distribution, the securitizer may resort to several different techniques of credit enhancement.

Standard & Poor's suggests that we conceive of credit enhancement in the following terms: "Think of credit enhancement as a kind of financial cushion that allows securities backed by a pool of collateral (such as mortgages or credit card receivables) to absorb losses from defaults on the underlying loans."[8] One of the most common techniques is subordination, which was introduced above. By having a structure that gives priority to some securities and a subordinated status to others, the securitizer legitimately enhances the credit quality of the top tranches, but reduces the credit quality of the lower tranches.

There are other techniques as well. The securitizer may over-collateralize a particular issue. In over-collateralization, the face value of the mortgage pool exceeds the face value of the securities in the securitization. For example, consider a mortgage pool of mortgages all bearing 7 percent coupons and totaling $1.1 billion in face value. If the securitizer issues only $1 billion of face value of new securities all with a 7 percent coupon, then the issue is over-collateralized. Importantly, the promised payments from the mortgage pool exceed the promised payments on the total securitization by 10 percent, which matches the over-collateralization in this example. Consequently, the securities of the securitization must deserve a better credit rating than the mortgage pool.

Another technique is to create a securitization that exploits an excess spread. Consider again the mortgage pool with $1.1 billion of mortgages having a 7 percent coupon. If the issuer creates securities that total $1.1 billion, but that have only a 6 percent coupon, the mortgage pool has an excess spread over the securities in the securitization, and the securitized instruments must have a higher credit standing than the mortgage pool itself. This is due to the simple fact that the mortgage pool promises to pay 7 percent on $1.1 billion, but the securitization securities only promise to pay 6 percent on the same principal amount.

Beyond credit enhancement through subordination, over-collateralization, or using an excess spread, the securitizer could simply purchase insurance that promises to make all the payments due on securities in the securitization in the event of default on the underlying mortgages.

Firms specializing in offering this kind of insurance are known as monoline insurers, because they operate in only one industry, such as insuring bonds. These monoline insurers insured many mortgage securitizations, and chapter 4 explores the story of their near collapse, which was due almost entirely to insuring securitized mortgages. In addition, a securitizer might use a *credit default swap* (CDS) as a tool of credit enhancement. A CDS functions like an insurance contract to pay if a "credit event" occurs. So if one of the tranches fails to pay as promised, a CDS might kick in to make up the deficiency. (CDS are explored more fully in chapter 7, and the CDS issuances it made lie at the heart of AIG's near-collapse, as chapter 7 also explains.) Thus with insurance through a monoline firm or with a CDS in place, the securitizer can also improve the credit quality of the instruments in the securitization.

The Subprime Difference

The years leading up to the subprime crisis saw two parallel developments that we have explored in this chapter, the extension of home lending to home purchasers with lower credit standing and the development of ever more sophisticated methods of securitization, as the market has gone from one with only pass-through securities to a market with tranches of securities that carve up the payments from the underlying mortgage pool in extremely diverse and innovative ways.

As a thought experiment, consider a pool of mortgages of the very highest quality, such that there is likely to be no, or at least very little, default. The securitization process could be applied to these mortgages with great confidence of success and with the creation of a very high proportion of AAA CMOs. If the cash flows from the mortgage pool have a high degree of certainty, then creating tranched securities that will perform as promised is a fairly easy matter. Of course, there is still the uncertainty over prepayments in the mortgage pool, but at least in this thought experiment there is little or no default risk.

In contrast, consider a pool of subprime mortgages. Compared to a pool of prime mortgages, subprime mortgages are virtually certain to have greater defaults, as the *subprime* designation implies. However, that does not necessarily mean that the securitization model will not work for these mortgages. The key to a successful securitization model is to estimate how bad the default rate will be and to exercise restraint in attempting to wring too high a proportion of AAA-rated securities from the pool. If there are two pools of mortgages that are similar except that one is composed of prime mortgages, while the other is made up of subprime mortgages, the two pools can support two sets of securities with different characteristics. For the prime pool, the proportion of higher-rated securities can justifiably be much larger, and the securitizer for the subprime pool will have to be satisfied with creating securities that have lower ratings overall.

However, these reflections in no way imply that a pool of subprime mortgages cannot support some AAA-rated securities. Accounts in the popular press sometimes make it appear as totally obvious that one cannot make AAA-rated securities from subprime mortgages, but this claim is patently false, as another thought experiment will show. Consider again the pool of mortgages discussed earlier in this chapter, which has an initial principal total of $500 million, an interest rate of 5.5 percent, and consists entirely of 30-year self-amortizing mortgages. As we have seen, the promised payments from the pool are $2,838,950 per month for the next 360 months.

Now assume that all of the mortgages in the pool are subprime, so the anticipated defaults are likely to be significant. To be more specific, let us assume that these mortgages would deserve a rating of BB from Standard & Poor's if they were to be rated as bonds, and strictly for convenience let us assume that there will be no prepayments. In this situation, it is reasonable to think that a securitizer could justifiably create securities from this pool that also had a rating of BB. However, now consider a securitization based on this pool that creates just three tranches. First, the senior tranche of securities collectively promise to pay $500,000 per month for 360 months. The junior (or middle) tranche securities promise $1,500,000 a month for 360 months, while the equity tranche securities receive the residual payments, which would be $838,950 per month for 360 months if there were no defaults at all.

Given this description of the subprime pool and the three tranches of securities, what ratings would be justifiable for the senior and junior tranches? For the senior tranche to suffer *any* loss, the default rate would have to exceed 82.39 percent. If just 17.61 percent of the home owners pay as promised, the senior security holders will receive every penny promised. (These numbers are derived from the fact that the payments promised to the senior security holders are just 17.61 percent of the total promised payments.) Might it be reasonable to think that the senior security truly deserves a AAA rating?

As we have assumed that the mortgages themselves were of BB quality, the next question is: What rating should the mezzanine security receive? Given that the senior tranche gets paid first and therefore siphons off the first payments every month, it might seem that the junior security should receive a rating lower than BB, which equals the quality of the underlying mortgages. However, this line of thought neglects the presence of the equity tranche, which will absorb the first losses. The proportion of payments promised to the senior and junior investors is 70.45 percent of the total. So if the default rate stays below 29.55 percent, the junior security holders will also receive every promised cent exactly on time. Thus, the junior security might well deserve a rating that is above BB as well—perhaps it would deserve an A rating.

In our example, it is certain that the equity tranche will suffer considerable defaults. After all, the mortgages are subprime, and the priority given to the senior and junior tranches focuses the default losses entirely on the equity tranche. With an average mortgage quality of BB for the mortgages in the pool and the protection given to both the senior and junior tranches, the equity tranche is sure to be in for a rough ride. If our informal suggestion that the senior tranche deserves an AAA and the junior tranche earns an A, and given the average quality of BB, the equity tranche is pretty surely of very low quality indeed. After all, in some sense, the rating for the equity tranche has to balance out the higher ratings for the other tranches. However, we have also seen that various techniques of credit enhancement can supplement the basic strategy of subordination and can improve the credit quality of all the issues in the securitization through over-collateralization, the technique of an excess spread, or by insuring payment on the securitized instruments.

One might reasonably disagree with the ratings suggested for this example. For example, one might insist that the payments to the senior tranche are too large for the security to deserve an AAA rating. But there is some promised payment that is a small enough percentage so that the senior security would really deserve AAA. If the right number is not a promise of $500,000 per month, might it be $250,000 or even $100,000? In spite of the alleged "financial alchemy" in creating AAA securities on a base of subprime mortgages, the principle is quite clear that such a security can be created in this manner with perfect legitimacy. The details of creating the portfolio of tranches and securing the appropriate rating for them are quite complex, of course, and we all know where the devil lives.

Before the Deluge

Subprime Lending: To the Peak

The subprime crisis did not occur overnight—it took years and much effort to lay the foundation for disaster. And much of the foundation building was accompanied by social indicators that were actually quite promising and thus helped to mask the shakiness of the towering debt of mortgage finance. Supporting this entire development was a general attitude among the U.S. public that gives home ownership a special place in the national psyche. We have already seen that broad public policy and frequent presidential pronouncements enshrined the virtues of home ownership, and this attitude has been embraced by the population at large.

A survey of the public in 2004 showed that 84 percent of Americans believed that a major reason to buy a home is because it is a good investment, and 74 percent opined that it provides the feeling of owning something of your very own, while 77 percent asserted that paying rent is a not a good investment. On certain issues, minority views differed from those of the general population, with African Americans and Hispanics having an even stronger view that owning a home gives the feeling of owning something of your very own and that owning a home was something that they always dreamed of doing. Further, there was a feeling that buying a home was a "safe investment with a lot of potential" among 61 percent of the population. By contrast, only 39 percent saw investing in an IRA in these terms, and only 26 percent saw a savings account as being both safe and as having a lot of potential.[1]

Against these generally favorable attitudes, it has always seemed natural, perhaps even obvious, to view increasing home ownership as a very good social outcome. In chapter 1 we noted a general rise in home ownership over the twentieth century and attributed it principally to rising societal wealth and the rapid formation of families. However, as figure 3.1 shows, the percentage of Americans living in their own home stagnated for the decade leading up to 1993, hovering right at 64 percent. In 1993, the Clinton administration inaugurated its National Home-ownership Strategy, and home ownership burgeoned for the next decade. This surge was due in part to the booming dot-com economy, in part to explicit federal action to encourage home ownership, and in part to the new techniques of securitizing mortgages, which made more funds available for mortgage finance.

Much of this gain in home ownership was achieved by non-white racial and ethnic groups. While the number of home owners rose by 14.1 percent for the 1994–2003 decade, black home ownership rose by 25.1

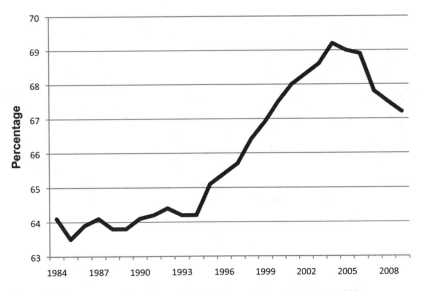

Figure 3.1 Percentage of Americans Living in Homes They Own, 1984–2008
Source: http://www.census.gov/hhes/www/housing/hvs/annual07/ann07t13.html

percent and Hispanic home ownership rose by 62.8 percent, while non-Hispanic white ownership rose only 7.6 percent.[2] Thus, much of the gain in home ownership was achieved by increasing African American and Hispanic participation. Even though non-white home ownership continued to lag behind that of whites, these years helped to close the gap. Further, for many families home ownership historically has been a primary vehicle of accumulating wealth, so the increasing non-white home ownership might have been expected to reduce wealth disparities among racial and ethnic groups as well.

Fueling this wealth accumulation was the surge in home prices shown in figure 3.2. Nationally, home prices rose by 115 percent from the end of 1993 to the end of 2004. So this period saw expanding home ownership, particularly among non-whites, and at the same time, a period of rapidly escalating home prices.

General conditions and technical developments in the housing finance market played an important role in the expansion of home ownership. In many respects, it became significantly easier to buy a home during this period. From 1985 to the present, mortgage interest rates

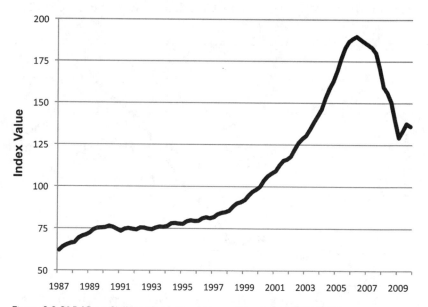

Figure 3.2 S&P/Case-Shiller U.S. National Home Price Index, 1993–2009
Source: http://www.macromarkets.com/csi_housing/data_download.asp. Accessed March 9, 2010.

have generally fallen, as figure 3.3 indicates, and this represents a very significant reduction in the cost of buying a home.

Of lesser, yet still significant, importance was a general reduction in the transaction costs and institutional frictions involved in acquiring a mortgage. A traditional method by which lenders garnered additional income from granting a mortgage was the inclusion of various fees at the inception of the mortgage, along with the payment of "points"—a point being one percent of the principal amount of the mortgage—with home buyers paying some number of points at closing, generally with some reduction in the interest rate charged on the mortgage. Over recent years, the total cost attributed to these points and fees have fallen substantially, as figure 3.4 shows. Not only did this cost reduction affect those simply buying a home as a permanent residence, it also made it much easier and less costly for a home owner to refinance a home or to exchange one home for another.

The traditional method of granting a mortgage required the painstaking gathering of relevant information and the submission of a mortgage application, which an experienced finance professional then examined in detail. Not surprisingly, this elaborate process took weeks

Figure 3.3 Mortgage Interest Rates, 1985–2008
Source: Geetesh Bhardwaj and Rajdeep Sengupta, "Did Prepayments Sustain the Subprime Market?" Federal Reserve Bank of St. Louis, *Working Paper Series*, October 2008.

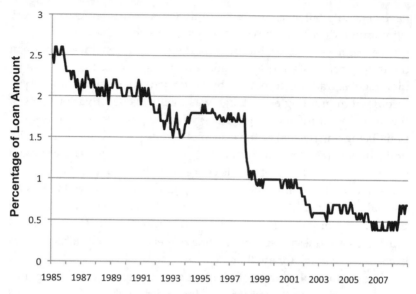

Figure 3.4 Points and Fees as a Percentage of Loan Amount, 1985–2008
Source: Geetesh Bhardwaj and Rajdeep Sengupta, "Did Prepayments Sustain the Sub-prime Market?" Federal Reserve Bank of St. Louis, *Working Paper Series*, October 2008.

and involved considerable cost. The 1990s witnessed the development of the automated underwriting system (AUS)—a computer program that accepts information about a mortgage applicant and makes a decision to grant a mortgage or to require additional screening of the application. Fannie and Freddie both developed their own AUS, called "Desktop Underwriter" and "Loan Prospector," respectively, and they used these computer programs to determine whether they would purchase a given mortgage. They also made their systems available to lenders to use in making loan decisions. According to one assessment, "The adoption of automated underwriting systems (AUSs) was the single most important technology development in the mortgage lending industry in the 1990s. Those systems, which use scoring technology to evaluate the credit risk of individual mortgages and loan portfolios, revolutionized the underwriting of prime conventional and later all single-family mortgages."[3]

Reducing the mortgage decision to an AUS speeds the decision and makes the assessment much less costly than having a knowledgeable person examine the mortgage application in detail. Fannie Mae conducted an analysis in 2001 that found that using an AUS reduced the cost of making an individual loan by $916,[4] and by that time Fannie and Freddie were using automated systems to evaluate fully 60 percent of the mortgages they considered for purchase.[5]

These systems were first developed for assessing conventional loans, but Edward N. Jones, a former NASA engineer, through his company Arc Systems, extended their application to subprime lending. Arc Systems acquired First Franklin Financial as its first big customer in early 1999. Thanks in large part to its AUS, First Franklin was able to evaluate as many as 50,000 mortgage applications a month by 2005. Using a competing AUS, Countrywide Financial pushed its mortgage operation to the granting of 150,000 mortgages per month.[6]

Virtually all of the big lenders used an AUS to evaluate loans, acquiring systems from the many small companies in the market, or by developing their own proprietary systems. New Century Financial boasted on its web site that due to its use of FastQual, its AUS: "We'll give you loan answers in just 12 seconds." (New Century Financial is now bankrupt.) These automated systems have been used to make favorable decisions on millions of mortgages, and their use accounts for 40 percent of all subprime loans, according to one estimate.[7]

Being simply a computer program, an AUS accepts data that can be rendered as a suitable input, such as a credit score, and applies rules to the input data, with the output being a decision to make the loan or to refer the application for human screening. Of course, the process is only as good as the quality and relevance of the input data and the rules the computer system applies to that data. Further, if the process is flawed, the application of an AUS merely makes a bad decision more cheaply and quickly. Nonetheless, at least before the subprime implosion, we might take the following as a representative assessment: "Borrowers have benefited from technological innovations. Automated underwriting systems have resulted in faster loan qualifications and processing—the time from mortgage application to approval has been reduced from months to minutes. New credit and mortgage scoring systems have allowed the mortgage market to serve some of those with weaker credit histories."[8]

Of course, this sanguine assessment was not shared by all of those who were intimately involved in using these systems. In 2003, Angelo R. Mozilo, who was the chairman, president, and CEO of Countrywide Financial Corporation at the time, was honored by being invited to present the John T. Dunlop Lecture, sponsored by the National Housing Endowment at the Joint Center for Housing Studies of Harvard University. In his speech Mozilo identified two problems with the industry's underwriting methodology, stating:

> The first is that the automated underwriting systems kick far too many applicants down to the manual underwriting process, thereby implying these borrowers are not creditworthy; and the second issue is that once arriving in the hands of a manual underwriter, the applicant is subject to basic human judgment that can be influenced by the level of a borrower's credit score. Let's address my first issue. I acknowledge that credit scoring uses proven statistical methods to provide lenders with the ability to quantify the risk of extending credit. And there is little question that the technique effectively and efficiently separates those with very good credit from those with questionable credit. However, far too many borrowers are being referred to an arduous manual and cumbersome underwriting process. To me, that is clear proof that the level deemed to be an acceptable risk by our automated underwriting systems is much too high.[9]

The development of AUS was one of the factors that accelerated the mortgage market in general and the subprime market in particular. By reducing the cost of evaluating and granting loans, the AUS increased the profitability of lending in general, and this had a large impact on subprime lending, as figure 3.5 shows. From 1995 to 2003, subprime lending went from $65 billion per year to $332 billion. As figure 3.5 also shows, the subprime industry became more concentrated over this period as well, with the largest 25 originators holding a 39 percent market share in 1995, which they expanded to a 93 percent share by 2003. However, in spite of its dramatic surge, subprime lending remained a relatively small share of the total mortgage market, as figure 3.6 shows. Even by the peak of the subprime market, subprime originations accounted for only 22 percent of new mortgages.

In some ways, subprime was catching up to the mortgage market in general. Figure 3.7 shows that from 1995 to 2006, the securitization of subprime mortgages advanced remarkably. In 1995 about 28 percent of subprime mortgages were being securitized, compared to 46 percent for agency mortgage purchases. But by 2006 the securitization rate for subprime mortgages was 78 percent, compared to the agencies' 87 percent. Of yet greater importance was the development and acceleration of securitization, particularly the extension of the technology of securitization to subprime in a massive way.

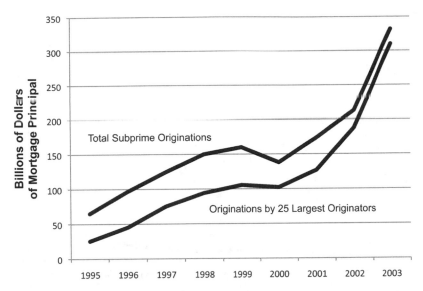

Figure 3.5 The Surge in Subprime Originations, 1995–2008
Source: Souphala Chomsisengphet and Anthony Pennington-Cross, "The Evolution of the Subprime Mortgage Market," Federal Reserve Bank of St. Louis, *Review*, January–February 2006, 31–56.

Table 3.1

Total Mortgage-Backed Securities Outstanding (Billions of U. S. Dollars)

| Year | Total MBS | Agency | Non-Agency | | | |
			Total	Jumbo	Alt-A	Subprime
2000	3,003	2,625	377	252	44	81
2007 Q1	5,984	4,021	1,963	468	765	730

Source: Gary Gorton, "The Subprime Panic," *European Financial Management*, 2009, 15:1, 10–46. See Table 2, p. 14.

Table 3.1 makes a similar point by comparing the total amount of mortgage securitization as well as market shares by types of mortgages for 2000 versus 2007. Over this seven-year period, the total amount of securitizations almost exactly doubled, from $3 trillion to $5.98 trillion. While the total amount of securitizations was doubling, the share held by the government-sponsored enterprises (GSEs) was

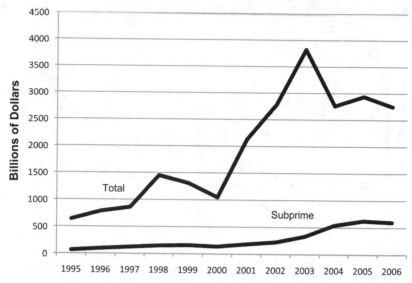

Figure 3.6 Mortgage Originations, 1995–2006
Source: Adapted and estimated from Adam B. Ashcraft and Til Schuermann, "Understanding the Securitization of Subprime Mortgage Credit," *Federal Reserve Bank of New York Staff Reports*, no. 318, March 2008; Souphala Chomsisengphet and Anthony Pennington-Cross, "The Evolution of the Subprime Mortgage Market," Federal Reserve Bank of St. Louis, *Review*, January–February 2006, 31–56; and Gary Gorton, "The Subprime Panic," *European Financial Management*, January 2009, 15(1): 10–46.

declining markedly, from 87 to 67 percent. Subprime securitizations grew from less than 3 percent in 2000 to more than 12 percent in 2007. The securitization of Alt-A mortgages made an even greater surge from less than 2 percent to almost 13 percent, while the securitization of jumbo mortgages held relatively steady. By 2007 subprime and Alt-A mortgages accounted for 25 percent of all mortgage securitizations.

The Height of Subprime Lending

In 2006, most contemporaneous assessments of the general economic situation and the housing market were quite optimistic. The previous years had witnessed a rapid recovery from the bursting of the dot-com bubble, there had been a rather large accumulation of wealth, and the presumed benefits of home ownership had been extended further than ever before and included a higher proportion of historically

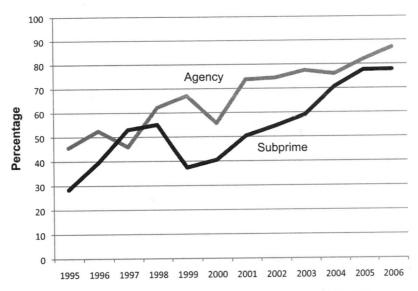

Figure 3.7 Federal Agency and Subprime Securitization, Proportions, 1995–2006
Source: Souphala Chomsisengphet and Anthony Pennington-Cross, "The Evolution of
the Subprime Mortgage Market," Federal Reserve Bank of St. Louis, *Review*, January–
February 2006, 31–56.

disadvantaged racial and ethnic groups that had lagged behind in
home ownership.

In retrospect, it seems obvious that those cheery assessments were
entirely misplaced. With the benefit of hindsight, it now seems apparent that much of this perceived increase in wealth was due to excessive leverage and to poor practices in the housing market. The same
period of increasing wealth had also seen a very steep decline in the
savings rate of individual households, as figure 3.8 shows. From 1992 to
2005, the savings rate fell from a very respectable 7.7 percent of income
to less than half of one percent. This meant that the cushion of wealth
available to households in adversity had been considerably lessened.
Perhaps more seriously, the declining savings rate also betokened a
more aggressive emphasis on consumption and even a frivolous attitude toward financial responsibility.

This trend was emphasized by the increasing mountain of debt
being borne by households. The same period began with American
households owing about one year's income on average, a debt load that
included home mortgages. But by 2006, this debt burden had increased

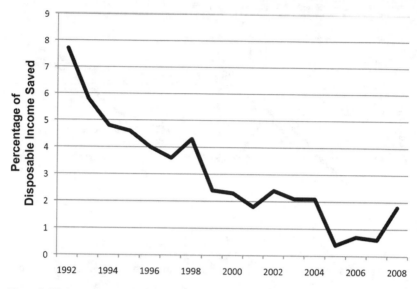

Figure 3.8 Personal Savings as a Percentage of Disposable Income, 1992–2008

by a full two-thirds, as figure 3.9 illustrates. All of this was visible in the period as it developed; all of it was published as Federal Reserve statistics each month, quarter, or year as it materialized. But now, with the benefit of hindsight, we can see that the debt burden was much too large and that it left many households in a position of extreme fragility, facing great risk of ruin if adverse economic events ever developed.

To a significant degree, this debt burden and financial fragility were built by increasing debt for home purchases. From 1990 to the height of the subprime frenzy, home owners increased the indebtedness for the homes the purchased. A study of all home purchases in Massachusetts from 1990 to 2007 shows a sharp increase in the ratio of the size of a home loan to the value of the property, the loan-to-value (LTV) ratio. In 1990, the typical (median) home loan was for 80 percent of the property's value, giving an LTV ratio of 0.80, but by 2007 this figure had increased to 0.90, as shown in figure 3.10. It is well-known that loans with higher initial LTV ratios tend to have higher default rates, a principle that figure 3.10 also illustrates. For the Massachusetts experience, loans that were originated in 1990 and eventually defaulted had a median LTV of 0.9, but by 2007 loans that were defaulting had an LTV

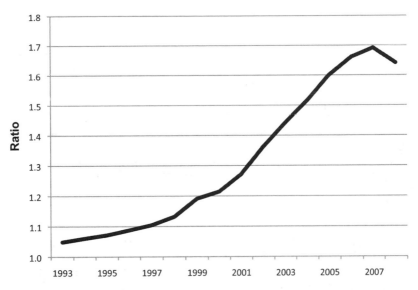

Figure 3.9 Ratio of Personal Financial Liabilities to Income, 1993–2008

ratio of 1.0, meaning that such home purchasers were borrowing the entire value of the home.[10]

Over the same general time span, from the early 1990s to the height of the subprime market in the 2004–2006 period, other practices developed in home mortgage lending that contributed to the financial fragility of households. To see how this developed, it is useful to recall the plain vanilla mortgage that dominated the housing finance system of the United States from the 1930s to the 1980s—the mortgage in which one borrowed 80 percent of the value of a home after an S&L carefully investigated the purchaser's financial position and income prospects. These traditional mortgages were self-amortizing and carried a fixed rate of interest, with a typical maturity of 30 years.

As we have seen, financial liberalization in the 1980s permitted adjustable rate mortgages for the first time. However, merely changing the rules did not lead to an immediate change in typical practices, and innovations such as adjustable rate mortgages spread slowly. Other innovations and practices followed and developed in turn. For example, it became possible for home owners to purchase a home with an "interest only" mortgage. As the name implies, such a mortgage merely requires the payment of the interest each month, and the home owner pays nothing toward the principal loan amount. Beyond interest only loans,

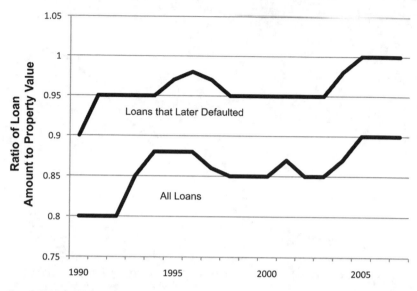

Figure 3.10 Initial Loan-to-Value Ratios, 1990–2007
Source: Christopher L. Foote, Kristopher Gerardi, Lorenz Goette, and Paul S. Willen, "Subprime Facts: What (We Think) We Know about the Subprime Crisis and What We Don't," Federal Reserve Bank of Boston, Public Policy Discussion Paper No. 08–2, 2008.

negative amortization loans also became available, in which the home owner makes a monthly payment that is smaller than the interest for the month, so the amount of indebtedness increased each month. In a negative amortization loan, the shortfall between the payment made and the interest accrued in a given month is merely added to the principal. Of course, this type of loan increased the amount of indebtedness and the amount of interest accrued each month. A negative amortization loan could be set up as a fixed rate loan with a fixed payment such that the home owner uses home equity to finance consumption that would otherwise be unattainable. In effect, such a loan allows the home owner to slowly spend the equity already accumulated in the home. Such loans might well make sense for some, particularly for the elderly, because this loan lets them stay in a home with a high value yet also have a reasonable level of consumption.[11]

Another type of negative amortization loan also developed, however, the "option ARM"—a type of loan that became quite prevalent in the subprime market. An option ARM is an adjustable rate mortgage that gives the home owner the option to pay less than the scheduled mortgage payment or even to skip a payment or payments altogether.

The shortfall in the payments is merely added to the principal balance of the loan. So a negative amortization loan that slowly reduces a substantial equity position in a home is a very different loan from an option ARM loan that begins with a zero equity position in a property. Consider an option ARM loan used to purchase a home with an LTV of 1.0, so that the entire value of the home is being financed. If the home buyer then decides to skip payments, the amount owed becomes larger than the value of the home—assuming the value of the home does not change. From the lender's point of view, this increases the risk of the loan, and it also increases the risk of insolvency for the home buyer. However, if home values rise consistently, the increase in the value of the home could outstrip the increase in the loan amount. It seems that a number of mortgages were granted on this basis—the presumption for both the lender and the borrower being that home values would continue to increase so that the rising value of the home would cover the increasing indebtedness on the loan.

While the loans just described pertained more to first mortgages, practices for second mortgages also changed over time. Of course, many second mortgages were granted as interest only or as adjustable rate mortgages. But beyond these simple developments, other more arcane second mortgages also developed. One of these was the "piggyback mortgage"—a second mortgage initiated at the time the home was bought, with the loan proceeds being used to cover the down payment on the first mortgage. Recall that conventional loans once had specific features that made them eligible for purchase by Fannie Mae and Freddie Mac. Two of the requirements were particularly important in this connection: the mortgage could not exceed a certain principal amount and could not have too great an LTV ratio. As an example, assume that the conventional mortgage limit happened to be $400,000, but the home purchaser wished to buy a house for $600,000 and only had $50,000 available for a down payment. The homebuyer could take a conventional mortgage for $400,000 (thereby capturing the favorable rates available on conforming mortgages—those that met the old standards of Fannie Mae and Freddie Mac, before they started purchasing subprime mortgages), take a piggyback second mortgage for $150,000 that would not qualify for purchase by Fannie or Freddie, and contribute a genuine $50,000 down payment from his or her own funds, thereby assembling the full amount of the purchase price. Of course, this technique allowed the home owner to increase the total amount of indebtedness on the home. The LTV for the conforming loan of our example might only be

0.667 ($400,000/$600,000), but the overall LTV for the home owner would be 0.917 ($550,000/$600,000).

Another important kind of second mortgage innovation was the "cash-out mortgage." In this type of second mortgage, a home owner with equity in a home takes a second mortgage against the home for the purpose of securing cash for some other use. In a period of rising home prices, the home owner uses the cash-out mortgage to treat the home as a piggy bank, withdrawing value from the home. As the value of the home continues to increase, the home owner can repeat this process with successive cash-out mortgages. The result of this process is the failure to accumulate equity in the home, leaving both the borrower and lender in a position of higher continuing risk.

By the height of the subprime market and the height of home prices, all of these practices had become quite prevalent. In 2000, only 2 percent of mortgages used to acquire a home were interest only or negative amortization loans, yet by 2005, 29 percent had at least one of these two features.[12] By the second half of 2004, two-thirds of all second mortgages being issued were piggyback mortgages.[13] In the second half of 2005, 53 percent of all subprime loans were cash-out mortgages, and 74 percent carried an adjustable rate.[14]

As noted in chapter 2, there is no standard definition of what it is to be subprime, and this imprecision leads to difficulties in analysis.[15] A typical analysis of the "subprime crisis" has been to attribute the debacle to ever more widespread lending to ever less qualified borrowers. As we have seen, one definition of a subprime loan is a mortgage made to a buyer with a FICO score below 620, while others define it as a loan made to a borrower with a score below 650. Table 3.2 shows that, in the first half of 2006, 23 percent of mortgages were made to borrowers with a FICO score of 650 or below. One study found that subprime mortgage originations accounted for 25.7 and 31.0 percent of all new mortgages in 2005 and 2006, respectively, and that outstanding subprime mortgages comprised about 13 percent of all mortgage loans.[16] This was supported in another study, which found that the percent of mortgage originations that were subprime diminished in 2001–2002, but were much larger in the 2003–2006 period.[17] For the period 2003–2006, subprime loans accounted for a very high percentage of mortgage originations, yet the percentage of outstanding mortgages that were subprime was much smaller. A reasonable consensus estimate for 2005 would be that about 12–13 percent of all outstanding mortgages were subprime, but that 20–30 percent of mortgages originations that year were subprime.[18]

One might well wonder how 20–30 percent of mortgage origina-tions could be subprime, yet only 12–13 percent of outstanding mort-gages could be subprime. First, some still outstanding mortgages were old, and they tended to conform to the old rules. Second, a further por-tion of this apparent discrepancy is resolved by recognizing that sub-prime mortgages tend to be paid off much earlier than other loans. The reason for this rapid repayment of subprime loans is that they were generally issued as adjustable rate mortgages, often with a fixed interest rate for two or three years, followed by a reset to a higher rate. For example, figure 3.11 shows that 80 percent of subprime mortgages bore an adjustable rate in 2005. As a result, the original subprime mortgage was extinguished (keeping down the percentage of outstanding mort-gages that were subprime) and replaced with a new subprime mort-gage (driving up the percentage of mortgage originations that were subprime).

Much has been made of this mortgage structure of adjustable rate mortgages, which has been disparaged as carrying a "teaser rate" fol-lowed by a higher reset rate. But according to many analysts, the pur-pose of this structure was to require these questionable subprime borrowers to refinance at the end of the initial period. On this model, the lender had the choice of whether to refuse refinancing and call the loan, an option that was particularly desirable if the home price had risen in the interim and if the borrower was not performing.[19] On this under-standing, the point of the mortgage structure was not to "trap" the bor-rower into a new higher rate after the teaser rate expired, but rather to make the borrower again pass the test of being worthy of receiving a

Table 3.2	
Credit Score Distributions for First Mortgages, First Half of 2006	
Credit Score	**Percentage of Mortgages**
Greater than 750	27
701–750	26
651–700	24
601–650	15
551–600	6
501–550	2
500 or less	0

Mortgage Bankers Association, "The Residential Mortgage Market and Its Economic Context in 2007," MBA Research Monograph Series, January 30, 2007.

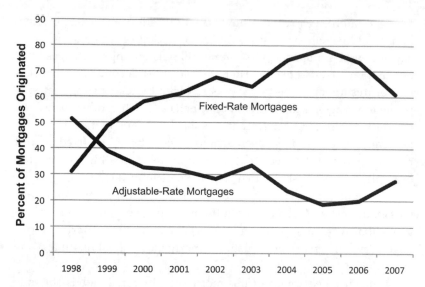

Figure 3.11 Proportions of Fixed-Rate and Adjustable-Rate Subprime Mortgages, 1998–2007

Source: Geetesh Bhardwaj and Rajdeep Sengupta, "Where's the Smoking Gun: A Study of Underwriting Standards for U.S. Subprime Mortgages," Federal Reserve Bank of St. Louis, *Working Paper Series*, October 2008.

new loan. In addition, the lender would expect to make fee income in the new origination. Obviously, the structure was designed for the benefit of the lender, but the prime motivation may well have been protection from a nonperforming borrower, rather than an effort to force a higher loan rate upon a hapless home buyer.

Some have claimed that the subprime crisis was due to deteriorating standards *within* the subprime category. For example, the policy statement by the President's Working Group on Financial Markets (2008) contains this claim: "The turmoil in financial markets was triggered by a dramatic weakening of underwriting standards for U.S. subprime mortgages, beginning in late 2004, and extending into early 2007."[20] However, figure 3.12 presents evidence that the proportion of subprime loans with a FICO score less than 620 was actually *decreasing* from 1998–2007. Somewhat supporting, yet also somewhat in contrast, another study found that FICO scores for subprime mortgages were steady to slightly rising for fixed rate subprime mortgages from 1995–2004 and that for the same period the FICO scores for subprime adjustable rate mortgages

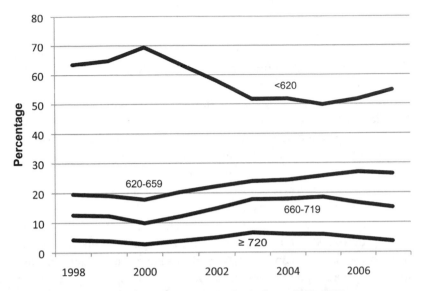

Figure 3.12 Proportion of Loan Originations by Credit Score, 1998–2007
Source: Geetesh Bhardwaj and Rajdeep Sengupta, "Where's the Smoking Gun: A Study of Underwriting Standards for U.S. Subprime Mortgages," Federal Reserve Bank of St. Louis, *Working Paper Series*, October 2008.

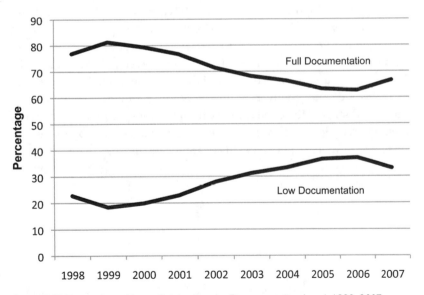

Figure 3.13 Proportion of Loan Originations by Documentation Level, 1998–2007
Source: Geetesh Bhardwaj and Rajdeep Sengupta, "Where's the Smoking Gun: A Study of Underwriting Standards for U.S. Subprime Mortgages," Federal Reserve Bank of St. Louis, *Working Paper Series*, October 2008.

first dipped and then rose, but did actually wind up being lower than they were at the outset of the period.[21]

However, in at least one important respect, there was a marked deterioration in underwriting standards—lenders started to care too little about the verifiability of their applicants' claims of wealth and income. Figure 3.13 shows the rise of low documentation loans among the subprime category. In a "stated-income loan" the borrower merely informs the potential lender about his or her income, but does not provide proof, such as pay stubs, letter from an employer, or so on. This kind of "no-doc loan" and its cousin, the "low-doc loan," became quite prevalent. By 2006, low-doc loans accounted for more than one-third of all subprime mortgage originations.

In sum, we have seen a variety of factors operated over the years leading up to 2006 to increase the financial fragility of many indebted home owners. Over many years, Americans have come to save less and to have a more highly leveraged personal portfolio. In large part, this increase in indebtedness was driven by, and was reflected in, a general increase in LTV ratios for home loans. Innovations in mortgage finance also contributed to this increasing riskiness and fragility. The development of interest only loans and negative amortization loans helped to keep LTV ratios high, as did option ARMs, cash-out mortgages, and piggyback mortgages. The widespread use of ARMs, particularly in the subprime market, made these home owners susceptible to the risk of rising interest rates as well. As the markets developed through 2000–2006, interest rates remained low, and the risk inherent in the prevalence of ARMs did not actually play its potentially dramatic role in creating financial distress. However, the very high leverage for home owners left them vulnerable to the shock of falling home values, and by the end of 2006, reality was ready to make its dramatic intrusion.

From the Subprime Crisis to Financial Disaster: An Overview

The Housing Peak to Hints of Something Wrong

Sometime between the second quarter of 2006 and first quarter of 2007, home prices in the United States reached an all-time high. These two quarters had the highest home prices recorded by the two most prominent home price indexes, prepared by the Office of Federal Housing Enterprise Oversight (OFHEO) and S&P/Case-Shiller, respectively. In January 2007 the Mortgage Bankers Association published an article entitled "The Perfect Calm," which extolled the wonderful real estate situation enjoyed at that moment in the United States.[1]

In another of its publications the same month, the Mortgage Bankers Association opined that after a period of slow home price appreciation that "The housing market is nearly back to normal. The housing market will regain its footing by mid-to-late 2007, depending on what measure is used. Home sales and starts will likely begin to increase in mid-2007, but, given the large inventory overhang, prices are unlikely to show any significant increase until late 2007 or early 2008. *The residential finance market is fundamentally sound and working efficiently.*"[2]

Reading such sanguine assessments that quickly proved to be so wrong provides wry amusements at this late date, but of course the

Mortgage Bankers Association was hardly alone in its rosy assessment. After all, the stock market climbed almost 14 percent from January 1, 2007, to its peak of 14,165 on October 9, 2007. From this height the market would immediately begin its sickening slide to 6,547 on March 9, 2009, losing 54 percent of its value in the process. Not only did the market make a woefully inadequate assessment of the status of the housing market and the economy, but some of the world's supposedly most sophisticated financial firms made faulty assessments that would prove fatal. In 2009, when the smoke began to clear, Wall Street was littered with corpses, and other once proud financial firms existed only as zombie institutions and governmental dependencies, subject to the whims of politicians, bureaucrats, and regulators.

This chapter chronicles the slide of the housing market and its impact on financial markets from the onset of the crisis, through the development of the subprime crisis, up to the point at which the problems that began in the housing market reached the proportion of a financial crisis that had the potential to plunge the economies around the world into a global recession or even depression. Thus, in terms of dates, this chapter focuses on the period from the beginning of 2007 until the fall of 2008. By October 2008 the entire financial system and the world economy stood in grave risk, and the difficulties in the real estate market, as large as they were, had come to seem quaintly small as the world faced an economic catastrophe with the potential to rival, or even exceed, the misery of the Great Depression. In telling the tale, this chapter relies on the detailed time line of the crisis prepared by the Federal Reserve Bank of St. Louis.[3] The Appendix to this volume was prepared by relying on this time line, by severely abridging it, and by supplementing it from the author's own research.

As is appropriate, the herald of the crisis was an institution that would come to play a pivotal role in the financial turmoil just around the corner, Freddie Mac, which issued a press release on February 27, 2007, that read in part: "Freddie Mac today announced that it will cease buying subprime mortgages that have a high likelihood of excessive payment shock and possible foreclosure." But the press release betrayed no particular urgency, as it continued by saying: "In keeping with its statutory responsibility to provide stability to the mortgage market, Freddie Mac will implement the new investment requirements for mortgages originated on or after September 1, 2007, to avoid market disruptions."[4] In other words: "We at Freddie Mac have been operating on false principles, now recognize that, and we promise to stop after six months after committing many more billions of dollars to bad purchases at the behest of Congress."

A few weeks later, in March 2007, the Mortgage Bankers Association reported that almost five percent of all mortgages and more than 13 percent of subprime loans had experienced late or missing payments. As summer 2007 came on, the pace of bad news accelerated with Standard & Poor's and Moody's announcing the first downgrade of securities based on subprime loans, and Bear Stearns suspended redemptions from two of its hedge funds that specialized in subprime-based securities. As the summer continued, Bear Stearns continued to bring forward bad news, and credit rating agencies announced further downgrades. By mid-summer, Countrywide Financial was warning of "difficult conditions," and Bank of America invested $2 billion in Countrywide to shore up its capital position.

The Slide Accelerates

As summer drew to a close, hints of difficulty outside the United States began to emerge. In the United Kingdom, Northern Rock, the UK's fifth-largest mortgage lender, experienced a classic bank run on September 14, 2007, with depositors lined up outside the Rock's various offices, desperately seeking to withdraw their funds. This was the United Kingdom's first bank run since 1866, and the Bank of England offered liquidity support to Northern Rock. Nonetheless, in the United States, the stock market continued its ascent toward its October 9 peak. On Friday, September 14, Northern Rock's share price fell by 38 percent, and the UK government stepped in to guarantee all of its deposits, effectively nationalizing the bank. Nonetheless, on Monday, September 17, the run continued and its share price fell another 31 percent.[5]

The fall of 2007 not only brought the peak of the stock market, but also further signs of distress. Citigroup, at that time the world's largest banking organization, announced previously unrecognized losses of $6.4 billion on October 15, and another $11 billion on November 4. That day Chuck Prince, Citi's CEO, resigned and was replaced by Robert Rubin.

In terms of the subprime crisis, Prince is perhaps best remembered for his remarks on dancing. Only a few months earlier, in July 2007, Prince had said there was little danger to Citi from subprime mortgages because the world's pool of liquidity was so massive, and Citi would be able to continue its aggressive program of expansion through the purchase of other firms saying, "The depth of the pools of liquidity is so much larger than it used to be that a disruptive event now needs to be much more disruptive than it used to be." He continued: "When the music stops, in terms of liquidity, things will be complicated. But as long as the music is playing, you've got to get up and dance. We're still dancing."[6] At the time of his resignation, Citi's stock price stood in the $35 range—it would subsequently fall to $1.02. Citi was not alone, as many of the world's other premier financial firms made successive announcements of losses, with Merrill Lynch confessing an $8.4 billion write-down on October 24 and Morgan Stanley acknowledging $3.7 billion of additional losses on November 7.

In the heyday of subprime, it had been customary for financial firms to create wholly owned, separately capitalized subsidiaries that were "bankruptcy remote." The idea behind these subsidiaries, often called *structured investment vehicles* (SIVs), or *special purpose entities* (SPEs), was to concentrate much of the firm's risky and highly leveraged investment activity in these off-balance-sheet entities. Because they were separately capitalized and claimed to be at a financial distance from the parent firm, financial distress in the subsidiary could not threaten the parent firm; they were "bankruptcy remote" from that parent. Further, these SIVs or SPEs were generally maintained outside the United States and were not subject to capital regulation, as were their parents based in the United States. Thus, they were freer to engage in riskier and more highly leveraged activities on behalf of the parent. This structure was intended to bring the parent the best of both worlds—the opportunity to engage in lucrative and high risk financial transactions without affecting the capital requirements or creditworthiness of the parent.[7]

As fall 2007 wore on to winter, Citi disclosed more bad news by announcing on December 13 that it would bring $49 billion in distressed assets onto its balance sheet from some troubled subsidiaries. Citigroup's bringing these assets back onto its own balance sheet was an essential admission that these SIVs and SPEs were not really so bankruptcy remote after all. Citi found itself unable, or at least unwilling, to let these subsidiaries fail because of the reputational damage it would suffer. After all, Citi had sponsored them, and all investors knew that they were really part of Citi and that the SIV/SPE structure was essentially merely a nod to accounting and capital regulations. As the crisis developed, other firms would also be forced to acknowledge their own bastard children, just as Citi had found itself compelled to do.

▨▨▨▨ Mortgage-Backed Securities and Foreclosures

The origins of these early signs of distress stemmed from the failure of borrowers to make payments on their mortgages as they had promised. In most instances, these mortgages had been collected into a pool and new securities had been created based on the cash flows from the pool of mortgages wrapped into various collateralized mortgage obligations (CMOs). As chapter 2 explained, these securities typically were issued in tranches organized into a structure in which some tranches received priority in payment. If all of the mortgages in the pool made every promised payment, then every security in every tranche would be paid in full. Of course, no one expected literally *every* mortgage to pay as promised, but reasonable expectations of defaults had been priced into the various tranches of securities—or so their creators and those who invested in them may have thought. Contrary to expectations, the default experience quickly developed to be much worse than the market had expected. Shortfalls in payments from the pool meant that the holders of securities in lower tranches started to receive diminished payments or no payments at all.

Figure 4.1 shows the overall foreclosure rate for the United States in 1990–2008. Up until 2000, the total number of homes in foreclosure never exceeded 0.4 percent, but the rate then increased modestly to be almost half of one percent in the early 2000s. Only in late 2006 and after was there a truly significant increase, so that more than one percent of U.S. homes were in foreclosure.

While this represents a very significant problem in the overall housing market, the most severe problem was concentrated in the subprime arena. Starting in 2006, subprime foreclosures escalated rapidly, while prime foreclosures also rose, but at a much more moderate pace. By the second quarter of 2008, almost 4.5 percent of all subprime mortgages were in foreclosure. Among subprime loans, foreclosures were much higher for adjustable rate mortgages (ARMs) than for fixed rate mortgages (FRMs), with ARMs entering foreclosure at a rate more than twice as high.

The cause of these failures to pay and the resulting foreclosures may have been that the mortgages were provided to those who were financially unworthy, or it may have been that the structure of the mortgage industry was predicated on housing prices that always rose, or the foreclosures may have been precipitated by the fall in housing prices that began in 2006. Whatever the causes, the failure of mortgages to pay as

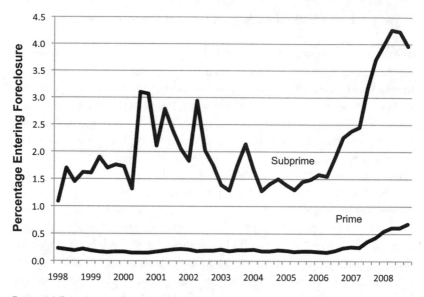

Figure 4.1 Foreclosures Started, 1990–2008

"Anatomy of a Train Wreck: Causes of the Mortgage Meltdown," The Independent Institute, *Independent Policy Report*, October 3, 2008. A special note of appreciation is due to Stan J. Liebowitz, who supplied the data for Figure 4.1. This information originally appeared in his article, "Anatomy of a Train Wreck: Causes of the Mortgage Meltdown," The Independent Institute, *Independent Policy Report*, October 3, 2008

promised made the mortgage-backed security (MBS) constructed from these nonpaying mortgages less valuable. Accounting rules require that firms holding such securities recognize the market value of those securities in their accounting statements—this is the *mark-to-market* accounting requirement that demands that accounting records show the true market value of securities, not the historical value of such instruments.[8]

Decreases in the market value of these MBS and collateralized debt obligations (CDOs) meant that firms had to show losses when they wrote down the value of these securities from their previous market prices to their current diminished value, in accordance with the mandate of mark-to-market accounting. These losses devastated the reported earnings of firms that held these mortgages, leaving them with a diminished capital position. These write-downs did not involve any actual cash flows or realized losses. As an example, consider a firm that has healthy operating earnings that are sufficient to reward shareholders and to maintain respectable capital ratios. If the value of the firm's MBS portfolio falls, the firm is obliged to report that fall in value, even if the firm keeps the portfolio intact. This write-down reduces the firm's earnings and so reduces the firm's capital position. A reduced capital position attracts the ire of regulators and also signals to the market that the firm is in a weakened position. This weakness makes counterparties less willing to leave funds on deposit with the affected institution, and it also attracts the interest of short sellers who speculate on further write-downs and the possibility of falling stock prices.

Because of these write-downs, some firms became desperate to sell CMOs to improve their cash positions and thereby strengthen their capital ratios. However, as foreclosures proceeded and as more and more firms sought to unload their failing mortgage portfolios, the market for these securities came under additional stresses for two reasons. First, the need of many players to sell caused the value of the mortgage-backed securities to fall. Second, as the prices quickly fell, players in the market became increasingly uncertain as to the value of any of these securities, and they therefore became reluctant to trade at any price. In effect, the rapid fall in prices, the complex nature of the MBS and CMOs, and the uncertainty over future defaults and foreclosures meant that the entire market for these mortgage securities was grinding to a standstill. For a typical financial firm, the falling value of their mortgage-backed portfolios required their sale and the raising of more cash, but the market in which they needed to trade was falling away beneath their feet, leaving them stuck with less cash than required and no reasonable way to raise those increasingly desperately needed funds.

No Relief in 2008

With the start of 2008, trouble quickly spread. Washington Mutual (WaMu) revealed that it had lost $1.87 billion in the fourth quarter of 2007, and Bank of America announced that it would purchase Countrywide Financial in an all-stock transaction worth $4 billion. But on January 18, a new kind of shoe dropped when Fitch Ratings downgraded Ambac Financial Group, and Standard and Poor's placed Ambac on CreditWatch Negative.

Ambac Financial Group is a *monoline* insurance company—an insurance company that writes insurance in a single industry. Ambac acts as a bond insurer that receives payment from the issuer of a bond, and Ambac then guarantees to the bond purchaser the timely payment of principal and interest. The incentive for the bond issuer to purchase insurance from a firm like Ambac is to be able to issue the bond with a lower interest rate and a higher bond rating. For the bond purchaser, the guarantee of the bond insurance provided by the monoline insurer makes the bond purchase safer than it otherwise would be. The value of the insurance promise can only be as good as the credit of the bond insurer, however, so it has always been critical for monolines to have the best AAA rating.

As the value of the instruments that the monolines insured became more and more suspect, the market started to fear that the insurance companies would not have enough capital to honor their insurance promises. Further, with these looming payouts hanging over the monolines, the market anticipated that credit rating downgrades might occur as well, an event that would cheapen the promise that the monolines were able to offer. Thus, the entire business of the monolines rested on two claims of credibility—that they could pay the insurance claims as promised, and that they would maintain a very high credit rating so that they could make credible promises in the first place.

Fitch's downgrade pierced this veil of credibility for Ambac, the oldest monoline insurer in the industry. MBIA, the world's largest bond insurer, did not receive a downgrade until April 2008, but these two largest and most important monoline firms both suffered successive downgrades through 2008 from Fitch, Moody's, and Standard and Poor's. Of course, much of the supposed new information of the monoline downgrades had already been anticipated by the market. The huge losses for Ambac and MBIA had already occurred in October 2007, with the stock of both firms tumbling more than 13 percent on a single day, October 25, 2007, the day after Merrill Lynch had announced its own $8.4 billion write-down. Much worse was to come for both firms, with both ultimately losing more than 90 percent of their stock's value, as figure 4.2 shows.

The loss of credible bond guarantees from Ambac and MBIA gave an unmistakable signal to the holders of insured bonds issued by financial firms, and that message was that bondholders could really only look to the resources of the troubled issuers of their bonds for fulfillment of those financial promises. But with almost daily announcements of huge subprime losses by the world's largest and supposedly most sophisticated financial firms, any bond investor had to have extreme concern about the viability of these firms to make their promised payments.

Through the first half of 2008, there was much more news—and almost all of it was bad. On February 17, the Treasury of the United

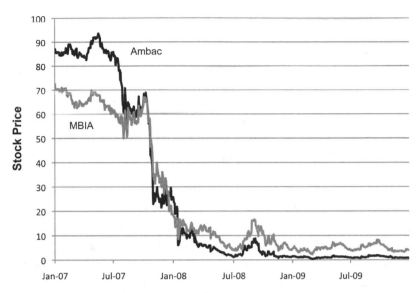

Figure 4.2 The Fall of the Monolines: Ambac and MBIA
Source: Yahoo! Finance.

Kingdom took over Northern Rock entirely. Recognizing the effects that the developing financial crisis would have on the real economy of the United States, President George W. Bush signed the Economic Stimulus Act of 2008 on February 13. The corpses of some firms moved toward burial, with the Federal Reserve Board approving the plan of JPMorgan Chase (often referred to in this book and elsewhere as just "JPMorgan") to take over Bear Stearns on March 14. The Fed issued a similar approval of Bank of America's plan to acquire Countrywide Financial on June 5. But on July 11, the Office of Thrift Supervision seized and closed IndyMac Bank. Before it failed, IndyMac was the seventh-largest mortgage originator in the United States, its rapid growth having been propelled by its specialization in Alt-A mortgages. At the time of its demise, IndyMac had $32 billion in deposits, and the FDIC estimated that the cost of the failure would be in the range of $4–8 billion.[9] The failure of IndyMac was reckoned as the second-largest bank failure in history, and would be one of 25 bank failures in 2008. By contrast, only three banks failed in 2007, and during the entire period of 2000–2007 only 27 banks failed, even though that period included the bursting of the dot-com bubble.[10]

The second half of 2008 opened with yet more signs of widening and deepening crisis. On July 13, the Federal Reserve Board authorized the Federal Reserve Bank of New York to lend to Fannie Mae and Freddie Mac. That same day, the U.S. Treasury increased the credit lines it extended to both GSEs and announced that it stood ready to purchase equity in both Fannie and Freddie if necessary. Given that Fannie and Freddie held about $5 trillion of mortgages between them, the difficulty of these two firms held out the prospect of a bottomless pit into which the government might feel compelled to throw dollars. On July 30, the Housing and Economic Recovery Act of 2008 became law, reforming the federal supervision of the GSEs under a new agency, the Federal Housing Finance Agency (FHFA). As one of its early actions, the FHFA placed both Fannie Mae and Freddie Mac under conservatorship on September 7, effectively recognizing that these two huge firms were bankrupt. In announcing this step, Treasury Secretary Paulson said, "Fannie Mae and Freddie Mac are so large and so interwoven in our financial system that a failure of either of them would cause great turmoil in our financial markets here at home and around the globe."[11]

These kinds of recognitions made it increasingly apparent that the world economy was facing a systemic crisis that threatened real economies everywhere. The next week, the crisis deepened, with Bank of American announcing its plan to purchase Merrill Lynch for $50 billion on September 15, the same day that Lehman Brothers Holdings Incorporated filed for Chapter 11 bankruptcy. Allowing Lehman to fail would quickly come to be regarded by many as a key decision that propelled the U.S. and world economies toward a potentially ultimate financial meltdown.

The next few days brought further bad news. On September 16, the Federal Reserve Board authorized the Federal Reserve Bank of New York to lend up to $85 billion to American International Group (AIG). In effect, this meant that the U.S. government was taking over AIG, receiving almost 80 percent of the firm in exchange for the investment. The next day, September 17, the Dow Jones Industrial Index fell 450 points, and the Securities and Exchange Commission imposed a temporary emergency ban on the short selling of all companies in the financial sector. Many of the distressed firms had lobbied with great intensity for this ban, believing that hedge funds were driving down the price of their shares by the intensity of their short-selling pressure. Perhaps responding to the ban on short selling, the Dow jumped 410 points on September 18, recouping almost all of the previous day's losses.

Interpreting the September 18 gains as some significantly positive signal was quickly shown to be a big mistake. On September 25, the

FDIC seized Washington Mutual Bank (WaMu) and its subsidiaries in the largest bank failure in U.S. history. With $307 billion in assets when seized, WaMu was ten times larger than IndyMac, which had failed only two months earlier. The FDIC transferred ownership of the bank's assets to JPMorgan for a payment of $1.9 billion.[12] Just four days later, on September 29, the FDIC announced that Citigroup would purchase the banking operations of Wachovia Corporation, and that the FDIC and Citi would share in Wachovia's losses. Citi would pay the first $42 billion in losses; the FDIC promised to pay the balance (whatever it proved to be); and Citi granted the FDIC $12 billion in preferred stock and warrants.[13] Wells Fargo quickly mounted a counteroffer that required no FDIC assistance or guarantees—although it did receive certain tax concessions—and it emerged as the ultimate victor in the battle to acquire Wachovia.

As the WaMu and Wachovia dramas unfolded, there were other significant developments. Both Goldman Sachs and Morgan Stanley applied to the Federal Reserve Board to become bank holding companies and to come under the Fed's regulatory aegis. The Fed granted this status on September 21. In short, Goldman and Morgan Stanley found a strategy by which they could weather the financial storm, but the price was a change in corporate form, becoming bank holding companies, which would include the onus of more intensive regulation. By becoming bank holding companies, Goldman and Morgan Stanley gained access to the Fed's discount window and became eligible to participate in the Treasury Department's Troubled Asset Relief Program (TARP), a program that had not yet been authorized by law, but that would pass Congress on October 3, 2008.

The Climax?

Each of these dramatic events—the demise of Bear Stearns, Lehman, Northern Rock, Wachovia, Countrywide, IndyMac, Washington Mutual, Merrill Lynch, and the near-death experiences of Fannie Mae, Freddie Mac, AIG, Ambac, and MBIA—had occurred in turn and had been addressed in a variety of ways, with differing degrees of success. But until the end of September 2008, while it was evident that the financial difficulties were serious, they did not yet appear to threaten the entire financial system in a dramatic way. However, all of these destructive events proved to be merely a prelude to the even greater problems that rapidly emerged in the first days of October 2008.

Figure 4.3 shows the performance of the Dow Jones Industrial Average from the beginning of 2007 through 2009. From the market peak on October 9, 2007, through September 2008, the Dow fell 27 percent, from 14,165 (the all-time high) to 10,851. But as figure 4.3 reveals, this was fairly gradual and really quite consistent with a normal bear market, in which losses of 25–30 percent in a single year are not uncommon. But the first 10 days of October 2008 were extraordinary. From September 30 to October 10, the Dow fell 22 percent, from 10,851 to 8,451—a drop of 2,400 points.

As dramatic as this drop was, the worst was not the mere loss of value that such losses implied. In addition, there were strong indications that the very structure of the market was extremely weak and that financial collapse had become a very imminent threat. One sign of the market's malfunctioning was an extreme spike in volatility. Figure 4.4 presents the VIX index as a measure of stock market volatility for the period from 2007 to mid-2009. It is based on option prices for the S&P 500 stock market index that expire in 30 days, so it provides a measure of how much the market expects the S&P 500 to move up or down over the next 30 days. These values are annualized. So the normal annualized volatility of the S&P 500 might be in the range of 0.15 to 0.20. A VIX value above that range indicates an expectation of higher than normal

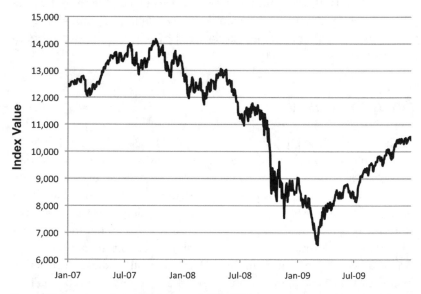

Figure 4.3 Dow Jones Industrial Average, 2007–2009

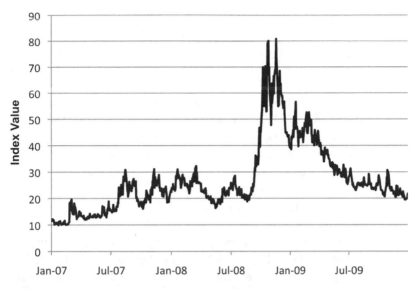

Figure 4.4 U. S. Stock Market Volatility, 2007–2009

volatility. Values of 0.40 or above indicate extreme volatility. As figure 4.4 shows, the VIX reached unprecedented highs in October and November of 2008.

Another way of understanding the extreme volatility of this period is by considering the typical number of percentage points that the entire market moved in a single day. In June 2008 a typical price move for the Dow Jones Industrial Average was about 1 percent in a day, either up or down; in October 2008, the typical price move routinely exceeded 5 percent and approached 6 percent per day. This extreme volatility implied that market participants were very uncertain about market values, and such persistent extreme volatility is a typical sign of a market in extreme distress.[14]

Developments in the credit markets were even more disturbing. A modern financial system relies on the rapid movement of funds from surplus units to deficit units with a minimum of friction, or transaction costs, in the process. (A surplus economic unit is one that generates more cash than it consumes, while a deficit unit has more spending or investment needs than available cash. Historically, households have been surplus units, earning more than they consume and thus saving, while businesses have been deficit units, needing to acquire funds from surplus units to fund their investment programs.) When conditions develop that impede the free movement of funds through the financial system, it is akin to throwing sand into the gears of a fine automobile. In a low friction market, major players must be able to trust each other's financial viability. This is especially true of large banks, who have frequent and very substantial cash flows among themselves. When these major banks start to question another bank's financial viability, they will refuse to lend and will seek a return of the funds on deposit with the suspect institution. At the very least, a prospective lender will have to charge a higher interest rate than otherwise to cover the additional perceived risk. For its part, a bank in distress will be willing to pay a higher interest rate to secure desperately needed funds.

Figure 4.5 provides a measure of credit conditions in the international money market from 2006 to mid-2009. The graph shows the difference between the three-month U.S. Treasury rate and the three-month London Interbank Offer Rate (LIBOR). LIBOR is essentially the rate at which the largest and most creditworthy international banks lend funds to each other. In the best of times, LIBOR is higher than the corresponding U.S. interest rate for dollars, because the creditworthiness of the U.S. Treasury exceeds that of even the most solid banking firm. As the period of 2006 well into 2007 shows, that differential tends to be about 50–75

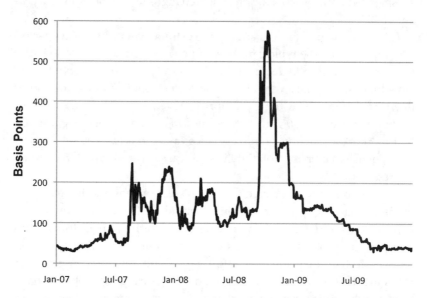

Figure 4.5 The TED Spread, 2007–2009 Source: Federal Reserve Board, Selected Interest Rates, http://www.federalreserve.gov/datadownload/Format.aspx?rel=H15. Accessed March 3, 2010

basis points, or one-half to three-quarters of one percent in normal times. (A full percentage point is 100 basis points.) This difference in yields between Treasuries and LIBOR, or equivalently between Treasuries and Eurodollar deposits, is also known as the TED spread.[15] The TED spread widened slowly through the first half of 2007 and stood at 95 basis points on August 13. In the next week, it escalated to 247 basis points. This period corresponds to the onset of difficulties of Bear Stearns and Countrywide Financial. This event ushered in a period of generally higher spreads for the next year. As figure 4.5 shows, the spread continued to fluctuate, but maintained a much higher level than observed in 2006.

On September 10, 2008, the TED spread was 138 basis points. Over the next month, the spread exploded, reaching 576 basis points on October 10, which is the peak shown in figure 4.5. Note also that this is exactly the same day on which the stock market hit its low for 2008, and it was the day that marked a 22 percent stock market drop in the preceding ten days.

While the quoted differential may have been 576 basis points, this should not be taken to imply that one could borrow or lend at such rates as freely as in normal times. In distressed markets, quotes often diverge from reasonable relationships, and in many cases it is a signal that no transactions can actually be made. That is exactly what was happening in October 2008. In effect, the enormous spread between Treasuries and LIBOR was a statement that the world's credit markets were at a standstill.

In the absence of functioning credit markets, ordinary firms cannot finance their inventories and cannot secure funds to meet their payrolls. Suppliers will refuse to ship products, and firms will be forced to lay off employees because of a lack of funds to pay them. When this happens in such crises, problems that started in the financial markets flood into the real economy, destroying production, consumption, and employment. If there was a single day in which the world looked into an economic abyss, it was October 10, 2008. That day the world's economy stood on the threshold of a depression that threatened to replay the experience of the 1930s.

During those early days of October, as the stock market spiraled downward and credit markets ceased to function, all observers came to realize that the United States economy, and thus the world economy, stood in the midst of a systemic financial crisis with potential for utter destruction. It also became clear that the federal government was fully engaged and prepared to undertake the most extensive and radical actions to forestall disaster.

On October 3, after much bitter debate, Congress passed and President Bush signed the Emergency Economic Stabilization Act of 2008, thereby establishing the Troubled Asset Relief Program (TARP). This law provided the administration with a pot of $700 billion to purchase "troubled assets." According to the underlying rationale of the TARP, if the Treasury purchased the "troubled" mortgage-backed assets, firms would receive cash, which would have three beneficial effects. First, the purchases of securities would take an illiquid asset off the balance sheet and replace it with cash, thereby improving the firm's liquidity. Second, with more cash on hand relative to their assets, the firms would be better capitalized and less leveraged. Third, by placing the problematic assets in the strong hands of the Treasury, the hope was that the market for MBS would stabilize, that an orderly market for MBS would resume, and that the Treasury might even make a buck by having bought the MBS at distressed prices and later being able to sell them at their presumably higher intrinsic values after the market stabilized. At the time of its creation, there was no publicly announced program for using the TARP, yet now $700 billion was in play, and the Treasury was understood to be fully engaged and frantically working on a plan to provide relief to the financial sector, a plan the Treasury unveiled on October 14.

During the same period, fears of bank runs in the United States quickly developed. Bank deposits had been insured by the FDIC up to $100,000, with amounts above that level either being uninsured or depending on private insurance acquired by the depository institutions. If bank runs were to develop, with depositors sucking their money out of banks, banks would be thrown into an even worse capital position and might be forced into liquidation. To forestall the development of runs, the FDIC increased its deposit insurance limit from $100,000 to $250,000. Perhaps more importantly, the FDIC insured other deposits and bank liabilities, with the result that the FDIC was insuring and guaranteeing virtually the entire banking system.

Back from the Brink

October 10 was a Friday. The market closed that week after one of the worst periods in financial market history. No one knew how things would develop on Monday or in the days that would follow. That Friday it was not unreasonable to think that the cascade would resume when markets reopened.

Contrary to reasonable fears, the stock market gained more than 11 percent on Monday, October 13, with the Dow climbing from its Friday close of 8,451 to 9,388 at close on Monday. Over the next weeks, stock market volatility remained high and the stock market fluctuated sharply from day to day. Eventually, the market resumed its downward march falling a further 23 percent from 8,451 on October 10, 2008, to a new low of 6,547 on March 9, 2009. But while a 23 percent drop in four months was certainly sharp, it proceeded in a fairly orderly fashion. Further, as figure 4.4 shows, volatility subsided substantially, although it remained high by historical norms.

In the months following the crisis of October 2008, the U.S. government enacted a number of programs to provide further relief to markets and the broader economy, as did governments around the world. By mid-2009, the TARP program had been revamped more than once and had been extended from the financial sector to the broader economy. The federal government entered the automobile business with a major stake in Chrysler and a 60 percent ownership of General Motors.

In response to the crisis, the federal government had initiated an extraordinary range of measures that brought its role in the economy to a dominance not seen since at least World War II. Over time, observers started to believe that the worst had been averted, and by late spring 2009 the market was enjoying a very sharp revival. Market commentators debated whether the stock market jump from the spring to autumn of 2009 was a "bear market rally"—an interlude of rising prices before a generally falling trend resumed—or whether we might be enjoying the beginning of a genuine bull market. Conditions in the real economy remained poor, with unemployment continuing to rise and housing prices continuing to fall through 2009. Nonetheless, by the second quarter of 2009, more and more economic commentators started to speak hopefully about "green shoots" of recovery starting to emerge in the real economy.

Extinctions

Among the Ruins

By mid-2009, with markets having regained substantial stability, it became possible to start to gain at least some historical perspective on the social meaning of the crisis. One part of this effort is to consider some of the firms that passed from existence. Some of the major extinctions were Bear Stearns, Lehman Brothers, Countrywide Financial, Washington Mutual, and IndyMac Federal Bank, FSB. In addition, Wachovia and Merrill Lynch ceased to be independent companies and were acquired by Wells Fargo and Bank of America, respectively.

Picking in these ruins, we find that the specific causes of collapse differed, but were all tied to problems that originated in the U.S. housing market. Bear Stearns, Lehman Brothers, and Merrill Lynch were heavily involved in the securitization and resale of mortgages, and their exposure in these areas was primarily responsible for their demise. The banking and mortgage lending firms, Countrywide, IndyMac, Washington Mutual (WaMu), and Wachovia, functioned more in the origination of mortgages, but they too were involved in securitization. This chapter focuses on the depository institutions that vanished from the scene (Countrywide, IndyMac, Washington Mutual, and Wachovia), while chapter 6 addresses the end of the investment banking industry.

From Countrywide to IndyMac

While the worldwide financial crisis may have grown to dwarf the subprime crisis, subprime remains a key element of the much grander financial crisis. After all, subprime provided the foundation upon which the global financial system built the bigger disaster. There is no single figure who played a more central role in the subprime debacle than Angelo Mozilo, a man who managed to found not just one, but two firms that contributed spectacular failures to the subprime fiasco— Countrywide Financial Corporation and IndyMac Bancorp, Inc. Mozilo founded Countrywide in 1969 and led it for four decades as it became the largest home mortgage lender in the United States. In the process, Countrywide spawned Countrywide Mortgage Investment in 1985. Countrywide spun off this investment arm in 1997 as an independent firm, and it later became IndyMac Bancorp, along with its subsidiary, IndyMac Federal Bank, FSB. IndyMac would have its own spectacular demise in 2008.

Countrywide came to be an enormous financial institution and one of the most prominent and aggressive firms of the subprime era. In 2006, Countrywide recorded revenues of $11.4 billion and net profits of $2.7 billion, along with total assets of $200 billion. At the end of 2006, Countrywide held $31 billion in loans that were to be sold, with another $78 billion of loans held for investment. It ended the year with a stock price of $42.45, reflecting a gain of 24 percent for the year. The next two years would be unkind, with losses in 2007 of $704 million and a stock price at year-end of $8.94 per share, reflecting a loss for the year of 79 percent. In just the third quarter of 2007, Countrywide lost $1.2 billion. Bad as 2007 was, 2008 would bring oblivion.

Mozilo took Countrywide to stardom (and ruin) on the back of the subprime mortgage. Honored at Harvard for his role in promoting the expansion of home ownership, Mozilo entitled his speech, "The American Dream of Homeownership: From Cliché to Mission." In that speech, Mozilo said that he had started Countrywide with ". . . the objective to lower the barriers and open the doors to homeownership."[1] He continued by explaining that he wanted Countrywide to be ". . . a force in making positive differences in people's lives." He called for the elimination of down payment requirements and advocated offering "customized programs to those borrowers who cannot meet the current down payment requirements." Other jewels from the speech include these statements "We must reduce the documentation required to make any and all loans"; and "We must all lean on the side of looking for every reason to approve applicants rather than the reasons to reject them." Harvard was not alone in honoring Mozilo; *Barron's* hailed him as one of the world's 30 most respected CEOs in 2005.

Countrywide's aggressive lending practices brought results. In 2004, Countrywide originated 13 percent of all U.S. home mortgages. By September 2006, it was issuing mortgages at a rate of $37 billion per month, almost $2 billion per business day.[2] During the heyday of sub-prime, 2003–2006, Countrywide followed loan-granting policies that today would make any observer's eyes pop. For example, in 2005, 19 percent of Countrywide's loans were pay-option ARMs—an adjustable rate mortgage that lets owners skip payments—which Countrywide recommended as a suitable loan for "anyone who wants the lowest possible payment." In 2006, Countrywide issued $470 billion in loans, 45 percent of which were nonconforming, with 46 percent of these being made in California. It continued making piggyback loans into 2007, frequently lending more than 95 percent of a home's appraised value. In mid-2007, Countrywide was still featuring a willingness to lend $500,000 to borrowers with FICO credit scores as low as 500—a credit score that is in the dark basement of the subprime range. (Recall that conventional benchmark FICO scores for subprime status range from 620 to 650.)

Mozilo's 2003 speech and Countrywide's liberal lending policies may suggest that the firm was flying blind. But that was not exactly the case. During 2006, Mozilo made a speech praising the payment-option ARM; the next day, in internal e-mails, he expressed concern that these same mortgages were based on borrower's statements of income that Countrywide knew were often lies.[3] While Mozilo may have praised zero down-payment loans in public, internal records now reveal that he regarded these loans as "the most dangerous product in existence and there can be nothing more toxic."[4]

When the housing market came into real difficulty in 2007, Countrywide found itself holding a huge portfolio of loans that it had issued under those incredibly liberal policies. Countrywide's deepening financial distress provided a clear answer to the rhetorical question that Mozilo posed at Harvard in 2003: "But from my point of view, if 80 percent of the sub-prime borrowers are managing to make ends meet and make the mortgage payment on time, then, shouldn't we, as a Nation, be justifiably proud that we are dramatically increasing home-ownership opportunities for those who have been traditionally left behind?"

In August 2007, Countrywide's financial distress led them to borrow the full $11.5 billion that it had pre-arranged as a credit line. A few days later, Bank of America invested $2 billion to secure a 16 percent owner-ship in Countrywide. Meanwhile, Countrywide maintained that its survival was assured and that it was not a takeover target. Matters did not improve. By early January 2008, 7.2 percent of the loans it serviced were delinquent, and Bank of America agreed to pay $4 billion (in addi-tion to its earlier $2 billion investment) to acquire Countrywide. In June 2009, the Securities and Exchange Commission charged Mozilo with securities fraud and insider trading.[5]

Why did Mozilo and Countrywide follow loan practices that they apparently knew were likely to lead to problems? After all, Mozilo knew in 2006 that about 70 percent of stated income loan applicants claimed income that was exaggerated by more than 50 percent; in the same period Mozilo referred to the no-money-down mortgages as "poison."

Perhaps Mozilo found posing as the friend of the poor and the pro-vider of housing to minorities and the disadvantaged quite intoxicating? Perhaps Mozilo's own financial incentives played a role in guiding his policies? Often criticized for his lavish compensation, Mozilo had for many years received and disposed of Countrywide shares, becoming a multimillionaire in the process. According to one reliable calculation, Mozilo had garnered more than $400 million from exercising options and selling shares since 1999; $300 million of that came just since 2005, and he accelerated his sales as Countrywide's stock price sank. Mozilo's pay in 2006 was $43 million. In 2007, Mozilo realized $122 million from exercising stock options, while receiving $22 million in annual compen-sation. That same year, Countrywide lost $704 million and suffered a 79 percent stock price decline.[6]

IndyMac

After its independence in 1997, IndyMac—a contraction of "Indepen-dent National Mortgage Corporation"—came to be a smaller, yet signif-icant, competitor to Countrywide. The IndyMac mortgage firm spun off by Countrywide acquired a bank in 2000 and became IndyMac Bank.

Throughout its history, IndyMac was led by Michael Perry, who had risen to prominence at Countrywide as a protégé of Angelo Mozilo.

While somewhat active in subprime lending, IndyMac specialized in Alt-A mortgages. These mortgages were supposedly offered to borrowers with good credit credentials, but the mortgages did not meet the requirements of conventional mortgages and were not eligible for purchase by Fannie Mae or Freddie Mac. For example, a quintessential Alt-A mortgage might be a jumbo mortgage made to a person with good credit, or a mortgage made to a financially worthy, self-employed person who chose not to prove income. At least, that is the theory behind Alt-A mortgages.

In 2006, IndyMac was already the number one originator of Alt-A loans, making more than 75 percent of its loans in that form; of its total $90 billion in lending, $70 billion was concentrated in Alt-A, and IndyMac accounted for 17.5 percent of the entire Alt-A market.[7] By 2008, IndyMac boasted assets of $32 billion. While supposedly not subprime, Alt-A mortgages were not free from their own difficulties, especially if they were made using subprime lending standards.

By early 2008, IndyMac realized it was in deep trouble, holding a mortgage portfolio of $10 billion that it was unable to sell. Frantically trying to raise capital, IndyMac met with several private equity firms, but none advanced capital. Perhaps facing eventual bankruptcy, the process was hastened by an extraordinary event. On June 26, Charles Schumer, senator from New York, made public a letter he had written to the Office of Thrift Supervision, the federal agency that supervised IndyMac. Schumer's letter read in part that he was "concerned that IndyMac's financial deterioration poses significant risk to both taxpayers and borrowers."

Up until this time, IndyMac's deposits had been increasing. But now reaction was swift. In the next 11 days, IndyMac suffered deposit outflows exceeding $1 billion. The director of the Office of Thrift Supervision publicly criticized Schumer's letter as "the immediate cause" of IndyMac's crisis and said that the letter "undermined the public confidence essential for a financial institution and took away the time IndyMac needed to pursue a recovery."[8] Whether Schumer's letter took away time or not, there was not much time left.

During this period, IndyMac took desperate actions, announcing that it was no longer accepting loan applications, that Michael Perry had asked the board to cut his base salary in half, and that it was dismissing more than half of its workforce over the next few months.[9] On July 11 the

Federal Deposit Insurance Corporation seized and closed IndyMac in a bank failure that wiped out shareholders and cost the insurance fund $8.9 billion. IndyMac's collapse ranked as one of the top five bank failures in U.S. history—at least up to that time.

IndyMac's problems were due largely to poor underwriting standards for mortgage loans. The problem is not with Alt-A loans per se. If Bill Gates chose to finance his mansion with a mortgage and refused to document his income, it would not be a prime mortgage. Instead, it would be an Alt-A mortgage for the simple reason that the loan amount would exceed the guidelines for a conventional mortgage and there would not be sufficient documentation of Gates's financial capacity. However, IndyMac's problems stemmed mainly from ignoring the financial capacity of its borrowers and therefore making loans to people who could not repay.

One IndyMac loan went to Ben Butler, an 80-year-old retiree in Savannah, Georgia. According to the loan application, Butler received $3,825 per month from Social Security, but the maximum Social Security payment is only about half that much. This suggests that Butler falsified the loan and that IndyMac failed to check it. As an alternative account, Butler's attorney maintains that someone in the loan origination process changed the application to ensure that Butler got the loan.[10]

Some have charged that IndyMac focused on making loans no matter how inadequate the borrower's resources. According to its own filings with the SEC, only 21 percent of IndyMac's mortgages had full documentation.[11] This was not a surprising result, as IndyMac trumpeted to prospective borrowers: "IndyMac NonPrime will accept a Verification of Employment for a full documentation loan with no pay stubs or W2s needed!"[12]

In its study, the Center for Responsible Lending documented numerous questionable lending tactics, including inattention to documentation, and various abuses of borrowers. According to the Center ". . . many of the problems at IndyMac were spawned by top-down pressures that valued short-term growth over protecting borrowers and shareholders' interests over the long haul."[13] Meanwhile, in his 2008 letter to shareholders, Michael Perry echoed a theme he had perhaps learned from Angelo Mozilo: "Most of us believe that innovative home lending served a legitimate economic and social purpose, allowing many U.S. consumers to be able to achieve the American dream of homeownership . . . and we still do."[14] After the seizure of IndyMac, the FDIC announced that it has retained the services of all of the bank's former top executives—except for Michael Perry, whose services were no longer required.[15]

Washington Mutual

Born in the aftermath of the "Great Seattle Fire" of 1889, Washington Mutual (WaMu) began its life as a tiny loan company based in Seattle, Washington. In the early 1900s it became a savings and loan association, then a mutual savings bank, and it incorporated as a public company in 1983. Through the 1990s, WaMu expanded rapidly, fueled largely by mergers that proceeded at a rate of about two per year. This rapid growth was led by Kerry K. Killinger, who joined WaMu in 1982, became president in 1998, and assumed the helm as CEO and chairman in 1990.[16] WaMu continued to expand into the new century and showed no signs of slowing down. From 2000 to 2003, WaMu's number of retail branches grew by 70 percent, reaching 2,200 in 38 states.

By 2006, WaMu had total assets of $346 billion and net income of $3.6 billion. At this point, the bank was a huge player in the mortgage market. In retrospect, much of this growth was achieved by making loans with little regard to the creditworthiness of borrowers: "At WaMu, getting the job done meant lending money to nearly anyone who asked for it—the force behind the bank's meteoric rise and its precipitous collapse this year in the biggest bank failure in American history."[17]

Court filings in a suit by the Ontario Teachers' Pension Plan contain testimony of 89 former employees of WaMu. A summary of their testimony concludes: "According to these accounts, pressure to keep lending emanated from the top, where executives profited from the swift expansion—not least, Kerry K. Killinger, who was WaMu's chief executive . . ."[18] One of those former employees who testified was Keysha Cooper, who had been a senior mortgage underwriter. She describes continuous intense pressure to approve loans, saying: "They didn't care if we were giving loans to people that didn't qualify. Instead, it was how many loans did you guys close and fund?" and "You were like a bad person if you declined a loan."[19]

Loan officers received free trips to Hawaii and Jamaica for granting loans, and mortgage brokers often offered WaMu loan officers bribes to approve loans. According to the Ontario Teachers' complaint, mortgage brokers could make 6–8 percent commission on a loan. Former employees speak of WaMu as a mortgage lending sweatshop. Some of the loans at

WaMu included elements of absurdity, including the mariachi singer who claimed a six-figure income.

The Orange County Register reported on the Soni family that acquired at least 43 mortgages from WaMu from early 2007 on. In July 2007, the Sonis bought a house for $440,000 and five weeks later resold it to their gardener and handyman for $660,000—raking in a 50 percent profit at a time when real estate values were falling. WaMu financed both mortgages. The gardener soon defaulted and WaMu foreclosed, losing approximately $300,000 on the round-trip.[20]

Perhaps there was reason behind such apparently mad lending policies. In good times, rapid expansion and aggressive lending translated into surging stock prices and lavish executive compensation. Killinger received more than $100 million while CEO, suggesting at least the possibility of a strong motive for lax lending standards. Over 2007, WaMu's stock price fell from $45.49 to $13.61; meanwhile, Killinger's compensation was $14.4 million.[21]

Matters did not improve in 2008, and WaMu's board became disenchanted with Killinger's leadership, forcing him to retire in September 2008 and sending him on his way with a severance package worth $17.7 million.[22] Killinger had made it almost to the end, but was replaced as CEO by Alan H. Fishman. More or less immediately, WaMu experienced a run on its deposits, with more than 10 percent of all deposits being withdrawn in a week. Just a few weeks after this transition, the FDIC seized Washington Mutual as insolvent on September 25, 2008, citing a deposit outflow of $17 billion as the main reason for closing the bank.[23] With its $307 billion in assets, WaMu's demise is the biggest bank failure in U.S. history.

The passing of WaMu had two noteworthy outcomes. The first is rather ironic. The tenure of the new CEO, Fishman, lasted less than three weeks, but it did make him eligible for an $11.6 million cash severance payment to accompany his $7.5 million signing bonus.[24] The second outcome was more serious. The failure of IndyMac had run down the FDIC's deposit insurance fund to $45.2 billion. A straight-out liquidation of WaMu was expected to cost the fund about $30 billion. Instead of liquidating the bank, the FDIC sold its banking operations to JPMorgan for $1.9 billion, which also agreed to absorb WaMu's losses. With this shotgun acquisition, JPMorgan became the largest deposit-taking institution in the United States.

Back in 2003, CEO and Chairman Kerry Killinger portentously predicted: "We hope to do to this industry what Wal-Mart did to theirs, Starbucks did to theirs, Costco did to theirs and Lowe's-Home Depot did to their industry. And I think if we've done our job, five years from now you're not going to call us a bank." WaMu may never have become the financial equivalent of Wal-Mart, but by the end of Killinger's five-year prediction horizon, no one was calling WaMu a bank. For Killinger's part, dismissed from the top spot at WaMu, he was free to pursue a new career as a seer.[25]

Wachovia

Wachovia National Bank began in 1879 in Winston-Salem, North Carolina, and remained true to its regional roots for more than a century. Following a multitude of smaller acquisitions, Wachovia became a truly large bank in 2001 when it merged with First Union, another large bank based in the Southeast. But Wachovia's most important acquisition was its 2006 purchase of Golden West Financial for about $25 billion.

At the time of the Golden West acquisition, Wachovia had a market capitalization of $90 billion and expected a resulting combined market capitalization of about $117 billion. By July 2008, Wachovia's total capitalization (including the *contribution* from Golden West) was $26 billion, or just about the same amount it paid for Golden West less than two years earlier. These unpleasant developments helped earn the Golden West acquisition the appellation of the "Deal from Hell."[26]

In 2006, the California-based Golden West was the second largest S&L in the United States and had just been named the "most-admired" firm in the mortgage business by *Fortune* magazine. Golden West got its start in 1963 when Herbert and Marion Sandler bought a small S&L for $4 million. The Sandlers stayed with the company for the next 43 years and built a huge business with a virtually single focus on issuing one type of mortgage loan—the option ARM—which constituted 99 percent of Golden West's entire $122 billion mortgage portfolio. Nonetheless, at the time of the acquisition, Ms. Sandler said of the option ARM that "we have been offering this product for over 20 years and we have a pristine portfolio . . . and we are not at all concerned about the risks in the portfolio."[27] Having just sold the bank, the Sandlers had much less reason to be concerned about the portfolio's risks, of course. Kenneth Thompson, CEO of Wachovia, apparently agreed, calling the acquisition a "dream come true."[28]

Other observers were less sanguine, with the market trimming $1 billion from Wachovia's market capitalization upon the merger announcement. Christopher Whalen at Institutional Risk Analytics noted at the time that Wachovia was buying at the top of a speculative bubble and wondered whether those at Wachovia were "going to regret this later on."[29] In less than two years, by mid-2008, "later on" had arrived. Wachovia announced a $23.9 billion loss for a single quarter and projected an additional $26 billion in mortgage-related losses for 2009. The quarterly loss, observed the *New York Times*, was one of the largest in banking history: "It is bigger than the market value of 422 companies in the Standard & Poor's 500-stock index, and slightly more than the gross domestic product of Panama."[30]

Even without the Golden West acquisition, Wachovia would have experienced considerable financial pain from its own unwise mortgage lending, but Golden West's option ARMs brought their own special pain and probably tipped Wachovia into oblivion. By September 2008, Wachovia was facing bankruptcy and desperately seeking a way out. WaMu had just been seized on Thursday, September 25, and Wachovia's stock responded by falling 27 percent the next day. The federal government, notably the FDIC and the Treasury department, were well aware of Wachovia's plight. Faced with another giant bank failure within a week of WaMu's implosion, informed market observers feared another wave of financial instability with uncertain, but potentially catastrophic, systemic effects.

Frantic merger talks went on all weekend, and Wells Fargo was prepared to buy Wachovia for $20 billion. But that Sunday evening, September 28, Wells suddenly backed out of the deal over concerns about the apparently bottomless pit of Wachovia's mortgage problems. This led to a frenzy of negotiations from Sunday night to Monday morning involving the FDIC, the Treasury, Wachovia, and Citigroup.

Before the markets opened on September 29, the parties were prepared to make a joint announcement. Sheila Bair, head of the FDIC, said: "This morning's decision was made under extraordinary circumstances with significant consultation among the regulators and Treasury."[31] Citi would acquire the banking operations of Wachovia for $2.2 billion, or about $1 per share. Citi promised to honor Wachovia's $54 billion in debt and to absorb the first $42 billion of losses on Wachovia's mortgage portfolio. The FDIC agreed to bear any greater mortgage losses. For the FDIC's taking that open-ended risk exposure, Citi would issue $12 billion in preferred stock and warrants to the FDIC.[32] Wachovia would continue in the securities business, but be out of banking. Wachovia's shareholders failed to express their gratitude, with Wachovia's shares falling 87 percent that Monday from $8.73 to $1.27, just a bit more than the price specified in the takeover plan.

Thus matters were resolved, or at least Citi thought so that bright Monday morning. The acquisition would have given Citi more than 4,300 branches in the United States and $600 billion in deposits. But that same day, Congress refused to pass the $700 billion Troubled Asset Relief Program (TARP) legislation. Citi had anticipated that this legislation would have allowed it to unload some of Wachovia's $54 billion debt to the federal government, but now that aspect of Citi's grand plan looked unreliable at best. Nonetheless, Citi announced on Tuesday that it was "committed to the orderly consummation of the transaction."[33]

So on Tuesday, September 30, everything was resolved, at least until Friday, October 3. That day, Wachovia and Wells Fargo—the same suitor that had abandoned Wachovia just five days earlier—announced a new plan. Wells would acquire Wachovia without any cash outlays from the government—but with valuable federally granted tax concessions— paying $15 billion for the privilege, along with accepting expected losses of $74 billion, which it promised to absorb. The FDIC was delighted at the prospect of being off the hook for all of the unknown risk it had shouldered in its assistance of the Citi-Wachovia deal. Citi, firmly believing it had a deal that had even been endorsed by the FDIC and Treasury, was outraged and initiated immediate legal action.

Receiving no support from the federal government and facing a protracted legal battle, Citi gave up the fight on October 9 and acquiesced in the loss of Wachovia to Wells Fargo. Perhaps treated unfairly in the entire process, Citi appears to have benefited by being jilted. On October 3, Citi's share price stood at $18.35, but even without the burdens and complications of absorbing Wachovia, it would fall as low as $1.02 within six months. For Wells Fargo, losses associated with the Wachovia acquisition continued, and the *New York Times* reported that Wells Fargo's ". . . hurried acquisition of the troubled Wachovia Corporation would be a long and difficult struggle."[34] Nonetheless, Wells Fargo has not visited the financial depths that Citi has explored, and it looks well able to continue in operation with an enormous deposit base.

Bank Extinctions, Banking Consolidation, and "Too Big to Fail"

Figure 5.1 shows the fate of these four huge banks—Countrywide Financial, IndyMac, Wachovia, and Washington Mutual—with their huge erosion of shareholder value. By the fall of 2008, all four of these banks would be gone. For its part, IndyMac passed from existence with the FDIC paying for the entire collapse. Three of these firms would be absorbed by larger and presumably healthier banks: Bank of America acquiring Countrywide, Wells Fargo absorbing Wachovia, and JPMorgan accepting the collapsed Washington Mutual, with a total of many billions of dollars being provided by the U.S. government to facilitate the transactions.

There has long been concern in the United States that some financial institutions are "too big to fail" in the sense that the collapse of these institutions would imply great distress for the entire financial system.[35] To a large extent, concern about the unsupervised bankruptcy of these large institutions drove government involvement in acting as morticians for these bankruptcies.

Figure 5.1 Banks Fall into the Subprime Abyss

However, the federal government adopted the solution of folding these failing banks into even larger, and presumably healthier, banks. If these four failing institutions were too large to be allowed to simply go bankrupt, what does this imply for the newly enlarged super-banks such as JPMorgan, Bank of America, and Wells Fargo Corporation, which were enlarged by these transactions, and Citi, which, while excluded from these transactions, was already an enormous bank? These failures contributed to an enormous banking consolidation in the United States, as we will see in chapter 15. If "too big to fail" was a problem in 2008, it is a much bigger problem at present, and the cause of growing public policy concern to escape from the too-big-to-fail trap.

6

The End of Investment Banking

Big Brains, Big Egos, and Big Pay

Investment banks have long been recognized as the world's greatest repository of practical financial wisdom. The largest and most sophisticated commercial banks and corporations in the world turn to these firms to guide their own financial affairs. Table 6.1 shows the status of the five major firms in this industry at the end of 2007. The subprime debacle and the ensuing worldwide financial crisis would bring this distinctive industry, with its $280 billion in revenue and $30 billion in profits, to an end within nine months. By the time the dust of crisis began to clear, not a single large U.S. independent investment banking firm would be left standing: Bear Stearns, Lehman Brothers, and Merrill Lynch were all gone, while Goldman Sachs and Morgan Stanley would change their corporate form in order to live to fight another day. Figure 6.1 shows the dramatic stock price drop of three prominent firms in the investment banking industry: Bear Stearns, Lehman Brothers, and Merrill Lynch.

Table 6.1		
Investment Banking in 2007		
Company	2007 Revenue ($ Millions)	Profits ($ Millions)
Morgan Stanley	76,688	7,472
Merrill Lynch	70,591	7,499
Goldman Sachs	69,353	9,537
Lehman Brothers	46,709	4,007
Bear Stearns	16,551	2,054
Totals	279,892	30,569

Source: http://money.cnn.com/magazines/fortune/fortune500/2007/industries/Securities/1.html.
Accessed October 14, 2009.

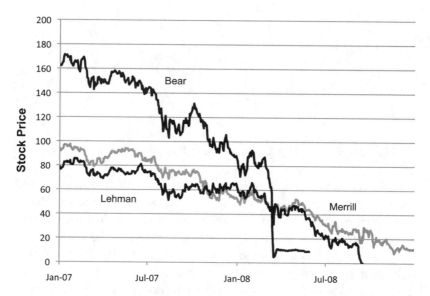

Figure 6.1 The Demise of Bear Stearns, Lehman Brothers, and Merrill Lynch, 2007 to Extinction

Bear Stearns

The Bear Stearns Companies originated in 1923 to trade equities. After surviving the crash of 1929, Bear managed to expand during the Great Depression. It continued to grow and began to offer brokerage services in the 1960s and went public in 1985. By 2000, Bear was a full-range securities and investment banking firm with offices around the world.

Near its apogee, at the end of its 2006 fiscal year, Bear employed about 14,000 full-time employees and held $350 billion in assets and total capital of $67 billion. Of this $67 billion, about $55 billion was in the form of long-term debt, leaving only about $12 billion free of this encumbrance. For the year, Bear collected revenues of $9 billion, paid $4.3 billion to its employees, and had profits of more than $2 billion. For 85 years, from 1923 until December 2007, Bear Stearns had reported profits in every single quarter. Less than three months later, Bear vanished from the financial landscape.

Leading up to 2007, Bear had been an aggressive player in the mortgage market, and said of itself in its SEC filing for 2006: "The Company originates commercial and residential mortgage loans through its subsidiaries in the US, Europe and Asia. The Company is a leading underwriter of and market-maker in, residential and commercial mortgages and is active in all areas of secured lending, structured finance and securitization products."[1]

Starting at the very end of 2006, some signs of distress in mortgage markets had started to appear. UBS, formerly the Union Bank of Switzerland, closed down one of its hedge funds in May 2007 due to losses related to subprime. But the market absorbed this news and other similar events without particular upset. Things started to get a bit more serious as the summer of 2007 began. Bear sent one of the very first signals of approaching catastrophe to the financial markets, although few were able to interpret the signal correctly. Bear had sponsored two hedge funds that focused on the mortgage business. Both funds were originated and managed by Ralph Cioffi, an apparently talented money manager who was reported to be pulling in more than $10 million in annual compensation.

The first of these funds was the Bear Stearns High Grade Structured Credit Strategies Fund, which Cioffi began and ran for a straight 40 months of profits, earning more than 12 percent per year. Total returns were 46.8 percent from October 2003 through March 2007.[2] Some investors were unhappy with these stable and modest profits and urged Cioffi to use more leverage. Partially in response, Cioffi started another fund in August 2006, the Bear Stearns High Grade Structured Credit Strategies Enhanced Leverage Fund. As the name of the funds implied, both invested almost entirely in structured mortgage products, but the "Enhanced Leverage" fund used invested monies as a basis on which to borrow yet more money in an effort to increase returns. Starting with $600 million in invested funds, it borrowed ten times that amount.[3]

Cioffi was so successful that other Bear employees invested about $35–40 million of their own assets in these two funds.

The Enhanced Leverage fund started earning returns right away in late 2006, but by the end of March 2007 the older fund was down 5 percent for the year, while the enhanced fund was down 10 percent. By the end of April, the enhanced fund was down 23 percent for the year, and some investors started to withdraw their funds. In fact, too many investors wanted to withdraw funds. On June 7, 2007, Bear sent a letter to investors saying it was suspending redemptions because the "investment manager believes the company will not have sufficient liquid assets to pay investors."[4]

In order to borrow, the two funds had posted collateral with lenders. Now these lenders, notably Merrill Lynch, JPMorgan Chase, and Deutsche Bank, feared that the collateral they were holding was not worth nearly as much as they had thought earlier. JPMorgan and Deutsche negotiated with the funds to unwind their positions. For its part, Merrill Lynch decided to sell some of its collateral. It put $850 million in collateralized debt obligations (CDOs) that it held from Bear up for sale, but was only able to sell $100 million.

The market for these CDOs was never very liquid, so no one should have expected Merrill to be able to sell the entire holding in a minute. But part of the problem was the market's unwillingness to pay anything approaching the supposed value of these instruments. The low prices that Merrill was receiving provided uncomfortable new information that the market was forced to recognize—these CDOs were not worth nearly as much as traders previously thought—at least not at present. Further, firms would soon be forced to recognize these new economic realities on their books. That is, under "mark-to-market" accounting, the firms were required to show the *true* market value of these assets in their financial statements. If there are no transactions for a particular asset, opinions can differ on that true value, but recorded transaction prices are much more constraining.

Now Bear Stearns, the parent of these two problematic hedge funds, started to come under pressure. Bear thought it could walk away from the funds legally, but only by accepting tremendous reputational damage. Further, if Bear refused to help, the funds would collapse, and lenders would flood the market with their collateral. This flood of mortgage-backed paper coming onto the market would lead to a "fire sale," generating yet lower transaction prices that market participants would be forced to recognize on their own books. Faced with these unpleasant choices, Bear loaned the original fund $3.2 billion on June 22, accepting some of the fund's CDOs as collateral. Now Bear was firmly holding the bag for the original fund, but with uncertain prospects for the Enhanced Leverage fund.[5]

The next months brought little good news for the subprime market generally. In these two Bear hedge funds, investors still lost $1.6 billion; lawsuits by angry investors began; and federal prosecutors began an investigation.[6] By October, the *New York Times* featured a headline: "Bear Stearns Denies Need to Seek Cash from Outside."[7] Soon the Bear co-president, Warren Spector, was forced out, and James Cayne, CEO at Bear since 1993, resigned his post in early January 2008, but stayed on as chairman of the board.[8] All during this time, more subprime revelations continued; financial stocks continued to sink, and Bear's stock price slid along with those of the crowd. More than other firms, however, rumors about Bear's financial stability continued to be murmured. Nonetheless, Bear was expecting to report earnings of about $1 per share for the quarter ending in February 2008.

On Friday, March 7, 2008, Bear's stock closed at $70.08, which was down substantially from the previous year's high of $171.51. This set the stage for the real action, which began on Monday, March 10, 2008. That morning, Moody's downgraded some of Bear's mortgage-backed bonds, but by March 2008, that was hardly news, as virtually all issuing firms had been hit by a wave of such downgrades.

The novel events started at about 11 A.M., when Bear's CFO, Sam Molinari, heard from the trading desks that Bear's stock was falling and that rumors were swirling about Bear's liquidity problems. But in Bear's view, this was nonsense, as it had about $18 billion in liquid capital. Through the day, CNBC featured repeated discussion of potential liquidity problems at Bear, and Bear's former CEO, "Ace" Greenberg, gave CNBC an interview at midday, labeling these rumors as "totally ridiculous."[9] In the view of some, this interview legitimated the rumors and kept the story alive. A little after 2 P.M., a story flashed across the wires that took the spotlight off Bear—Governor Eliot Spitzer was involved with a prostitution ring. Bear staggered to the close of the day, finishing Monday with a stock price of $62.30, a loss of more than 11 percent since Friday.

On Tuesday, March 11, several hedge funds, anxious not to wait until Bear's capital diminished, pulled their deposits. Three big Wall Street firms, Goldman Sachs, Credit Suisse, and Deutsche Bank, started getting numerous novation requests pertaining to Bear. If one of Bear's trading partners has a contract with Bear and wishes to eliminate that position, it could simply unwind the trade with Bear. (In finance parlance, to "unwind" a trade is to make off-setting transactions to eliminate the economic exposure of the original transaction.) Alternatively, Bear's trading partner could ask another firm to accept a fee and stand in as a trading partner to Bear for the obligation—a novation request.

That Tuesday, many firms started asking Goldman and the others to take their places as Bear's counterparty. (A *counterparty* is just a trading partner. In a transaction between two trading partners, each is a counterparty to the other.) Normally, firms would be happy to do so, as it represents another way of making profits. But once a company suddenly starts receiving a wave of novation requests pertaining to a single firm, say Bear, that firm has to be suspicious that others know something that it does not. Perhaps they have privileged knowledge of trouble at Bear and consequently wish to pay a fee to get some other firm to take its place as a creditor to Bear. That afternoon, Goldman and Credit Suisse both decided to delay action on any novation requests involving Bear, pending approval from upper management. The market closed, with Bear's stock down only a penny for the day.

Wednesday, March 12, Bear's CEO, Alan Schwartz, appeared on CNBC to deny that Bear was facing any liquidity problem. Hedge funds continued to move their deposits from Bear to other firms, and Bear closed the day with $15 billion in capital and a stock price of $61.58.

While Bear may have started Thursday, March 13, with $15 billion in capital, that day's trading radically transformed its prospects. Bear, like other investment banks at the time, operated with huge leverage, supporting assets many times as large as its capital base. According to some calculations, Bear held more than $30 in assets for every $1 in capital. In essence, this means that Bear had to borrow the difference between its total assets and total capital.

That leverage—the ratio of total assets to total capital—implied that Bear had to finance the difference, which it, like other firms, did through the repurchase, or *repo*, market. (In the repo market, one firm lends a security to a second firm as collateral and receives cash in return. The firm receiving cash promises to repurchase the security at a certain date for a somewhat larger amount, the price difference being the interest payment. Most repos are overnight, or one day, commitments.) This practice of short-term financing means that securities firms have to meet a market test every day. Will a lending firm agree to accept the borrower's securities as collateral for a loan and then give the borrower cash? Will they do it tomorrow, and the next day, and the day after that? If a lender refuses to roll over (i.e., renew) a repurchase agreement, the borrower has to get cash from another source and pay the lender who refuses to renew. Otherwise, it is in default.

Spurred on by the rising tide of rumors of Bear's difficulties, more firms and hedge funds accelerated the pulling of money on deposit with Bear, while others refused to renew financing that Thursday. Billions of dollars were flying out the door over the course of the day, with a single client, D. E. Shaw, pulling $5 billion and Fidelity Investments refusing to renew its financing. By 4:30 P.M., Bear's cash position was about $3 billion. However, the market as a whole was generally unaware of Bear's plight, and its stock closed at $57.00.

But inside Bear, knowledge of the cash situation revealed that the situation was now desperate. Bear realized it would have to immediately find new financing or file for bankruptcy. Alan Schwartz contacted JPMorgan about 7 P.M. that evening, seeking an emergency $25 billion line of credit. Schwartz then called Timothy Geithner, president of the Federal Reserve Bank of New York, to apprise him of the situation and to solicit his help in arranging new financing. By 9 P.M., one Bear executive described the situation as "end of the world bad."[10] Now Bear confronted the necessity of obtaining financing from JPMorgan, or Bear could not open for business on Friday morning. JPMorgan began to review Bear's books at about midnight, joining representatives of the New York Fed already in Bear's office.

JPMorgan was essentially unwilling to extend credit to Bear on its own, but overnight the Fed and JPMorgan cobbled together an emergency loan. At 5 A.M. on Friday, March 14, Geithner, Secretary of the Treasury Henry Paulson, and Federal Reserve Chairman Ben Bernanke conferred by phone. The lengthy discussion centered on the effect of Bear's potential bankruptcy on the financial system. With time running out before markets opened, a deal had to be struck.

About 6:45 A.M. on Friday morning, JPMorgan emailed the outline of an agreement to Bear. Essentially, JPMorgan would serve as a conduit by which the Fed could lend to Bear. This complicated structure was necessary, as the Fed believed it did not have the power to lend directly to an investment bank. (In future months, as the crisis worsened, both the Treasury department and the Fed would come to take an expanded view of their powers.) The exact terms of the loan were not immediately disclosed, but they boiled down to the Fed extending a line of credit of about $30 billion for 28 days. When the markets opened that Friday, March 14, Bear thought it had a month to secure new and more permanent financing. Nonetheless, Bear's stock price fell almost 50 percent that day, closing at $30.00. Worse still, the overall market was in turmoil, and it became increasingly apparent through the trading day on Friday that the market interpreted the lifeline thrown to Bear as a sign of weakness rather than strength.

That evening, Treasury Secretary Paulson called Alan Schwartz and told him that Bear would need to find a buyer for itself before the markets opened on Monday morning, March 17. That weekend, bankers from Bear and JPMorgan worked around the clock to consummate a deal. By Sunday morning, a tentative offer from JPMorgan was in place, but it was withdrawn before Bear could accept or reject. JPMorgan ultimately feared that its brief examination of Bear's books gave inadequate information to make such a huge commitment.

Further frantic efforts continued through Sunday, with JPMorgan contemplating a purchase of Bear in the $4–5 per share range, given that the Fed would provide some additional financial guarantees. Reporting this plan to Paulson elicited the response: "That sounds high to me. . . . I think this should be done at a low price."[11] By mid-afternoon on Sunday, JPMorgan gave the news to Bear: it would offer $2 per share. But even the $2 would not be in cash; instead, the offer would take the form of 0.05473 shares of JPMorgan for each share of Bear. Faced with no alternatives, Bear's board accepted the offer in the early evening of Sunday, just as the Asian markets opened for Monday morning trading. Market observers were incredulous at the purchase price—a 93 percent discount from Friday's closing price—and recriminations began immediately. Bear's employees held more than one-third of Bear's shares, and they began to consider refusing approval of the deal, thinking they might do better in bankruptcy.

On Monday, March 17, Bear closed at $4.81, well above the $2 offer. But the offer, being expressed as a certain number of shares of JPMorgan, had actually risen, as JPMorgan's shares increased in value. Further, speculation swirled about the emergence of another bidder. In addition, the quickly negotiated agreement for the purchase soon proved to have some defects that JPMorgan was anxious to cure. Amazingly, the agreement required JPMorgan to guarantee Bear's trades, even if shareholders voted down the deal. This inclusion left JPMorgan in an extremely risky position. The reaction to the $2 deal quickly made it apparent that something would have to be done. Within a week of the $2 announcement, JPMorgan quintupled its offer to $10 per share and Bear, JPMorgan, and the Fed ultimately consummated the deal.[12]

(JPMorgan's willingness to pay $10 per share seems to be a clear indication that Bear was worth much more than the $2 per share that Paulson had urged.)

So, what killed Bear Stearns? Was it subprime exposure, lack of capital, bad management, or a crisis of confidence leading to a run on the bank? Bear's subprime exposure was certainly a problem, and those investments did embody huge losses, but the ultimate share price of $10 per share suggests that the firm clearly was not truly bankrupt but, instead, held considerable actual value. Bear was highly leveraged, but so were other firms that managed to survive. As Christopher Cox, chairman of the Securities and Exchange Commission, observed, ". . . at the time of its near-failure Bear Stearns had a capital cushion well above what was required to meet supervisory standards . . ."[13] In retrospect, it would be easy to fault Bear's management for not having even more capital—enough to be sufficient to withstand the crisis of confidence that actually developed. But there is no particular reason to think that Bear's management was worse than that of other similar firms that did survive.

Rather than pointing the finger at low capital, subprime exposure, or bad management, the SEC offered a "run on the bank" explanation. As Christopher Cox testified before the Senate Committee on Banking, Housing and Urban Affairs on April 3, 2008:

> What happened to Bear Stearns during the week of March 10th was likewise unprecedented. For the first time, a major investment bank that was well-capitalized and apparently fully liquid experienced a crisis of confidence that denied it not only unsecured financing, but short-term secured financing, even when the collateral consisted of agency securities with a market value in excess of the funds to be borrowed. Counterparties would not provide securities lending services and clearing services. Prime brokerage clients moved their cash balances elsewhere. These decisions by counterparties, clients, and lenders to no longer transact with Bear Stearns in turn influenced other counterparties, clients and lenders to also reduce their exposure to Bear Stearns.

In retrospect, it seems that Bear was brought low by something akin to a classic bank run, such as the run that precipitated the demise of Northern Rock in England. But instead of retail depositors running to withdraw, as with Northern Rock, Bear's institutional counterparties refused to believe that the firm was solvent and refused to continue to extend credit.[14]

As Bear plummeted toward ruin during the week of March 10, rumors of a smear campaign against Bear persisted. Some thought that a bear raid was in process against Bear, with large short positions being placed and then rumors of Bear's financial weakness being spread in order to drive down the price of Bear's shares. In fact, some very large negative bets were placed on Bear by trading put options against the firm. (Buying a put option on a stock gives the purchaser the right to sell the underlying share at a given price for a certain period. Buying a put on a stock is generally a bet that the value of the underlying stock will fall.) In the immediate aftermath of Bear's demise, the SEC moved to initiate an investigation of a potential manipulation of Bear's stock price. But it appears that this investigation produced no evidence of stock manipulation.[15]

In facilitating the rescue of Bear, the federal government took virtually unprecedented action. The Treasury and the Fed were torn between two conflicting concerns. If they bailed out a firm such as Bear, it would encourage moral hazard—the alteration of behavior that often occurs when one has some kind of insurance against bearing the full responsibility for one's actions. In other words, Paulson, Geithner, and Bernanke feared that bailing out Bear would signal to other firms that it was permissible to take big risks, knowing the federal government would intervene. This fear was one of the factors that led Paulson to insist on the initial $2 offer price.

The second concern focused on the effects that a Bear bankruptcy would have on the entire financial market. The market was already extremely fragile, and the sudden collapse of Bear might cause untold damage to the entire financial system, leading to tremendous effects on the real economy. As Paulson had noted at the time, "Every situation is different. We have to respond to the circumstances we are facing today."[16] In March 2008, given all the unknowns about the effect of a total collapse of Bear, the federal government bet that they had to act; in six months they would find out what would happen if a similar firm was not rescued. The bankruptcy of Lehman brothers would provide a valuable course of instruction.

The Bankruptcy of Lehman Brothers

There really were Lehman brothers, two German immigrants who settled in Alabama in the middle of the nineteenth century, got their start by running a general store, and moved into cotton trading. After the Civil War, they moved their business to New York, entered the financial advisory industry, and the firm joined the New York Stock Exchange in 1887. Active in the investment banking business since the late 1880s, Lehman went through a series of mergers and divestitures, both as an acquiring firm and as a target. For a while, it was part of American Express, but it went public in the mid-1990s and was an independent company until its demise in 2008.[17]

Lehman focused much of its real estate securitization activity in commercial real estate and was widely admired for its strategy in that area. But Lehman was also a big player in residential real estate, carrying as much as $25 billion in residential mortgages of highly questionable value as the end neared. Like other players on Wall Street, Lehman used extremely high leverage to earn profits of $4 billion in 2006.[18]

Following the collapse of Bear, Lehman possessed all the information one can imagine about the seriousness of the problems it faced. By June 2008, the public too received the message, if they did not already have it: Lehman posted a quarterly loss of $2.8 billion. At a time when other firms were scrambling to unload assets and secure partners, Lehman's CEO Richard Fuld still was insisting that Lehman can "go it alone."[19]

As summer wore on and fall approached, the crisis deepened and Lehman's prospects deteriorated. Despite Fuld's proud go-it-alone stance, Lehman was seeking a merger partner in the summer and was scouring the Middle East and Asia for investment funds. Ironically, in hindsight, Lehman even tried to sell itself to AIG.[20] In the summer, Lehman proposed to the Federal Reserve that Lehman could transform itself into a bank holding company subject to regulation by the Federal Reserve, a transformation that would allow Lehman to borrow from the Federal Reserve. However, the Fed rejected this plan.[21] Later, Treasury Secretary Paulson explained this decision by saying that Lehman lacked good assets to deposit as collateral and that the federal government lacked the powers to offer Lehman support.[22]

By September, matters were clearly worsening rapidly. Shortly after Labor Day, other Wall Street firms began to demand additional collateral for loans they had extended to Lehman. On September 9, the Korea Development Bank announced conclusively that it would not be investing in Lehman, and Lehman's stock fell a further 37 percent on the news.[23]

Realizing its desperate straits, Lehman intensified discussions with Barclays and Bank of America, seeking to be acquired. A key question in such matters turned on whether the Federal Reserve would offer guarantees to limit the potential losses of acquirers. Both Barclays and

Bank of America were clearly looking for such a guarantee to make an acquisition palatable.

The Fed faced the following question: Is Lehman too big to fail, given current market conditions? After all, Lehman was bigger than Bear, and market conditions were worse in September than they had been in March, when the Fed put itself on the hook for $30 billion to get the Bear deal done. The Fed certainly had its hands full at the moment, that week of September 8–12, as Merrill Lynch, a much larger firm, was under simultaneous pressure. Also, the shares of Washington Mutual contributed to the stress by falling 30 percent that Wednesday and another 21 percent the next day, while AIG tottered on the brink of collapse.[24] By September 11, a Thursday, Lehman's survival depended on whether the Fed would guarantee some of its assets to help get a deal done, and Lehman was trying to limp to the weekend, when it would try to finalize a deal.[25] The *Wall Street Journal* reported on September 12 that Lehman had experienced $10 billion in paper losses in 2008, had a market capitalization of $2.86 billion, and was holding a bonus pool of $3 billion, more than its entire market capitalization.[26]

The weekend brought resolution, and it was not a victory. On Saturday night, the Fed refused to offer support for a Lehman deal, and Barclays and Bank of America abandoned their talks to acquire Lehman, proving that their pleas for Fed assistance were not mere bargaining ploys. Lehman had no alternatives remaining, and it filed for the largest bankruptcy in U.S. history on September 15, 2008, ending its more than 150-year history.[27]

The collapse of Lehman led almost immediately to bitter recriminations. Had the Fed and Treasury erred in not finding a way to save Lehman? Was the government trying to send a message of market discipline to show that some firms were not too big to fail? Could Lehman have done a better job for itself by acting more aggressively and wisely to restructure its miserable finances as the magnitude of the crisis developed?[28] All these issues would attract much attention in time, but the market and public policy analysts had little leisure to reflect on these broader issues that were now of historical concern, for other larger shoes were already threatening to drop the same weekend.

Merrill Lynch: The Herd Goes to the Abattoir

Founded in 1914, long one of the most prominent firms in retail brokerage, widely known by its bull logo, and billing itself as the "thundering herd,"

Merrill's herd thundered over the horizon and into oblivion as an independent company in mid-September 2008. Merrill consisted of two main divisions, an asset management company and a trading company. The asset management arm of the firm employed 16,000 brokers and managed $1.4 trillion in assets. For its part, the trading side of the firm focused on fixed-income instruments and became heavily involved in the securitized mortgage market.[29]

During the heyday of subprime, Merrill, like other firms, believed that everything was in good order, with CEO E. Stanley O'Neal asserting in 2005, "We've got the right people in place as well as good risk management and controls."[30] In 2006, with its shares up 40 percent for the year, Merrill plunged deeper into subprime by paying $1.3 billion for First Franklin, a lender specializing in subprime loans. But First Franklin was just the largest of 12 major purchases of mortgage-related companies that Merrill acquired from January 2005 to January 2007.[31]

Merrill, like many firms, started to experience problems with its MBS portfolio in 2007. However, even in 2007, as problems started to emerge, Merrill reported a 31 percent increase in quarterly profits to $2.1 billion. According to Merrill at the time, subprime business was less than 2 percent of its revenues, and growth in other lines of business much more than offset the problems in subprime. Merrill also reported that it had taken strong action to limit its subprime exposure; Merrill's CFO, Jeff Edwards, said that while the subprime market was likely to remain "in flux for a period of time," that "the majority of our exposure is now in the highest credit segment of the market."[32]

But the future did not materialize as projected. In October 2007, just a few months after its rosy forecasts, Merrill announced a write-down of $8.4 billion to acknowledge the declining value of its mortgage-related securities. This led to the ouster of O'Neal as CEO and his replacement by John Thain, CEO of the New York Stock Exchange and a former president of Goldman Sachs. Thain moved aggressively to improve Merrill's balance sheet and to address the problems in Merrill's mortgage security business. For example, Thain disposed of $31 billion of mortgage securities, receiving only pennies for each dollar of their face value. In the summer of 2008, Merrill sold its investment in the Bloomberg financial news and data firm and raised almost $10 billion in new equity.[33]

But none of this was enough to stop the bleeding. In July 2008, Merrill took another write-down of $9.4 billion on its mortgage portfolio and reported a loss of $4.6 billion for the quarter. At this point, Merrill had lost $19 billion over the preceding year.[34] Through the summer of

2008, the stock market continued to slide, and the financial news was full of dreadful stories of more difficulty everywhere. In early September, the federal government took the mortgage giants Fannie Mae and Freddie Mac into receivership. As late as September 10, Thain was still out promoting Merrill in public and assuring employees that things would work out well. He predicted that the pain should end by 2009.[35]

At the same time, Lehman approached dissolution, and by the weekend of September 12–14 Lehman's fate was sealed when the Fed refused to assist in a takeover. At that point, both Barclays and Bank of America walked away from Lehman, and Bank of America immediately turned its attention to exploring an acquisition of Merrill.

By contemporary accounts, the deal between Merrill Lynch and Bank of America was initiated and concluded with stunning swiftness. Apparently, talks between the two CEOs, Kenneth Lewis for Bank of America and John Thain for Merrill Lynch, were initiated only on Saturday, September 13. The government's refusal to help with a Lehman acquisition apparently concentrated the mind of Merrill's chief. The next day, the two companies announced that Bank of America would acquire Merrill.[36]

The terms of the deal required Bank of America to exchange 0.8595 shares for each share of Merrill in an all-stock transaction. The implied value of the deal was $50 billion in total, valuing Merrill at $29 per share. This price represented a huge 70 percent premium over Merrill's closing share price on Friday, which Lewis defended on grounds of an urgent desire to complete the deal and exclude rival bidders.[37] For his part, Thain could only say: "We have over 60,000 people working every day. All the efforts of these people were overwhelmed by the write-downs in the mortgage-related assets."[38]

This hasty marriage of Bank of America and Merrill Lynch produced difficulties right away. Immediately, some maintained that Lewis and Bank of America overpaid for Merrill. After all, they offered a 70 percent premium over the current share price of Friday, September 12, and it was after this price was recorded that Lehman went into bankruptcy. Further, it soon became clear that the deal had been done in haste, without a full understanding of all the problems that faced Merrill. By the end of the year, before the deal closed, Bank of America was considering invoking a Material Adverse Change (MAC) clause in the merger contract that would allow Bank of America to cancel the transaction.

It is at this point that the facts become obscure and the real controversy begins. First, did Ken Lewis know of Merrill's difficulties and decline to disclose those to shareholders before they formally ratified the deal on December 5, 2008? Failing to disclose such critical information to shareholders would have been a serious breach of fiduciary duty at least, and perhaps a felonious act as well as a violation of federal securities laws. Against this charge, Lewis asserted that he only became concerned about Merrill's deteriorating position in mid-December. As a further complicating factor, the Treasury and the Fed may have encouraged Lewis to delay reporting the adverse information to shareholders. The information was disclosed only after the deal closed on December 30, with the announcement coming on January 16, 2009—perhaps only coincidentally the day that the Treasury Department announced that it would provide $20 billion in new capital to Bank of America and provide guarantees of $118 billion against additional losses on Merrill's mortgage-related assets.[39]

Lewis also alleged that the U.S. Treasury and the Federal Reserve pressured him to consummate the transaction, even if he wanted to invoke the MAC clause. Lewis informed the Treasury and the Fed on December 17, 2008, that he was considering invoking the MAC clause to cancel the acquisition of Merrill—after all, Lewis had learned that Merrill's losses were $7 billion more than anticipated.

It seems clear that the Fed and the Treasury "strongly encouraged" Lewis to consummate the transaction. In congressional testimony, Lewis spoke of being pressured in this manner, but refused to go so far as to call it a threat. Behind the spoken testimony, the suspicion lingers that the Fed and the Treasury may have threatened to fire Lewis and the entire board, but nothing is ultimately clear on this matter. Not surprisingly, the Fed and the Treasury maintain that they acted appropriately.[40]

Another enduring controversy concerns the ever-troublesome question of bonuses and huge paychecks. Just before the merger with Bank of America, Merrill paid $3.6 billion in bonuses, a timing that was earlier than usual. Almost 700 Merrill employees received bonuses of $1 million or more, with the top four bonuses totaling $121 million, prompting an investigation by New York attorney general Andrew Cuomo. Bank of America was aware of these pending payments and reported that it had succeeded in persuading Merrill to reduce the amounts from its original plan.[41] But the matter did not die there. Concerned that Bank of America may have lied to or misled its shareholders about the matter of bonuses, the SEC filed suit against Bank of America. Later, the two parties reached a settlement of the matter, but this was rejected in court in a stinging opinion, and the matter was ordered to trial.[42] The matter was resolved in early 2010, with Bank of America agreeing to pay $150 million in penalties.

Goldman Sachs, Morgan Stanley, and the Week That Remade Wall Street

With the demise of Lehman Brothers and Merrill Lynch, only Goldman Sachs and Morgan Stanley remained among the former leaders of the investment banking industry. Both Goldman and Morgan had experienced their own difficulties in the subprime fiasco and mortgage securitization, and of the two, Morgan traveled a rougher road.

Morgan Stanley traces its existence to the empire of John Pierpont Morgan in the nineteenth century, and was spun off from J. P. Morgan & Company in 1935 when the Glass-Steagall Act (also known as the Banking Act of 1933) forced the separation of commercial and investment banking. Goldman Sachs and Morgan Stanley have long occupied the two premier spots in the industry, with Morgan Stanley as a distinct second. The usual history of acquisitions and growth brought Morgan Stanley to the twenty-first century, and John Mack became CEO in 2005 with a commitment to become more aggressive in taking risk, as he made clear in the 2007 annual meeting: "Do we take a lot of risk? Yes, . . . I think this firm has the capacity to take a lot more risk than it has in the past."[43]

Finding more risk proved to be all too easy, and in late 2007 Morgan was forced to write down its subprime portfolio by $9.4 billion. By the end of 2007, the write-downs totaled almost $11 billion, and Morgan reported its first quarterly loss in its 72-year history.[44] In spite of this $3.59 billion quarterly loss, its huge write-downs, and the fact that Morgan still had $1.8 billion in its subprime portfolio, the firm still made $3.2 billion for the full year. Even though Morgan's stock price lost 20 percent of its value in 2007, it still finished the year as a quite profitable and viable firm, with no special worries on the horizon.

Not only profitable and viable in 2007, Goldman Sachs was in much better shape than Morgan. Goldman got its start in 1869 by Marcus Goldman, who brought his son-in-law, Samuel Sachs, into the business in 1882. By 1906, Goldman Sachs was prominent in investment banking and brought one of the largest initial public offerings of all time to market—that of Sears, Roebuck and Company. Rising to preeminence among

Wall Street firms, Goldman alumni include Robert Rubin and Henry Paulson, both former Treasury secretaries; Jon Corzine, senator and then governor of New Jersey; Gary Gensler, now head of the Commodity Futures Trading Commission; Joshua Bolton, former White House chief of staff; and John Thain, former chairman of the New York Stock Exchange and CEO of Merrill Lynch at the time of its demise. All of these men held positions at or near the top of Goldman Sachs at one point. But Goldman alumni also include many other prominent people outside government, including financial news personalities Jim Cramer, Erin Burnett, and Guy Adami.

In the second half of 2007, while other firms were starting to take huge write-offs of their subprime positions, Goldman was reporting no difficulties, having largely off-loaded the offending mortgage securities. In fact, Goldman reported a 79 percent increase in profitability for the third quarter, earning $2.85 billion. Further, it had set aside a $16.9 billion compensation pool to cover the first three quarters of 2007.[45] Comparing Goldman and Morgan for 2007, table 6.1 shows that Goldman's revenues were smaller than Morgan's, but Goldman was substantially more profitable, earning more than $9.5 billion.

Even in 2008, a year that witnessed the destruction of Merrill Lynch, Bear Stearns, Lehman Brothers, AIG, Fannie Mae, Freddie Mac, and a host of the nation's largest banks, both Morgan and Goldman reported full-year profits of $1.7 and $2.0 billion, respectively. Further, both firms achieved quarterly profits in the first three quarters, and experienced a loss only in the fourth quarter of 2008. These statistics make it appear that Morgan and Goldman skated through the crisis unscathed, but that is far from the truth.

Figure 6.2 shows the stock price slide for Morgan Stanley and Goldman Sachs from their respective highs in 2007 to the lows of 2008. Morgan Stanley hit its high on June 14, 2007, at $70.09, while Goldman reached its zenith of October 31, 2007, at $243.83. From those respective highs, the stocks of both firms fell through 2007 and most of 2008 as the financial crisis deepened. They both hit their lows on the same date, November 20, 2008, with Morgan Stanley at $9.05 and Goldman at $51.58, a loss of 87 and 79 percent, respectively.

It is hard to square the profitability of Goldman and Morgan in the first three quarters of 2008 with the price punishment that the market doled out to the shares of both firms. Hard, that is, until we consider the fear and panic that was gripping the market in the summer and early fall of 2008. This period witnessed the repetition of a fearful scenario in

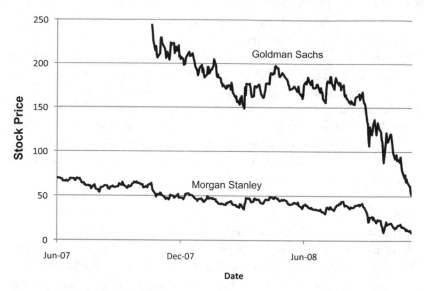

Figure 6.2 The Stock Price Slide for Morgan Stanley and Goldman Sachs, 2007–2008

which a financial firm would come under attack, its shares would be driven down by relentless selling, and its counterparties would demand additional collateral to maintain the firm's trading positions. When a firm such as Bear or Lehman came under market suspicion, its trading partners would seek to abandon relationships with the suspect firm by closing all possible positions. This flight would require the beleaguered firm to sell securities to raise cash. But, of course, the securities it had to sell were already suffering from depressed prices, and attempting to sell them would simply drive their prices down further. As a result, a firm that was thought to be weak could face a massive liquidity squeeze that would drive the firm into bankruptcy, even if the firm were completely viable in some broader sense. That is, a firm could fail because of the market's seizure that removed liquidity from the market and that rendered an otherwise viable firm unable to meet its obligations at a particular moment.

As was becoming increasingly clear, in a panic no one wanted to be confused with facts. That became clear in the middle of the week of September 14–21, from Tuesday, September 16, to Thursday, September 18. In the aftermath of the weekend that saw the bankruptcy of Lehman and the end of Merrill, both Goldman and Morgan reported quarterly profits of $845 million and $1.425 billion on Tuesday, with Morgan even registering an increase in profits from the previous quarter.

Against that background, table 6.2 shows the closing stock prices for five financial firms on September 16 and 17 and the percentage of stock price change. By this date, AIG and Lehman had already ceased to exist as viable firms, with September 16 stock prices of $.30 and $.48, respectively. Nonetheless, the shred of value left to these firms was further decimated with a 57 percent drop for Lehman and a 10 percent drop for AIG. In spite of the announcement that Bank of America would acquire it, Merrill fell by another 13 percent. But now Goldman and Morgan were the only large investment banks left, and that same day the market trimmed 14 percent from Goldman's share prices and 24 percent from Morgan's.

At this point, the market was clearly coming completely unhinged from the underlying economic realities, as the lead from a story in the *New York Times* on September 18 emphasizes:

> Even Morgan Stanley and Goldman Sachs, the two last titans left standing on Wall Street, are no longer immune. To the surprise of executives within those firms, and their rivals, the stocks of these powerful companies were drawn into the crisis of investor confidence on Wednesday. Morgan Stanley, whose stock fell almost 25 percent . . . Goldman Sachs's stock fell almost 14 percent, and it had to rebuff rumors that it was seeking a capital infusion.
>
> The assault on these two companies underscored how quickly a sense of fear is spreading through Wall Street. Both firms just reported respectable profits on Tuesday, and were considered in a separate class from weaker banks like Bear Stearns and Lehman Brothers that saw the value of their businesses evaporate.[46]

Table 6.2			

The Day that Remade Wall Street in the Week that Remade Wall Street, September 17, 2008

	Closing Stock Prices		
Firm	Tuesday, September 16	Wednesday, September 17	Percentage Change
AIG	0.48	0.43	−10.42
Lehman Brothers	0.30	0.13	−56.67
Merrill Lynch	22.18	19.36	−12.71
Goldman Sachs	131.55	113.24	−13.92
Morgan Stanley	27.87	21.12	−24.22

Goldman and Morgan were both quickly realizing that their recent profits and their genuine financial soundness were not necessarily proof against collapse. Both firms realized that drastic action was required. The same story from the *New York Times* reported that Morgan was seeking a merger with either Wachovia or Citicorp and quoted John Mack, CEO of Morgan, as saying: "We need a merger partner or we're not going to make it."[47] These considerations led both firms to a drastic decision that meant the end of investment banking. The following weekend, on Sunday night before the markets in Asia would open for Monday, September 22, the Federal Reserve announced that it had approved the application of Goldman Sachs and Morgan Stanley to become bank holding companies.

Becoming a bank holding company had several strong implications. First, as bank holding companies, both Goldman and Morgan would have potential access to enormous short term borrowing from the Fed. Second, and perhaps more important than the short-term borrowing facility, the acceptance of the two firms as bank holding companies by the Fed sent a signal to the markets that the Fed stood firmly behind both firms. Third, becoming bank holding companies brought both firms under the regulatory purview of the Fed and implied that in the future they would have to operate their businesses in a different manner and be subject to considerably more stringent capital requirements. As the *Wall Street Journal* summarized the implications of this move, the demise of Bear, Lehman, and Merrill and the transformation of Goldman and Morgan ". . . effectively mark the end of Wall Street as it has been known for decades."[48]

Both firms had long resisted regulation, and becoming bank holding companies was a bitter pill to swallow. As they became bank holding companies, both Goldman and Morgan had more than $20 of assets for every $1 of capital they possessed, but commercial banks typically have only $10–$12 dollars of assets per $1 of capital. Thus, both firms faced the prospect of having to operate their businesses in a much more conservative and potentially much less profitable manner. That both firms were willing to become bank holding companies signals how truly desperate times had become.

In the aftermath of this transformation, the shares of both firms continued to fall for several weeks until November 22, as figure 6.2 shows. After that low, both firms rebounded remarkably, as shown in figure 6.3, and by mid-2009 both firms were reporting substantial profits and preparing to pay large bonuses.

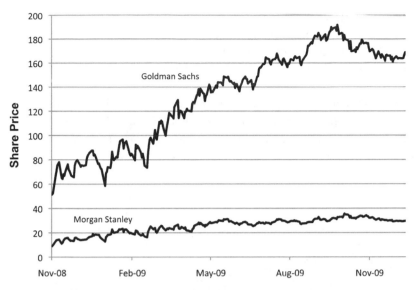

Figure 6.3 The Recovery of Goldman Sachs and Morgan Stanley

Yet in some quarters there remained a legacy of bitterness, for example concerning Lehman, which just a few weeks earlier had itself petitioned the Federal Reserve to become a bank holding company and had been denied. The *New York Times* reported: "But Timothy Geithner, then New York Fed president, now Treasury secretary, didn't like the idea of letting an investment bank become a bank holding company—so he said no. Immediately after the Lehman default, however, that is exactly what he allowed Morgan Stanley and Goldman Sachs to do, which helped stabilize both firms."[49]

There are at least three possible explanations for this difference in treatment. First, one might point to a difference in the true underlying financial position of the three firms, Lehman, Goldman, and Morgan. The correct explanation may simply be that Lehman really was insolvent, whereas Goldman and Morgan were quite solvent but were facing a temporary liquidity crisis due to the general market meltdown. Second, it might be that the intervening weeks and developing crises between the refusal issued to Lehman in mid-July and the acceptance of Goldman and Morgan in mid-September may have given the Fed good reason to change its mind to avoid the complete destruction of the financial markets. The third possible explanation is more sinister and turns on the allegations that Goldman's unique connection with the federal government means that its tentacles extend into the heart of the government's decision making. We have already seen the honor roll of Goldman alumni with prominent government connections, and the charge of Goldman Sachs possessing undue influence over the government has been raised by a number of publications, earning Goldman the unappealing sobriquet of "Government Sachs."[50] Whatever the true explanation or explanations, one fact remained after September 2008— the investment banking industry as it was had come to an end.

When Zombies Walk the Earth

While a *zombie* was first a snake god of voodoo cults, at least according to the *American Heritage Dictionary of the English Language*, the word has a much broader and richer meaning. Béla Lugosi, for example, starred in the 1932 film *White Zombie*, and this cinematic triumph was followed by a succession of other zombie films, such as *Plague of the Zombies* (1966), *Night of the Living Dead* (1968), *Dawn of the Dead* (1978), and many others. The connection of the zombie motif to finance comes from Edward Kane, who focused on the idea of a zombie as a dead person (or financial institution) that continues to walk the earth, perhaps not even being aware of its status. In his research into the savings and loan crisis of the 1980s, Kane claimed that quite a few savings and loan associations were zombie institutions, by which he meant that they were essentially insolvent, but that their insolvency was not generally acknowledged.[1]

Kane's conception of zombies has an all too immediate relevance to the current financial crisis. Surely, some of the financial institutions that continue to haunt our economy are zombie firms. While there may be some doubt as to exactly which firms are viable and which are zombies, this chapter focuses on four huge firms that have come to the brink of extinction, with their share prices falling to the one dollar range: Fannie Mae, Freddie Mac, AIG, and Citigroup.

▬▬▬ Fannie Mae and Freddie Mac

We have already seen how the U.S. federal government created Fannie Mae in 1938 and Freddie Mac in 1970 with the mission of supporting the housing market and making mortgage financing more generally available. As previously discussed, these institutions became government-sponsored entities (or GSEs), with private ownership, a public purpose, an implicit guarantee of the obligations by the federal government, and in the case of Fannie Mae, a board of directors that was, in considerable part, appointed by the president of the United States. Freddie Mac created the first collateralized mortgage obligation (CMO) in 1983, and both institutions became gigantic and dominating players in the U.S. mortgage finance system. As such, they are two of the largest financial institutions in the United States and the world.

One measure of their dominance is that they essentially defined the world of U.S. mortgages, with their definition of a "conforming mortgage" as one meeting a certain size limit, possessing a certain structure, meeting rigorous documentation standards, and going to a borrower with a sufficiently high credit rating. Fannie and Freddie regarded loans that did not meet those requirements as "nonconforming" and outside their sphere of interest; at least that was the case for many years. Loans that were too big to be conforming were "jumbo loans"; loans made to supposedly solid borrowers but lacking complete documentation were "Alt-A loans"; and loans made to borrowers with sub-standard credit were "subprime loans." All of these loans bore a higher interest rate than they otherwise would, simply because Fannie and Freddie, for many years, would not buy them. Fannie and Freddie's reluctance to purchase these mortgages made it more difficult for lenders to recycle their funds, and they were stuck holding these kinds of mortgages in their own long-term portfolios—at least until the flowering of mortgage securitization.

GSEs have long been controversial, and long-standing arguments have raged in academic and policy circles about the subsidies they receive, the benefits that they are supposed to confer on the housing industry and the American public, the risks that they pose to the financial system, and the threat that the federal government's implicit guarantee would become explicit. Debate on these questions has also long been marred by politicization between those who wish to see a smaller governmental role in markets and those who seek an expansive federal footprint in the economy. Recent history has provided a painful answer to many of the questions in disputes, and in the present grim aftermath of the demise of the GSEs there is little point in rehearsing arguments about these issues.

However, it is important to recognize that these questions have long been in the public domain, as reflected in the 1991 publication of a 300-page report by the Congressional Budget Office, entitled *Controlling the Risks of Government-Sponsored Enterprises*, which stated: "The implicit federal guarantee of GSE obligations transfers to the government a large portion of the risk that creditors normally bear. Federal risk bearing conveys an implicit subsidy and creates a permanent potential for federal losses."[2] In 1996 the director of the Congressional Budget Office testified before Congress, saying that the ". . . subsidy consists of billions of dollars of reduced costs conferred on Fannie Mae and Freddie Mac annually by the federal government's grant of GSE status to the enterprises . . . CBO [the Congressional Budget Office] estimates that the government's implicit backing was worth $6.5 billion to the housing GSEs in 1995."[3] The GSEs and some scholars offered a spirited defense of these issues, summarized in Freddie Mac's 2006 publication, "Revisiting the Net Benefits of Freddie Mac and Fannie Mae." This document concluded that ". . . these two housing-related government sponsored enterprises (GSEs) confer substantial benefits on homeowners while posing manageable risks to the financial system and minimal costs to taxpayers," and that their risk is ". . . contained with strong safety and soundness regulation."[4] Further, both firms had strong political support, with Barney Frank, congressman from Massachusetts and ranking Democrat on the Financial Services Committee, opining in 2003: "These two entities—Fannie Mae and Freddie Mac—are not facing any kind of financial crisis . . . The more people exaggerate these problems, the more pressure there is on these companies, the less we will see in terms of affordable housing."[5]

While economists and politicians debated, Fannie and Freddie grew at a rate that far exceeded the expansion of the mortgage market as a whole. From 1970 to 2000, Fannie and Freddie grew from owning 5 percent of single-family residential mortgages to owning 38.8 percent of these mortgages.[6] Similarly, over a portion of this same period, in 1980–2003, Fannie and Freddie went from holding no MBS to owning more than $2 trillion worth between them. By this time, Fannie and Freddie were the second- and third-largest U.S. companies, measured by total assets.[7]

Both firms came into political and legal difficulty over fraudulent accounting in the early 2000s. First came Freddie Mac, with a 2003 criminal investigation of its accounting and the resignation of its CEO. As a consequence, Freddie had to restate its earnings for a three-year period and agreed to pay a $125 million penalty. Ironically, the firm had *under-stated* its earnings by about $5 billion in an effort to build a fund that would allow it to smooth its reported earnings over time.[8]

Fannie Mae quickly followed with its own more conventional accounting scandal—conventional in that it involved overstated earnings. In 2004 the Securities and Exchange Commission (SEC) ordered Fannie to restate its earnings for four years to reveal previously undisclosed losses in the range of $9–11 billion. One effect of the exaggerated earnings was to increase the firm's executive compensation. According to the SEC, CEO Franklin Raines, former director of the federal Office of Management and Budget, received $90 million in compensation from 1998 to 2003, and at least $52 million of this pay was facilitated by the accounting irregularities. Fannie Mae eventually paid a $400 million fine in the matter.[9]

Given their size and the problems that developed in the mortgage market, Fannie and Freddie would surely have suffered to some extent, but their problems were exacerbated by an interaction of public policy goals, defective regulatory oversight, political pressure, and the political weakness of both GSEs in the aftermath of their accounting scandals. The Federal Housing Enterprises Financial Safety and Soundness Act of 1992 established the Office of Federal Housing Enterprise Oversight (OFHEO) within the Department of Housing and Urban Development (HUD). The Act established OFHEO as the regulator for Fannie and Freddie and required that HUD set goals for Fannie and Freddie to meet in support of housing for low-income participants and underserved housing areas. During the hearings leading up to the passage of the act, Fannie and Freddie worked hard and with considerable success to reduce their requirements in the area of affordable housing. These goals were only established in 1995, and this rule permitted Fannie and Freddie to receive credit toward their affordable housing goals by purchasing CMOs backed by subprime mortgages.

This was a significant break with previous policy that required Fannie and Freddie to focus only on conforming loans with high credit standards and substantial down payments. With an initial foray into subprime that was quite modest, Fannie and Freddie soon expanded their subprime activities, largely in response to strong encouragement from HUD and politicians. Affordable housing goals that were mandated to become an increasingly large part of the GSEs' mission provided a key justification and an important motivation for their focus on subprime. While the rules were complicated and compliance proved difficult to measure, the stated affordable housing goals were increased over time and exceeded 50 percent by the early 2000s—meaning that over half of the mortgages that the GSEs were supposed to buy should support affordable housing. Such a mandate fully justified, or even required, Fannie and Freddie to plunge ever more deeply into subprime. From 2000 to 2004, Fannie and Freddie's purchase of subprime-backed securities increased tenfold and the affordable housing goal was increased again, such that the two GSEs' combined purchases of subprime CMOs were $175 billion in 2004 and $169 billion in 2005. This led a Freddie Mac spokeswoman, Sharon McHale, to say that the higher goals ". . . forced us to go into that market to serve the targeted populations that HUD wanted us to serve."[10] However, weakness from the accounting scandals at both firms also made them vulnerable to pressure from Congress that pushed in the same direction. The large anticipated profits in subprime may have made the firms more than willing to plunge ever deeper into the subprime arena.[11]

Whatever the exact motivation, by 2003 Fannie and Freddie were among the very largest firms in the United States, and together they held assets of almost $2 trillion, owned or guaranteed a mortgage portfolio of $3.6 trillion, and made more than $12 billion for their shareholders, as table 7.1 shows. In 2003–2008, as shown in table 7.1, Fannie and Freddie increased their mortgage holdings by 46 percent, a much faster rate of growth than the market as a whole. In 2003–2006, Fannie and Freddie earned more than $30 billion for their shareholders, and by 2007 the two firms held or guaranteed the payments on more than half of all U.S. mortgages. Further, the two firms had always been highly leveraged, which was permitted by their regulatory mandate, which required only 2.5 percent capitalization. The two firms typically were more highly leveraged than investment banks, but if one considers their positions in MBS, the two were even more highly leveraged, with a capital structure akin to that of the most highly leveraged hedge funds. On February 7, 2008, their chief regulator testified that the two firms taken together had ". . . only 1.2 percent of equity backing their mortgage exposure."[12]

As a consequence of their huge size, high leverage, and extreme concentration in mortgage securities, both firms were extremely exposed to changes in the housing market, and their share prices responded very quickly when housing prices started to fall in 2007. Figure 7.1 shows the share price performance for Fannie and Freddie in 2007–2008.

Table 7.1

Fannie Mae and Freddie Mac, 2003–2008

Net Income ($ Millions)

Year	Fannie Mae	Freddie Mac	Combined
2003	7,931	4,809	12,740
2004	4,802	2,392	7,194
2005	5,861	1,890	7,751
2006	3,548	2,051	5,599
2007	−2,563	−3,503	−6,066
2008	−59,776	−50,795	−110,571
Entire Period	−40,197	−43,156	−83,353

Total Assets ($ Billions)

Year	Fannie Mae	Freddie Mac	Combined
2003	1,022	788	1,810
2004	1,018	780	1,798
2005	832	799	1,630
2006	841	805	1,646
2007	879	794	1,674
2008	912	851	1,763

Total Mortgage Portfolios—Owned or Guaranteed ($ Billions)

Year	Fannie Mae	Freddie Mac	Combined
2003	2,223	1,415	3,638
2004	2,340	1,506	3,846
2005	2,356	1,685	4,041
2006	2,526	1,827	4,353
2007	2,888	2,107	4,995
2008	3,109	2,207	5,316

Source: 10-K reports of Fannie Mae and Freddie Mac, various years.

During 2007, as problems with the mortgage market came to be more obvious, the share price of both firms fell quickly, and by Thanksgiving, shares of both firms had lost half their value compared to earlier in the year. Nonetheless, both firms—and their regulator, OFHEO—were still subject to considerable pressure from lawmakers and lobbyists to increase the size of their mortgage portfolios, as the *Wall Street Journal* reported on October 24, 2007. Amazingly, OFHEO largely acceded to these requests.[13]

In 2008, as Fannie and Freddie's prospects dimmed, Fannie Mae reduced its dividend from $.35 to $.05 per share, strove to cut operating

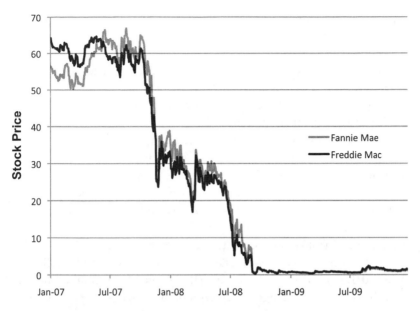

Figure 7.1 Stock Prices: Fannie Mae and Freddie Mac

costs, and announced its intentions to slow the growth of its mortgage portfolio and to stop buying nonconforming loans. Nonetheless, on March 19, 2008, the chief GSE regulator, James B. Lockhart, head of OFHEO, argued for reducing capital requirements for the two firms and allowing them to expand their role in the U.S. mortgage market. Such actions, Lockhart said, would ". . . make the idea of a bailout nonsense in my mind. The companies are safe and sound, and they will continue to be safe and sound."[14]

Freddie lost $821 million and Fannie lost $2.3 billion in the second quarter of 2008.[15] On June 7, Freddie Mac's CEO predicted that Freddie's 2008 financial results would be better than those of 2007: "The revenue engine is showing more horsepower . . . We are quite confident that the positive changes will offset the negative."[16] Against this background, Fannie Mae managed to raise $7 billion in new funds, but Freddie had difficulty with its plan to attract new capital. Meanwhile, the Treasury made new lending available to the firms in the summer, and Congress considered extending a $300 billion line of credit to the firms.[17] On July 10, 2008, OFHEO reported that both Fannie and Freddie were "adequately capitalized," the highest capital ranking category in the regulator's classification, a remark trumpeted that day by Treasury Secretary Henry Paulson in a press conference.

In spite of protestations to the contrary, the end for Fannie and Freddie was near. In August 2008, Freddie again failed in its attempt to raise new capital and started to realize that its fate was sealed. Paulson briefed President Bush on August 26, and Bush agreed that the firms must be taken in conservatorship—effectively a form of bankruptcy, which was announced on September 7, 2008. As part of the takeover by the federal government, CEOs of both firms were required to resign. At that time, the government provided lines of credit of $100 billion to each firm, thinking that these huge amounts would be sufficient.[18] In less than two months, both firms had gone from receiving the best grades on capitalization from their regulator to total bankruptcy. As table 7.1 shows, the losses swelled, with Fannie and Freddie losing $111 billion in 2008 and $98 billion in 2009. Note also that Fannie Mae and Freddie Mac have become the mortgage purchasers of last resort—as private firms fled the market in 2008-2009, Fannie and Freddie were buying, with their combined mortgage portfolios (owned plus guaranteed) growing by almost $800 billion from year-end 2007 to year-end 2009. While this engorgement may be in line with their public mission, it could well spell even greater financial losses ahead.

One of the most amazing survivors of the GSE episode was James B. Lockhart, head of OFHEO. As the GSEs headed toward collapse, their regulatory structure was revised, retiring OFHEO and replacing it with the Federal Housing Finance Agency (FHFA) on July 30, 2008, with no one other that Lockhart as its head. (Replacing the OFHEO with the FHFA might be likened to renaming the *Titanic* the *Good Ship Lollipop*, as the director and many other key personnel were kept in place.) Thus, mid-2009 found Lockhart testifying about the state of the mortgage markets and the GSEs' activities. He reported that in mid-2009 Fannie and Freddie's mortgage exposure was still $5.4 trillion, representing 56 percent of all single-family mortgages in the United States. Further, Fannie and Freddie were continuing to acquire newly originated mortgages, accounting for 73 percent of originations in the first quarter of 2009.[19] Clearly, the working out of the problems of Fannie and Freddie would prove to be neither simple nor rapid. Meanwhile, the federal government expanded its guarantee for Fannie and Freddie to a total of $400 billion.

AIG

Beginning in Shanghai in 1919, AIG became one of the first Western firms to sell insurance to the Chinese. AIG was based in Shanghai until 1949, but with Mao Zedong and the Communist army rapidly approaching the city, AIG quickly relocated to New York. In 1962, leadership of the firm devolved to Maurice "Hank" Greenberg, who led AIG in a tremendous expansion of the firm until 2005, when the firm became embroiled in an accounting scandal. During this period, AIG grew to be one of the largest insurers in the world, and by the onset of the financial crisis in 2007, AIG clearly was the world's largest insurer with 116,000 employees, 74 million customers, 2007 revenue of $110 billion, and profits of more than $6 billion for the same year.

In many respects, it appears that AIG's difficulties date from 2005 and the accounting scandal of that year, as these events led to the forced departure of Greenberg from the firm and a downgrade of AIG's credit rating from AAA to AA. However, events of the financial crisis revealed that AIG's downfall was latent in business decisions made before 2005.

In 1987, AIG established its AIG Financial Products division (AIGFP) to trade a variety of sophisticated financial products such as swap agreements, a contract that was relatively new at the time but that soon became a multi-trillion dollar worldwide market.[20] Headquartered in London, AIGFP was a clear success by 1998 with $500 million of revenue. Upon request by JPMorgan that year, AIG entered the nascent credit default swap (CDS) business by first issuing a CDS to guarantee debt held in JPMorgan's portfolio.

Although not an insurance policy, a CDS functions analogously to an insurance policy, with the insured event being a "credit event." The best model for understanding a CDS is to think of it by analogy with an ordinary insurance policy, like fire insurance on a house, except that the insured event is a default rather than a fire. For example, assume a bond investor holds a risky bond in its portfolio and is nervous about the bond issuer's ability to make all of the promised payments. The bond investor can turn to a financial institution and purchase credit protection through a CDS. The protection buyer, the bond investor in our example, makes a regular periodic payment to the protection seller. If the risky bond makes all of its payments as promised, the insurance payment becomes pure profit to the protection seller, and this pattern continues through time, just as with fire insurance on a house. However, if the risky bond defaults, the protection seller has the obligation to pay the protection buyer according to the terms of the CDS agreement. The CDS may require the protection seller to continue making the payments that the defaulting bond issuer had promised, or it might require the protection seller to make a one-time cash payment to the protection buyer.

Just as with fire insurance, the protection buyer will want to ensure that the protection seller actually has the financial ability to pay as promised if a credit event occurs. Therefore, the protection seller must have financial credibility, in the form of a sterling credit rating, in order to make a viable promise to pay off if the risky bond defaults.[21]

Just as the holder of a risky bond can acquire insurance through a CDS, so can a bond issuer. A firm with a risky credit rating has a choice of two different ways to float a bond issue. First and most simply, the firm can issue its risky bond and pay bond buyers the high yield that such risky bonds require. Second, the firm could issue the same risky bond, but also engage in a credit default swap to accompany the bond. In this case, an issuer might buy protection from a firm with an AAA rating, like AIG before 2005, and back its own bond with AIG's promise as well as its own.

With this CDS in place, if the issuer defaults, the bondholder has the AAA promise from AIG that it would make the payments originally promised by the issuer of the risky bond. From the issuer's point of view, the question is finding the cheapest way to acquire the needed funds from the bond issue. Which is cheaper: Issue the straight bond, accept a lower credit rating on the bond, and pay the higher yield such bonds require; or issue the same bond, buy AIG's guarantee, and get a higher credit rating and a lower yield for the bond based on AIG's guarantee?

The practice of selecting the approach that gives the best credit rating at the lowest cost is known as ratings arbitrage. To get a better credit rating for the bonds it issues, the issuer could simply raise more capital for the firm and thereby earn a better credit rating. However, it often turns out to be much cheaper to effectively rent a higher rating from an AAA firm like the former AIG. For AIG, insuring the risky bond is a way to get more income out of its AAA rating. After all, collecting payments from the issuer for the default insurance is free money—as long as the issuer does not default. In its actual business, AIG insured the bonds of very creditable issuers, but these were issuers that had solid credit ratings, just not the golden AAA rating that AIG enjoyed. And what was the chance that a firm with a solid credit rating was going to default?

From 1998 to the end of 2007, AIG enlarged this model of guaranteeing debt, expanding the business both in absolute size and aggressively extending the CDS model to guarantee CDOs. After all, a CDO really is just a debt obligation with a series of promised payments, and those payments can be guaranteed just like the promised cash flows from an ordinary corporate bond.

AIGFP's business was greatly aided by bank regulators in Europe, with their particular requirements for bank capital. Under the European bank regulatory structure known as the Basel Accords—Basel I and Basel II—a bank holding a risky bond or CDO in its investment portfolio was required to hold a certain percentage of capital to cover the risk associated with that investment, the required percentage varying with the risk of the bank's investment portfolio. However, if the bank purchased a CDS to cover the risk of its portfolio, it could reduce its capital requirement. Often the reduction in required capital was huge, reducing the demanded capital from 8 percent of the value of the risky bonds or CDOs to just 1.6 percent if a CDS were in place. Again, the matter became one of cost. Which was worse, having a high amount of dead capital per the regulation, or meeting regulatory requirements by buying a CDS and freeing up some capital? The cheaper alternative often turned out to be to buy credit protection through a CDS, and AIGFP was there to sell the needed CDS.[22]

And sell protection AIGFP certainly did, under the leadership of Joe Cassano, who saw these transactions as extremely safe in August 2007: "It is hard for us, without being flippant, to even see a scenario within any kind of realm of reason that would see us losing one dollar in any of those transactions."[23] By the end of 2007, AIG had CDSs on $527 billion worth of risky debt outstanding, much of this debt being in the form of CDOs backed by home mortgages.[24]

The range of possibilities in AIG's position was enormous. Theoretically, all of the bonds could default, AIG would owe $527 billion, and it would clearly be bankrupt. At the other end of the range, no bonds could default, AIG would never have to pay on the protection it had sold, and it could keep pocketing the payments on the CDSs it had sold—this seemed to be the obvious scenario contemplated by Joe Cassano.

Of course, there would be *some* defaults in a half-trillion dollar portfolio, but as long as they were modest, AIG's business could be quite profitable. But there was one other possibility that few saw as realistic. In a CDS, the protection is only as good as the financial soundness of the protection seller. The typical CDS contract contained a clause in contemplation of this fact, but without any real expectation that the clause would become operational. A CDS contract typically requires the protection seller to post collateral if the protection seller suffers a credit downgrade. In other words, the promise of an AAA firm is sufficient, but if the firm loses that crown, it needs to replace that golden promise with hard cash. And the worse the protection seller's credit rating becomes, the more collateral the protection seller has to post. Further, as the risk of default on the insured instruments increases, CDS contracts typically require the protection seller to post more collateral, so that a protection seller that is absolutely sound in a normal market can still experience collateral calls if the firms that it insures start to have troubles.

We have already seen that AIG lost its AAA rating in 2005 due to an accounting scandal, but the firm entered 2008 with its AA rating well in hand, and this was sufficient to sustain its business as a credit protection seller. Further, for 2007, AIG earned $6.2 billion after taxes, in spite of a fourth-quarter loss of $2.08 billion, and it ended the year with more than $1 trillion in assets and almost $100 billion in shareholder equity. AIG enjoyed its highest stock price of $72.65 per share on June 1, 2007, with a total equity value of $188 billion. As figure 7.2 shows, AIG lost value from this point forward.

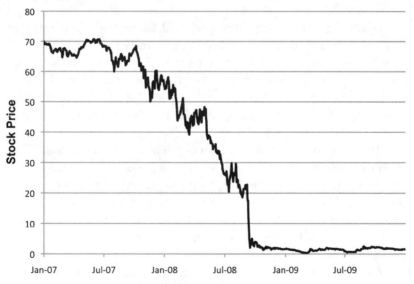

Figure 7.2 AIG's Share Price, 2007–2009
For consistency, this graph does not reflect the 20:1 reverse split of AIG's shares that occurred on May 30, 2009.

The first hints of trouble arrived in the third quarter of 2007, when AIG wrote its swap portfolio down by $352 million and then reported a $5.3 billion loss for the fourth quarter. But even bigger difficulties started in May 2008, when AIG reported a loss of $7.8 billion for the first quarter, which the firm attributed to the weak housing market and credit market volatility. Standard and Poor's and Fitch both issued a credit downgrade from AA to AA-, and S&P put AIG on CreditWatch negative, signaling the prospect of further downgrades if AIG did not raise $12.5 billion in new capital as it planned. So far, AIG had suffered no dramatic external effects, such as being forced to make collateral deposits that threatened its capacity. Most of those collateral demands would come if AIG were to suffer a further downgrade to A. On a brighter note, if earnings improved, everything could still be all right.

As bad news continued to arrive, matters were still not desperate. True, AIG's stock price had fallen steadily from the $70s in 2007 into 2008 and further into the summer of 2008, and by mid-2008, AIG's total losses on its swap positions had reach $25 billion.[25]

But, unlike some other firms, AIG retained significant value. For instance, at the end of the second quarter of 2008, AIG's stock price had fallen from its 2007 high of $72.65 to $26.46 and its shareholder value still stood at $70 billion (even though that represented a loss of 62 percent over the previous year's high). Faced with losses, a firm must shore up its capital position in some way. It can start accumulating profits, it can sell assets, or it can raise new funds from investors. To raise new funds, strong firms can go to the capital markets, while weaker firms can go to private borrowers, and AIG was pursuing both avenues aggressively, but without particular success.

Matters did not improve, and on August 18, 2008, AIG announced its second quarter results—a loss of $5.36 billion. If losing more than $13 billion in six months—a rate higher than $2 billion in losses per month—was not enough to tank AIG completely, what would it take? AIG's mounting losses made it impossible to go to the capital markets and made it less likely that the firm could find private lenders. So shoring up capital seemed unlikely. Further, as AIG's struggles became more acute, its CDS agreements started to become an ever more serious financial drain.

Now AIG's CDS counterparties started to demand more collateral to protect them from AIG's weakened condition and to reflect the deteriorating position of some of the firms that AIG was insuring. Already suffering from a lack of capital, these demands were the last thing that

AIG needed. While the collateral demands are specified in the CDS contract, they are also somewhat negotiable, and the actual collateral that is posted reflects the relative strength and bargaining positions of the two parties. But with mounting losses, AIG faced increasingly insistent demands for collateral, and one of the most strident of AIG's counterparties was Goldman Sachs. According to one report, Goldman had succeeded in collecting $8–9 billion of collateral from AIG during the summer of 2008.[26] By August 2008, AIG reported that it had posted a total of $16.5 billion in total collateral on its portfolio of swaps.[27] Gary Gorton, a Yale professor and consultant to AIG, said "It is difficult to convey the ferocity of the fights over collateral."[28]

Torturing collateral out of AIG was one thing, but the big event for collateral demand would be a ratings downgrade, a fate that befell AIG on September 16, when both Moody's and S&P downgraded AIG. S&P issued a downgrade from AA- to A- and warned that it might be forced to issue a further downgrade to BBB. This reduced credit rating implied that AIG would have to post an additional $14.5 billion in collateral for the CDS protection it had sold.

That same day, New York governor David Paterson agreed that AIG could borrow $20 billion from its insurance subsidiaries. These funds had previously been set aside by the insurance subsidiaries to guarantee that AIG could pay on its ordinary lines of insurance business, so this change helped AIG as a firm, but weakened protection for those who had purchased insurance from AIG for risks such as fire and auto.

Anticipating this ratings move, AIG had been meeting with the federal government the previous weekend to try to secure additional financing from private sources, but met with no success. Faced with the fait accompli of the ratings downgrade, the federal government determined on September 16 that it had no choice but to help AIG avoid out-and-out bankruptcy. The reasoning went as follows: AIG stands at the center of the web of global finance and owes billions to other large financial institutions. If AIG declares bankruptcy and is unable to pay its counterparties, then those firms will suffer increased financial distress. AIG's problems would quickly prove contagious and infect its immediate counterparties, as well as the counterparties of AIG's counterparties. Even though AIG presumably had assets sufficient to pay the $14.5 billion, it was unable to convert them into cash in time to meet its obligations. Faced with this reality, the federal government determined that the financial system could not afford to allow an AIG bankruptcy, and the government agreed to lend $85 billion to AIG at LIBOR plus 8.5

percent. In return for making the loan, the government received a 79.9 percent ownership stake in AIG in the form of warrants.

In anticipation of the downgrade, and then in response to the actual event, AIG's share price fell from $17.55 on September 11, 2008, to $2.05 per share on September 17, a loss of 88 percent in a few days, giving shareholders a loss of $42 billion.

In extending assistance to AIG, the Fed used its authority to lend to nonbanks under the "unusual and exigent" terms of the Federal Reserve Act. These were the same terms that the government had used to assist Bear Stearns in March and had refused to extend to Lehman Brothers just a few days before dealing with AIG. The $85 billion lifeline quickly proved to be too little. In a series of supplements and restructurings, the government's commitment to AIG quickly ballooned to $182.5 billion, and by March 2, 2009, AIG had drawn on $126.1 billion of that total commitment.[29]

What became of these billions of taxpayer dollars? To a great extent, AIG received funds from the government and immediately paid those monies to its counterparties—large financial institutions in the United States and abroad, including $12.9 billion to Goldman Sachs, $6.8 billion to Merrill Lynch, $5.2 billion to Bank of America, $2.3 billion to Citigroup, $1.5 billion to Wachovia, $12 billion each to Société Générale of France and Deutsche Bank of Germany, $8.5 billion to Barclays of Great Britain, and $5 billion to UBS of Switzerland.[30] Not surprisingly, the publication of this information engendered a new sense of outrage on two counts. First, AIG paid many billions of dollars to firms that were seen as miscreants in the financial crisis, and second, so much of American taxpayer funds went to foreign banks (43.5 percent was paid to U.S. firms, with French, German, and United Kingdom firms receiving 19.1, 16.7, and 12.7 percent, respectively).[31]

Of course, to a considerable extent, these complaints miss the point of the bailout, which was to protect the financial system. Many of the U.S. firms receiving payments from AIG were already wards of the government to a large extent, so permitting AIG to pay them was just another way of shoveling money to them. Further, with AIG at a critical nodal point in the web of international finance, refusing to pay foreign banks would have merely encouraged those banks to force AIG into bankruptcy. In short, the purpose of the AIG bailout was to prevent AIG's bankruptcy with its attendant systemic implications, and that could be achieved only by helping AIG fulfill its financial promises, even if that meant directing money to unworthy firms that happened to be AIG's trading partners.

A more salient objection to the AIG bailout focuses on the question of "haircuts." Often, when a firm is in financial distress, its creditors accept less than 100 percent of what is promised. Instead of forcefully negotiating for such "haircuts," the Fed paid AIG's counterparties in full. This decision generated immediate criticism and also led the Special Inspector General for the Troubled Asset Relief Program to conclude that the Federal Reserve Bank of New York made ". . . limited efforts to negotiate concessions . . ." and that its ". . . negotiating strategy to pursue concessions from counterparties offered little opportunity for success, even in the light of the willingness of one counterparty [UBS of Switzerland] to agree to concessions."[32] To many, this approach was particularly galling, as other creditors of AIG, most notably its employees, were making concessions in compensation and even losing their jobs. However, during September 2008, the federal government was busy shoveling money to a variety of financial firms in an effort to save the financial system, and making AIG's counterparties whole was one more way of achieving the same goal. The perhaps sad truth of the matter is that making employees whole has little systemic effect, but keeping large financial firms from going into bankruptcy has widespread effects, and federal policy clearly focused on these systemic concerns.

While the counterparties were made whole, the shareholders certainly were not. From the peak in 2007 to the end of 2008, AIG's shareholders lost $184 billion, more than 97 percent of the shares' earlier value. Even worse was to come, as AIG's stock price sank further in 2009 to the $1 per share level.

▬ Citigroup: The Biggest Zombie of Them All

Today's Citigroup grew out of a bank formed in 1812 as City Bank of New York; it eventually became First National City Bank in 1962, and the firm and its bank became Citicorp and Citibank in 1976. With Citibank already a huge bank, the firm became a "financial supermarket" through a series of mergers and acquisitions, picking up other financial firms such as Primerica, the stock brokerage firms Smith Barney and Shearson Lehman, and the bond dealer and investment banking firm Salomon Brothers. Citi acquired Travelers Insurance Group in 1998 in the largest merger in history.[33] At this time, the firm became Citigroup, hereafter merely "Citi."

Managing such a huge array of diverse financial businesses proved an enduring challenge, with Citi having continuing difficulties with risk management and the integration of its many computer systems. Yet Citi was profitable, recording almost $18 billion in net income in 2003, and Citi continued to grow, largely through acquisitions. Concerned about its risk management practices, the Federal Reserve Bank of New York forbade it to engage in any more mergers for a year (2005–2006). At the end of 2006, Citigroup was the largest banking firm in the United States, with $1.8 trillion in total assets—25 percent more than Bank of America and twice as much as JPMorgan. That year, Citi earned revenues of $86 billion, reported net income of $21.5 billion, and employed 327,000 people.

On top of the world in 2006, Citi's CEO, Charles Prince, said: "Our job is to set a tone at the top to incent people to do the right thing and to set up safety nets to catch people who make mistakes or do the wrong thing and correct those as quickly as possible. And it is working. It is working."[34] Citi continued its merger habit, and Prince learned in September for the first time that the bank owned $43 billion in mortgage-related assets."[35] Nonetheless, his managers assured him that everything was all right. Shortly thereafter, Citi told a concerned SEC that ". . . the probability of those mortgages defaulting was so tiny that they excluded them from their risk analysis."[36]

If things were all right, they did not stay that way. For the fourth quarter of 2007, Citi reported subprime losses of $18 billion, an overall loss of $9.8 billion in net income for the quarter, and Prince was out as CEO. This was the beginning of a string of losses for Citi that would persist for many quarters. Through 2008, Citi posted billions of dollars of losses for net income in every quarter: $5.1 billion in quarter one, $2.5 in quarter two, $2.8 in quarter three, and $17.3 in quarter four. Because Citi did have some profitable operations, the net income figure understates the subprime and MBS losses, which eventually exceeded $65 billion, including reserves for future losses. As Citi lurched through the year, its share price sank, as figure 7.3 shows. During one trading day it fell below $1 per share, and Citi had its lowest closing price of $1.02 on March 5, 2009, a loss of more than 98 percent of its high value for 2007.

In the fall of 2008, as the federal government prepared to dish out assistance to the financial system, no one could doubt Citi's need. In October 2008, Citi received a first tranche of $25 billion from the TARP program and a second helping of $20 billion a month later. In exchange for these two cash infusions, Citi gave the government dividend-paying

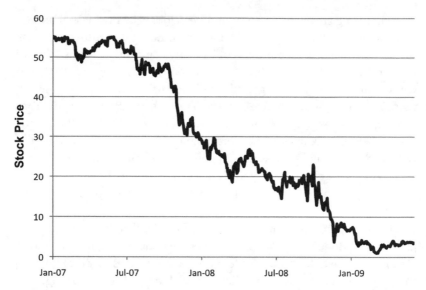

Figure 7.3 Citigroup's Stock Price

preferred shares. Paying the dividend on these preferred shares proved a difficult cash drain for Citi, and in February 2009, the government agreed to convert a portion of those preferred shares into common stock. As a result, the federal government owns 36 percent of the firm. This conversion marks the depth of Citi's difficulties, because it signals an acceptance of shareholder dilution in order to escape the necessity of making regular dividend payments on the preferred shares. Of all the TARP recipients, only Citi and General Motors Acceptance Corporation, the financing arm of General Motors, engaged in such a conversion.

Citi managed to eke out a $1.6 billion profit in the first quarter of 2009, and followed that with profits of $4.3 and $0.1 billion in quarters two and three; by the end of 2009, its stock price was in the $3.50 to $4 per share range. As 2009 drew to a close, some still questioned Citi's viability.[37]

Zombies and the Future

The four firms discussed in this chapter, Fannie Mae, Freddie Mac, AIG, and Citigroup, are four of the clearest examples of zombie firms—firms that still exist, but that may not be able to survive. Beyond the financial sector, General Motors and Chrysler Corporation, along with their two financing units, General Motors Acceptance Corporation and Chrysler Financial, are also deeply troubled wards of the government, with uncertain futures.

While other firms received federal assistance and while quite a few have initiated or even completed repayment, these zombie firms are important for what they reveal about the U.S. economy and the relationship between the federal government and supposedly private businesses for the future. In essence, they showcase the vastly altered terms on which companies in the United States now do business.

Fannie Mae and Freddie Mac, it has turned out, had much more than an implicit guarantee from the federal government. When matters came to a head, the federal government took these quasi-private firms firmly onto the books of the taxpayer, thereby making explicit that these really were creatures of the federal government. For these two firms, the federal government now has a stated commitment of $400 billion (and an unstated commitment that could be much larger) and operates them completely.

Before the financial crisis, the federal government had regulated AIG with a light hand, refraining from exercising the full regulatory authority it already possessed. Part of the reason for this is that AIG was principally an insurance company, and insurance firms have generally been subject to supervision by the states in which they are located. But because of AIG's connections to the international web of finance, the federal government suddenly found itself compelled to commit almost $200 billion to the firm's assistance. So sudden, deep, and troubling was the government's entanglement with AIG that Federal Reserve Chairman Ben Bernanke was led to say: "Of all the events and all of the things we've done in the last 18 months, the single one that makes me the angriest, that gives me the most angst, is the intervention with AIG."[38]

Policy Responses and the Beginnings of Recovery

Even in retrospect, the six weeks from early September to mid-October 2008 must be reckoned as a time of near financial catastrophe. Living through that time made the likelihood of disaster appear even more present. During this period, the financial leaders of the U.S. government, Timothy Geithner at the New York Federal Reserve Bank, Henry Paulson at the U.S. Treasury, and Ben Bernanke at the Federal Reserve System cooperated to take unprecedented actions in a frantic attempt to rescue the financial system as it stood on the brink of ruin.

In 1998, as Long Term Capital Management imploded and threatened the world's financial system, the federal government refused to intervene on the grounds that it lacked authority to do so. After assisting JPMorgan Chase's purchase of Bear Stearns in March 2008, the federal government demurred to assist Lehman in a similar transaction and refused to let it become a bank holding company during the summer of 2008. But faced with the enormity of the developing crisis in the fall of 2008, the federal government seemed to find previously undiscovered powers, and Congress granted new authority through legislation.

The market turmoil in the days immediately following Lehman's bankruptcy may have convinced the government that AIG could not be allowed to go bankrupt without destroying the financial system. At any rate, the government suddenly found authority on September 16 to provide $85 billion to, and to take an almost 80 percent ownership stake in, AIG, which many had viewed as being fairly remote from federal regulation, although it was subject to regulation by the Office of Thrift Supervision. The Securities and Exchange Commission (SEC) followed the AIG rescue with a stronger ban on short selling on September 17. Nonetheless, the Dow fell 449 points that day.

Before dawn on Thursday, September 18, the Fed announced a plan to provide $180 billion to financial markets through a cooperative arrangement with the European Central Bank, as well as central banks in Canada, Japan, Great Britain, and Switzerland. The same day rumors began to circulate that the Treasury and the Federal Reserve were considering a massive bailout plan that envisioned the establishment of something like the Resolution Trust Corporation, which had proved an effective bailout mechanism during the S&L crisis of the 1980s and early 1990s. These actions led to a substantial stock market surge that day, with the Dow gaining 410 points, which almost offset the losses of the previous day. Henry Paulson, Ben Bernanke, and Christopher Cox, chairman of the SEC, met with key leaders of Congress on Thursday evening, and Senate majority leader, Harry Reid, said he expected a proposal within hours, not days.[1] On Friday morning, the SEC banned all short selling in 799 financial sector stocks, to take effect immediately.

Unfurling the TARP

That same Friday morning, Secretary Paulson acknowledged the reactive nature of the policy makers' previous efforts, when he announced a "Comprehensive Approach to Market Developments," which read in part:

> We have acted on a case-by-case basis in recent weeks, addressing problems at Fannie Mae and Freddie Mac, working with market participants to prepare for the failure of Lehman Brothers, and lending to AIG so it can sell some of its assets in an orderly manner. And this morning we've taken a number of powerful tactical steps to increase confidence in the system, including the establishment of a temporary guaranty program for the U.S. money market mutual fund industry. . . . Despite these steps, more is needed. We must now take further, decisive action to

fundamentally and comprehensively address the root cause of our financial system's stresses.

In this announcement, Paulson tracked the main problem to poor-quality mortgage assets that were impeding the flow of credit in the financial system:

> The underlying weakness in our financial system today is the illiquid mortgage assets that have lost value as the housing correction has proceeded. These illiquid assets are choking off the flow of credit that is so vitally important to our economy. . . . The federal government must implement a program to remove these illiquid assets that are weighing down our financial institutions and threatening our economy. This troubled asset relief program [TARP] must be properly designed and sufficiently large to have maximum impact, while including features that protect the taxpayer to the maximum extent possible.

The announcement included no details, but did include the promise that details would be worked out over the weekend of September 20–21, with legislative action expected in the next week. The market responded to these two moves with a surge on the Dow of 369 points.

This same weekend, the government allowed Goldman Sachs and Morgan Stanley the comfort of the bank holding company designation, a relief that had been denied to Lehman only weeks before. (The stated ground for the different treatment was that Goldman and Morgan Stanley had collateral with actual value and that Lehman did not, but one might reasonably think that the market's reaction to the Lehman collapse and the quickly worsening crisis had the effect of broadening the thinking of the government's financial team.)

Details on the government's plan followed soon, with the *New York Times* publishing over the weekend the text of a three-page "Legislative Proposal for Treasury Authority to Purchase Mortgage-Related Assets." This was the beginning of the soon-to-be-famous Troubled Asset Relief Plan (TARP), which would allow the federal government to purchase "troubled assets" from financial institutions. The three most notable features of this proposed legislation were the sweeping authority it gave to the secretary of the Treasury, the huge cost of the plan, and the brevity of the proposal—three pages in its original typography. (See Appendix B, Original TARP Proposal, which reproduces this brief document.)

Perhaps most stunning was the following sentence, which gave un precedented authority to the secretary of the Treasury: "Decisions by the Secretary pursuant to the authority of this Act are non-reviewable and committed to agency discretion, and may not be reviewed by any court of law or any administrative agency." Beyond giving the secretary sweeping power, the proposal urged the establishment of a $700 billion fund that the Treasury could use to buy these assets. This was essentially a $700 billion line of revolving credit, in that it set a limit of $700 billion at any one time, so that purchase and subsequent resale of an asset would free the line of credit up to its maximum of $700 billion. Further, the proposal included an increase in the federal public debt to $11.315 trillion, up from the $10.615 trillion limit that had just been approved in July 2008.[2] If this was not enough for the market to digest in a single weekend, this was the same weekend that Goldman Sachs and Morgan Stanley both became bank holding companies.

The Market Reacts

The proposal brought a swift and unfavorable market reaction, which was almost immediately supplemented by a firestorm of criticism. First, the market responded by falling 532 points (4.7 percent) over the Monday and Tuesday, September 22–23, after the weekend announcement. Ben Bernanke testified before a Senate Committee on Tuesday, September 23, on behalf of this TARP plan, saying: ". . . removing these assets from institutions' balance sheets will help to restore confidence in our financial markets and enable banks and other institutions to raise capital and to expand credit to support economic growth."[3]

Deviating from his prepared remarks, Bernanke also explained the underlying rationale behind the asset purchase plan: "Accounting rules require banks to value many assets at something close to a very low fire-sale price rather than the hold-to-maturity price, which is not unreasonable in itself, given their illiquidity. However, this leads to big write-downs and reductions in capital, which in turn forces additional sales that send the fire-sale price down further, adding to pressure."[4]

The accounting rule FAS 157 requires financial institutions to show the market value of assets on their books. In his testimony, Bernanke distinguished between the "fire-sale" price and the "hold-to-maturity" price and implicitly conceded that the fire-sale price *is* the market price, given their illiquidity. So the essential proposal was to pay financial institutions an above-market price. As Bernanke also implicitly noted, paying the fire-sale price would expose just how little the assets were truly worth, which would exhibit just how capital-impoverished these institutions were, and would demonstrate how much more capital they needed.

The vision, Bernanke explained, would be to create an auction mechanism to reveal the hold-to-maturity value:

> If the Treasury bids for and then buys assets at a price close to the hold-to-maturity price, there will be substantial benefits. (1) banks will have a basis for valuing those assets and will not have to use fire-sale prices. Their capital would not be unreasonably marked down. (2) liquidity should begin to come back to these markets. (3) removal of these assets from balance sheets and better information on value should reduce uncertainty and allow the banks to attract new private capital. (4) credit market should start to unfreeze. New credit will come available to support our economy. And, (5) taxpayers should own assets at prices close to hold-to-maturity values, which minimizes their risk.[5]

In essence, this bold TARP legislative proposal urged that the taxpayer should buy assets from troubled financial institutions at a price that would reflect the returns that would actually be realized if the assets were held until their ultimate maturity. This "hold-to-maturity" price was, of course, unknown. The great uncertainty in the markets was identical to the uncertainty over the value of this entire class of "troubled assets." As only estimates of the "hold-to-maturity" price were possible, various parties were sure to have different assessments of the worth of these assets. If the government thought an asset had a "hold-to-maturity" value that was higher than the estimate of the owner of that asset, the owner would happily sell. If a financial institution thought the "hold-to-maturity" price exceeded the government's offer, the financial institution would refuse to sell—unless it was compelled to do so by the precarious state of its financial position.

However, let us assume that the Treasury was able to correctly estimate the true "hold-to-maturity" price and buy assets at that price. By maturity, the Treasury would be made whole and would suffer no loss and enjoy no gain. But it would have undertaken a tremendous risk in the process and would have transferred tremendous wealth from taxpayers to financial institutions, with no prospect of any gain for taxpayers at all. For its part, the selling financial institution would receive the "hold-to-maturity" price for an asset that could otherwise only be sold at the "fire-sale" price. This difference constitutes an immediate wealth transfer from the public to the financial institution. Further, the financial institution would have also transferred all the risk of the volatile assets from its balance sheet to the public.

The TARP proposal had one further benefit for the many distressed financial institutions. With FAS 157 requiring that assets be shown on firms' books at market values, selling an asset at the "hold-to-maturity" value would create a transaction price that firms could use to pretend that the value of their other assets was much higher than the "fire-sale" price, which was a much better representation of the actual market price of the assets. (This aspect was explicitly embraced in Bernanke's analysis, quoted above.) In sum, the original TARP plan helped financial institutions in three main ways: by transferring wealth from the public to the banks, by improving the capital position of the banks by replacing unmarketable assets with ready cash, and by helping them pretend that their other assets were worth more than their current market values.

The TARP Evolves

In the last days of September 2008, the actual economics of the TARP legislation became increasingly apparent to policy makers and the public and generated tremendous outrage at a plan that was essentially designed to enrich financial institutions at public expense without any chance for public gain. As a particularly clear example, Paul Krugman wrote in the *New York Times* that Ben Bernanke had "let the cat out of the bag" and called the proposal "fundamentally disingenuous." After noting that a Treasury purchase of these assets at prevailing market prices would reveal losses that are ". . . much larger than the banks have already acknowledged, so that their capital position would be severely weakened," he went on to say: "So the plan only helps the financial situation if Treasury pays prices well above market—that is, if it is in effect injecting capital into financial firms, at taxpayers' expense. What possible justification can there be for doing this without an equity stake? No equity stake, no deal."[6]

Krugman was far from alone in his analysis. At the web site 247wallst.com, Douglas McIntyre had a similar immediate and trenchant analysis:

What has become clear is that Treasury plans to purchase bad assets from banks at prices very near their original value. The risk to taxpayers under this program would be tremendous. If housing prices continue to fall, so will the value of the paper the government has purchased. Under this set of circumstances the public could be at risk for underwriting the great majority of the Treasury's purchases and never having a chance to recoup their investment. Buying troubled bank assets at above where they would be valued in a free market now and at a price which is near to the potential price when they mature is a great handout to the banks, but undermines almost any chance that the Treasury will ever get any meaningful yield from the bailout. Taxpayers lose any chance of being made whole.[7]

The *New York Times* summed it up quite well by Friday, September 26, with Floyd Norris writing: "But coming up with any kind of fair value was not the real objective. Instead, the goal was to recapitalize the banking system by placing a floor under the prices of securities that never should have been issued."[8]

With reactions such as that of Krugman, McIntyre, and Norris, it was not surprising that the three-page bill was in deep trouble less than a week after its unveiling. On Wednesday night, President Bush made a prime-time television address warning that "Our entire economy is in danger."[9] Thursday, September 25, brought a flurry of meetings, with Paulson reportedly going on one knee to beseech Nancy Pelosi, Speaker of the House, to support the plan. For his part, President Bush said: "If money isn't loosened up, this sucker could go down."[10]

The plan immediately became perceived as an ill-conceived "bail-out," with the plan's sweeping authority and the proposal's three-page brevity contributing significantly to this impression, These factors led to the plan's rejection in the House of Representatives on September 29, 2008.[11] The stock market immediately registered its disappointment by dropping the Dow Jones Average 778 points (7.0 percent) that day, the largest point drop in history.

The market's reaction helped to concentrate the mind of federal politicians and bureaucrats, and over the next week the plan was re-crafted, with its length increasing to 169 pages, while keeping the basic tenor of the plan. On October 3, 2008, just one tumultuous week after its initial rejection, Congress approved the TARP, formally named the Emergency Economic Stabilization Act. During the next week, October 3–10, 2008, the crisis continued with the market falling significantly every day. During that week, the Dow lost 1,874 points, or more than 18 percent of its value, and then rose by 936 points on the following Monday.

Policy makers, most notably Paulson, Geithner, and Bernanke, were trying to hit a moving target, with events outracing their planning. Just days after the passage of the TARP, Paulson moved to revamp the plan drastically. Instead of attempting to purchase troubled assets, Treasury would use TARP funds to inject capital directly into financial institutions by taking an equity stake in firms. This was a dramatic change that many with a free-market orientation had opposed and tried to avoid, because it amounted to a partial nationalization of the recipient financial institutions.

Paulson summoned the CEOs of the nine largest banks in the United States to a meeting at Treasury on the afternoon of Monday, October 13, 2008. Representing the government were Paulson, Bernanke, Geithner, and Sheila Bair, head of the Federal Deposit Insurance Corporation. The bank CEOs in attendance represented huge firms such as JPMorgan, Goldman Sachs, Morgan Stanley, Citibank, Wells Fargo, Bank of America, and Merrill Lynch.

In essence, Paulson unveiled a plan that all nine banks would be forced to accept. Refusal to participate would bring regulatory wrath, with Paulson directly informing the head of Wells Fargo that "your regulator is sitting right there," referring to Sheila Bair. Refusal to participate would lead to a regulatory demand that firms raise new capital, a virtual impossibility under prevailing market conditions.[12] Before the meeting ended in the early evening, all nine CEOs had signed and committed their firms to participate. Forcing all of these key firms to take this assistance would mask the firms desperately in need of assistance. If funds were extended only to those banks facing runs, the government feared that identifying those firms as weak would itself promote runs.

In essence, the Treasury would commit $250 billion to buy senior preferred shares. Banks would pay a dividend rate of 5 percent per year for the first five years, followed by a 9 percent dividend thereafter. Although the shares represented an ownership interest in the firms, the shares would be non-voting. In addition, the Treasury would receive warrants to purchase common stock at a price equaling the market price at the time the warrants were issued. As an additional condition of this enforced participation, firms had to agree to accept corporate governance standards set by the government and to accept restrictions on their executive pay practices.[13]

Citigroup, Bank of America (which now included Merrill Lynch), JPMorgan, and Wells Fargo each received $25 billion, with Morgan Stanley and Goldman Sachs receiving $10 billion each, Bank of New York Mellon taking $3 billion, and State Street Bank participating by receiving $2 billion. Reaction to the plan varied tremendously by bank circumstance. Wells Fargo unequivocally viewed the mandatory capital as unwelcome, while for Citigroup it was an absolute lifeline. In the following months, hundreds of additional financial institutions would also receive funding. Some would receive billions, and some small firms would receive less than $1 million. In addition, some of the largest institutions, such as Citigroup and Bank of America, would receive additional billions in infusions.

The market's reaction on October 15 was hardly encouraging, with the Dow dropping 733 points (7.9 percent) to the lowest level attained since the crisis began, standing at 8,578. In the following weeks, the stock market drifted, but credit markets remained completely shuttered, leading the Federal Reserve and Treasury to announce a new program in late November 2008.

Introduction of the TALF

On November 25, the Fed and the Treasury announced the creation of the Term Asset-Backed Securities Loan Facility (TALF). In essence, this was a plan for the Fed and the Treasury to accept asset-backed securities as collateral and to lend the owners of these securities the market value of those assets less a small percentage (a "haircut") of their value. In contrast to mortgage-backed securities (MBS), these asset-backed securities (ABS) are securities created based on underlying student loans, auto loans, credit card loans, and loans guaranteed by the Small Business Administration. So, while MBS and ABS are created through a similar process of securitization, they differ in the type of loan that ultimately underlies the two types of instruments.

The Federal Reserve explained the rationale for the move in the following terms:

> New issuance of ABS declined precipitously in September and came to a halt in October. At the same time, interest rate spreads on AAA-rated tranches of ABS soared to levels well outside the range of historical experience, reflecting unusually high risk

premiums. The ABS markets historically have funded a substantial share of consumer credit and SBA-guaranteed small business loans. Continued disruption of these markets could significantly limit the availability of credit to households and small businesses and thereby contribute to further weakening of U.S. economic activity. The TALF is designed to increase credit availability and support economic activity by facilitating renewed issuance of consumer and small business ABS at more normal interest rate spreads.[14]

While the ABS market had issued about $1 trillion per year in 2005 and 2006, and even $750 billion in 2007 with the start of the crisis, total ABS securitization in 2008 fell well below $200 billion, grinding to only $8 billion in the last quarter of 2008.[15] Without the ability to create ABS, financial institutions were limited in their ability to lend to consumers, so consumers were unable to spend, and economic activity was sharply curtailed, leading to increased unemployment.

The initial scope of TALF was $200 billion. Whereas the TARP involved legislation to authorize $700 billion to purchase troubled as-sets (later modified to take the form of direct capital injections into banks), the TALF was undertaken by the authority of the Federal Reserve and the Treasury, with the Treasury using some of the TARP funds for its portion of the lending, and the Federal Reserve using its existing authority to lend against good collateral. The Treasury pro-vided 10 percent of the total projected funds from the TARP, so that with the "haircut" of 5 to 16 percent, the view was that the Federal Reserve would be fully protected against losses. As an additional ironic condi-tion, lending was restricted to securities bearing an AAA rating. How-ever, firms that lent the collateral would only be exposed to losing the 5–16 percent "haircut" from the market value that formed the basis for the loan.

The stock market continued to be unimpressed in the months that followed. After recovering slightly from its low on October 10, 2008, the overall direction of the stock market was downward, reaching the low for the crisis on March 9, 2009, at 6,547. From its 2007 high of 14,164 on October 9, 2007, the Dow lost 40 percent of its value in the following year, and then lost an additional 23 percent from October 2008 to March 2009. Over the entire crisis, the stock market lost 53 percent of its value as measured by the Dow (from 14,164 on October 9, 2007, to 6,547 on March 9, 2009).

The government continued to respond with more programs. For example, as early as November 2008, the government committed $600 billion to buy assets from Fannie Mae and Freddie Mac. In March 2009, the Fed and the Treasury expanded the TALF to $1 trillion. Also in March 2009, the government expanded its asset purchase plan to cover up to $2 trillion in real estate assets. In essence, in March 2009 the government sponsored a plan to lend money to private investors, a Public-Private Investment Program, so that they could purchase MBS. These investors included traditional fund managers, hedge funds, private equity funds, pension funds and banks.[16] In May 2009, the Federal Reserve extended the TALF program to buy securities backed by commercial real estate loans.

Support for the Auto Industry

In 2008, the U.S. automobile industry fell into serious difficulties, due to long-standing financial, management, product development, and labor problems, in addition to legacy costs and high oil prices, issues that all were exacerbated by the recession. Problems were most severe for General Motors, followed by Chrysler, and then Ford. Of the three, Ford was the only firm not to receive government assistance and was the only firm to avoid bankruptcy.

Federal support for Chrysler and GM began in December 2008, with loans of $4 billion to each firm. Chrysler quickly moved to sell 35 percent of the firm to Fiat, but this deal hit serious legal difficulties. Chrysler filed for bankruptcy on April 30, 2009, becoming the first U.S. automaker to go bankrupt since 1933. General Motors quickly followed an even worse trajectory. GM's original federal loan of $4 billion in 2008 was followed by more federal loan support: $5.4 billion in January 2009, $4 billion in February, and a request for yet another $11.6 billion in April 2009. Unsuccessful in its efforts to reorganize and trim costs, General Motors filed for bankruptcy on June 1, 2009, and emerged from bankruptcy later in the summer with the federal government as the majority owner. The United Auto Workers and the Canadian government became minor shareholders.

Support for the automobile industry also helped the financing arms of GM and Chrysler, General Motors Acceptance Corporation (GMAC) and Chrysler Financial. In addition, $5 billion was committed to the

Auto Supplier Support Program, with all of these funds being drawn from the TARP's $700 billion kitty. Further, the federal government also moved to guarantee the warranties on GM and Chrysler cars. By the fall of 2009, the federal government owned 61 percent of the "New GM," the firm that emerged from bankruptcy, and 8 percent of the "New Chrysler," based on federal commitments of $52.4 billion to GM and $13.8 billion to Chrysler.[17]

Support for Home Owners

In February 2009, the government introduced the Making Homes Affordable (MHA) Program to help struggling homeowners. The MHA involves a loan modification program, a loan refinancing program, and support for lowering mortgage interest rates. Of these three, only the first falls under TARP and has been targeted at $75 billion, with $50 billion coming from the TARP funds. The largest recipients of these funds are mortgage servicers with names that have been prominently featured in the crisis: Countrywide, GMAC, JPMorgan Chase, Wells Fargo, CitiMortgage, and Wachovia Mortgage. Funds for these six ranged from $4.5 billion down to $1.4 billion as of fall 2009.[18] In the second quarter of 2010, the federal government was still struggling to devise a program for home owners that would be both politically palatable, yet provide meaningful assistance.

Green Shoots in the Financial Sector

In the months following the height of the crisis in September–October 2008, conditions remained generally poor, with severely truncated availability of credit. Yet some sectors of the financial industry started to improve, particularly following the market lows of March 2009. In June 2009, the Treasury announced that the ten largest firms participating in the Capital Purchase Program would be permitted to make repayments if they wished. Some firms, such as Goldman Sachs, JPMorgan, and Morgan Stanley, for instance, rushed to redeem their shares and cancel their warrants as soon as the government permitted. Reluctance to repay signaled continuing difficulties at some of the biggest banks, notably Citigroup and Bank of America.

Through the second half of 2009, the stock market continued to recover, and many financial firms returned to profitability. Yet the recovery was spotty at best, with almost weekly bank closings continuing through the year and continuing disturbances in the credit markets. Nonetheless, by October 2009, the Treasury was starting to develop plans for winding down its support of credit markets, with one Treasury official saying of the contemplated exit: "You do it incrementally, where and when you think you can, and not sooner."[19]

While the economic problems clearly originated in the housing sector and then moved to imperil the entire financial sector, they inexorably spilled over to the broader real economy. With the financial turmoil and the withdrawing of credit that began in 2007 and accelerated in 2008, economists and policy makers were well aware that a serious recession loomed on the horizon, or was already under way. Officially, the economy fell into recession in December 2007, where it remained well into 2009. The last quarter of 2009 showed some economic growth, but by the end of the year the National Bureau of Economic Research, which determines the official dates for recession, had not yet called an end. With the real sector of the economy in distress, unemployment rose steadily. Starting from a low of 4.1 percent in October 2006, the unemployment rate rose steadily and hit a peak of 10.2 percent in October 2009, and still stood at 10.0 percent well into 2010. In 2010 the Congressional Budget Office predicted that an unemployment rate above 5.0 percent would persist until 2016. Many states were particularly hard hit, especially Nevada, due to its overextended real estate market, and Michigan, due to the bankruptcies of Chrysler and General Motors, along with contraction at Ford, all of whose problems affected their suppliers and other related firms, and led to support for the auto industry.

Initial Cost Assessment

In spite of the appearance of green economic shoots, the entire year of 2009 progressed with continuing fear of renewed crisis. Yet matters did seem to be improving, and various observers began to attempt to reckon the damage and the cost of recovery.

A final assessment was impossible, of course. The real economy had suffered very significant damage, as persistently high unemployment showed. Further, trillions of dollars of real estate value had evaporated, at least measured from the real estate peak of late 2006. Perhaps a great deal of that peak value was merely illusory wealth, but millions of Americans had thought and acted as though it were real and had spent and consumed as if they were much wealthier than the financial crisis would reveal them to be.

In the fall of 2009, the *New York Times* published an initial assessment of the cost, the basics of which appear in table 8.1. On this accounting, the federal government had committed almost $12.5 trillion

Table 8.1

An Initial Assessment of the Federal Cost of the Financial Crisis ($Billions)

Item	Committed	Spent	Interest and Profits
Capital for Financial Firms	290.0	244.5	10.0
Guarantees on Bank Debt	789.0	0.0	9.3
Guarantees on Deposit Accounts	736.0	4.3	0.0
Backing Citigroup Assets	$249	0.0	0.0
Backing Bank of America Assets	98.0	0.0	0.0
Fed Loans to Financial Firms	1,340.0	239.0	0.7
Term Asset-Backed Loan Facility (TALF)	1,000.0	50.1	0.1
Public-Private Investment Program	1,000.0	0.0	0.0
Fannie Mae and Freddie Mac	400.0	95.6	2.2
Debt and MBS Purchase Programs	1,450.0	1,130.0	0.0
Support for Money Markets	3,000.0	0.1	1.3
Funding for Commercial Paper	1,800.0	41.0	0.0
A.I.G.	183.0	145.1	1.4
Automakers	82.6	75.9	0.4
Totals	**12,417.6**	**2,025.6**	**25.4**

Source: Adapted from Amy Schoenfeld and Dylan Loeb McClain, "The Bailouts: An Accounting," *The New York Times*, September 14, 2009. Available at: http://www.nytimes.com/interactive/2009/09/14/business/bailout-assessment.html; Accessed on December 6, 2009.

through its various programs and had disbursed more than $2 trillion. On the other hand, some recipients had started to repay funds they had received, and federal officials hoped for much more in such repayments. Chapter 15 attempts to offer an assessment of the economic world left behind as the financial tsunami appears to shrink back into the sea.

Causes of the Financial Crisis:
Macroeconomic Developments
and Federal Policy

What caused the financial crisis of 2007–2009? Such an apparently straightforward question calls out for a direct answer. Yet no simple one-sentence response is both informative and meaningful. We might as well ask what caused the Renaissance or the Industrial Revolution and expect a response as simple and satisfying as an answer to a question like "What caused the car accident?" While the financial crisis may not compare to the world historical developments of the Renaissance or the Industrial Revolution, the crisis is nonetheless a complex social event with many strands.

More than 70 years after its inception, scholars continue to debate the causes of the Great Depression of the 1930s. No doubt, 70 years from now, academics will still be scribbling about the causes of the financial crisis of our time, an event that many now call the "Great Recession." Even such "medium scale" social phenomena, such as our financial crisis, can only come about through a multiplicity of causes. (One recent attempt by the Congressional Research Service to assess the cause of the crisis lists 26 causal factors.[1]) Yet it is possible to draw together the causal threads that played a role in creating the crisis, and it is possible to begin an assessment of these causes that achieves a broad understanding of the underlying causes of this financial disaster.

Three critical factors were key in setting the scale of our financial crisis: the price collapse of a major asset class, residential real estate in the United States; heavy exposure to the failing asset by investment banks, depository institutions, and other financial firms that, when taken together, were sufficiently large and important so that their sudden demise threatened the entire financial system; and a lack of transparency in the financial system that kept financial institutions from knowing which other institutions were sufficiently sound to receive credit and which were truly imperiled. Against this basic story of asset price collapse, large financial exposure, and poor transparency, this chapter examines the causal role played by macroeconomic factors, public policy, and governmental efforts to encourage home ownership. Later chapters consider other important causes.

The Basic Story

Residential housing in the United States is at the center of the crisis, because it constituted the major asset class that experienced a collapse in prices. In its entirety, the housing stock of the United States is a huge asset class, at one time worth $22.9 trillion dollars.[2] By the end of 2006, housing prices had reached heights never seen before, the result of a pro-longed rise in prices over many years. In sober hindsight, it now appears that prices reached a level that was far beyond the intrinsic values of the homes they represented. In short, it now seems apparent that housing prices in the United States were caught in a speculative bubble. Of course, few observers realized the extent of the overpricing back in 2006. Therefore, to understand the first causal element of the financial crisis, we need to understand what drove housing prices to such unjustified levels. In short, what caused the bubble in housing prices?

For the fall in housing prices to cause major losses for the financial system, financial institutions had to have substantial risk exposure to real estate. If every home in the United States had been fully paid for by its owners, so that there was no mortgage debt, the fall in housing prices would have caused huge losses for many individuals and for society as a whole, but it need not have caused a financial crisis. Home owners would still have suffered massive losses, but the financial system as a whole would have suffered much less than it did in the financial crisis of 2007–2009. Thus, the fall in value of a major asset class is not sufficient to cause a *financial* crisis. The second major ingredient in the financial crisis was the excessive exposure of financial institutions to this asset class.

Before 2007, prevailing opinion maintained that "housing prices only go up." Yes, there had been episodes of falling housing prices, such as the experience of Texas in the 1980s, but the unpleasantness in the Texas housing market had been locally contained. This kind of observation led to a second element of common wisdom about residential real estate in the United States. The favorite saw of real estate agents has long been: "There are only three things you need to know about real estate: 'Location, location, location.'" The idea that the location of a home was the key to understanding its value tied in with the mantra that "all real estate is local," implying that the fate of the housing market in one geographical area was largely independent of that of other areas. Seeing real estate values as being locally determined, financial institutions found it reasonable to believe that prices for real estate in various parts of the country were largely independent. From this perspective, there is not a single market for U.S. residential real estate, but rather, there are many local markets.

From the point of view of an investor, seeing U.S. residential real estate as divided into many local markets effectively suggested that investors could treat real estate in different cities as different asset classes, so even an investor committed to maintaining a diversified portfolio could hold a concentrated real estate investment, as long as the pieces of real estate in the portfolio were geographically dispersed. This kind of reasoning, combined with factors such as government encouragement of home ownership and the development of securitization (which caused the very efficient recycling of mortgage loan funds) led financial institutions to enlarge the proportion of their portfolios that they committed to real estate. This massive exposure was an important element in making the home price collapse a *financial* crisis, rather than merely a general economic event.

The crisis that developed and its accompanying desperation also required a lack of transparency on the part of the financial institutions that were suffering losses. Here, "transparency" is a shorthand expression for how easily one financial institution could accurately perceive the true financial situation of other institutions. Because of this poor transparency, one financial institution could not know or trust the financial condition of its trading partners. As a consequence, the soundness of all financial institutions became suspect, so each institution reacted by refusing to trade in the normal manner with other financial institutions.

This lack of trust, itself a direct result of poor transparency about the financial condition of each institution, led to the freezing of credit. This credit freeze exacerbated and largely constituted the financial crisis.

Macroeconomic Developments

In our internationally integrated financial system, macroeconomic factors constitute the giant economic tide that raises and lowers all financial ships. Not surprisingly, some have pointed to macroeconomic developments as being key to the financial crisis. Attention has focused on the issue of "global imbalances" in particular. The basic idea is that for developing countries, most notably China and the petroleum exporting countries, a high savings rate accompanied rapid economic development, and this saving created huge pools of capital. Much of this amassed capital was concentrated in sovereign wealth funds, and much flowed to the capital markets of developed countries, most notably the United States. As Ben Bernanke put the point: "Like water seeking its level, savings flowed from where it was abundant to where it was deficient, with the result that the United States and some other advanced countries experienced large capital inflows for more than a decade, even as real long-term interest rates remained low."[3]

Thus, the main global imbalance to which Bernanke is pointing is a high savings rate abroad and deficient savings in the United States, which resulted in large capital inflows to the United States that had to be invested. (Figure 3.8 in chapter 3 shows how the savings rate in the United States fell from a healthy rate of almost 8 percent in 1992 to less than 1 percent in 2006–2007. At the same time, personal indebtedness rose from parity with income to approach 1.7 times income for the average American, per figure 3.9.)

In Bernanke's analysis, ". . . the responsibility to use the resulting capital inflows effectively fell primarily on the receiving countries, particularly the United States," but the United States and some other industrial countries ". . . failed to ensure that the inrush of capital was prudently invested."[4] Putting the point even more starkly, the problem stemmed from developing countries being awash in capital that they invested in countries like the United States, and instead of investing those funds wisely, we in the United States plowed those funds into residential real estate investments that made no sense. As a result, this excessive investment drove real estate prices higher than reasonable, setting the scene for an inevitable price correction. For Bernanke, this was an issue of the first magnitude: ". . . it is impossible to understand this crisis without reference to the global imbalances in trade and capital flows that began in the latter half of the 1990s."[5]

This view was sustained by Secretary of the Treasury Henry Paulson, who argued that the high savings rate in China and among oil exporting countries helped to depress global interest rates, which encouraged investors to seek higher yields and to underprice the risk of those investments:

> Over a period of years, persistent and growing global imbalances
> fueled a dramatic increase in capital flows, low interest rates,
> excessive risk taking and a global search for return. Those excesses
> cannot be attributed to any single nation. There is no doubt that
> low U.S. savings are a significant factor, but the lack of
> consumption and accumulation of reserves in Asia and oil-
> exporting countries and structural issues in Europe have also fed
> the imbalances.[6]

In sum, the global imbalances story points to high consumption in the United States, accompanied by rapid growth and a high savings rate in the developing world, especially in China. Figure 9.1 shows the current account deficit for the United States and surplus for China, indicating that China and other countries were financing high consumption in the United States. (Roughly, the current account reflects the difference between exports and imports, but it also includes remittances from migrant workers and aid grants. Between the United States and China, exports and imports are the driving determinants.) The developing country savings created a pool of capital that sought safe investment, and these funds flowed into the United States. Instead of investing those funds prudently in productive investments, this money flowed into residential real estate with two effects. First, the huge pool of investable capital helped to keep interest rates low in the United States, and second, the Federal Reserve's policy of "easy money" (low interest rates) in the United States helped to fuel the surge in home prices.[7]

There can be little doubt that a large pool of global capital seeking investment in the developed world acted as financial fuel that propelled the surge in housing prices. But most scholars clearly agree that other causal factors are an important part of the story. For example, even in the matter of relatively low interest rates, many observers believe that the "easy money" policies of the U.S. Federal Reserve also played an important role.[8]

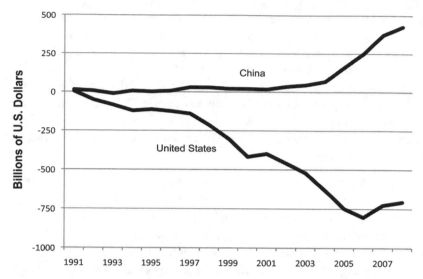

Figure 9.1 Trade Deficits (U.S.) and Surpluses (China)
Source: Current account information for the United States is provided by the Bureau of Economic Analysis. Data for China are drawn from: http://www.chinability.com/CurrentAccount.htm.

Federal Stimulative Policy and Legislation

For many decades, federal regulation and general public policy in the United States have aimed to stimulate and expand home ownership. This activity dates from the Great Depression, so the efforts to escape the economic horror of that period set in course a general policy and regulatory outlook that laid the foundation for our financial crisis and the Great Recession. Chapter 1 discussed some of the Great Depression initiatives: the creation of the Federal Home Loan Bank Board in 1932 to provide liquidity to S&Ls and to stimulate mortgage lending; the 1933 creation of the Home Owner's Loan Corporation to buy defaulted mortgages and help home owners stay in their homes; the creation of the Federal Housing Administration in 1934 to provide protection to mortgage lenders in case home owners defaulted; and the creation of the forebearer of Fannie Mae to stimulate a secondary market for mortgages. The Great Depression saw the beginning of presidential pronouncements valorizing home ownership, a presidential predilection that runs from Roosevelt to the present day. Expanding wealth in the

United States, supported by policies that encouraged home ownership, led to a persistently higher percentage of Americans living in homes they own, a trend captured in figure 1.1 in chapter 1.

We have seen that without securitization, a financial institution generally keeps the mortgage it issues on its books for the life of the loan, which was 30 years for the typical mortgage in the years since the Great Depression up until the 1990s. Such a system limits the growth in home mortgages to a rate that parallels the growing size of the lending institution. But securitization played an important role in eliminating that restriction. The financial institution that can issue a mortgage and sell it thereby frees its own funds to make new mortgages, thus making mortgage financing more widely available and helping to encourage home ownership.

From the beginning, the federal government played a critical role in expanding securitization. The National Housing Acts of 1934 and 1938, along with subsequent legislation, created and propelled the governmental and quasi-governmental entities that dominated mortgage finance through the twentieth century and into the twenty-first. These most prominently included the following institutions, with their alphabet soup of acronyms and abbreviations: Federal Housing Administration (FHA), the Federal National Mortgage Association (FNMA, or Fannie Mae), the Federal Home Loan Mortgage Corporation (FHLMC, or Freddie Mac) and the Government National Mortgage Association (GNMA, or Ginnie Mae). These federally sponsored enterprises, agencies, and associations became ever more important fixtures in U.S. mortgage markets. In 1952, all of these entities together owned less than 5 percent of residential mortgages, but in 2006 they owned a full 40 percent of all mortgages and were accounting for more than 40 percent of all mortgage originations. By 2006, these creatures of the federal government, all with the mission of supporting and expanding home ownership, were the dominant players in the U.S. mortgage market. Soon thereafter, Fannie Mae and Freddie Mac owned or guaranteed over half of U.S. mortgages between them.

Attempts to Combat Mortgage Lending Discrimination and to Expand Home Ownership to Minorities

Given the history of race relations in the United States, there can be little doubt that many businesses throughout our history have made decisions based on race, to the detriment of the financial interests of the firm. For a simple example, for many decades after the end of slavery, many businesses refused to hire any black worker without regard to a black job candidate's abilities or required wage. Thus, it is not difficult to believe that such non-economic factors have played a role in mortgage lending. Strongly believing that race and prejudice were a factor in the allocation of mortgage credit, Congress passed laws to fight that discrimination and to extend mortgage credit to "underserved" groups. Two early pieces of legislation were the Home Mortgage Disclosure Act of 1975 (HMDA) and the famous and controversial Community Reinvestment Act of 1977 (CRA).

The HMDA is a reporting statute, which has been amended and expanded since its original passage to eventually cover most home mortgage lenders.[9] By 1992, the law required lenders to report the race, ethnicity, gender, locale, and income of mortgage borrowers. The law was originally intended to help combat lending based on non-financial grounds, with the act itself charging that banks and thrift institutions had "contributed to the decline of certain geographic areas by their failure . . . to provide adequate home financing to qualified applicants on reasonable terms and conditions."[10] As amended over the years, the HMDA became a tool for expanding mortgage lending. If mortgage lending to various racial, gender, or ethnic groups differed, this variation was often attributed to prejudicial grounds of race, gender, and ethnicity. As Patricia McCoy notes: ". . . HMDA evolved from an obscure reporting statute to a flashpoint for debates over lending discrimination and subprime lending."[11]

More important is the Community Reinvestment Act of 1977 (CRA), which also was designed to combat discrimination in mortgage lending. In particular, the act's principal author, William Proxmire, said: "The main purpose of the CRA is to eliminate the practice of redlining by lending institutions."[12] According to the Congressional Record of 1977, "redlining" refers to a practice in which a financial institution would ". . . draw a red line on a map around certain geographic areas, and decline to make loans in those areas on the basis of the racial composition, age of the housing stock, or other factors, regardless of the creditworthiness of the individual loan applicants."[13] This red line could be metaphorical or actual. Following its passage, the act was not used extensively, but the act did receive modification that, in one estimation of 2004, ". . . transformed CRA from a dormant legislation to a vibrant act that has become one of the most significant tools for community activists in the community development and regeneration efforts."[14]

One factor that gave impetus to the CRA as a tool for social change was the publication of a study in 1992 by the Federal Reserve Bank of Boston that examined HMDA data and found significant evidence of discrimination in mortgage lending. The study concluded in part that the data: ". . . showed substantially higher denial rates for black and Hispanic applicants. . .," that "these minorities were two to three times as likely to be denied mortgage loans as whites," and that ". . . high-income minorities in Boston were more likely to be turned down than low-income whites."[15] According to the study, part of this difference in application results was due to differences in economic factors such as debt burdens, loan-to-value ratio, and credit histories, but that even after accounting for all economic factors ". . . black and Hispanic mortgage applicants in the Boston metropolitan area are roughly 60 percent more likely to be turned down than whites."[16]

Although the methodology of this study has been questioned,[17] the publicity garnered by the Boston Fed's report was influential in bringing the Community Reinvestment Act to the forefront of public consciousness, and it helped lead to the establishment of new regulations during the Clinton administration that gave the act more force.[18] The strengthening of the act was part of a new initiative, the National Homeownership Strategy, which would itself constitute a major effort to expand mortgage lending to minorities by forcing lenders to change their lending policies.

National Homeownership Strategy

While the federal government had long supported the expansion of home ownership, the proportion of Americans living in their own homes had been relatively stable in the decade from 1984 to 1994 at about 64 percent (see figure 3.1 in chapter 3). The National Homeownership Strategy came into play in 1993, as detailed in the Urban Policy Brief of the Department of Housing and Urban Development, entitled "Homeownership and Its Benefits," which begins:

> At the request of President Clinton, the U.S. Department of
> Housing and Urban Development (HUD) is working with dozens
> of national leaders in government and the housing industry to

implement a National Homeownership Strategy, an unprecedented public-private partnership to increase homeownership to a record-high level over the next 6 years." The document also makes clear that the goal of the Strategy is to ". . . increase ownership opportunities among populations and communities with lower than average homeownership rates.

The HUD document specifies some of the methods that will be used to achieve this goal and includes, among others: "The National Home-ownership Strategy is committed to: . . . reduce regulatory barriers . . . making financing more available, affordable, and flexible . . . cut transaction costs through streamlined regulations . . . reduce down-payment requirements and interest costs . . . increase the availability of alternative financing products . . . opening the home buying market to underserved populations . . . [and] . . . promote fair housing and lending . . ."

The Strategy was comprehensive and, in may ways, successful in its specific goals. A subsequent 1995 HUD document listed 100 actions to further the strategy.[19] Some of the specific strategies that were implemented included a reduction in proof of stable income from five to three years and allowing borrowers to use their own appraisers instead of having lending institutions hire the appraiser, a change that raised the risk of appraisal fraud.[20] In sum, the CRA proved to be an important tool in an attempt to expand mortgage lending. According to its many critics, the CRA forced financial institutions to make loans to customers who were uncreditworthy or who would have been denied loans on purely business grounds.[21] Others challenged the alleged evidence of discrimi-nation and called for repeal of the act.[22]

At the same time, the act has vociferous defenders. Some believe that the act helps borrowers receive more favorable terms.[23] In recent months, the defense of the CRA has focused on absolving the CRA from a causal role in fomenting the financial crisis, with substantial defense of the act coming from those in government who are tasked with enforcing the law, such as Sheila Bair, head of the FDIC; Randall Kroszner, a Fed-eral Reserve Board governor; and to a limited extent, Ben Bernanke— with Bernanke's lukewarm defense coming in March 2007, before the crisis exploded.[24] Ironically, some who support the intentions behind the act point out the act's unintended consequence of fostering predatory lending.[25] Still others who support the act's intentions find it woefully inadequate.[26]

One way of assessing the ultimate intentions of the CRA with respect to the lending policy of financial institutions is to examine the guidance that federal agencies and regulators offered. Recalling that the Federal Reserve System is the regulator of all bank holding companies and is the bank examiner for all state-chartered commercial banks, there is no document more instructive than the publication "Closing the Gap," by the Federal Reserve Bank of Boston, which offers ". . . recommendation on 'best practice' . . ." for closing the mortgage gap among races.[27]

The document acknowledges that overt discrimination is rarely observed, so it focuses on unintentional discrimination when a lender's ". . . underwriting policies contain arbitrary or outdated criteria . . ."[28] While "Closing the Gap" contains much unobjectionable and even reasonable advice, it also contains a number of recommendations that show the extent to which public policy strove to change the underwriting standards on mortgage loans in order to increase the rate of home ownership and to ensure that loans were made to those who ultimately could not afford them. The document urges that "Special Consideration could be given to applicants with relatively high obligation ratios who have demonstrated an ability to cover high housing expenses in the past," and recommends that "loans from relatives" be allowed to count toward a down payment. More amazingly, it counsels, "Lack of credit history should not be seen as a negative factor."

Also, "For lower-income applicants in particular, unforeseen expenses can have a disproportionate effect on an otherwise positive credit record." One might think that a lack of income and a poor credit record would be exactly the best reasons to deny a loan, rather than being part of an apology or excuse for why a bank might nonetheless make a loan. The document goes on to counsel: "Successful participation in credit counseling or buyer education programs is another way that applicants can demonstrate an ability to manage their debts responsibly." In other words, having a history of paying debts is one way to demonstrate responsibility, but failing that, one can demonstrate responsibility by attending classes about paying debts.

Beyond focusing on the institution's own underwriting polices, "Closing the Gap" goes on to remind: "In addition to primary employment income, Fannie Mae and Freddie Mac will accept the following as valid income sources: overtime and part-time work, second jobs (including seasonal work), retirement and Social Security income, alimony, child support, Veterans Administration (VA) benefits, welfare payments, and unemployment benefits." Some of these income items are solid and reasonably secure (retirement income, Social Security income), while some are fragile (overtime, seasonal work, alimony, child support). The truly absurd "income categories" are welfare payments and unemployment benefits, suggesting that being a ward of the government should not be a bar to undertaking a huge financial commitment and that financial institutions should lend to those in such dire financial straits.

In saying that Fannie Mae and Freddie Mac will accept such income sources as valid, the Boston Fed is reminding institutions that they can make these dubious loans and then sell them to the GSEs, thereby offloading the risk inherent in such weak loans to these federally sponsored enterprises. In other words, the federal government advises in the clearest terms a scheme for making money, complying with regulators' desires, and appearing socially virtuous by combating discrimination: make bad loans to minorities, sell them to the government, collect fees, and count profits.

While the CRA, other similar legislation, and the encouragement offered by legislators aimed to expand lending to minorities, the effect of these policies ran beyond helping the disadvantaged and underserved. Once underwriting standards were compromised for the benefit of the disadvantaged, those same standards were naturally extended to poor credit risks of all ethnic groups. Not merely was this extension natural—it was mandated by the government as well. "Closing the Gap" also reminds financial institutions: "To ensure fair treatment, it is important that the lending institution document its policies and practices regarding acceptable compensation factors. If an institution permits flexibility in applying underwriting standards, it must do so consistently." That is, lenders could make the same bad loans to everyone and sell all the loans to Fannie and Freddie—enthusiastically complying with regulatory encouragement, simulating virtue, and making money all the way.[29]

Defenders of the CRA insist that the legislation and its accompanying regulation were not the cause of the subprime debacle. Kevin Park, in a study for Harvard's Joint Center for Housing Studies, points out that: "The vast majority of subprime lending to lower-income borrowers and neighborhoods was outside the requirements and scrutiny of the CRA," and that the contribution of the CRA to the housing collapse and financial crises "appears marginal."[30]

But the point here is not that the CRA forced financial institutions to make all the bad loans that the subsequent subprime collapse and financial crisis revealed. Instead, federal policy included both the push of the CRA and similar legislation, along with the pull of an easy method of disposing of these bad loans by having Fannie and Freddie serve as willing buyers. Together, this push and pull provided a set of incentives that eviscerated underwriting standards, increased the demand for housing, helped to increase the prices of housing through this increased demand, and played a major role in creating the subprime meltdown and the ensuing financial crisis.[31]

The Causal Role of the GSEs

Consider a world with the CRA and its companion legislation, but without Fannie Mae and Freddie Mac serving as a means whereby mortgage originators could dispose of their loans. Under these circumstances, the lender would be forced to keep all the loans it made in its portfolio for the life of the loans. In such a hypothetical situation, financial institutions might well have resisted pressure to collapse their underwriting standards and to make bad loans, because they would have borne the risk of those loans themselves.

Instead, Fannie Mae and Freddie Mac provided eager outlets for lenders to dispose of the bad paper they were writing. They did this by compromising their own standards for purchasing loans, and they were spurred to do so by the regulatory regime they served.

Having created Fannie Mae in 1968 and Freddie Mac in 1970, Congress revamped the regulation of these entities in 1992 with the passage of the Federal Housing Enterprises Financial Safety and Soundness Act (FHEFSSA), also known as the GSE Act. The act required HUD to ensure that the GSEs met goals for affordable housing and fair lending and it prescribed ". . . a set of escalating performance goals that measured, as a percentage of the GSEs' total business, the availability of housing financing for low-and moderate-income families; for very-low income families; and for families living in central cities, rural areas, and other underserved areas."[32] In 1995, HUD promulgated new regulations that raised the percentage of business that had to be directed toward the achievement of these public policy goals.

Not only were these new rules an imposition on the management of the GSEs, but they proved to be an important new business opportunity. Clearly participating in the drive to improve mortgage-borrowing access by reducing underwriting standards, Franklin Raines, CEO of Fannie Mae, said in 1999: "Fannie Mae has expanded home ownership for millions of families in the 1990's by reducing down payment requirements.

Yet there remain too many borrowers whose credit is just a notch below what our underwriting has required who have been relegated to paying significantly high mortgage rates in the so-called subprime market."[33]

By 1998, at Fannie Mae 44 percent of the loans it purchased were from those originated to low- and moderate-income borrowers. Yet HUD was urging that Fannie and Freddie increase that rate to 50 percent by 2001, and the target was raised to 55 percent for 2007. Even in 1999, some were recognizing that this move into subprime involved serious risks, and at least one commentator already feared that another thrift crisis was in the making.[34] By 2002, the GSEs were aggressively expanding their foray into subprime.[35] This move was supported by studies,[36] and even more by political pressure. If anything, pressure from the federal government for the GSEs to do more in subprime intensified, with Congressman Barney Frank, ranking democrat of the House Financial Services Committee, saying in 2003 that he believed the federal government had ". . . probably done too little rather than too much to push them [Fannie and Freddie] to meet the goals of affordable housing and to set reasonable goals." On the same occasion, the congressman whom the *Wall Street Journal* has described as "Fannie Mae's Patron Saint,"[37] went on to stress the financial soundness of Fannie and Freddie and to deny that the federal government would incur a financial liability were the GSEs to experience financial distress.[38]

In 2000–2006, the GSEs continued to expand their footprint in subprime and Alt-A mortgage financing. For 2006, the GSEs' regulator, OFHEO, reported that both firms were adequately capitalized. In 2006, the GSEs purchased $90 billion in private-label MBS backed by subprime, taking 20 percent of all such securities issued, and they also purchased $113 billion of low-documentation loans. At the same time, the average loan-to-value (LTV) ratio of the mortgages purchased by the GSEs increased, as did the proportion of loans with LTV ratios exceeding 90 percent.[39]

By mid-2007, problems with subprime were becoming increasingly apparent, and many mortgage-related firms were reducing their commitments. For the second half of 2007, almost the entire decline in mortgage originations stemmed from a sharp decline in subprime and Alt-A originations.[40] In this collapsing market, Fannie and Freddie also reduced the dollar volume of loans they purchased, but they still increased their share of the market to almost 58 percent, by ". . . purchasing mortgage assets shunned by many traditional market players."[41] For 2007, Fannie and Freddie together lost more than $11 billion in accounting terms, but their regulator, OFHEO, reported that their true market fair value losses were $40 billion taken together.[42]

To an extent that is seldom realized, and one that the federal government is loathe to emphasize, the GSEs are at the very center of the financial crisis, both as a cause and as a locus of loss. As the crisis developed and its seriousness became increasingly apparent, most private firms headed for the exits as quickly as their circumstances would allow, but not Fannie Mae and Freddie Mac. The director of OFHEO, James Lockhart, testified in early 2008 about the management and condition of the GSEs, saying:

> Their business expanded rapidly in 2007 with their market share rising to record levels in the fourth quarter of 2007. The GSEs have become the dominant funding mechanism for the entire mortgage system in these troubling times. They are fulfilling their missions of providing liquidity, stability, and affordability to the mortgage markets. In doing so, they have been reducing risks in the market, but concentrating mortgage risks on themselves.[43]

He might have added that Fannie and Freddie were *very* actively concentrating risk on themselves. He did point out that the GSEs were expanding their mortgage dominance as the crisis grew: the two firms were securitizing mortgages at the rate of $100 billion per month and that the two together purchased over 60 percent of all new mortgages originated in the United States in the second half of 2007. This proportion continued to grow, reaching 76 percent for the fourth quarter of 2007. Testifying in mid-2009, Lockhart stated the true proportion of the mortgage market represented by Fannie and Freddie when he said that these two firms ". . . own or guarantee 56% of the single family mortgages in this country or $5.4 trillion."[44] By late 2009, Lockhart was no longer in charge, and Edward DeMarco, the new director of FHFA testified to the magnitude of the disaster at the GSEs: "In the first two full years of this housing crisis—from July 2007 through the first half of 2009—combined losses at Fannie Mae and Freddie Mac totaled $165 billion." By the end of 2009, the federal government had committed $400 billion to take the two firms into conservatorship, and had actual outlays totaling $111 billion to the two.

One might well wonder why Fannie and Freddie plowed ahead as other firms abandoned the sinking ship of the mortgage market. The *Wall Street Journal* supplied at least part of the answer in late October 2007. It reported that senators, congressmen, and interest groups urged

OFHEO to loosen the limits on Fannie and Freddie so that they could play an even more dominating role in the mortgage markets.[45] As creatures of government and subject to congressional oversight, the GSEs were extremely susceptible to political pressure. The *New York Times* reports that "Between 2005 and 2008 Fannie purchased or guaranteed $311 billion loans to risky borrowers," which was five times as much as in its entire previous history. Speaking of this period, a former Fannie Mae executive said: "Everybody understood that we were now buying loans that we would have previously rejected, and that the models were telling us that we were charging way too little. But our mandate was to stay relevant to and to serve low-income borrowers. So that's what we did."[46]

This demand for relevance stemmed from political pressure, reports the *New York Times*: "Lawmakers, particularly Democrats, leaned on Fannie and Freddie to buy and hold those troubled debts, hoping that removing them from the system would help the economy recover." As the crisis accelerated, OFHEO permitted the GSEs to purchase an additional $40 billion of subprime loans. For his part, Barney Frank said: "I'm not worried about Fannie and Freddie's health, I'm worried that they won't do enough to help out the economy."[47]

As political entities by their very nature and subject to the continuing regulation of the federal government, the GSEs will always be subject to political pressure. However, both Fannie Mae and Freddie Mac embroiled themselves in massive accounting scandals in the early 2000s that made both firms subject to even more political pressure. In assessing Freddie Mac's accounting scandal, an Associated Press report makes the connection between regulation, scandal, and political pressure crystalline: "Freddie Mac was accused of illegally using corporate resources between 2000 and 2003 for 85 fundraisers that collected about $1.7 million for federal candidates. Much of the fundraising benefited members of the House Financial Services Committee, a panel whose decisions can affect Freddie Mac."[48]

For his part, James Lockhart, director of OFHEO, referred to the ". . . misadventures and misdeeds at Fannie Mae, which led to a consent agreement listing 81 areas for correction."[49] Even as it was being taken into conservatorship in September 2008, Freddie Mac was up to its customary tricks, with regulators finding that it had overstated its capital position.[50] In sum, the political character of the GSEs, the implicit (now explicit) backing of the obligations of these firms by the federal government, the huge financial size of both Fannie Mae and Freddie Mac, and the public mission of increasing home ownership proved a toxic brew that stimulated non-economic behavior by these firms and created a fertile field for both financial and political corruption.

Thus, the fruits of the federal government's efforts to promote home ownership in the United States were largely mature, and the size of the "harvest" was becoming all too apparent as 2010 approached. In sum, the federal government and its creations stood at the very center of the financial crisis, with its GSEs representing over half of the entire U.S. mortgage market and the losses of its GSEs dwarfing public losses to all private financial firms, with the exception of AIG.

Causes of the Financial Crisis: The Failure of Prudential Regulation

In the United States, as in all developed nations, the financial system is subject to close regulation. At least there are numerous laws stipulating this exacting regulation, and in the United States many federal agencies are tasked with supervising a variety of elements of the finance industry, including the Federal Reserve System, the Office of the Comptroller of the Currency, the Federal Deposit Insurance Corporation (FDIC), the Department of the Treasury, the Federal Housing Finance Agency, the Commodity Futures Trading Commission, the Securities and Exchange Commission (SEC), the Financial Industry Regulatory Authority, the National Credit Union, and the Office of Thrift Supervision (OTS). These agencies operate under so many articles of legislation that enumerating them is essentially impossible. In spite of this elaborate structure and the numerous personnel these agencies employ, the failure of federal financial regulation to detect and counteract the growing problems of the financial firms they regulate played an important role in causing the financial crisis.

Perhaps the most popular narrative of the financial crisis maintains that it was caused by the dismantling of the regulatory structure from 1990 to 2005, and that this deregulation enabled greedy financial institutions to take excessive risks that imperiled the financial system and the world economy. Consistent with this diagnosis, the most widely heralded corrective is the institution of a tighter regulatory regime to constrain greed and risk taking by reckless financial institutions that are heedless of the needs of the societies they exploit.

While there is a case to be made for deregulation contributing to the financial crisis, that is only a part of the story of the failure of prudential regulation in the financial crisis, and the failure of regulation in total is just one causal factor in creating the crisis. As this chapter explains, the main problem with regulation is not that regulation was attenuated by free-market ideologues, which left committed and diligent regulators without the tools they needed to perform their regulatory tasks effectively. Instead, the failure of regulation was essentially a failure of regulators to perform their duties and to exercise the regulatory powers that they possessed before the crisis, possessed at every moment through the crisis, and continue to possess to the present day. The failure of regulation was primarily a failure of regulators, not a failure to pass legislation or to fund regulatory agencies.[1]

However, this is not to say that the regulatory structure in place was ideal, nor is it to say that regulatory failures were all solely due to the failure of regulators to perform their duties. As this chapter also details, there are clear deficiencies in the regulatory structure that was in place as the crisis developed. Some policy correctives seem fairly clear, while others are more difficult to stipulate, and there exists a danger of instituting new and well-intentioned regulations that can do more harm than good.

We have already seen that the creation of Fannie Mae and Freddie Mac by the federal government and inadequate supervision by their regulatory body, now called the Federal Housing Finance Agency, led to such massive losses that the federal government took these essentially bankrupt businesses into conservatorship and has committed $400 billion to allowing them to meet their obligations. Reflection on these brute facts should give pause to anyone who thinks that giving more power to federal regulators is the panacea that will prevent future crises. If the past is any guide, the financial disaster that the GSEs have become would indicate that the federal government can create—and its regulatory bodies can midwife—financial crises of enormous proportion. More specifically, the very worst two offending financial institutions in the financial crisis, measured by the likely total cost to the public, were the two institutions most closely associated with the federal government. So looking to greater regulation to solve the problem of financial crises may be seeking comfort in exactly the wrong direction.

Regulation of Depository Institutions

Every commercial bank, every savings institution, and every credit union in the United States holds a charter from a state government or from the federal government. Every such depository institution is inspected by a federal agency and is subject to capital requirements and other regulations imposed by state and federal agencies. In addition, every such institution with deposits insured by the Federal Deposit Insurance Corporation (FDIC) is subject to seizure and closure by the FDIC, as the 140 such bank closures in 2009 attest. As such, these institutions exist only by the sufferance of governments and are subject to the most stringent regulatory regimes our governmental bodies have to offer.

When they run amok or go bankrupt, their failure also provides information on the performance of their regulators. The purpose of regulation is not to prevent the failure of every bank, but rather to provide a framework that protects society from the serious harm that bank failures can perpetrate on their depositors, the financial system, and the economy at large. So a single bank failure need not be interpreted as a failure of regulation in any way. However, if general disruption among depository institutions causes serious problems for those beyond the management, employees, and owners of the institution, questions of regulatory competence naturally arise.

The financial crisis of 2007–2009, which featured depository institutions in starring roles, calls into serious question the adequacy and competence of depository institution regulation. While the focus here is on bank regulation in the United States, highly developed financial systems in other countries have a broadly similar style of regulation, most notably in Great Britain and in the euro zone, so the argument here applies generally to these other countries as well. Four aspects of bank regulation are most relevant to the financial crisis of 2009: regulation of lines of business in which banks may engage; the capital requirements that banks must meet in order to be permitted to operate; restrictions on the size and scope of depository institutions; and restrictions on concentration of risk.

Regulation of Lines of Business

In the great wave of government programs and regulations that accompanied and grew out of the Great Depression, the Bank Regulation Act of 1933 (the Glass-Steagall Act) in the United States established the FDIC and required the separation of commercial and investment banking.[2] The essential thinking behind this legislation was to provide deposit insurance and, given that the federal government began to guarantee most deposits, to limit the risk that banks could undertake. Thus banks were allowed to continue the core functions of taking deposits and making business loans, but the act sharply restructured their activities in the riskier business of investment banking. This policy held in effect for more than 50 years in almost unabated form.

External pressures stemming from the development of more sophisticated financial markets started to erode this rigorous separation of commercial and investment in the 1980s.[3] The Glass-Steagall provisions were weakened by the Depository Institutions Deregulation and Monetary Control Act of 1980 and the Garn–St. Germain Depository Institutions Act of 1982, but the ultimate abandonment of Glass-Steagall is typically attributed to the Gramm-Leach-Bliley Act, which received broad bipartisan support and was signed into law in 1999.

Some of the largest commercial banks responded to the relaxation on their investment policies by becoming major players in the mortgage-backed security (MBS) market. Losses at Citigroup, Bank of America, and Wachovia would probably have been much smaller had the Glass-Steagall restrictions been kept intact, but this is not to say that the crisis would have been prevented or even that it would have been less major. Had commercial banks been kept from participating in the MBS market, other financial institutions may simply have had greater market shares, with the overall volume of MBS business—and its excesses—being of the same ultimate scale. If this surmise is true, the restrictions on commercial banks would still have limited the federal government's direct exposure through deposit insurance. However, as matters developed, the federal government undertook to rescue or support nondepository financial firms anyway, so the public exposure might not have been much altered even had Glass-Steagall been kept in place.

Capital Requirements

For any business, capital not only provides the resources to undertake investment, but capital also provides a buffer against losses, and an adequate capital base allows a firm to continue operating for some time even in the face of losses. The capital position of depository institutions is subject to direct regulation, and for these banks with insured deposits, the FDIC, the OTS, and the Federal Reserve stipulate the necessary capital positions that banks must maintain. Outside the United States, many European banks fall under the capital requirements recommended by the Basel Committee on Banking Supervisions and promulgated under the two Basel Accords. The Basel Committee consists of representatives from central banks and regulatory authorities from the Group of Ten (G10) countries, which includes the major industrial powers of the world.[4] While capital requirements specified by the Basel Accords are not themselves binding on individual financial institutions, central banks and regulatory authorities in the various countries generally follow those recommendations in their own regulatory practices. The regulatory regime in the United States generally demands higher capital ratios for commercial banks than those maintained by most European and Japanese banks operating under the guidance of the Basel Accords.

The key principle of capital risk management is that the capital position of any firm must match the size of the firm and its risk appetite, such that a large firm with risky activities needs much more capital than a small firm with a low-risk operating policy. When the abandonment of Glass-Steagall restrictions freed commercial banks from restrictions on their lines of business, they moved into riskier lines of business, but they did not increase their capital positions.

The long sweep of capital regulation has witnessed a sharp historical slide in the ratio of capital to assets. Circa 1850 the ratio of capital to assets for banks in the United States and the United Kingdom was approximately 50 percent. For the last 50 years, the ratio has generally been less than 10 percent, and this period includes the period of our financial crisis.[5] Improved techniques of financial management and the development of more robust credit markets over the last 150 years certainly justify some diminution of capital requirements for all financial firms, but the key is always to set the right level of capital for a firm of a given size and operating policy. Because capital is expensive, firms want to hold the optimal level, but determining that optimum exactly is generally not possible.

Regulatory authorities are supposed to use capital regulation as a key tool to protect the public from excessive risk-taking by financial institutions. When financial institutions come into financial distress, that is a sign of deficient capital, and when the financial distress of these firms threatens the well-being of society, that is a sign of failing regulation. In the financial crisis, the failure of large commercial banks and savings institutions (Countrywide, IndyMac, Wachovia, Washington

Mutual), the near-failure of other such institutions (Citicorp), the financial distress experienced by still others (Bank of America, JPMorgan Chase, and, to a lesser extent, Wells Fargo), the 25 bank failures in 2008, and the 140 failures in 2009[6] collectively demonstrate the inadequacy of the capital positions of these institutions.

Capital regulation is supposed to be under the control of financial regulatory bodies in the United States, and it is difficult to argue that the problem with capital regulation was an external limitation on the proper exercise of regulation or a weak regulatory regime that prevented diligent regulators from pursuing a wise course of action to keep the system safe. As George Kaufman and A. G. Malliaris summarize the point:

> There is neither a law nor a regulation that prevents bank regulators from requiring banks to maintain higher regulatory capital ratios. Ironically, before the meltdown, some regulators actively argued for lowering the minimum regulatory capital requirements for many large U.S. commercial banks through the adoption of Basel II regulatory capital requirements, despite the fact that many recognized bank analysts and scholars were arguing that the banks were already at that time undercapitalized, not overcapitalized.[7]

A similar failure of regulation occurred in other countries, and for a similar reason. Regulatory personnel abroad failed to use the existing regulatory framework in an effective manner, as in the United States. As a result, these countries also experienced their own bank failures and near-failures in the crisis. Thus, the stunning record of failures points to an inadequacy of capital regulation of depository institutions in the United States and in other industrialized countries.

For emphasis, the point is not that isolated bank failures demonstrate poor capital regulation. Because capital is expensive, regulators should not attempt to demand that banks hold enough capital to prevent all possible failures. Rather, numerous failures, large failures, and failures that threaten the broader economy provide the evidence of a problem in bank capital regulation. As we will see later in this chapter, capital regulation was a problem for other financial institutions besides those with insured deposits. Also, to say that regulation of capital was poorly managed is not to absolve financial institutions of their own responsibilities. Banks are always free to hold more capital than regulations demand, and each financial institution has an obligation to manage its capital position in a manner that serves its shareholders and other stakeholders.

Interaction Between Capital Regulation and Credit Derivatives.

The extremely rapid development of credit default swaps into a multi-trillion dollar industry and the collapse of AIG have brought this previously arcane and obscure corner of the financial markets into the limelight. As we have seen, the actions of AIG's trading arm in London wrote massive amounts of credit default swaps that generated large income for AIG but exposed the firm to massive risk that came home to roost during the financial crisis. Less known is an important incentive to the development of this market that stemmed from bank capital regulation under the Basel II Accords and pertained most strongly to G10 banks outside the United States.

Consider a risky bond held in a bank's portfolio. Such a bond requires an allocation of capital under banking regulation. However, if that instrument embodied less risk, the capital requirement for holding that instrument would be diminished. One way of reducing the capital requirement would be to sell the risky bond and replace it with a safer bond, such as a government-issued instrument, for which regulations require less capital. However, the innovations in Basel II permitted banks for the first time to reduce the capital requirements associated with a risky investment by insuring the investment against default. The simple idea is that a risky bond accompanied by a credit default swap (CDS) that pays if the risky bond defaults has less risk than the bond itself, so the bond plus CDS requires less capital than the bond alone.

According to some critics, this capital-reduction provision of Basel II stimulated the rapid development of the CDS market. This rapid market expansion, with AIG occupying such a central role, set up significant counterparty risk, which led to widespread financial distress as one after another large financial firm came into difficulty. Thus, this argument maintains that the capital substitution regime of Basel II played an important role in generating the crisis. Beyond increasing counterparty risk, this increasing reliance on the use of CDS instead of actual capital contributed to the lack of transparency that played such a critical role in the entire crisis. Not surprisingly, the Basel Accords also have their staunch defenders, and there is little consensus on the validity of this argument.[8]

Regulation of Size and Scope—"Too Big to Fail."

Among financial economists, the phrase "too big to fail" signals a particular problem of financial regulation that played a major role in the financial crisis, and one that is a continuing challenge to regulators and the economy. A financial institution is too big to fail if its sudden demise would be so horrific for the broader economy that the government feels compelled to prevent such a failure. In the financial crisis, some banks and other financial institutions were at least implicitly judged as being too big to fail. When these large banks came into crisis, regulatory bodies employed a variety of actions to prevent their sudden collapse. As examples, the U.S. federal government brokered a takeover of Countrywide Financial by Bank of America, Wachovia by Wells Fargo, and Washington Mutual by JPMorgan Chase.

As matters developed during the crisis, other nondepository institutions proved themselves also too big to fail, leading to a government-assisted takeover of the investment bank Bear Stearns by JPMorgan Chase, the government-supported acquisition of the brokerage firm of Merrill Lynch by Bank of America, the conservatorship of Fannie Mae and Freddie Mac, and the effective nationalization of AIG. Although large, IndyMac was allowed to fail with a cost of about $9 billion to the FDIC's insurance fund.[9] In addition, the federal government allowed the investment bank of Lehman Brothers to declare bankruptcy in September 2008, implicitly judging that it was not too big to fail. However, in the controversial view of many, permitting Lehman to fail was a signal error on the part of the federal government, one that badly exacerbated the financial crisis.[10]

When a financial institution becomes too big to fail, the problem of moral hazard may become acute. An institution that regards itself as too important to the economy to be allowed to fall into bankruptcy may take risks that it otherwise would avoid, confident that the government will rescue the institution rather than let it fail with potentially disastrous consequences for the broader economy. There is a rich literature on this problem, and regulators and policy makers have long been aware of this issue. However, essentially nothing has been done to address this issue to date. In the run-up to the financial crisis, financial institutions were allowed to become so large and their scope so extended that the federal government blanched at the prospect of their demise. This fear led to the extension of billions of dollars of support to a wide range of firms as we have seen in the previous chapters, ranging from the $400 billion committed to Fannie and Freddie, down to the $185 billion of financing granted to AIG, and even down to the paltry tens of billions for firms like Citigroup, Bank of America, Wells Fargo, and many others.

Of the many ironies of the financial crisis, perhaps none is more absurd than the effect of the government's policy response on this issue. In essence, the federal government reacted to the imminent failure of firms that were too big to fail by folding them into yet larger firms. Among depository institutions, Washington Mutual went to JPMorgan Chase, Wachovia fell to Wells Fargo, and Countrywide was absorbed by Bank of America, with all of these combinations and enlargements being brokered or financed by the federal government. In addition, the federal government kept large and desperate investment banks and brokerages from declaring bankruptcy by assisting their acquisition by commercial banking firms, as in the case of JPMorgan Chase acquiring Bear Stearns with $30 billion of federal assistance and Merrill Lynch being folded into Bank of America under controversial terms that have already become the subject of litigation. All of these actions exacerbated the problem of these firms being too big to fail. If firms that were smaller than JPMorgan, Bank of America, and Wells Fargo were already too big to fail, then JPMorgan plus Washington Mutual plus Bear Stearns, Bank of American plus Countrywide plus Merrill Lynch, and Wells Fargo plus Wachovia must surely be too huge to fail. Thus, one very serious outcome of the federal government's response to the financial crisis is a worsening of the problem of banks being too big to fail, along with a much heightened concentration of firms in the financial sector.

To date, the failure of the federal government to resolve, or even seriously to address, the problem of financial institutions being too big to fail stands as a signal regulatory failure. However, in early 2010, this issue started to receive serious attention. Some argue that the largest institutions should be broken up to keep them small enough to fail. Others regard this prospect as unlikely, but urge that larger institutions should have higher capital requirements or should pay into the FDIC insurance fund at a higher rate than smaller institutions. The political forces arrayed on every side of this battle are powerful. As a consequence, it remains uncertain whether this problem of large firms being able to hold the federal government hostage by threatening the stability of the entire financial system will be addressed in a meaningful way, or whether it will be allowed to stand and to cast a shadow over the future.

Restrictions on Concentration of Risk

If there is any one established principle of investment management, it is the principle of diversification—the reduction of total risk in an investment portfolio by the allocation of funds to a variety of different investments. Federal regulators of depository institutions are empowered to prohibit the concentration of investments and loans. For example, in the United States, depository institutions are generally prohibited from lending too much to a single borrower. The broad purpose of such authority is to prevent banks from lending so much to one party that it imperils the soundness of the bank, and the same principle holds true for restricting the concentration of the bank's investment portfolio. For if the lending or investment concentration is severe enough to threaten the bank's soundness, then that bank runs the risk of imposing costs on the depository insurance program and thereby harming the public interest.

These regulations are extensive, convoluted, and exacting. For example, just one fragment of the lending restrictions imposed by the FDIC reads, in part:

> *Combined general limit.* A national bank's total outstanding loans and extensions of credit to one borrower may not exceed 15 percent of the bank's capital and surplus, plus an additional 10 percent of the bank's capital and surplus, if the amount that exceeds the bank's 15 percent general limit is fully secured by readily marketable collateral, as defined in § 32.2(n). To qualify for the additional 10 percent limit, the bank must perfect a security interest in the collateral under applicable law and the collateral must have a current market value at all times of at least 100 percent of the amount of the loan or extension of credit that exceeds the bank's 15 percent general limit.[11]

The full statement of these and related restrictions goes on for pages in excruciating detail. But this brief excerpt shows the depth of control that banking regulators are permitted to exercise. At all times prior to, during, and after the financial crisis, regulators of depository institutions in the United States had ample authority to restrict the concentration of lending and investment by the institutions that they regulate. Of course, the managers of the various banks had a correlative duty, as prudent managers, to avoid such excessive concentration of risk.

The events of the crisis revealed both that the regulators failed to exercise the powers they already possessed to prevent excessive investment concentration in home mortgages, and bank managers extended their investment concentration in the housing sector to too great a degree as well. As we have seen, this concentration of investment in the housing sector by financial institutions was a significant cause of the crisis. With the benefit of hindsight, we can see that regulators failed to exercise their authority to restrain bank managers from making foolish investment decisions that incurred large, but not disastrous losses (Bank of America and Wells Fargo, for example), brought some banks to the brink of ruin (Citigroup), compelled the government to broker a merger (Wachovia), and pushed yet others into actual or effective bankruptcy (Countrywide, IndyMac, Washington Mutual, and many others). In short, this regulatory failure, coupled with actively bad management at many financial institutions, helped to increase portfolio risk by enabling the risky concentration of investment in the housing sector.

Regulation of Securities Markets and Supporting Institutions

While the Comptroller of the Currency, the Federal Reserve, and the Federal Deposit Insurance Corporation are the headline federal regulators of depository institutions in the United States, the Securities Exchange Commission plays a similar role for U.S. securities markets and financial institutions active in those markets. Created by the Securities Exchange Act of 1934, the SEC announces that its mission is ". . . to protect investors, maintain fair, orderly and efficient markets, and facilitate capital formation."[12] Under this mandate, the SEC has had considerable say over capital requirements for brokerage firms and investment banks, the oversight of credit rating agencies, and the accounting rules that govern most firms. Each of these areas has proven problematic in the financial crisis.

Capital Regulations

We have already seen that insufficient capital at depository institutions left them without adequate resources to weather the financial storm brought about by the fall in housing prices and the ensuing credit crunch. These perceived deficiencies in ready funds resulted in runs on banks thought to lack funds to meet their immediate obligations.

As the housing boom surged to the peak, the SEC contributed to the problem of weak capital by relaxing the capital requirements that it imposed on broker dealers. It did this explicitly on June 8, 2004, with the promulgation of its "Final Rule: Alternative Net Capital Requirements for Broker-Dealers That Are Part of Consolidated Supervised Entities." The SEC stated the key feature of the new rule in its first two sentences: "We are adopting rule amendments under the Securities Exchange Act of 1934 that establish a voluntary, alternative method of computing deductions to net capital for certain broker-dealers. This alternative method permits a broker-dealer to use mathematical models to calculate net capital requirements for market and derivatives-related credit risk."[13]

While the elaboration of this new regime circumscribed the privilege to some extent, this new rule essentially allowed the largest broker-dealers in the United States to set their own capital requirements. As some have uncharitably remarked, the SEC seemed to be outsourcing its own regulatory function to its regulatees. Five firms qualified—Bear Stearns, Goldman Sachs, Lehman Brothers, Merrill Lynch, and Morgan Stanley—and all five voluntarily converted to the new regulatory regime.[14] Indeed, the industry had actively lobbied for the change in rules. As part of this voluntary conversion, the participants agreed to submit to regulation of their parent entities by the SEC, not just their broker-dealer functions.

All five firms also responded to the regulatory regime by increasing their leverage—as measured by the ratio of total assets to total stockholders' equity. Figure 10.1 shows the leverage ratios for each firm over the years 2002–2007. For these five major firms, the leverage ratio rose from 22.51 to 30.53 over the 2002–2007 period. Thus, by the end of 2007, for every dollar of assets on the books of these firms, there were only 3.3 cents of capital, implying that a fluctuation of less than 4 percent in the value of those assets could wipe out the equity of the major players in the industry. Averaging across firms, the typical increase in the leverage ratio was over 40 percent, and Merrill Lynch increased its leverage ratio by more than 78 percent.[15]

According to the SEC, this new regulatory approach had a number of anticipated benefits: "protect investors," "maintain the integrity of the securities markets," "improving oversight of broker-dealers," "providing an incentive for broker-dealers to implement strong risk management

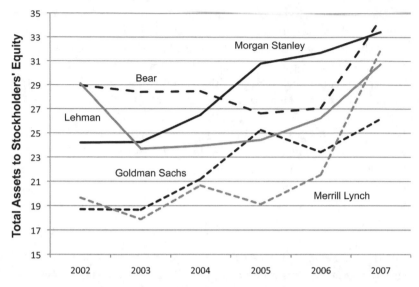

Figure 10.1 Increases in Investment Banking Leverage Ratios, 2002–2007
Source: *10-K Reports* filed with the Securities and Exchange Commission; *Annual Report to Stockholders* filed with the Securities and Exchange Commission, various years.

practices," and "reduce regulatory costs for broker-dealers."[16] Whatever the intentions, the result was an increase in industry leverage that increased financial fragility and made individual firms and the entire industry extremely vulnerable to the blast of the financial crisis. In the span of a few months in 2008, three of these firms disappeared through bankruptcy (Lehman Brothers) or vanished in distressed sales (Bear Stearns and Merrill Lynch). For their part, Goldman Sachs and Morgan Stanley were forced to change their corporate form and seek shelter from the Federal Reserve by becoming bank holding companies, which meant submitting to a more cumbersome, unwelcome, and onerous regulatory regime.

As the financial system became unhinged in late September 2008, the SEC conceded its mistake, with its chairman, Christopher Cox, acknowledging that the program "was fundamentally flawed from the beginning," and he terminated the program.[17] But by that time, five firms had ceased to exist, and the remaining two had collapsed into the arms of the Federal Reserve. While the SEC may have great responsibility for this fiasco, the culpability of the five investment banking firms must also be acknowledged. These firms actively sought the new regulatory regime, and once the SEC enabled the new policy, they recklessly rushed to increase their leverage and financial risk, which led to their own destruction, as well as imperiling the financial system and the entire world economy. Perhaps the industry set some kind of speed record: four years from regulatory relaxation to oblivion.

Off-Balance-Sheet Corporate Entities

Closely related to the leverage increases just discussed is the issue of off-balance-sheet corporate entities. These special-purpose vehicles (SPVs), structured-investment vehicles (SIVs), or special-purpose entities (SPEs) are essentially shell corporations created for a special and limited purpose, usually designed to achieve some tax, regulatory, or legal objective, as opposed to conducting some substantive business. As one commentator notes, "SPVs have no purpose other than the transaction(s) for which they were created and they can make no substantive decisions. . . . Indeed, no one works at an SPV and it has no physical location."[18] For example, a bank may decide to offer a mortgage to a customer, but it may have its SPV be the legal entity that officially makes the loan.[19]

While the legalities of SPVs are complex, they can be extremely useful in helping a parent company reduce the capital requirements mandated by regulators. The SPV is created as an independent firm outside the scope of regulatory authority. For example, the SPV might be incorporated in the Cayman Islands. While the SPV might be entirely sponsored by its parent, the parent constructs the relationship so that the default of the SPV imposes no explicit financial obligation on the parent. However, the SPV is supported by the idea of "implicit recourse" or "moral recourse"—the idea that the parent company will exceed its strictly legal obligations to the SPV and will rescue the SPV if it comes under stress. Thus the parent wishes to deny any financial obligation to the SPV from a regulatory perspective, but tries to convey to investors the belief that it will support the SPV financially if difficulties arise, even though it is not technically or legally obligated to do so. As Gorton and Souleles make the point: "Investors in SPVs know that, despite legal and accounting restrictions to the contrary, SPV sponsors [the parents] can bail out their SPVs if there is the need."[20]

One potential motivation for using SPVs is to economize on regulatory capital. An SPV can be extremely highly leveraged, but if it is incorporated in a friendly regulatory regime outside the United States (e.g., the Cayman Islands) it may not require much capital at all to support a very large asset base. In essence, the idea is that the sponsoring firm can use the SPV to hold assets outside of the purview of its regulators so it will not have to maintain capital against the assets in the SPV. It is generally recognized that using SPVs can be a way of circumventing regulation—a kind of "regulatory arbitrage" in which the capital position of the parent can appear better from a regulatory perspective than it is in fact.

In general, the idea of an SPV is not to deceive investors or to appear better capitalized than it is, but rather to avoid capital regulation. However, Enron created more than 3,000 SPVs, fraudulently kept these entities off the books and unobservable to investors, thereby inducing investors to provide funds to an entity that was economically bankrupt.[21] Rather than defrauding investors, the idea of SIVs, SPVs, and SPEs in the financial crisis was to collude with investors to circumvent regulatory capital requirements. Investors are apparently willing to invest in a sponsored SPV, confident that the sponsoring firm will rescue the SPV if necessary, because the investors believe that the parent company's failure to effect a rescue would have severe reputational damage that would limit the parent's future access to the capital markets.

In the financial crisis, firms with troubled SPVs did indeed bring the SPVs back onto the parent's balance sheet just as expected. This practice first came to widespread attention with the Bear Stearns rescue of its two failing hedge funds in 2007. Citigroup also brought massive quantities of assets back onto its balance sheet, as did many other firms caught up in the crisis. By the time the SPV was rescued, it consisted of large amounts of assets and virtually no equity, so consolidating the SPV back to the parent's balance sheet made the even greater leverage of the parent more obvious and sometimes forced the parent to attempt to raise new capital.[22]

Credit Rating Agencies

The role of credit ratings and the agencies that issue them have been mentioned in previous chapters, and we have seen that a ratings downgrade often has serious financial consequences for a firm. The role of the big three credit rating agencies, Standard & Poor's (S&P), Moody's, and Fitch, in the financial crisis would be difficult to exaggerate. This section focuses on regulatory issues surrounding credit rating agencies, while chapter 12 examines their business practices and how inaccurate, and perhaps even dishonest, ratings by these agencies helped to cause the crisis and make the disaster worse than it otherwise would have been.

The history of today's credit ratings goes back at least 100 years. Poor's Publishing Company published *Poor's Manual* as early as 1890, which reported on the quality of various investments, including bonds. John Moody began to publish ratings for railroad bonds in 1909.[23] These ratings were originally published and sold to interested parties seeking guidance for their investing. As such, a reputation for accuracy and relevancy of information was essential to generate revenue. Over time, ratings became much more widely accepted, and by the 1970s, changes in ratings generally merely reflected the current market perception of the quality of the debt issue. Thus, the informational content of ratings had been eroded.[24] Ironically, by the mid-1970s, credit ratings had been incorporated into investment policies, just as the informational value of those ratings had diminished. It is common for the investment policy of financial institutions to specify that the portfolio can contain only "investment grade" securities, where this means that the securities must have received a rating of a sufficiently high level from one or more of the three main credit raters: S&P, Moody's, or Fitch. This entrenchment guarantees business for the rating firms.

Whereas the rating firms originally published information and generated revenue from interested investors, today the overwhelming majority of credit rating agency income is paid by the issuers of securities. Part of the reason for this switch in sources of revenue is that information has become largely a public good, due to improved communication, which makes it difficult for a rater to capture income from the public. As a result, rating agencies today garner 95 percent of their revenues from issuers of securities.[25]

The ability of credit rating agencies to extract revenue from bond issuers stems in part from the requirement that financial institutions hold bonds with certain ratings. However, this entrenchment also stems from federal regulation. In 1975 the SEC designated some firms as "nationally recognized statistical rating organizations" (NRSROs). At one point, there were nine such firms, but just prior to and through the period of the financial crisis, 2001–2008, there were only five such firms: Standard & Poor's (S&P), Moody's, Fitch Ratings, A.M. Best Company, and Dominion Bond Rating Service Limited. Among them, S&P, Moody's, and Fitch account for 90 percent of the market, with Fitch being a much smaller player among the three. In essence, S&P and Moody's dominate the market.[26]

The importance of NRSRO designation is critical. As the SEC notes ". . . ratings by NRSROs today are used as benchmarks in federal and state legislation, rules issued by financial and other regulators, foreign regulatory schemes, and private financial contracts. Many of these uses specifically refer to the term NRSRO as used in the Commission's rules and regulations."[27] As Frank Partnoy has persuasively explained,[28] this designation and the role it plays in the investment world grants a "regulatory license"—a property right that allows NRSROs to "determine the substantive effect of legal rules." Given the oligopolic structure of the credit rating industry and the dominance of just a few firms, this approach gives tremendous market power in this arena to S&P and Moody's.[29]

In a sense, credit rating agencies serve a gatekeeper function—they presumably certify the credit condition of securities by assigning an alphabetical rating. In doing so, they put their reputational capital on the line, such that they should have a strong incentive to provide an accurate rating. However, Frank Partnoy explains that credit rating agencies are very different from other financial market gatekeepers. He writes: "Why are credit rating agencies so different from other gatekeepers? Part of the reason is that the most successful credit rating agencies have benefited from an oligopoly market structure that is reinforced by regulations that depend exclusively on credit ratings issued by National Recognized Statistical Rating Organizations (NRSROs)."[30]

This market power gave rating agencies an important role in the securitization of mortgages and other financial instruments, because each of the newly created securities required a rating from an NRSRO. In large part, this market power was a gift from the SEC through its regulatory structure. The rating agencies turned this regulatory license into cash during the period of the credit crisis. Figure 10.2 shows the growth in profitability for S&P and Moody's during the first years of the twenty-first century. Starting from a 2001 level of profits of about $400 million each, Moody's almost doubled its profits by its peak year of 2006, while S&P actually tripled its profitability by 2007. Further, both businesses had extremely high operating profit margins through the period 2001–2007, ranging from 30–50 percent of revenues. Much of this profitability came from the surge in ratings business due to the explosion in securitization of the early 2000s. With the collapse of securitization that began in 2007 and continues to this date, profits of both businesses have receded sharply.

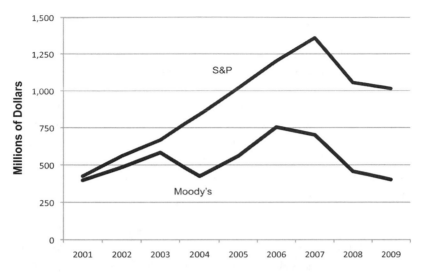

Figure 10.2 Profitability of S&P and Moody's 2001–2008
Source: Annual Reports of Moody's and McGraw-Hill, various years. Standard & Poor's constitutes the Financial Services division of McGraw-Hill and includes the credit rating business as well as various information services. The credit rating business dominates the other portion of that division. Fitch is part of a privately held firm, which does not publish separate profitability figures.

There are two problems with credit rating agencies during this period. First, by exploiting their regulatory licenses, they were able to amass profits over and above those that they could have earned without a regulatory license, so these excess profits came at the expense of society at large. The second problem is more severe, as chapter 12 explores in more detail. There is strong evidence that the agencies exploited a business model in which they cooperated with securitizers to help ensure high ratings for the collateralized deposit obligations (CDOs) they rated, and these high ratings helped to mislead investors into believing that many securities were much more secure than they actually were.

As a result of ratings that turned out to be highly inflated, financial institutions and other investors acquired more CDOs for their portfolios, thinking that these instruments that were rated AAA or Aaa were comparable to corporate securities with comparable ratings. This proved to be disastrously false. Thus, these inflated ratings encouraged excessive exposure to the housing sector, the very area of the economy that was soon to experience a rapid fall in prices, and this greater exposure exacerbated the severity of the crisis.

Mark-to-Market Accounting Rules

In traditional accounting, a financial asset acquired as an investment by a financial institution was acquired at a particular price and kept on the books at that price until it was sold. At sale, the transaction price was recorded as the true value of the asset, and gains and losses were incorporated into accounting statements only at that point. This contrasts with the accounting treatment for physical assets that would be depreciated or have their accounting value marked down as the asset was consumed. The idea behind mark-to-market accounting is to more closely match the accounting value of financial assets to their economic value or their true market value.

If assets are kept on the books at their historical acquisition price, but the market value of those assets fluctuates, there can be a disparity between accounting statements and economic reality. For example, consider two different financial assets, bonds perhaps, that are acquired for $1,000 each. Over time, let us assume that due to normal market fluctuations one asset appreciates to $1,100 and the other falls to $800. The true economic value of the two assets taken together is now $1,900, but with historical accounting they will still be carried on the books of the firm as being worth a total of $2,000.

Assume that management knows the true value of the assets, but it wishes the firm to appear more profitable than it is. With historical accounting principles, the firm simply sells the appreciated asset for $1,100 and continues to carry the depreciated asset at its historical value of $1,000. After the sale, it appears that the value of the two is now $2,100 ($1,000 of historical value and $1,100 realized in cash on the sale). However, the true value of the two is still obviously $1,900. This practice is called "gains trading," and mark-to-market accounting is designed to foil such accounting manipulations and to ensure that the accounting reports more closely resemble the real economic position of the firm.

When markets function normally and trading is frequent, the best indicator of the value of the security is the price at which it trades in the market. However, if markets are illiquid and there is no trading, the value of an asset that must be liquidated immediately can potentially fall far below its normal market value.

Consider a bond that a firm acquires for $1,000, has no intention of selling, and that continues to make its payments as promised. Assume also that because of a financial crisis there is no normal market for the security and the only price being offered for that particular bond is $500.

Under mark-to-market accounting, the holder of the asset may be compelled to mark the asset down to only $500, generating an accounting loss. This loss in turn may trigger regulatory demands for additional capital. Also, such accounting losses may require the firm to post additional collateral with its trading partners based on its contractual requirements. To acquire more ready cash, the firm then may be compelled to actually sell the asset for its depressed price, and the recording of this sale establishes a new market price that other firms must honor in their own mark-to-market accounting. During the financial crisis, many firms were caught in just such a cascade of temporarily falling market values that caused holders of securities to dump additional assets onto the market to raise ready cash, and these forced sales in turn depressed prices yet further, leading to a vicious cascade of prices.

The accounting profession, bolstered by the SEC, has been moving toward mark-to-market accounting for quite some time, and some firms voluntarily adopted this system some time ago. In implementing accounting standards, the SEC works with the accounting profession's Financial Accounting Standards Board that issues Financial Accounting Standards, such as FAS 157, *Fair Value Measurements*, which came into effect for firms with fiscal years beginning after November 15, 2007. (It would have been almost impossible to time this implementation to have a worse effect on the financial crisis.) The essence of the standard is to require that firms carry assets at their "fair value," which is determined in terms of "the price in an orderly transaction between market participants. . . ."[31] While the standard does contemplate using estimates in times of illiquid markets, the invocation of this new standard gave a strong push to using any recorded transaction price as a basis for marking other assets on the firm's book to their new market value. If the observed transaction price happened to be a depressed price, that recorded price still gave an impetus to writing down the assets.

Almost immediately upon coming into effect, the new rule caused problems. In early 2008, ". . . auditors forced AIG to mark to market at valuations provided by a US investment bank."[32] This caused an increase in accounting losses in the range of $1–5 billion. Credit Suisse was the victim of a similar problem. These incidents led *Euromoney* to opine: ". . . the present crisis in financial markets is not just about actual credit losses. . . . Marking to market when no real market exists can seem nonsensical, especially when the asset is performing. Far from helping to make markets more efficient, it amplifies problems."[33]

By March 2008, the SEC acted to soften the effects of FAS 157 by reminding firms that prices that are the result of a forced liquidation or distress sale might be ignored, a recommendation that the *New York Times* labeled an "invitation to fudge."[34] The strict accounting rule continued to be a problem, and in September 2008, 60 members of Congress united to urge the SEC to suspend the rule immediately, and the SEC issued new guidance further softening the implementation of the rule:[35] "When an active market for a security does not exist, the use of management estimates that incorporate current market participant expectations of future cash flows, and include appropriate risk premiums, is acceptable."[36] Summing up the matter so far, a former chair of the FDIC, William Isaac, wrote that same week: "The SEC has destroyed $500 billion of bank capital by its senseless marking to market of these assets for which there is no marking to market, and that has destroyed $5 trillion of bank lending."[37]

This problem continued throughout the financial crisis with great controversy over the effect of such mark-to-market accounting. At the end of 2008, the SEC issued its own 259-page study of the issue, which reached the conclusion ". . . that fair value accounting did not appear to play a meaningful role in bank failures occurring during 2008" and that "for the failed banks that did recognize sizable fair value losses, it does not appear that the reporting of these losses was the reason the bank failed."[38] In spite of this self-exculpating finding, many other seasoned market observers disagreed strenuously, and many large financial institutions suffered the pain of the mark-to-market regime.

In evaluating the impact of mark-to-market accounting on the financial crisis, it should be remembered that this accounting innovation did not cause the crisis. As long as markets are orderly, most economists would agree that mark-to-market accounting helps to give a truer picture of a firm's financial position than does historically based accounting. The only way that mark-to-market rules can have an effect is if they force firms to mark down assets to nonrepresentative prices that are themselves the product of a financial crisis that is already underway. Thus, the accounting regime may have exacerbated an already existing problem, but it was not a root cause of the crisis itself. Nonetheless, the imposition of this accounting regime was another way in which the hand of regulation played a causal role in the financial crisis.

Complex Financial Derivatives

Two types of complex financial derivatives played major roles in the financial crisis, CDS and CDOs, particularly collateralized mortgage obligations (CMOs). Earlier in this chapter, we explored the role that CDS played in reducing the cost of banks' meeting their capital requirements, and it is clear that CDS played an important role in the collapse of AIG, which induced the federal government's effective takeover of that company at the cost of more than $100 billion. Later chapters chronicle how financial firms created CMOs and the role that they played in stimulating mortgage finance, while at the same time making the ownership of mortgages more opaque and the resolution of mortgage defaults much more difficult. In both cases, these markets developed extremely rapidly to become gigantic world financial forces, and both were largely unregulated. For example, in April 2008, the CDS market had reached a size of $44 trillion in nominal value.[39] Despite the large size and worldwide importance of this market, it has been essentially unregulated. Though the market was largely unregulated, many of the most significant institutions in this market were regulated, however, with AIG being a prime example.

Some have pointed to the development of these large and sophisticated unregulated markets as a failure of regulation. It is clear that both types of instruments developed swiftly, fostered markets of enormous size, and played intimate roles in the crisis. However, the development of regulations generally lag behind the pace of financial innovation, with new instruments being developed more rapidly than regulatory structures can be put in place to control them. In retrospect, it seems that there was a regulatory failure to control these instruments in the financial crisis of 2007–2009, and the tendency of finance to outpace regulation is a concern for the future as well.

The Regulation of AIG

A common narrative of the crisis focuses much of the blame on complex financial instruments such as CDS and CMOs and focuses on the light regulation that characterizes these markets. Some who emphasize this point go on to imply that key firms in these markets were able to run amok because they were not regulated. Among these firms, none was more spectacularly and problematically involved than AIG, especially through the many CDS written by its London subsidiary, AIGFP.

In the United States, insurance companies are principally regulated by agencies of the various states. Thrift institutions (savings banks and S&Ls) are regulated by the Office of Thrift Supervision (OTS), a branch of the U.S. Treasury. The OTS also regulates holding companies that own thrift institutions, so the OTS is the primary federal regulator of AIG, which owns a thrift institution. Scott M. Polakoff was the acting director of the OTS during the crisis and presented testimony before a Senate committee in March 2009. Polakoff's testimony is remarkable for his frankness, his willingness to acknowledge the responsibility of OTS for regulating AIG, his admission of the scope of his agency's regulatory powers over AIG, and for acknowledging the regulatory failures of OTS.

In particular, Polakoff acknowledged that OTS had the duty to oversee AIG to ensure that it complied with regulations on permissible activities and transactions, capital requirements, risk-taking, and to identify systemic issues and weaknesses. Polakoff reports that his agency recognized the need for intensive regulation of a large complex institution like AIG, including a "dedicated examination team and continuous onsite presence." Polakoff reports:

> OTS conducted continuous consolidated supervision of the AIG group, including an on-site examination team at AIG headquarters in New York. Through frequent, ongoing dialogue with company management, OTS maintained a contemporaneous understanding of all material parts of the AIG group, including their domestic and cross-border operations.[40]

The supervision of OTS extended to AIGFP, the London branch of AIG most responsible for its book of CDS business. About AIGFP, Polakoff says:

> With respect to AIGFP, OTS identified and reported to AIG's board weaknesses in AIGFP's documentation of complex structures transactions, in policies and procedures regarding accounting, in stress testing, in communication of risk tolerances, and in the company's outline of lines of authority, credit risk management and measurement.[41]

These and many other statements made by Polakoff in his testimony show the far-reaching authority of OTS to investigate AIG and to compel changes in its behavior. Polakoff is also fairly frank in admitting the inadequacy of OTS's efforts with respect to AIG.

In his Congressional testimony on AIG, Treasury Secretary Geithner summed up the problem pretty succinctly:

> Despite regulators in 20 different states being responsible for the primary regulation and supervision of AIG's U.S. insurance subsidiaries, despite AIG's foreign insurance activities being regulated by more than 130 foreign governments, and despite AIG's holding company being subject to supervision by the Office of Thrift Supervision (OTS), no one was adequately aware of what was really going on at AIG. . . . Moreover, neither AIG's management nor any of AIG's principal supervisors—including the state insurance commissioners and the OTS—understood the magnitude of risks AIG had taken or the threat that AIG posed to the entire financial system.[42]

The point here about AIG and regulation is not to single out the OTS for doing a poor job. Rather, it is important to realize that there was a federal agency charged with regulating AIG all through the crisis, that the agency had broad powers, and that the regulatory effort was inadequate in crucial respects. So, the regulatory problem with respect to AIG is not the absence of a regulator, but rather poor regulatory performance.

Poor Regulation of the Mortgage Industry

As we have seen, the federal government is intimately involved in the housing industry, and this intense intercession ranges from supervision of lenders to a multitude of rules regarding disclosure of terms of loans, as well as legislation supervising the provision of loans to various geographical areas, and the making of loans available to underserved demographic groups. In spite of this extensive involvement in almost all aspects of housing finance, deception and dishonesty played an important role in the crisis. While the next chapter explores this issue in more detail, this brief section considers the regulatory structure that failed to prevent such abuses.

In retrospect, it seems undeniable that many home mortgages were made to borrowers in amounts and on terms that were completely inappropriate to the borrower's circumstances. In many instances, the loan amount was impossibly large relative to the borrower's means. In other instances, loans were structured in a manner unsuited to the borrower's resources and prospects. For example, a buyer might be given a loan with a low "teaser" rate for the initial years that reset to a higher rate after a couple of years. The buyer might be able barely to afford the low teaser payments, but would be left in an impossible situation once the loan reset to the higher rate. For their part, many borrowers and mortgage brokers consciously lied in order to secure loans. These instances of predatory lending on the one hand, and predatory borrowing on the other, are explored more thoroughly in the next chapter. The point here is that regulation failed to forestall all of these problems in spite of the elaborate regulatory structure and the deep intrusion of regulation into the mortgage market.

Emergency Responses to the Crisis and "Really Too Big to Fail"

Desperate times are said to require desperate measures, and the actions of the federal government, particularly the U.S. Treasury and the Federal Reserve, must be measured in that light. However, there can be no doubt that emergency responses to the crisis exacerbated one of the most serious problems in our financial system—the problem that some institutions are too big to fail.

This account of the financial crisis has focused on 16 firms (and to a lesser extent on MBIA and Ambac), and table 10.1 highlights their fate as falling into one of three categories—merger, stasis, or bankruptcy. As the table shows, emergency actions led to the merger of Countrywide Financial and Merrill Lynch into Bank of America, Bear Stearns and Washington Mutual into JPMorgan Chase, and Wachovia into Wells Fargo. All of these mergers were accomplished with the active intervention and assistance of the federal government, and all of them were financially assisted by the federal government, with the exception of Wells Fargo's acquisition of Wachovia, which was supported by tax concessions but no actual transfer of immediate cash.

If there was a problem of financial institutions being too big to fail before the crisis, the mergers midwifed by the federal government during the crisis have exacerbated this problem tremendously by creating much greater concentration in the financial sector. Before the crisis, no U.S. financial firm had assets exceeding $2 trillion, now both Bank of America and JPMorgan Chase exceed that figure. In addition, Wells Fargo more than doubled in size, and now has assets of $1.25 trillion. The 16 firms in table 10.1 have now been reduced to just 9 companies. In the process, the average asset size of these behemoth firms has gone from $797 billion to $1.3 trillion, an increase of 60 percent in asset size.

Table 10.1 shows six firms that remained in stasis, but all of these firms proved their credentials as being too big to fail. Citigroup and AIG received bailouts from the TARP fund; Fannie Mae and Freddie Mac became explicit wards of the federal government; and Goldman Sachs and Morgan Stanley received shelter from the Federal Reserve by transforming themselves into bank holding companies. Of the big firms involved in the crisis, only Lehman Brothers and IndyMac were allowed to go into bankruptcy. If "too big to fail" was a problem before the crisis, the regulatory response to the crisis has made it a really big problem now.

Table 10.1				
Really Too Big To Fail				
	2006		**2009**	
	Firm	**Assets ($ Billions)**	**Firm**	**Assets ($ Billions)**
Merger	**Bank of America**	**1,463.7**	**Bank of America**	**2,224.7**
	Countrywide	199.9		
	Merrill Lynch	841.3		
	JPMorgan Chase	**1,351.5**	**JPMorgan Chase**	**2,032.0**
	Bear Stearns	350.4		
	Washington Mutual	346.3		
	Wells Fargo	**482.0**	**Wells Fargo**	**1,243.6**
	Wachovia	707.1		
Stasis	Citigroup	1,884.3	Citigroup	1,856.6
	AIG	979.4	AIG	847.6
	Fannie Mae	843.9	Fannie Mae	869.1
	Freddie Mac	813.1	Freddie Mac	841.8
	Goldman Sachs	838.2	Goldman Sachs	849.3
	Morgan Stanley	1,120.6	Morgan Stanley	773.4
Bankruptcy	Lehman Brothers	503.5		
	IndyMac	29.3		
Average Asset Size		**797.2**		**1,282.0**

Defects in Regulatory Architecture

As the financial crisis abated in late 2009 and the first half of 2010, attention has turned increasingly to an assessment of the causes of the crisis and remedies for the future. In retrospect, it has seemed to many that a defective regulatory architecture both failed to prevent and even helped to cause the financial crisis. This chapter and chapter 9 have chronicled some of the deficiencies in regulation.

Current attention focuses most particularly on three areas of problems with regulation. First, many cite the various instances of deregulation of the financial sector, instances of which these chapters have addressed. Second, many commentators point with despair to the fragmented regulatory regime that governs U.S. financial markets and maintain that an integrated system of regulation is needed. Third, there are increasing calls for a regulator of systemic financial risk. These areas of concern have led to considerable ferment in discussions of how the regulatory structure should be repaired to regulate markets in a manner that will forestall the next crisis. However, reflection on the role of regulation in causing and failing to prevent the financial crisis of our time should give pause to those who see regulation as a panacea for our future problems.

Causes of the Financial Crisis: From Aspiring Home Owner to Mortgage Lender

Beyond governmental housing policies, flawed macroeconomic policies, and defective regulation of financial firms, the focus now turns to the all too human failings outside the regulatory structure that also played a dramatic causal role—the roles of private individuals seeking personal advantage, those individuals operating in firms, and firms themselves. These failings ranged from the grasping of individuals to the implementation of business policies that were almost designed to fail. Among individuals, the personal failings were exemplified by corporate titans and the most humble. The institutional arrangements that dominated the mortgage market—the originate-to-distribute (OTD) model of mortgage production and the placing of credit rating agencies at the nexus of the securitization process—performed as if created by an evil genius. As Richard Bookstaber said in a somewhat different context, the mortgage market became a "demon of our own design."[1]

In their telling, Richard Thaler and Cass Sunstein assert that the financial disaster was caused by "human frailty," and this is certainly true to a great extent.[2] But this human frailty played upon an institutional stage that created incentives that led individuals to act in certain ways. In the institutional setting of the OTD system of mortgage production, individuals who pursued the narrow incentives that lay before them, in ways that must have seemed rational at the time, fed into the maw of an infernal machine that led to destruction. This part of the story of the causes of the crisis begins at the head of the mortgage-generation process that came to dominate the mortgage market from the 1990s to the catastrophe that began to unfold in 2007, and the new set of incentives that this new organization of the mortgage market created is the key to understanding the subprime part of the financial crisis.

It is far too facile to ascribe the financial crisis to greed or cupidity alone, as some have done, for these failings are constants in the human condition. Greed did not emerge as a new feature of human nature with the turning of the millennium and suddenly lead to financial disaster. Instead, we must look to a new institutional order that provided a backdrop of incentives against which the ordinary actions of people operated in a setting that led to financial disaster. The incentive effects of the OTD model of mortgage production provided an intricate mechanism within which ordinary humans responded to clear incentives that collectively led to disaster. Thus the basic story of the subprime part of the crisis is how the constant of human nature met a new economic and institutional environment, within which ordinary and typical human responses led to ruin.

The OTD model of securitization provides a narrative thread for exploring the faults that did so much to create the crisis. It is in the securitization process that all of the actors from the private sphere come together—the aspiring home owner, the mortgage broker, the appraiser, the initial lender, the securitizer and its staff, the credit rating agencies, the risk management specialists, and the ultimate investors who purchased the CDOs that were the ultimate product of the securitization process. This chapter focuses on the first part of the OTD chain, from home buyer through the initial lender, while chapter 12 explores the process of securitization down to the ultimate purchaser of the newly created securities.

As we have seen, long-standing national public policy aimed at increasing home ownership expressed itself in aggressive policies to change the terms of lending beginning with special intensity in the 1990s and extending into the twenty-first century. These policies met individuals and families anxious to embrace this part of the American dream—to live in a home they owned that provided a high level of comfort and reflected the owners' wealth, success, and achievement. To some extent, the national policy of spreading home ownership to a wider public met with reluctance or even resistance by some financial institutions, but it was readily embraced by other firms and soon became widely accepted by almost all lenders. A key part of the mechanism of expanding home ownership was the process of securitization. With securitization, the lenders' capital could be recycled and could support the origination of many more mortgages, which had a dramatic effect in expanding the total pool of capital available for mortgage lending.

These developments led to a society of home owners who borrowed heavily and pushed household leverage to unprecedented heights. For their part, financial institutions also accelerated their borrowing and increased their leverage to a pinnacle never seen previously. This precarious reliance on debt made the entire system, both households and financial institutions, reliant on a principle that had always held before: that taking the United States in its entirety, housing prices would never fall, and they would even continue to rise as they always had done before. Not surprisingly, this massive bet proved far from a self-fulfilling prophecy. As events have demonstrated, it was actually a self-falsifying prophecy, in that the massive borrowing of individuals and institutions to fund housing investment pushed housing prices far beyond their fundamental values. The bubble started to deflate in late 2006 and continued to collapse in the ensuing months, leading directly to the crisis of the financial system.

To explore the cause of this massive leveraging, the house price bubble, the price collapse, and the financial crisis, we must look beyond the encouragement of public policy and focus on the actions of individuals and firms. After all, no government policy forced citizens to buy houses they could not afford or to pay more for houses than they were worth. While federal pressure may have encouraged lenders to weaken lending standards, these modest forces were surely too weak to induce lenders to rush to the self-destruction of wild lending and massive leveraging that they in fact all too readily embraced.

The old originate-to-hold (OTH) model of mortgage production essentially involved two key parties: the aspiring home owner, or mortgagor, and a lender, typically a local savings and loan (S&L). The appraiser, hired by the lender, was a peripheral third party. This small network of actors, functioned in a cocoon of tight regulation, as depicted in figure 2.1 in chapter 2.

The Borrower

In this setting, the mortgagor had three principal reasons to seek a home loan. In most cases, the mortgagor sought a loan simply to fund the purchase of his or her own home. In addition, a home owner might apply for a new loan to obtain a better financing rate, or to secure additional funds on a second mortgage to enhance the value of the property through renovation. The mortgagor's interest in the character of the loan was equally straightforward—simply to secure the best financial terms available.

With the development of the mortgage market of the 1990s and early 2000s, characterized by easier credit, lower transaction costs, lower interest rates made persistent by federal policy, and home prices perceived to be rising steadily, the prospective home buyer had a richer set of incentives. The old incentives still pertained: to secure a home, to refinance to better terms, to secure a home improvement loan. But the home owner now had other reasons to consider obtaining a loan. If the mortgagor already owned a home with substantial equity, the home owner could refinance and gain access to that equity by a "cash-out refinancing." The equity in the home that was thus converted to cash could be used for any purpose the home owner desired. In the old world of mortgage finance, the lender would certainly have resisted such a move by the home owner, because this would reduce the equity in the home that provided a financial cushion for the mortgage held on the lender's books. The lower transaction costs for obtaining a mortgage and the greater liquidity the OTD model brought to the entire market created these new possibilities.

In the old world of mortgage finance, lenders aggressively limited their financing to only owner-occupied housing. Any other financing would be offered on much less favorable terms, if at all. This earlier policy was a reflection of the much more conservative nature of the industry and was induced in part by the relative scarcity of funds available for mortgage lending. In the new world of mortgage lending, the prospect of buying residential real estate as a pure investment property became alluring in a way it never had been before. The prospective home buyer might now contemplate the purchase of a house as a pure investment with the intention of quickly reselling it for profit—the process of "home flipping." The previous policies of lenders demanding occupancy of homes that they financed became ever looser in the 1990s and early 2000s, so some buyers found they could even buy several homes, as it was all the more profitable to flip several houses at a time, instead of merely the one that the home buyer occupied. Even if a home buyer was too conservative or "financially backward" to consider flipping a home, the same market conditions created incentives for a home purchaser to stretch to buy a larger and more expensive home. Low interest rates, confidence in rising home prices, and expectation of higher personal income all conspired to suggest that one should buy the largest and best home for which one could get financing, and then plan to "grow into" the house financially.

All of these factors—low interest rates, low mortgage transaction costs, readily available credit under the OTD model, the chance to use the expanding equity in a home as a source of financing for other pursuits, the conception of a home as an investment vehicle—helped to create a much expanded demand for housing. This accelerated demand for housing expressed itself in surging housing starts, as shown in figure 11.1. In 1991, across the United States, construction began on just over one million houses, but this rapidly accelerated to a peak of just over two million by 2005, before collapsing to 550,000 in 2009. At the same time, from 1991 to 2005, the size of homes increased rapidly. The average new house started in 1991 was 1,890 square feet, but reached a peak of 2,277 in 2007, an increase of more than 20 percent.[3] Over this period, the increasing number of homes being built, a surge in the size of homes, and an increase in the level of finish, including fancier kitchens and more bathrooms, all expressed a rising demand for, and a burgeoning national investment in, housing.

The Lender

The accelerated push for mortgages from home buyers met a pull from lenders, for they too faced exciting fresh incentives in the new world of housing finance. Urged by governmental pressure to lend to those they previously would have denied, lenders' new economic opportunities in a world of securitized mortgages proved a much more powerful incentive.

By contrast with the coming world of securitized mortgages, the lender operating in a mortgage world characterized by the OTH model faced a simple set of incentives and a clear rationale for making lending decisions. Of course, the lender had an incentive to lend funds at the highest feasible rate and charge as much as possible, but this desire was

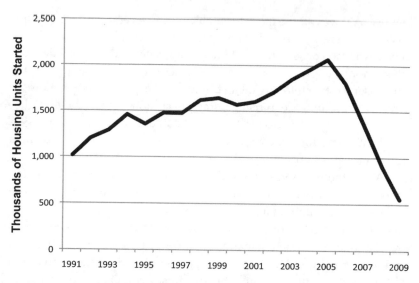

Figure 11.1 Annual Housing Starts
Source: U. S. Census Bureau, New Privately Owned Housing Units Started. Available at: http://www.census.gov/const/www/newresconstindex_excel.html. Accessed: March 9, 2010.

not unconstrained. With the typical lender operating in the same community as the borrower, the lender, like any merchant, faced some competition and feared being perceived as too rapacious, so the ordinary constraints that many merchants feel held for the lender as well. Further, the lender had a strong incentive to ensure that the mortgagor could actually meet the obligations of the mortgage agreement. Eviction and repossession is costly and unpleasant—even for heartless financial institutions. After all, these financial institutions want to operate in the financial industry, not in the property management or real estate workout industry. To ensure that the mortgagor would honor the terms of the mortgage agreement, the lender carefully assessed the financial capacity of the mortgagor and confirmed that the mortgagor has sufficient cash flow to cover the loan payments. Beyond that, the lender would usually demand a substantial down payment, so that the mortgagor has sufficient "skin in the game" to militate against abandonment of the property. To protect against the worst outcome of foreclosure, eviction, and repossession, the lender would want to establish terms to ensure that the property was worth more than the loan value. A significant down payment and a property fully worth the sale price both help to ensure that the lender cannot lose. If the mortgagor paid as promised, the lender achieved the best outcome. If the mortgagor defaulted and the lender was compelled to take over the property, the down payment and high value of the property relative to the loan amount assured that the lender could recoup the principal balance of the loan, along with payment for the expenses of repossession and re-marketing the home.

The lender had a strong incentive to test the creditworthiness of the borrower and the adequacy of the home as collateral. This was especially important, given the extent of the lender's commitment. Typically a mortgage was a level-payment, self-amortizing loan, with monthly payments and a maturity of 30 years. The S&L would collect payments on the loan (including escrow payments for taxes and insurance) and would hold the mortgage as an asset on its balance sheet for the entire life of the mortgage. The lender had only so much capital to use to support its mortgage portfolio, so it was important to select the best lending opportunities. Thus the prospective home owner came to the lender as petitioner, with the lender holding the balance of power and granting loans to the best credit risks available on terms that ensured a generally safe profit.

If the lender planned to retain the mortgage in its permanent portfolio, it had the same essential incentives that prevailed under the OTH model. But, if the lender plans to originate and then sell the mortgage straightaway, the OTD model completely alters the lender's incentives. For a lender planning to sell a mortgage soon after origination, the lender mainly desires to create a highly salable mortgage with the characteristics that potential purchasers demand. As in the OTH model, the lender wants to create a mortgage with an attractively high interest rate and features that hold out the possibility of additional fee income to the purchaser of the mortgage, such as prepayment penalties that will accrue to the ultimate investor.

For the lender planning to sell a mortgage, some factors that were crucially important in the OTH model now hold little interest. First and most crucially, the OTD model frees the lender from concern over whether the mortgagor can make the promised payments. For the initial lender who sells a mortgage, the typical sale is made on a no-recourse basis after an initial period of 45–60 days. So if the mortgagor avoids immediate default, the originator's sale of the mortgage is final. Further, the lender now has virtually no concern about the value of the property relative to the loan amount. After the sale is final, any problem of default, repossession, and extraction of value from the house will be the financial problem of the subsequent purchaser of the mortgagor. (The initial lender may well be involved in the process as the servicer of the mortgage, but it will not bear the principal risk if the mortgagor defaults.)

Thus, the move from the OTH to the OTD model essentially erases the initial lender's insistence that a mortgagor actually be able to pay as promised, and it also makes the adequacy of the home as collateral almost a matter of indifference. But at the same time, this shift in the model of mortgage production makes new incentives become very important, and transforms some of the lender's incentives completely. Consider a house that sells for $200,000 and that is worth exactly the sales price. The lender in the OTH model might demand a 20 percent down payment, making the mortgage balance $160,000, and this would be the maximum the originator might finance if it planned to retain the mortgage. However, if the intention is to sell the mortgage, these scruples are not merely a matter of indifference, but they actually become adverse to the initial lender. The initial lender can make more money by securing an inflated appraisal and permitting a lower down payment. Let us assume that the lender secures an inflated appraisal stating that the property is worth $220,000 and also reduces the down payment to 5 percent, both of these being fairly conservative assumptions compared to many actual practices. With these assumptions, the mortgage balance will be $209,000, or 31 percent more than the amount the lender would be willing to finance if planning to hold the mortgage. Assuming the same interest rate on the mortgage, the lender would receive 31 percent more for selling this risky mortgage than it would for selling a mortgage that was more conservative—such as a mortgage it would be willing to hold in its own portfolio.

In addition to inflating the appraisal amount and reducing the down payment to increase the principal balance for resale, the initial lender also has a strong incentive to originate a mortgage with a higher interest rate. A mortgage originated with an interest rate above the prevailing market rate is said to bear a *yield-spread premium*—the excess of the rate on the mortgage over the market rate. In the OTH model, this same incentive to lend at high rates exists, but it is constrained by the fact that the lender does not want the mortgagor to fail. So there is less benefit from inflating the interest rate to a point that the mortgagor cannot meet the payments. In the OTD model, subsequent defaults will not be the problem of the lender, but will fall on investors further along the securitization chain, and the higher the interest rate on a given mortgage, the more valuable it is for the initial lender to sell.

Originating a mortgage under the OTD model brings other profit opportunities to the initial lender. It is quite common for the initial lender to service the mortgage—that is, to collect the monthly payments and to manage the escrow account for taxes and insurance—and the initial lender typically acts as mortgage servicer under both models. The annual fee for this service is 25 basis points, or one-fourth of one percent of the mortgage initial principal amount. Thus, selling the mortgage does not mean that the originator had to give up the servicing fee. In fact, the increased generation of mortgages brought the initial lender ever more mortgages to service. Further, many subprime mortgages were structured in a way to encourage periodic refinancing, which brings repeat business to the originator, with more fees and more opportunities for profit.[4] All of these factors just discussed benefit the originator under the OTD model by offering more income and less risk than the originator would bear under the OTH model.

In sum, the development of the OTD model brought a host of new and beneficial incentives to mortgage lenders: potential for a greater volume of mortgage originations, an opportunity to reduce the risk of holding mortgages, less need for careful due diligence, greater profits by weaker mortgage underwriting standards, an incentive to increase loan sizes, benefits from increasing mortgage rates beyond the home buyer's capacity to pay, more frequent refinancing opportunities, and greater mortgage servicing fees. Every one of these new incentives redounded to the financial benefit of an unscrupulous lender, and even the most upright lending institution would benefit from many of these new incentives.

The Appraiser

One minor player—but one with a huge effect—in the origination process is the home appraiser. Under both the OTH and the OTD models, the initial lender typically hires an appraiser to visit the property and opine on its value, and the appraiser takes his or her orders from the lending institution.[5] Under both models, the mortgagor undoubtedly ultimately pays for the appraisal if the loan goes through, with the appraisal cost being imbedded in the terms of the mortgage. Under the OTH model, the lender has good reason to instruct the appraiser to value the property accurately or perhaps even conservatively, because the lender ultimately looks to the true value of the property to recoup the mortgage principal if the mortgagor defaults. The appraiser must serve the financial institution, which can choose among many appraisers, so the appraiser has an incentive to provide the kind of appraisal that the financial institution desires. Happily for the appraiser, the financial institution had every reason to want an honest appraisal under the OTH model, freeing the appraiser from the conflicts that arise in other contexts.

We have already seen that a lender who originates and sells a mortgage benefits if the mortgage has a higher principal amount, so the lender benefits from a higher appraised value in this case. So while the lender's incentives in the OTH model are consistent with an appraiser's interest in being an honest professional, the situation is just the opposite in the OTD model. The lender intending to originate and immediately sell a mortgage can benefit by encouraging the appraiser to inflate the value of the property. The appraiser's sole source of income derives from lenders, so the appraiser working for an unscrupulous lender has little choice but to deliver the kind of appraisal the lender demands or to leave the profession for another line of work.[6]

In 1989, Congress tightened federal regulation of appraisers used by federally insured depository institutions, but these strictures were quickly relaxed during the early 1990s under that push for greater home ownership by the National Homeownership Strategy.[7] The Federal Reserve Bank of Boston's *Closing the Gap* publication in a section on "ways to eliminate the unjustified disparities that have been documented" poses a list of questions for lenders, including: "Do we encourage the brokers and appraisers with whom we do business to be constructively active in minority communities?"[8] The clear goal was to ensure that unfavorable appraisals not impede mortgage lending, as the same document instructs lenders that "Management should consider having all appraisal reports that would cause an application to be denied reviewed by another experienced appraiser." In other words, if an appraisal indicates that it is unwise to make a loan, get a new appraisal. *Closing the Gap* also recommends that lenders should work with appraisers who are committed to the goals of expanding markets to a more diverse customer base.[9]

These relaxed appraisal standards, introduced about 1994, quickly led to inflated appraisals, which were well recognized as early as 2000–2001. A HUD report published in 2000 was so concerned with inflated appraisals that it spoke of forming "Swat Teams" ". . . to target abusive appraisal practices . . ."[10] In 2001, the *Chicago Tribune* reported,

"Appraisers, however, say their mission is in jeopardy and the risk to the market is great because they're under pressure to raise prices as high as possible so brokers and lenders can make more and bigger loans and thus collect more fees."[11] The same year, a research report ripped the weakening of the appraisal process and concluded that ". . . the changes in the appraisal process, over the past decade, have jeopardized the soundness of the process and skewed real estate prices."[12]

The seriousness of false appraisals is difficult to overstate, as the appraisal largely determines the size of the loan. If the appraised valuation is corrupt, then the collateral value of the home may be too small for the size of the loan, imperiling the lender. At the same time, an appraisal that is too high may leave the purchaser stuck with a mortgage unsupported by the value of the home. A mortgage principal that is too large relative to the value of the home also strips value from the ultimate purchaser of the mortgage when it is securitized. At the same time, a faulty appraisal can benefit some parties in the process. When a mortgage is first originated, an inflated appraisal harms the home buyer, but it can create larger fees for the mortgage broker and a higher sales price for the initial lender when the loan is securitized. In a cash-out refinancing, the inflated appraisal helps a home owner extract more funds from a lender than the true equity in the home would support. The ultimate beneficiaries and victims of inflated appraisal are thus unclear. However, it is certain that faked appraisals corrupt the entire mortgage process and cause financial harm to at least one of three parties: the home owner, the initial lender, or the purchaser of the mortgage.

The Mortgage Broker

Given these much more complex and varied incentives for both mortgagor and lender, the introduction of a mortgage broker into the relationship creates many potentially toxic opportunities. As the name implies, a mortgage broker arranges or facilitates mortgages, rather than being a lender or borrower. In essence, a mortgage broker acts as an information intermediary, who uses superior market knowledge to connect prospective mortgage borrowers with prospective lenders. Possessed of valuable knowledge about prospective borrowers and lenders, the mortgage broker is in a position to provide a valuable service to both the borrower and lender. For the prospective borrower, the mortgage broker could help the borrower complete the mortgage application and direct the borrower to the financial institution most likely to fund the loan at a reasonable rate. In the happiest situation, the mortgage broker might even help the borrower secure the most favorable terms available in the market. The mortgage broker could also benefit the lender by helping the lender make more loans than would otherwise be possible. From the lender's perspective, the mortgage broker could also provide a valuable service by pre-screening prospective borrowers and helping them to get all necessary information in order, thereby reducing the lender's cost of vetting the borrower and completing the loan. By providing such services, the mortgage broker would earn a reasonable compensation.

The mortgage brokerage industry is a fairly recent development. It was only in 1960 that the first trade association for mortgage brokers was formed,[13] with the National Association of Mortgage Brokers not being established until 1973. In 1991, there were about 14,000 brokerage firms, but by 2004–2006, approximately 53,000 mortgage brokerage firms employed somewhere in the range of 200,000 to 420,000 people. By the early 2000s, brokers originated about two-thirds of all residential loans.[14]

In our society, with a bank on every corner, one might reasonably wonder why a mortgage broker is at all necessary. Those with financial resources and even middling financial sophistication are unlikely to need a mortgage broker to find a loan or complete the mortgage application. While it is possible that a mortgage broker might be of some service to such a borrower in finding the best possible loan, it is much more likely that mortgage brokers will work with poorer or less sophisticated prospective home purchasers.

Virtually without exception, mortgage brokers are paid by the lending institution at the time the loan is funded and the transaction closes, but the source of all revenue for any mortgage stems ultimately from the mortgagor. The mortgage broker typically receives a fee expressed in "points" or one-hundredths of the principal balance on the mortgage, so that a fee of two points on a $100,000 mortgage would bring the mortgage broker a payment of $2,000. The broker receives payment if and only if the mortgage loan is consummated, an incentive arrangement that encourages mortgage brokers to ensure that the deal goes through. In the subprime market, the financial institution that funded the loan would pay more to the mortgage broker for a mortgage with more desirable financial terms, with the broker's compensation ranging from one to as many as four or, in extreme cases, seven points.

As the name implies, a mortgage *broker* is not a principal in the lending transaction, but a facilitator, who owes no fiduciary duty to either the prospective borrower or the initial lender. At least that was the conceit of the mortgage broker industry. The recommended disclosure practice of the National Association of Mortgage Brokers of 1997 includes the following language:

> In connection with this mortgage loan we are acting as an independent contractor and not as your agent . . . we do not distribute the products of all lenders or investors in the market and cannot guarantee the lowest price or best terms available in the market. . . . The lenders whose loan products we distribute generally provide their loan products to us at a wholesale rate. The retail price we offer you—your interest rate, total points and fees—will include our compensation. In some cases, we may be paid all of our compensation by either you or the lender. Alternatively, we may be paid a portion of our compensation by both you and the lender. For example, in some cases, if you would rather pay a lower interest rate, you may pay higher up-front points and fees. Also, in some cases, if you would rather pay less up-front, you may be able to pay some or all of our compensation indirectly through a higher interest rate in which case we will be paid directly by the lender. We also may be paid by the lender based on (i) the value of the Mortgage Loan or related servicing rights in the market place or (ii) other services, goods or facilities performed or provided by us to the lender.[15]

Of course, whether such disclosures were made is a different question. But the disclosure, if made and understood, certainly makes the potentially adversarial relationship between the prospective mortgagor and mortgage broker quite clear. Starting in 2008, more and more states have passed laws to insist that mortgage brokers owe a fiduciary duty to borrowers.

Even in the heyday of the OTD model, many mortgages were originated without any mortgage broker. For such mortgages, creating a mortgage began in the old-fashioned way—a prospective home buyer applied directly to a financial institution for a loan. One of the most distinctive features of the mortgage finance crisis turns on the role played by the mortgage broker, so the subsequent discussion considers only those mortgages that were originated with the assistance of a mortgage broker.

As we have seen, from the point of view of the originating financial institution, at least in the OTH era, a given mortgage proposition is more attractive if the mortgagor is wealthier, has a greater income, and has a higher credit rating; if the property is more valuable; if the down payment is larger; if the fees that the mortgagor will pay are higher; and if the interest rate on the mortgage is higher. In the subprime market, as it developed in the early twenty-first century under the dominance of the OTD model, the originating lender did not, or even could not, verify the information about the mortgagor or the property, due to the interposition of the mortgage broker. Thus, the financial institution often funded mortgages based on representations made by the mortgagor or the mortgage broker.

The financial institution's lack of direct knowledge of the mortgagor means that the mortgage broker occupies a crucial position in the chain running from the mortgagor to the ultimate investor. In many instances, only the mortgage broker really knows the mortgagor and his capacity to fulfill his obligations. Because the mortgage broker stands between the mortgagor and the originator, the loan originator may feel less concern about how it treats the mortgagor. The mortgage broker's privileged information position and the greater remove of the originator from the mortgagor gives the mortgage broker opportunities and incentives to play three dishonest games. First, the mortgage broker might cooperate with the originator to create a mortgage that harms the mortgagor, a practice usually known as predatory lending. Second, the mortgage broker might cooperate with the mortgagor to abuse the lender, a practice known as mortgage fraud or predatory borrowing. Third, the mortgage broker might cooperate with both the borrower in a refinancing and the lender to enact a charade in which the borrower receives a larger refinancing loan for more cash out of the property, the broker receives a larger fee because the loan size is larger, and the lender sells the larger loan for a higher price.

"Predatory lending" is a controversial term, subject to competing definitions, some of which are absurdly expansive and include as predatory many practices and loan features that can be quite desirable for particular borrowers and quite injurious to others.[16] Without striving for absolute precision, the following can serve as a working definition of predatory lending: "knowingly creating a mortgage that the mortgage broker and originator know, or should know, is financially injurious to the mortgagor." HUD characterizes predatory lending as ". . . involving engaging in deception or fraud, manipulating the borrower through aggressive sales tactics, or taking unfair advantage of a borrowers' lack of understanding about loan terms."[17] Without trying to give an exhaustive account, two common practices seem to provide clear examples of predatory lending. First, creating a mortgage with a yield spread premium—an interest rate above the going market rate of interest for which the borrower could qualify—clearly injures the borrower. Second, creating a mortgage with a principal balance having implied payments that the borrower cannot financially sustain also clearly injures the borrower, as such a practice can be expected to lead to default. These practices harm the borrower but benefit the mortgage broker and the originator by improving their income from the mortgage. As the mortgage broker receives a number of points for helping to originate the loan, a higher principal balance benefits the mortgage broker. Further, the number of points received will be larger, and sometimes significantly larger, for mortgages with a yield spread premium.

Predatory lending became a gigantic problem in the mortgage lending frenzy from the mid-1990s to the housing price peak in 2006–2007. Thousands of people, often the less wealthy and unsophisticated, were financially abused and even ruined. The personal stories of some of these individuals are heartbreaking. For example, a predatory loan might start with an inflated appraisal of the property, and continue by steering the borrower into a loan with a higher interest rate than the borrower could obtain elsewhere, loading the mortgage up with high fees, starting the mortgage payments with a low "teaser" rate that the purchaser can barely meet, and building into the mortgage terms an escalation to a much higher rate in two years. Such abuse is obviously easier to perpetrate if the purchaser has low educational attainment and lacks financial acumen. Among the thousands of mortgagors who have now defaulted and those who continue to make payments on mortgages with balances above the value of the underlying properties, it remains unclear how many of those were victims of predatory lending. Part of the reason for this is that predatory lending conceptually strays into other forms of mortgage misconduct. That is, it is not always possible to distinguish predatory lending from attempts at predatory borrowing—a practice in which mortgage brokers also often play an important role.

A dishonest mortgage broker might exploit a second set of perverse incentives to cooperate with the borrower to defraud the lender. Two of the most common abuses are to commit owner-occupancy fraud or to falsify the mortgagor's financial resources. Based on decades of experience, defaults tend to be lower for owner-occupied dwellings, so conscientious lenders prefer to lend on homes that are to be occupied by the mortgagor, and they give better terms for such mortgages. In the now seemingly distant and happy world of steadily rising home prices, many participants sought to buy homes as pure investment properties with no intention of ever occupying them, so lying about occupancy intentions yielded financial advantages for the borrower as it helped to secure better terms for the mortgage. Mortgage brokers sometimes assisted in this fraud.

Compared to typical borrowers, particularly those in the subprime market, mortgage brokers have a superior understanding of what financial resources the borrower must have to secure a particular mortgage. The mortgage broker can use this knowledge to help the borrower secure a mortgage for which they might not actually qualify. Two examples illustrate the point. First, the mortgage broker might encourage the borrower to secure down payment monies by borrowing from a relative and then cooperate with the borrower to hide this additional indebtedness from the lender. Second, it became a frequent practice for lenders to grant mortgage loans based on the mere statement of income by the borrower. (These loans were known as "stated-income loans" or more commonly as "liars' loans.") Knowing what the lender needs to hear, the mortgage broker can guide the borrower in making a false statement sufficient to qualify for the desired loan.

This section closes by drawing from a story about a subprime borrower told by David Faber in his book, *And Then The Roof Caved In*.[18] Faber interviewed a Mexican immigrant, Arturo Trevilla, who bought his first home in San Clemente, California, for $584,000 in 2005. He signed loan documents totaling more than 100 pages, all in English, that he understood poorly, if at all. He reports that he just signed them, based on his total trust of his mortgage broker. The area where he and his family lived previously had been dangerous, and he was delighted to have a nice home in a safe area. Further, Trevilla reports that the mortgage broker led him to believe that he could refinance in a year and should expect to be able to get a cash-out loan that would allow him to withdraw about $70,000. This money Trevilla planned to use to realize his lifetime dream— he wanted to launch a business. Trevilla signed a mortgage document in which he claimed $16,000 in monthly income. However, he actually only earned $3,600 per month. Predatory lending? Mortgage fraud? Both? It all depends on the proper understanding of Trevilla's story.

In the case of mortgage fraud, there is a question as to which party is defrauded. If the initial lender merely intends to sell the loan, the initial lender might not object to these practices of mortgage fraud or predatory borrowing. After all, the initial lender will profit just by getting the deal done, so the initial lender might connive with the mortgage broker to help the mortgage fraud along, confident that a subsequent investor in the mortgage will be the party that actually bears the cost of the fraud.

In many cases the mortgagor, mortgage broker, and initial lender all cooperated to secure what each wanted: the mortgagor lied about his occupancy intentions and financial resources; the mortgage broker helped to fashion the lies and then transmitted them to the lender; and the lender pretended to believe the mortgage broker's representations. In this case, the mortgagor got the loan he wanted, the mortgage broker got a fat fee, and the lender originated a mortgage that it immediately resold for a significant profit.

This conflicted incentive relationship between initial lender and mortgage broker relates to the interpretation of the payment scheme that initial lenders offered to mortgage brokers—paying them a percentage of the loan's principal amount when the deal goes through. Did these lenders offer incentives to mortgage brokers with the understanding that they were inducing brokers to engage in predatory lending and predatory borrowing? Or was the pay design merely the lazy and witless creation that inadvertently pointed mortgage brokers toward predatory lending and borrowing? There seems little doubt that both behaviors were in play, with different lenders falling into each category. For some lenders, it now seems clear that they consciously engaged in a game to generate new mortgages of poor quality so that they could sell them into the securitization pipeline, and studies of lending standards seem to support this understanding.

The Mortgage Frenzy, the Originator, and Underwriting Standards

The President's Working Group on Financial Markets, "Policy Statement on Financial Market Developments," published in March 2008, contains the following statement: "The turmoil in financial markets clearly was triggered by a *dramatic weakening of underwriting standards for U.S. subprime mortgages, beginning* in late 2004 and extending into early 2007."[19] We have seen that federal policies, legislation, and regulation all contributed to a weakening of underwriting standards. To date, a number of studies have examined lending standards leading into and through the financial crisis. These studies certainly do not agree on every point, but they generally concur that lending standards were weak. For the most part, they find a pattern of weakening throughout much of the period.[20]

We have already met the poster child for poor lending standards, Countrywide Financial Corporation, the creation of the pitchman Angelo Mozilo. Mozilo and Countrywide were the perfect counterpart to the call for relaxed lending standards of the National Homeownership Strategy and the push for expanding home ownership to minorities and the less affluent. Countrywide embraced the lower standards with glee, while Mozilo reaped awards at Harvard for his concern for the poor, and claimed the moral high ground, saying that ". . . I founded Countrywide with the objective to lower the barriers and open the doors to homeownership" and ". . . it has always been our intention to be more than a corporation that makes mortgage loans; we wanted to be a force in making positive differences in people's lives."[21]

The truth appears to be quite different. Instead, Countrywide posed as the champion of the little man in need of a home, while following a course of absolute rapaciousness, as the *New York Times* reported: "Countrywide's entire operation, from its computer system to its incentive structure and financing arrangements, is intended to wring maximum profits out of the mortgage lending boom no matter what it costs borrowers, according to interviews with former employees and brokers who worked in different units of the company and internal documents they provided."[22] Based on internal documents from Countrywide's subprime lending unit: ". . . Countrywide was willing to underwrite loans that left little disposable income for borrowers' food clothing and other living expenses. A different manual states that loans could be written for borrowers even if, in a family of four, they had just $1,000 in disposable income after paying their mortgage bill. A loan to a single borrower could be made even if the person had just $550 left each month to live on, the manual said."[23]

While Countrywide may have been the most prominent lender following such destructive policies in the subprime market, they certainly were not alone. At the huge Washington Mutual and IndyMac and at thousands of smaller and obscure lenders across the country, the story was much the same—urgent demands of staff to make and fund loans with high interest rates, high fees, and no regard for the consequences their customers might suffer. As figure 11.2 shows, subprime originations surged in 2000–2006, with $630 billion in subprime originations in 2005 alone, and more that $2.5 trillion in subprime loans being originated over the 2000–2006 period. As a consequence, the end of 2006 witnessed the completion of a subprime time bomb created courtesy of firms in the mold of Countrywide, WaMu, and IndyMac.

But what made mortgage originators fail so spectacularly? After all, if a mortgage originator—a Countrywide, WaMu, IndyMac, or any other such firm—merely makes a subprime loan and then immediately sells the mortgage into the securitization process, it seems it should have little subprime exposure. There are two reasons that these kinds of firms failed. First, every such lender has a mortgage pipeline for loans in the process of being securitized, so there will necessarily be subprime exposure from loans originated but not yet sold. Further, the originator might sell the loan, but the buyer typically had the right to return the loan to the seller if the borrower fails to make any of the first three payments. After the mortgagor makes the first three payments, the purchaser of the loan would have no recourse to the originator and would be stuck with the loan permanently. So big mortgage originators are sure to be stuck holding some loans that are returned to them when mortgagors fail to make those first payments. Second, for a variety of

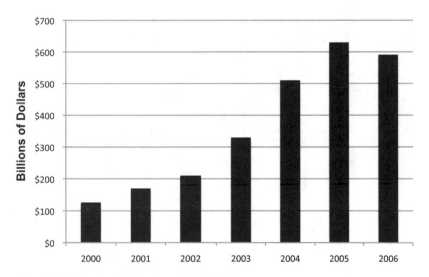

Figure 11.2 Subprime Originations, 2000–2006
Source: "Data360.org, Subprime Originations," Available at: http://www.data360.org/dsg.aspx?Data_Set_Group_Id=1362. Accessed February 9, 2010. These data are based upon *USA Today*, "In 2005, Half of Minorities Purchased Their Homes with Subprime Loans," May 18, 2007.

reasons, the originator kept a significant percentage of loans it originated on its own books.

Table 11.1 provides a snapshot of Countrywide, Washington Mutual, and IndyMac at the end of 2006 as representatives of the subprime
lending industry. Together, the three firms held almost $400 billion in
loans on their books, most of which were probably mortgage securities
and an unknown proportion of which were subprime loans. Considered
individually, each firm had well over half of its total assets in loans, and
collectively they held almost 70 percent of their total assets as loans.
Thus, when the value of mortgages started to collapse in 2007, each was
exposed to huge losses. They had created toxic mortgages but utterly
failed to pass them to a buyer before the poison began to act. For each,
its own brew proved fatal. Yet when one views the wreckage of so many
financial institutions destroyed by their own actions, it also seems
equally clear that some institutions had little understanding of the ultimate effects of their actions.

Of course, in some instances, CEOs of financial institutions may
have led their institutions down an ultimately destructive path because
excessive mortgage lending fattened their own pay checks. The incentives faced by such managers could be quite compelling. For example,

Table 11.1

**Loans Held by Countrywide Financial, Washington Mutual,
and IndyMac, Year-End, 2006**

(Dollar values in billions)

	Countrywide	Washington Mutual	IndyMac	Total
Loans Held for Sale	31.27	44.97	9.47	85.71
Loans in Portfolio or Held for Investment	78.09	224.96	10.11	313.16
Total Loans Held	109.36	269.93	19.58	398.87
Total Assets	199.95	346.29	29.50	575.74
Loans as Percentage of Total Assets	54.7%	78.0%	66.4%	69.3%

Source: Consolidated Statements of Financial Condition, 10-K filings for 2006.

one observer noted that at Washington Mutual "Kerry [Killinger] has made over $100 million over his tenure based on the aggressiveness that sunk the company."[24] For Mozilo, the Complaint filed against him by the SEC points out that from May 2005 to the end of 2007, Mozilo exercised Countrywide stock options and sold the underlying proceeds for a total of $260 million.[25] This was a portion of the $410 million that Mozilo took home from 1999 to the end of 2007.[26] In addition, Mozilo garnered many awards, including being listed as one of Barron's 30 most respected CEOs in 2005 and receiving the 2006 American Banker's Lifetime Achievement Award. Yet 2010 found Mozilo awaiting trial on SEC charges, and while he may keep many of his millions, that is still quite a fall for a man who fraudulently postured as a champion of the poor and was lionized in that role.

Causes of the Financial Crisis: From Securitizer to Ultimate Investor

Further steps beyond the origination of the mortgage take the created mortgage from the originator through the securitization process to the ultimate investor in the originate-to-distribute (OTD) model. In briefest terms, a securitizer acquires many mortgages from initial lenders to form a pool of mortgages, and the promised cash flows from that mortgage pool form the income stream that funds payments on new securities that the securitizer creates and issues. Those new securities tend to be of diverse levels of default risk, so the various tranches have different credit ratings and different promised payment rates. The creation of these securities is mediated by a credit rating agency that typically consults with the securitizer to design the securities and then issues a credit rating as the new securities are created. The securities are then ready for sale to the ultimate investor, which can be a municipality, pension fund, or hedge fund. The securitizer typically retains a portion of the new security issue for its own portfolio.

At each step in this process, the various participants face incentives that are often in conflict and that can lead to perverse outcomes. Exploring these incentives deepens the understanding of how the securitization process and the poor management of financial institutions helped to cause the crisis.

▨▨▨ Purchasing Mortgages

The securitizer must first assemble a pool of mortgages. In a multi-divisional financial firm, this can be accomplished by having a mortgage origination arm issue mortgages, but it is also quite typical for the securitizer to purchase mortgages from independent firms that make mortgage loans throughout the country. By purchasing mortgages from diverse geographic areas, the securitizer expects to reduce the risk of many mortgages experiencing payment difficulties at the same time, so this practice offered the benefits of geographical diversification.

As a purchaser of mortgages, the securitizing firm has every incentive to ensure that the mortgages are of good quality, so the securitizer undertakes due diligence to test the quality of the mortgages before purchase. Securitizing firms—Bear Stearns, Merrill Lynch, Morgan Stanley, Lehman Brothers, and the like—almost all outsourced the work of testing the quality of mortgages to due diligence firms that specialize in this work. Of the six or so firms most prominent in the business, the three largest at the height of the subprime frenzy were Clayton Holdings of Shelton, Connecticut, Bohan Group of San Francisco, and Opus Capital of Chicago. The prospective purchaser (e.g., Merrill) would send its own manager to accompany its due diligence firm (e.g., Clayton) to the site of a mortgage originator with loans to sell, and the due diligence firm would examine mortgages as the prospective purchaser directed.

Members of the due diligence team—contract underwriters—typically received a two-week training course and were then sent on site. These underwriters received about $30–$40 per hour plus expenses, and the prospective mortgage purchaser typically paid a flat fee of about $150 for the review of each file. Arithmetic implies that spending four hours reviewing a file would cause the due diligence firm to lose money, while spending an hour per mortgage was pretty much the upper bound of time consistent with good profitability for the due diligence firm. From 2000 to 2006, Clayton's revenues skyrocketed from $19 to $239 million. At the peak, Clayton had about 900 contract underwriters working at any given time, while Bohan had about 350.[1] Clayton Holdings reviewed about one million files in 2006.[2]

The due diligence firm would review a particular mortgage file and assign it a score of 1 to 3, with a "1" being the highest quality, and a "3"—a fail—implying that the mortgage had serious problems and should not be purchased. However, as one contract underwriter explained: "You weren't supposed to fail loans unless they were horrendous."[3] Even a "fail" did not necessarily mean the loan would not be purchased and securitized—instead, the prospective purchaser could use the loan's poor rating as grounds to offer a lower purchase price for the low-quality loan. In a typical assignment, the due diligence firm reviewed 5–20 percent of the loans being purchased, with the supervisor for the due diligence firm urging speedy reviews and the on-site representative of the purchaser urging approvals.

Over time, as the subprime mania accelerated, prospective purchasers asked for a smaller percentage of loans to be reviewed, relaxed their standards for purchasing mortgages, and tilted the balance of their concerns further away from quality and ever more toward purchasing a greater quantity of mortgages. One former managing director for Bear Stearns characterized the process this way: "Bear didn't really care about quality. They wanted volume." As for the due diligence firm, the former Bear executive went on: "But Clayton was hardly an innocent party. . . . They told the client what they wanted to hear."[4] In sum, the prospective purchaser would pay the due diligence firm to conduct a hasty pretense of review and then approve the loans for purchase. If a loan received a "fail," that judgment was often revised to be more favorable, and the securitizer purchased the loan anyway.

Why did the prospective purchaser pay for this charade of due diligence? There are several reasons. In the heyday of subprime, and in spite of the rapid generation of loans, securitizers competed for the acquisition of raw loans to feed their securitization machines. Often an originator would have competing prospective purchasers on site with their respective due diligence teams reviewing mortgages so the securitizer could prepare a bid for a batch of mortgages. As one subprime executive from Irvine, California, put it, "From Monday to Thursday you would make the loans, put all the data in a spreadsheet, and send it to the [Wall] Street, and they'd call you back with their bids. By Friday your mistake would be in the marketplace."[5]

A second reason for lax diligence stemmed from the compensation system at the securitizers. Pay for managers was largely a function of volume, so they had strong incentives to acquire the mortgages that the securitizer needed to keep the securitization process rolling. Third, with the intensification of the subprime market ". . . Wall Street firms and their investor customers accepted increasing levels of default and fraud in sub-prime loans as they grew to trust software designed to offset those risks by charging higher interest rates, extra fees and penalties for paying off mortgages early."[6] Fourth, these incentives for workers at securitizing firms were not necessarily the same as those that motivated shareholders or the CEO. Many CEOs had a substantial portion of their monetary wealth and human capital tied to their firms, so their interests were at least fairly well-aligned with those of the shareholders and the firm as a whole. But CEOs also received compensation based on quarterly results in the form of salary, bonus, and stock-based incentive compensation, so their personal fortunes were not always completely aligned with the well-being of the firm. In some cases, this diversity of incentives may have led those with different roles in the securitizing firm to favor poor decisions about the quality of mortgages that they purchased.

The due diligence firms maintain that they did nothing wrong. Their job, they say, was to provide to the prospective purchaser the kind of review that was requested. In addressing the issue, the CEO of Clayton asserted that "The client really drives the process."[7] In early 2008, Andrew Cuomo, New York attorney general, granted Clayton Holdings immunity from civil and criminal prosecution in exchange for documents and testimony. If Clayton had liability, Cuomo apparently decided that they were less culpable than other parties, and he recruited Clayton to provide information on the securitizers to help investigate questions such as: Did the securitizers provide sufficient disclosure to the rating agencies and to the purchasers of the collateralized debt obligations (CDOs), or did the securitizer weaken standards and reduce the quality of the securities it was issuing while keeping that change a secret?[8]

Creating Securities and Obtaining Ratings

Chapter 2 offered a brief, nontechnical explanation of the process of securitization. In essence, a pool of mortgages promises a sequence of cash flows. The owner of that pool of mortgages issues a variety of new securities—the various tranches in a securitization. The promised cash flows from the new security are themselves based on the promised receipts from the mortgage pool. It is perfectly reasonable that some of the new securities can be less risky than the average risk of the mortgage pool, and it is also perfectly legitimate for the new securities to offer stated interest rates and maturities that differ from those payments that are scheduled to be received from the mortgage pool. By offering new securities that are better suited to the tastes and needs of the end investor with respect to risk, maturity, and coupon rates, the securitization process can create value. That is, the newly created tranches can have a value greater than the sum of the underlying mortgage values themselves. While this feat of financial engineering may seem magical, it is sound at base, and there is nothing inherently illegitimate, dishonest, or deceitful about the venture.[9]

Yet matters went horribly wrong, leading the world's economy to the brink of disaster, and securitized home mortgages are undeniably at the heart of the crisis. Not surprisingly, incentives are the key to understanding how matters developed, and the two key players at this juncture are the securitizer and the rating agency.

The securitizer's goal is to take an existing pool of home mortgages and use them as the raw ingredients to create a new portfolio of securities that has higher value. In the process, the profit is the value of the new securities, less the cost of acquiring the home mortgages, minus the cost of the securitization process. The securitization process is somewhat expensive in terms of the compensation paid to those who devise and market the new securities, but that cost is subsumed in the vast dollar amounts inherent in the securities themselves.

The securitizer surveys the market, analyzes its tastes and needs, and then offers various tranches of new securities. One key distinguishing feature of each tranche is its risk of default—the risk that the security will not make all of its promised payments in full and at the time promised. Creating a security that receives a triple-A rating (AAA from S&P or Fitch, or Aaa from Moody's) has long meant that a security has an extremely low risk of default.

So a triple-A security is worth considerably more than a double-A, all other matters being equal. To illustrate the importance of these ratings and their financial implications, figure 12.1 shows the difference in yields between bonds that receive a Aaa and a Baa from Moody's over recent years. The difference in yields has been about 1.2 percent historically. For a 30-year industrial bond, this implies a price difference of about 12 percent. So if an Aaa bond issue with a principal amount of $100 million sells at that full face value, an otherwise similar Baa issue would only fetch about $88 million. Of course, the difference in yields and prices for a triple-A versus a double-A would not be so great, yet it would still mean real money.

Given these financial realities, the securitizer typically intends to create a triple-A tranche, as well as others. To ensure that the particular tranche gets the coveted triple-A rating, enough of the payments from

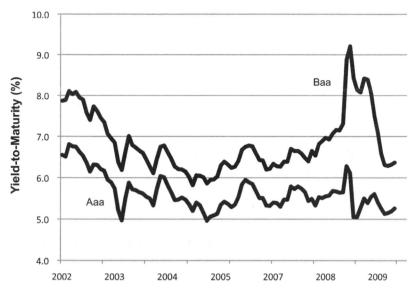

Figure 12.1 Aaa vs. Baa Industrial Bond Yields
Source: Federal Reserve Board. Data are available at: http://www.federalreserve.gov/
releases/h15/data/Monthly/H15_BAA_NA.txt

the mortgage pool must be dedicated to that tranche to garner the triple-
A rating. But how much is enough? The more that the securitizer commits to the triple-A tranche, the less cash flow is available to backstop
other tranches, so the securitizer's incentives are clear: the securitizer
wants to devote the least possible value to the triple-A tranche, while
still ensuring that it gets the desired rating. The same logic applies to the
other tranches with double-A and weaker ratings.

This is where the credit rating agency starts to play an active role. As
every new CDO that the securitizer creates must receive a rating, who
better to advise the securitizer on securing the desired rating than the
firm that will provide the rating? As a consequence of the obvious answer
to this question, credit rating agencies developed a huge business as
consultants to securitizers. Figure 2.2 captures this dual role, in which
the credit rating agency consults with the securitizer in the creation of
the CDO and also rates the CDO upon its creation.

The credit rating agencies seized this opportunity, and Moody's
can serve as an example of an explosion in this line of business. As a
benchmark, consider Moody's rating business for corporate debt issues
compared to the structured finance arena. In 1994, Moody's issued 2,747

corporate debt ratings, and this number grew steadily to a total of about 5,580 total corporate debt ratings in 2007.[10] In 1993, Moody's rated about 4,000 global structured finance issues, with about 90 percent of these applying to residential mortgage-backed securities issued in the United States. In 1993–2006, this business accelerated. In the peak year of 2006, Moody's rated about 29,000 total structured finance issues. Of these, about 20,000 were based on U.S. homes, and by this time securities based on home equity loans had become a big part of Moody's ratings business. With the onset of the financial crisis in 2007, new issues in structured finance fell to less than 20,000 total, and this number collapsed in 2008 to about 2,500, almost a 90 percent decrease in one year. Nonetheless, the total number of structured finance ratings outstanding at the beginning of 2008 exceeded 100,000; of these, about 61 percent were based on U.S. residential real estate mortgages, with another 9 percent being based on commercial property mortgages.[11] Both S&P and Fitch had a similar pattern of growth and decline in their number of ratings as well.

While the explosive growth of ratings for securitized instruments far outstripped that of corporate bonds, ratings for the two kinds of securities differed in another important dimension. For corporate bonds issued in 2007 and rated by Moody's, fewer than 4 percent earned a triple-A rating, and the most common rating was single-A, as panel A of figure 12.2 illustrates. For structured finance products, Panel B of figure 12.2 shows that the distribution was completely different. At the beginning of 2008, half of all structured products outstanding that Moody's had ever rated had a triple-A rating. Almost 60 percent were rated either triple- or double-A. Either a corporate triple-A was not the same as a triple-A for a securitized instrument, or the structured finance products that Wall Street had been fabricating were truly creations of genius.

At first, and for quite a while, it looked like geniuses really had been at work. Initially, the credit performance of structured products was at least as good as those of corporate bonds. Continuing to focus on those instruments rated by Moody's, from 1994 through 2008, the number of defaults in the corporate sector varied from a low of just 16 in 1994, to a high of 188 in 2001, with four of the highest years being concentrated in the years of the dot-com bubble (1999–2002). So for 2008, with 101 defaults and 5,580 ratings, the ratio of defaults occurring that year to the new ratings issued that year was less than 2 percent. On this measure, the worst year was 2001, with a ratio of defaults to new issues of 3.76 percent.[12]

Panel A

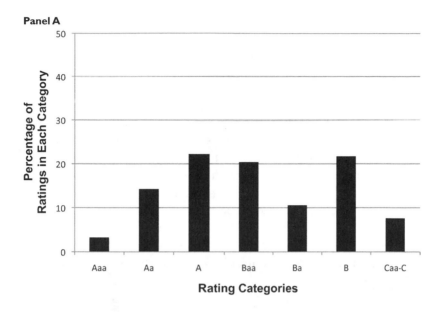

Rating Categories

Panel B

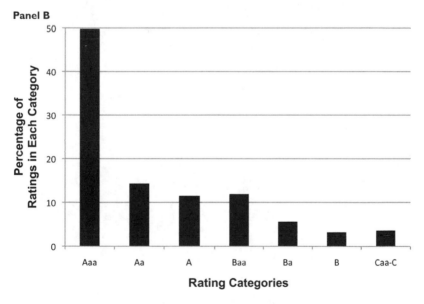

Rating Categories

Figure 12.2 Panel A—Distribution of Industrial Bond Ratings Panel B—Distribution of Structured Products Ratings
Source: Data are drawn from Moody's Investors Services, "Corporate Default and Recovery Rates, 1920-2008," February 2009, p. 49. Available at: http://www.moodys.com/cust/content/content.ashx?source=StaticContent/Free%20Pages/Credit%20Policy%20Research/documents/current/2007400000578875.pdf. Accessed February 13, 2010.

In the world of structured finance, Moody's defines an "impairment" as either an actual default—the failure to make an interest or principal payment as promised—or as a downgrade to Ca or C, indicating the expectation of an actual default. Table 12.1 shows the number of impairments in each year. In 1994, Moody's rated about 4,000 structured finance issuances and there were exactly three impairments. From 1994 to 2006, the business of rating structured securities accelerated tremendously, as we have seen, but the impairment rate was extremely low, never exceeding 300 impairments in a single year. For example, in that boom ratings year of 2006, the total number of impairments was only 105, with about 29,000 issuances, so the ratio of impairments to new ratings was about one-third of one percent. Thus, for the 1993–2006 period, the loss experience in structured finance was at least comparable to, and arguably better than, the default experience in the corporate sector. This remarkably light default experience suggested that all was going well.

Table 12.1

Defaults and Impairments for Corporate Issues and Structured Products Rated by Moody's Investors Services, 1994–2008

Year	Corporate Bond Defaults	Structured Finance Impairments
1994	16	3
1995	27	1
1996	17	17
1997	25	37
1998	50	25
1999	101	54
2000	126	50
2001	188	103
2002	145	276
2003	81	209
2004	38	235
2005	32	90
2006	31	105
2007	18	2,141
2008	101	12,666

Sources: Moody's Investors Services, "Corporate Default and Recovery Rates, 1920–2008," February 2009. Moody's Investors Services, "Default and Loss Rates of Structured Finance Securities: 1993–2008, August 2009. An 'impairment' is either a default (the failure to make a promised principal or interest payment) or a downgrade to Ca or C.

Starting in 2007, the number of impairments in structured finance exploded, rising almost 20 times over the 2006 experience. In 2008, matters became even worse, with more than 12,000 impairments, meaning that almost 12 percent of all rated global structured securities outstanding at the beginning of the year suffered an impairment. Of these impairments in 2008, 77 percent were based on residential mortgages in the United States, with over half of all impairments being based on U.S. home equity loans. In the disaster year of 2008, 65 percent of the impairments that occurred were for securities issued in the "go-go" years of 2005 and 2006, with 28 percent of the impairments occurring for securities that had been issued very recently in 2007, or for securities that had just been issued in 2008 and thus failed to make it a whole year before impairment.[13]

Thus the history of credit troubles for corporate debt issues and structured finance products started out similarly, but the experience leading into and through the financial crisis was completely different, with a sudden and massive acceleration in impairments starting in 2007 and pertaining mostly to securities of very recent issuance. While the early experience offered confirmation of the brilliance of financial engineering by the creation of so many highly rated securities, and while the low impairment rates seemed to validate the accuracy and reliability of the ratings process, the financial crisis revealed that something was rotten. Suddenly, it was hard to escape the conclusion that Wall Street had been grinding out garbage all along and that the rating agencies were saying that it all smelled as sweet as roses.

There are two leading explanations for how the ratings went so terribly wrong. A first account is that the ratings technology was flawed, even though it seemed to work correctly initially. Further, the surge in securitization created a boom business that was poorly managed and also led to inaccurate ratings. Second, some insist that the regulatory franchise granted to these agencies by their status as NRSROs gave these agencies (most importantly, S&P, Moody's, and Fitch) an oligopolistic position, and that these agencies used this privileged market position to amass huge profits by knowingly partnering with securitizers to provide the ratings that securitizers desired. These two explanations are complementary, and they actually work together to provide a pretty complete picture of the disaster that ratings became.

To begin to understand how the credit rating agencies could have been so wrong, consider this statement from Moody's *Code of Professional Conduct* from June 2005 as a representative posture of the industry:

Moody's Credit Ratings are based on information obtained by Moody's from sources believed by Moody's to be accurate and reliable, including but not limited to Issuers and their agents and advisors (e.g., accountants, legal counsel, and other experts). Moody's relies on Issuers and their agents to provide accurate, timely, and complete information.

Moody's has no obligation to perform, and does not perform, due diligence with respect to the accuracy of information it receives or obtains in connection with the rating process. Moody's does not independently verify any such information. Nor does Moody's audit or otherwise undertake to determine that such information is complete. Thus, in assigning a Credit Rating, Moody's is in no way providing a guarantee or any kind of assurance with regard to the accuracy, timeliness, or completeness of factual information reflected, or contained, in the Credit Rating or any related Moody's publication.[14]

In other words, Moody's, along with other credit rating agencies, merely accepts the information given to it by the issuer and bases its ratings on that information. As we have seen, the securities that performed so poorly in the financial crisis were complex instruments based on pools of underlying mortgages. In producing their ratings for such products, the credit rating agencies never examined the underlying mortgages themselves. The last examination of the mortgages conducted by any party were the frequently half-hearted due diligence efforts of firms hired by securitizers as they prepared to purchase the mortgages. By circumscribing the scope of their efforts, the credit rating agencies essentially ensured that they did not have proper information on which to base a rating that investors could regard as reliable. Because the entire rating process is based on information received from others and never tested by the agencies, the rating can only be as reliable as the information.

As a next step, the agencies applied their analytical models to the information as it has been provided to them. So the next potential problem lies in the quality of the analytical procedure applied by the agencies. If the analytical process is poor, the result of the rating will be suspect, even if the agencies receive full and accurate information as a starting gift from others.

In July 2008, the Securities and Exchange Commission (SEC) released its report on the performance of the credit rating agencies in the subprime debacle. This "Summary Report of Issues Identified in the Commission Staff's Examinations of Select Credit Rating Agencies" includes a fairly detailed description of the rating process, one which the report indicates is substantially similar at the three (unnamed) agencies it studied.[15] In essence, the process starts with information provided by the securitizer, and this information is fed into a quantitative analytical model developed by the agency. The agency then performs various scenario analyses and stress tests to determine how well the security is likely to perform under stress, and then the agency further examines the capital structure (i.e., all the tranches) of the security.

Next, the agency would then report to the securitizer, or arranger, a preliminary conclusion about the rating of the security. At this point: "The arranger could accept that determination and have the trust issue the securities with the proposed capital structure and the lower rating or adjust the structure to provide the requisite credit enhancement for the senior tranche to get the desired highest rating."[16] After the securitizer's adjustment to secure the desired rating, if any, the agency finishes a cash flow analysis and issues a rating.

The SEC "Report" also documents that agencies typically did not have written policies about how to rate these securities, had difficulties in adapting to the increased volume and complexity of the new instruments they were rating, made adjustments to the rating that were inconsistent with their own quantitative models, and that they lacked policies and procedures to identify, address, and correct errors in their methods and quantitative models. Beyond the SEC "Report," additional information about flaws in the ratings process have come to light. In 2008 the *Financial Times* reported: "Moody's awarded incorrect triple-A ratings to billions of dollars worth of a type of complex debt product due to a bug in its computer models, a *Financial Times* investigation has discovered. Internal Moody's documents seen by the *FT* show that some senior staff within the credit agency knew early in 2007 that products rated the previous year had received top-notch triple-A ratings and that, after a computer coding error was corrected, their ratings should have been up to four notches lower."[17] Further, Moody's acknowledged violating its own code of conduct in rating some complex European securities, and S&P also discovered errors in the models it used to rate some debt obligations.[18]

Given the vast number of defaults and impairments, plus the evidence presented in the SEC "Report" and in other sources, it seems fair to say that the processes followed by the agencies proved defective in serious respects. One potential explanation for these deficiencies stems from the explosive growth in the ratings business. From 1986 to 1995 the number of analysts working at S&P went from 40 to 800, with similar growth at Moody's, and from 1975 to 1999 the number of issues rated by Moody's went from 600 per year to more than 20,000 per year, with similar growth at S&P.[19] Not surprisingly, given this surge, the SEC "Report" concluded that ". . . some of the rating agencies appear to have struggled with the growth."[20]

However, there are aspects of the credit rating agencies' performance that are more disturbing than failed processes and an inability to manage the happy problem of surging demand for services. In its investigation, the SEC uncovered disturbing evidence of malfeasance as well as error. The "Report" includes portions of intra-staff e-mails from credit rating agencies. Quoting from the SEC "Report": "One analyst expressed concern that her firm's model did not capture 'half' of the deal's risk, but that 'it could be structured by cows and we would rate it'"; "In another email an analytical manager in the same rating agency's CDO group wrote to a senior analytical manager that the rating agencies continue to create an 'even bigger monster—the CDO market. Let's hope we are all wealthy and retired by the time this house of cards falters.'"[21]

One key to this apparent malfeasance stems from the blatant conflicting incentives faced by a credit rating agency that opines on the structuring of the security, rates the security, and is paid for both services by the issuer of the security. The SEC "Report" spends considerable time on this issue—one it explicitly calls a conflict of interest—and points out: "While each rating agency has policies and procedures restricting analysts from participating in fee discussions with issuers, these policies still allowed key participants in the ratings process to participate in fee discussions"; "Analysts [at the credit rating agencies] appear to be aware, when rating an issuer, of the rating agency's business interest in securing the rating of the deal"; and "Rating agencies do not appear to take steps to prevent considerations of market share and other business interests from the possibility that they could influence ratings or ratings criteria."[22] Of course, much prior to the SEC "Report" this blatant conflict of interest on the part of the rating agencies was well known, and perhaps best analyzed by Frank Partnoy.[23] Given the huge profit potential of the ratings process and the very lucrative profits realized by the rating agencies, as documented in figure 10.2 in chapter 10, the seriousness of these conflicts of interest is clear.

To the Ultimate Investor

For good or ill, the new securities at this point in the process are created, rated, issued, and ready for the investor. For the most part, the ultimate purchasers of these securities were financial institutions, investment companies, hedge funds, and municipalities. Few of these complex securities were purchased directly by individuals, except for the very wealthy. However, millions of individuals owned pieces of these securitized mortgages indirectly through investment in retirement plans and investment companies. Ownership of a mutual fund, participation in a retirement plan, or coverage under a pension fund made indirect ownership of these securities an incredibly widespread phenomenon. The failure of this market had direct investment impacts on all of these millions of people, beyond the economic effects suffered around the world by all, without regard to whether they invested in securitized mortgages, even indirectly.

We have seen that mortgage originators such as Countrywide, Washington Mutual, and Indymac carried subprime mortgages, mortgage-backed securities (MBS), and collateralized mortgage obligations (CMOs) on their own books. For these firms, losses were particularly intense in the instruments at the simpler end of the scale—mortgages that they failed to sell or chose to hold in their own portfolio, along with some more straightforward MBS. However, they also held some more complex securities such as CMOs. For example, Countrywide reported $3.3 billion of CMOs on their books at the end of 2006 and still held $2 billion of these instruments even at the end of 2007. For its part, Washington Mutual held $225 billion in mortgage-backed securities at the end of 2006, but does not distinguish which portion of these might be CMOs—in fact, their 10-K report for 2006 does not even mention such instruments.

Among investment banks, CMOs were a way of life. One of the big events that brought the financial crisis to public attention starting in June 2007 was the attempt by Bear Stearns to save its hedge funds that were facing difficulties. The names of the funds say it all: "Bear Stearns High-Grade Structured Credit Fund" and "Bear Stearns High-Grade Structured Credit Enhanced Leverage Fund." With these funds held off its balance sheets up until this time, Bear had been reporting less than $1 billion in exposure to these collateralized obligations. When they became an obvious part of Bear, the firm's exposure to CMOs and CDOs became palpable. In 2006, Lehman showed $219 billion in collateralized agreements as assets, along with $170 billion in collateralized financing, making their net exposure to CMOs and CDOs far from clear. Only in the first quarter did Lehman indicate that it actually had $6.5 billion in CDO exposure. At that time, at least one web site oriented toward finance professionals seriously questioned even that admission.[24]

At this late date, there is little point in attempting to ascertain the actual exposure of investment banks to these assets that have proven to be so toxic. The financial landscape is littered with the remains of these firms, and the recollection that the original purpose of the $700 billion TARP program was to purchase toxic assets from financial institutions is powerful testimony to the size of their holdings of these kinds of instruments.

While it is easy to say that these originators and packagers of sub-prime got what they deserved when their own financial excesses made them fail, there are many other less sophisticated and more removed investors who were also harmed or destroyed. Brief accounts of two investors and their woes gives a flavor of the lack of sophistication of many investors and illustrates how quickly and completely a "stretch for yield" led to investment disaster.

One of the most poignant and colorful of these investors was the municipality of Narvik, Norway, which was featured on the CNBC special "House of Cards" and also receives a chapter of attention in David Faber's excellent book, *And Then the Roof Caved In*.[25] Faber tells how he traveled to Narvik, a town inside the Arctic Circle that was the scene of an important battle in World War II, to meet with the mayor and learn of Narvik's foray into the deep waters of international finance.

Faber learned that Narvik tried to stretch its budget by borrowing money to invest in high-yielding securities. To obtain the loan, Narvik pledged its future tax revenues, and based on this excellent collateral, it was able to borrow very cheaply. Relying on advice from the Norwegian brokerage firm Terra Securities, Narvik decided to invest in very safe triple-A instruments based on CDOs that were marketed by Citigroup. Thus, it would make a spread between the higher return on the CDO-based instruments and its own borrowing cost.

When the investment started to go bad, Narvik quickly lost $15 million, a quarter of its annual budget. Before its problems ran their course, Narvik was forced to close school classrooms, reduce personnel at the local nursing home, and close the museum dedicated to the battle of Narvik. As it turned out, Narvik had thought its investment was tied to subprime. As Narvik learned from David Faber's investigation, it was not invested in mortgages. Instead, it had unknowingly invested in a CDO based on other CDOs—and the securities it actually purchased were not even triple-A after all.

While Narvik's story is a sad one, and one that could be replicated around the world many times, it must be acknowledged that part of the blame for this catastrophe lies at the feet of these unsophisticated ultimate investors. First, in many instances these investors, like Narvik, made investments that they completely failed to understand, thereby violating the first and most fundamental rule of investing. Second, many investors in subprime and other instruments "stretched for yield" and tried to capture a yield differential. If a corporate bond and a CDO are both rated triple-A, but one yields considerably more than the other, a more circumspect investor might become suspicious. The higher yield on the CDO just might signal a higher level of risk. All too many investors merely observed the solid credit rating and grabbed the higher yield, thinking they were getting a free investment lunch. In doing so, they committed a second grave error, refusing to recognize that something that was too good to be true certainly wasn't.

Narvik was far from alone as an investor in over its head. In 2006 the school board in Whitefish Bay, Wisconsin, met to seek a way to meet its obligation to the teachers' retirement plan. Their investment adviser, Dave Noack, recommended a low risk investment, a CDO that would generate a quarterly payment that would be very safe—telling the board that there would have to be 15 Enrons for the investment to lose money. Noack described the CDO as a "collection of bonds from 105 of the most reputable companies." Based on Noack's guidance, the school board at Whitefish Bay and four other nearby school districts amassed $200 million, $165 million borrowed from a bank in Ireland, combined with $35 million of their own funds.

Dave Noack had only received two hours of training in CDOs, but nonetheless the five school boards relied on him in going forward. Acknowledging that he had not read the prospectus, one board member said: "We had all our questions answered satisfactorily by Dave Noack, so I wasn't worried." The actual investment of the $200 million went into a synthetic CDO that effectively insured the corporate bonds of more than 100 firms. Defaults by these corporations would mean that the school boards could lose part or all of their $200 million, and a default rate of 6 percent on the corporate bonds would imply a complete loss of all invested funds for the boards. If there were no defaults, the total cash inflows, less the financing cost for the borrowed $165 million, would be about $1.8 million per year. This compared with a $1.5 million annual return on investing their own $35 million in Treasury securities. In effect, the boards had "stretched for yield," hoping to get $1.8 million per year, rather than $1.5 million. In the process, they had agreed to bear a certain amount of risk—a negligible risk, according to their adviser.

The safety of the investment ultimately depended on the performance of the corporations whose bonds the school boards were effectively guaranteeing. These corporations included GE, 3M, and Exxon Mobil, but also in the mix were Lehman Brothers, Washington Mutual, Fannie Mae, and Freddie Mac. As these firms defaulted, collapsed, or received credit rating downgrades, the value of the school boards' investment shrank, losing 90–95 percent of its value, implying a loss of $180–190 million. This not only wiped out the boards' own $35 million, but most of the borrowed $165 million as well.

As the fiasco came to public attention, it not surprisingly caused an uproar in the affected Wisconsin communities. One teacher asked, "If millions of dollars are gone, what happens to my retirement? Or the construction paper and pencils and supplies we need to teach?" Shawn Yde, the director of business services in the Whitefish Bay district, says: "The local papers and radio shows call us idiots, and now when I go home, my kids ask me, 'Dad, did you do something wrong?' This is something I'll regret until the day I die."

Facing a desperate situation, the school boards sued the investment banking firm that recommended the investment, Stifel Nicolaus, but refrained from suing Dave Noack, who is cooperating with the boards in their litigation effort. The boards seek to have the entire investment rescinded on the grounds that the boards were not "accredited investors" or "qualified institutional buyers." In early 2010, the judge presiding in the case refused to dismiss the charges against Stifel Nicolaus, clearing the way for the matter to go to trial.[26]

Incentives from Securitizers to Ultimate Investors

The chain of perverse incentives that characterized the beginning of the securitization chain continues through the second half of the chain as well, from packager, to due diligence firm, to rating agency, to the ultimate investor. The securitizer has an incentive to buy the bad mortgages that the originators created, because the securitizer expects to package them and pass them on to the ultimate investor. The due diligence firm has incentives to bless all manner of poor mortgages because those arc the instructions, whether explicit or implicit, that it receives from its client, the securitizer. The credit rating agency knows that it will profit by cooperating with the securitizer, because cooperation brings a double payday. The agency makes a buck when it helps the securitizer design a security that just barely gets a desired rating, and it gets paid again when it provides the rating. The ultimate investor appears to make out well, too, by securing a higher return than would otherwise be obtainable for bearing a given level of apparent risk. This appearance of good financial wisdom holds for all of the ultimate investors—the originator that consumes its own product, the securitizer that eats its own cooking, and the outside investor, like Narvik, that stretches for a higher yield— at least until a financial crisis reveals the folly in which all these investors were engaged.

Causes of the Financial Crisis: Financial Innovation, Poor Risk Management, and Excessive Leverage

As we have seen, the OTD model of mortgage production brought a system of complex incentives into the businesses of mortgage lending and mortgage investing. This process expanded the size of mortgage lending and brought new investment vehicles into play. Three fairly technical developments played important enabling roles in making the financial crisis the huge disaster that it has proven to be. First, the development of complex new financial instruments—the collateralized debt obligation (CDO) and the credit default swap (CDS)—offered methods for investing, taking risk, and managing risk that proved to be opaque to external observers and poorly understood even by those most intimately involved in creating and managing these new instruments. Second, at the outset of the mortgage securitization surge in the late 1990s and early 2000s, financial firms succeeded in developing more sophisticated mathematical techniques of measuring and managing risk. While these risk management methods were elegant, the financial crisis proved that they had some real-world limitations that would contribute to disaster. Third, the opportunity to recycle capital through mortgage securitization, combined with an overweening confidence in the sophistication of risk management techniques, encouraged financial firms to take more risk, which they did with glee and for great profit—at least in the early years of the 21st century.

Financial Innovation and the Creation of Complex Instruments

Of the many problems that plagued financial firms in the early twenty-first century, one that is somewhat less important was the development of complex financial instruments. These new instruments are less important because they are merely tools that firms used inappropriately to contribute to their own destruction, rather than being flawed instruments that lie at the heart of the financial crisis. The two most prominent new financial instruments that played a role in the financial crisis fall into two families—collateralized debt obligations (CDOs) and credit default swaps (CDS).

It is not at all unusual for new financial powers or new financial instruments to lead to troubles. Starting in the 1980s, the granting of new powers to savings and loan (S&L) institutions in the United States was quickly followed by those S&Ls engaging in lines of business that they understood only poorly. Not surprisingly, their ruin followed in many instances, and the United States suffered the S&L crisis of the 1980s.

The development of more robust financial options and futures contracts in the 1980s led quickly to the stock market crash of 1987, in which the theoretically elegant risk management technique of portfolio insurance (which utilizes futures and options) proved to create additional risk in real markets under some circumstances. Similarly, the debacle of Long Term Capital Management (LTCM) featured Myron Scholes and Robert Merton, two Nobel economic laureates, among its principals. LTCM essentially came to ruin by pushing perfectly valid financial theory beyond its practical limits with excessive leverage.[1] Compared with the powers and instruments featured in these earlier debacles, CDOs and CDS are much more complex, and the entire financial system was already rendered more fragile by its increased complexity, as Richard Bookstaber eloquently explained just before the onset of the crisis in his *Demon of Our Own Design*.

The mathematics of CDOs are complex, yet the essential potential problems of CDOs are apparent without deep mathematical understanding.[2] The entire process of securitization allows the rapid recycling of a lender's capital, so a given capital base can support much more lending in a market that permits securitization than would be possible otherwise. We have seen the beneficial effects that this can have on the expansion of home ownership through the extensive use of one type of CDO, the collateralized mortgage obligation (CMO). Because the creation of a CMO allows ownership of fractions of many mortgages, this kind of securitization can have important risk management benefits. By participating in a CMO, an investor can effectively hold exposure to many mortgages diversified by home type, price level, and location. In normal circumstances, a portfolio of so many diverse underlying exposures should have less risk than a commitment of the same amount to a single property.

However, the diversification and risk management advantages of CMOs helped to induce investors to believe they could bear a much higher degree of leverage with these new instruments. Further, the inherent complexity of a CMO means that mortgage defaults are much more difficult to resolve than would be the case with a simple mortgage. If a bank lends to a home owner and holds the mortgage in its own portfolio, the ownership of the mortgage is clear, and the bank is free to negotiate with the particular debtor who defaults. The bank may allow new terms or seize the collateral at its choice. However, with a CMO, a default on a property that is embedded in the CMO is a problem for all CMO investors. Further, almost all investors in a CMO have very little information and even less say about how the delinquency or default should be resolved.

A typical CMO might have hundreds of investors, each with a very indirect claim on a fraction of the cash flow from each of the properties in the pool of mortgages that supports the CMO. As a result, if a mortgagor in the United States defaults and the mortgage is part of a mortgage pool that supports a CMO, the resolution of that default affects all of the investors in that CMO. Of course, some municipality in Europe might be one of the CMO investors, and they would have essentially no information about that particular property or the defaulting mortgagor. Further, with so many investors being affected, they are sure to have divergent interests and opinions about how the default should be resolved. For example, should the mortgage be restructured or should the property be seized and resold?

As mortgage markets came under stress in 2007, it became increasingly clear that the methods for managing these mortgages and the securities built upon them were completely inadequate. The servicer of the mortgage is the point of contact with the mortgagor, but servicers were ill-equipped to handle the demands of so many defaults, and the methods for properly resolving such defaults were not adequately established in advance.

Nothing illustrates the point of carelessness and poor management in the securitization process as well as the simplest matter of paperwork—the maintenance of records to show who owns a particular mortgage.[3] When a mortgage is sold to a pool, there must be an adequate record of that transfer. However, it appears that ". . . the vast flow of notes into the maw of the securitization industry meant that a lot of mistakes were made."[4] That is, the paperwork was not maintained properly. Later, when a home owner defaults and the owner of the mortgage seeks redress, the owner of the mortgage must be able to prove title to the mortgage. As it turns out, in many cases the paperwork has been lost—"perhaps a third of the notes 'securitized' have been lost or destroyed."[5] Further, judges are becoming more demanding of proof, perhaps in sympathy with the plight of home owners slipping into the abyss of delinquency and default.

For example, in Miami, Florida, a home had been foreclosed and repossessed by Chevy Chase Bank, which claimed to own the mortgage note on the house for $225,000. However, the bank was unable to prove ownership, and the judge in the case intervened and allowed the home owner to remain in the home.[6] This sloppiness is not a small matter: "Depending on the documentation defect, lawyers say, investors in the trust could try to force the institution that sold the loan to the trust to buy it back. Many of these institutions would be unable to do so, however, because they are defunct. In the meantime, when judges are not persuaded that the documentation is proper, troubled borrowers can remain in their homes even if they are delinquent."[7]

Thus, the complexity of CMOs was poorly managed from the outset, both in the "small" matter of recordkeeping, but also in the essential design of the instruments. As we will see later in the context of risk management, the entire design of CMOs is predicated on the idea of diversification and a lack of correlation among the underlying mortgage instruments. When property values in many diverse locales fell at the same time, these beliefs about correlation proved false, and simple defects, such as poor recordkeeping, were magnified by the complexity of the instruments.

Along with CMOs, credit default swaps (CDS) were the other principal financial innovation that caused trouble in the crisis. Simple in concept, CDS are nonetheless complex to price and manage.[8] As Gerald

Corrigan, former president of the New York Federal Reserve Bank, noted: "Anyone who thinks they understand this stuff is living in la la land."[9] The CDS also had the honor of being described as "the bet that blew up Wall Street" in a segment of *60 Minutes*. Credit default swaps came to the most concentrated public attention with the collapse and rescue of AIG. In bailing out AIG, the federal government supplied it with many billions of dollars, principally to allow it to fulfill its obligations on CDS contracts it had written on financial firms that were themselves failing, as we have seen in some detail in chapter 7.

If we evaluate the causal role of CDS in the crisis, it seems fairly clear that they had little or nothing to do with causing the financial difficulties that began to beset firms in late 2007, but it also seems apparent that they were important in exacerbating the systemic effects of the crisis. Unexpected cash flows come into play on a CDS only when a firm defaults and the protection seller has to pay, or when an insured firm comes under stress and the protection seller has to post additional collateral. Both of these events arose for AIG.

In September 2008, virtually all major U.S. financial firms were in significant distress. AIG was forced to post additional collateral for some of the CDS contracts it had written even before Lehman filed for bankruptcy. Later, the failure of Lehman Brothers led to massive flows on CDS contracts in two ways. First, in many CDS contracts, the protection seller essentially promises to purchase securities if a "credit event" (default, bankruptcy, conservatorship, or so on) occurs. According to one source, CDS losses triggered by the Lehman default were $300–$400 billion, and one German bank apparently received $1 billion in face value of Lehman bonds in fulfillment of a CDS contract at a time when the bonds were only worth $30 million in the market. Second, beyond actual deliveries of bonds and payment for them, there is a second manner of settling CDS contracts, used mainly by dealers and hedge funds, and that is by a process of netting in an auction. The outcome of the auction is that only the difference between the value of the CDS promise and the current value of the bonds is paid. Apparently, this method of settling the Lehman CDS involved about $6 billion.[10] Thus, the actual effect of Lehman's bankruptcy on CDS flows fell somewhere between $6 and $400 billion.

As these figures show, even in the aftermath of Lehman's default, the true exposure is extremely difficult to gauge. In the heat of the crisis, many involved parties had little idea as to whether those who would owe on the CDS contracts could honor their obligations. Further, if the protection writer failed to perform, what would happen to the financial position of the protection buyer who was holding the underlying defaulted securities?

The Lehman default emphasized this uncertainty. When it defaulted, Lehman had about $600 billion in outstanding debt, and the total volume of outstanding CDS contracts with Lehman debt as the reference entity totaled somewhere in the range of $400–$500 billion. But market participants generally did not know which other financial institutions held positions among these hundreds of billions of dollars of obligations. Further, some unknown amount of these contracts involved positions that would be netted out—that is, a particular firm might have been a protection seller for one counterparty and a protection buyer in a second contract with a different counterparty. Such a firm would have a smaller net position than it might at first appear, and it might not be in such a deep risk position—if both of the two CDS contracts were honored in full.

But, of course, a key problem was the lack of transparency in this market. No one really knew who owed what amount to whom. Further, because of the general financial stress and great uncertainty, various banks had little idea which other institutions would be in a position to honor their obligations. In the course of events, all CDS contracts were honored, but this was probably due only to the governmental funds extended to AIG and other institutions that allowed them to keep their CDS promises. As former Secretary of the Treasury Hank Paulson noted, "If any company defined systemic risk, it was AIG, with its $1 trillion balance sheet and massive derivatives business connecting it to hundreds of financial institutions, governments, and companies around the world."[11]

Thus, CDS instruments may not have caused the financial crisis, but they certainly appear to have exacerbated the uncertainty that paralyzed the credit markets in late 2008 and threatened to lead to a meltdown of the entire system. Even though CDS contracts did not cause the crisis, they made it worse than otherwise would have been the case, and they almost certainly caused the federal outlays to be larger than they otherwise would have been.

The AIG bailout has continued to cause anguish ever since it occurred. Much of the public became enraged that much of the federal money that went to AIG was used to pay banks that were viewed as miscreants in the crisis, including many foreign banks. For his part, Bernanke said in Senate testimony in 2009: "I think if there's a single episode in this entire eighteen months that has made me more angry, I can't think of one, than AIG."[12]

Faced with displeasure from the public and Congress, the understanding of the purpose (or at least the explanation) of the AIG bailout has also morphed. The original view was the one given above—that AIG's massive counterparty risk through its opaque CDS contracts was the issue that threatened the financial system. However, in late 2009, a contradictory explanation emerged from the office of the inspector general for the TARP. Now the real problem was said to be the vast number of ordinary insurance policies that AIG had written around the world, and Treasury Secretary Geithner now claims that "the financial condition of the counterparties was not a relevant factor."[13] Yet others point out that these insurance contracts were generally covered by separate capitalization and would not have been at risk from AIG's problems with its CDS. Perhaps the real motivation for the bailout of AIG—probably the most controversial of all expenditures of federal monies in the crisis—will never be known.

▰▰▰ Poor Risk Management

There is an emerging discipline of risk management—enterprise risk management—which attempts to develop a unified framework for managing all types of risk. While there are numerous possible taxonomies of risk, one standard risk grouping especially connected with financial institutions is to think of risks as falling into one of three risk "buckets"—market risk, credit risk, or operational risk. This approach is codified by the Basel II risk framework and is used in formulating capital requirements for financial institutions, particularly in rich industrial countries outside the United States.[14] Prior to the financial crisis, risk managers believed that market risk management was sophisticated, well developed, and could serve as a model that other areas of risk management could strive to match. Today, that illusion has been shattered.

The long history of risk management can be read as a struggle to bring quantification to this critical endeavor, a story that Peter Bernstein tells in his excellent account, *Against the Gods*.[15] In the years running up to the financial crisis, many in the field thought that the practice of risk management was making remarkable strides, and much mathematical risk measurement had been incorporated into the risk management framework used by financial institutions and the rules that regulators imposed on those same institutions.

Foremost among those approaches has been *Value-at-Risk* (VaR), a method that measures risk with the following kind of precision for a portfolio and allows statements such as: "There is an x percent probability that losses on this portfolio will not exceed $y over the next z days" or similarly, "We can be 95 percent confident that our portfolio will not incur a loss greater than 5 percent of its value over the next 10 days."[16] The computations necessary to make such a statement are complex. In essence, computing the VaR of a large portfolio requires estimating the level of risk of each constituent security, along with understanding how the future returns of each security are correlated with those of the other securities in the portfolio. Always controversial, VaR nonetheless became the most standard and universally accepted technique of quantitative financial risk management.

VaR has been most trenchantly criticized by Nassim Taleb in his book *The Black Swan*. Taleb charges the finance profession with an excessive reliance on the assumption that asset returns follow a normal distribution, generally a key assumption in the application of VaR. It has long been well-accepted that asset returns are not normally distributed, and that there is a greater chance of extreme events (big losses or big gains) than a normal distribution would suggest. This is the phenomenon of "fat tails"—the tails of a graph of the normal distribution underestimate the chance of events far away from the mean, and the correctly rendered graph of the distribution of security returns would show more area of the total probability distribution at the extremes. However, the use of the assumptions of the normal distribution seemed appropriate nonetheless, because it was thought that the normal distribution was a sufficiently close approximation to the unknown "true" distribution of security returns. Further, the mathematics associated with the normal distribution are well-understood, and there is essentially no well-behaved mathematical method of dealing with the true distribution of security returns, even if we knew what the true distribution might be.

For Taleb, however, relying on technologies that are built on an assumption of normality, such as VaR, merely asks for trouble. In his metaphor, a black swan is a completely unanticipated discovery that is beyond the bounds of previous experience. (Europeans thought all swans were white, but were disabused of this prejudice when they arrived in Australia.) Taleb likens such reliance on the normal distribution to "picking up nickels in front of a steamroller." Everything goes well and many nickels are collected, until the day one fails to evade the steamroller. That is, when markets perform in the normal range, VaR works well to generate small reliable returns, but when an extreme event occurs—a black swan arrives or the steamroller catches the gatherer of nickels—the normal techniques of risk management fail completely at the moment of greatest need. The collapse of housing prices and the ensuing financial crisis certain qualify as black swan or steamroller events.[17]

The large sophisticated commercial banks and the Wall Street investment banks pushed the mathematical technology of risk management far beyond VaR. For the last 30 years, much of the hiring on Wall Street has been focused on brilliant physicists and mathematicians, who have been deployed to devise trading and risk management strategies. As noted above, the 1987 crash has largely been attributed to "portfolio insurance"—a technique built on the Black-Scholes option pricing model, and the LTCM debacle was a second harvest of bitter fruit from the financial technology revolution. These harsh experiences proved no impediment to increasing quantification of trading strategies and risk management regimes.[18]

The publication of an article that was to prove instrumental in extending mathematically based risk management techniques to portfolios of mortgage-backed securities of all kinds occurred shortly after the LTCM debacle. David X. Li, born Xiang Lin in China, worked on Wall Street in the 1990s and well into the twenty-first century. In 2000, he published a paper in *The Journal of Fixed Income* entitled "On Default Correlation: A Copula Function Approach." This article had been circulating previously in various versions as a working paper, and was already well-known before its formal publication in 2000.

In essence, the paper provided a way to compute the probabilities that two or more assets would default at the same time. Li started with an actuarial problem from the world of life insurance. The probability of any 50-year old dying in the next year is quite small (about 0.6 percent), but given that a 50-year old spouse dies, the probability that the surviving spouse will die within the next year goes up considerably. Thus, the probability of the two deaths are correlated. Similarly, the probability of multiple defaults of related financial instruments defaulting over a given period depends very much on the default correlation among those assets. Li's big contribution was the devising of an elegant mathematical model to assess those default probabilities.

Like all mathematical models, it was built on assumptions, and its practical application required data inputs from the real world.

The assumptions used to derive the model and the real-world inputs to apply the model provide two sources of possible error. First, if the assumptions that are key to deriving the model do not match the real world pretty well, the application of the model to practical problems will be fraught with error. Second, the real-world inputs to the model must be derived from past experience or present understanding. If these inputs do not match the unknown experience to occur in the future reasonably well, the model may give faulty predictions.

Li's model was built on assumptions of normal distributions, a limitation of which he and many others were aware, and an assumption that Li acknowledged as a limitation of his approach. In fact, Li very clearly emphasized these limitations of his model in his article. This is not a fault with the model—every mathematical model of the world is built on assumptions that are necessary to secure any kind of result. This is highly analogous to Galileo's and Newton's approaches to physics, with their assumptions that the study of events in a vacuum and without friction could still have important real world uses.

For inputs to his model, Li recommended that his model should not be used with historical data, such as Moody's published survival statistics for bonds. Rather, he urged that the inputs should be based on current market information, because "This current market information reflects the market agreed perception about the evolution of the market in the future, on which actual profit and loss depend. The default rate derived from current market information may be much different that historical default rates. . . . In practice we usually use market spread information to derive the distribution of survival times."[19] Using historical information implicitly assumes that the future will be like the past. Using current market information implicitly assumes that the future will be like what we now expect it to be. Again, Li was completely aware of this limitation and said of his model: "The most dangerous part is when people believe everything coming out of it."[20]

So the model had two inherent limitations: its reliance on the normal distribution and its implicit assumption that the future default experience would be similar to what traders now expected it to be. But the model gave *answers*, and it could be put into operation. The model quickly swept Wall Street, and in 2004, Moody's incorporated Li's mathematical approach into its rating model for CDOs.[21] So now

Moody's was estimating CDO default probabilities based to a considerable extent on what the market thought those default probabilities were at a given moment. To the extent that ratings were based on this mathematical model, the future was now predicted to be like whatever the market thought it would be, as expressed in prices that prevail at a given moment.

As is now all too obvious, the future turned out to be very much unlike the past and almost completely different from the market expectations that prevailed at the beginning of 2007. Of course, a few people foresaw problems, but their views were subsumed by the much more dominant expectations of continuing house price gains. Market prices continued to reflect this rosy expectation—or at least that was what market prices were telling the market—until prices suddenly starting shouting a quite different forecast in 2007.

Equipped with a mathematical model, with its apparently precise measurement of risk, reliance on such a tool seemed only wise. Further, if one had great confidence in the precision of risk measurement, then one could reasonably expand operations to the bounds of what the model indicated was safe. Thus, the market came to rely all too heavily on its mathematical risk models, and this dependence encouraged an expansion of leverage that was to prove disastrous. In short, financial institutions adopted risk management principles that ignored judgment and common sense in favor of theoretical elegance and mathematical precision, even though the intellectual limitations of that approach were well understood and clearly expressed by those who developed those sophisticated techniques.

Excessive Leverage

We have seen in chapter 10 how prudential regulation failed to restrain investment banks from increasing their leverage in the early years and how the investment banks rushed to take advantage of this weakened regulatory regime by markedly expanding their leverage ratios in the run-up to 2007. Similarly, we explored how a lax regulatory regime allowed the widespread use of off-balance-sheet financing with its fiction that the parents were somehow not really responsible for their offspring. This ability to keep substantial portions of their risky positions off the books of the parent allowed these firms to reduce their holdings of capital and to increase their leverage.

A further incitement to greater leverage stemmed from the excessive confidence that firms placed in their supposedly rigorous risk management regimes, and part of this risk management hubris stemmed from the utilization of complex mathematical models that at least gave the appearance of exact measurement and control of risk. Even though much of this increased leverage was made possible by weak regulation, no firm was forced to use extreme leverage and take enormous risks, yet the major firms universally did so, no doubt in large part because they were so confident of their risk management expertise.

Figure 10.1 in chapter 10 illustrates how the five major investment banks increased their leverage from 2002 to 2007. But as we have seen in chapter 6, even Goldman and Morgan Stanley were forced to change their corporate form and become bank holding companies. Figure 13.1 shows this buildup in leverage for Goldman Sachs and Morgan Stanley, but it also shows the massive deleveraging for these firms that characterized the entire financial industry from the end of 2007 to the end of 2009. Both Goldman Sachs and Morgan Stanley cut their leverage ratios in half, with the major drop occurring in the final quarter of 2008 as they became bank holding companies. Bank of America, which was a bank holding company throughout the period, appears in Figure 13.1 to provide a basis of comparison. At the end

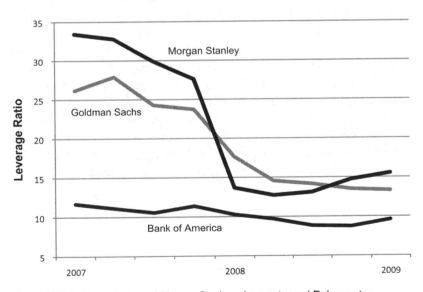

Figure 13.1 Goldman Sachs and Morgan Stanley—Leveraging and Deleveraging
Source: Financial statements of respective firms for various years, all available at SEC.gov.

of 2009, Goldman Sachs and Morgan Stanley were still more highly leveraged than Bank of America, but the differences were much smaller than previously.

The history of reports from firms that were bank holding companies over this entire period does not show a similar pattern of increasing and falling leverage, but they were actually experiencing quite an analogous pattern in reality, even if it was not quite as severe. Bank holding companies (e.g., Citigroup, JPMorgan Chase, Bank of America) were subject to tighter capital regulations than investment banks over the entire period. Consequently, these holding companies had to report a position in compliance with the more rigorous capital requirements that applied to depository institutions, and they always reported capital positions that complied with regulations. Nonetheless, for these firms their true leverage was much higher than they reported, because so many risky assets were held in structured-investment vehicles (SIVs) and not reported on the books of the bank holding company. This practice was understood and permitted by regulatory authorities, so such reports were not dishonest in the fullest sense, even though they understated the true risk position of the firms.

Citigroup is the best exemplar of this practice and problem. Near the end of 2007, Citi was the largest sponsor of SIVs in the world and held no equity in them. In the fall of 2007, these entities had assets in the range of $80–100 billion, with undisclosed liabilities. At year end 2007, Citi took $49 billion of its SIVs assets back onto the books of the parent, with a dramatic effect on its reported leverage and the consequential necessity of raising new capital to maintain its mandated capital ratios.[22]

Why, then, did virtually all major financial institutions in the United States adopt such high leverage, with all of the risk that such a strategy implies? Beyond the belief that their risk management systems were bulletproof, we can look to the incentives that the Wall Street compensation schemes gave to their top executives and managers, and we can consider the effectiveness of corporate governance for these firms as well.

Causes of the Financial Crisis: Executive Compensation and Poor Corporate Governance

If there is any delightful irony in the entire financial fiasco that we have all endured, it is the realization that some of the firms that perpetrated bad mortgages and worse financial instruments also suffered their own demise (Countrywide Financial, Washington Mutual, IndyMac, Wachovia, Bear Stearns, Lehman Brothers, Merrill Lynch, and many others), reduction to zombie status (Fannie Mae, Freddie Mac, AIG, Citigroup) or near financial ruin (Goldman Sachs and Morgan Stanley). That these firms, supposedly among the most sophisticated in the world, fell on such hard times is a testament to a plague of poor management that ran throughout these firms and infected almost all dimensions of their corporate cultures.

If an ordinary corporation pays executives exorbitantly, takes huge chances, and suffers destructive losses, that can be a concern just for those most intimately involved with the firm: shareholders, managers, employees, customers, and suppliers. But when firms are extremely large and thus systemically significant, or when they are insured by the public, either explicitly or implicitly, they are subject to a much wider legitimate concern. This is especially apparent with firms that have received direct public assistance or are owned by the public to a significant degree, so that it is perfectly legitimate for the supplier of those funds to have a direct say about the management of such a firm. Thus, when the public supplies funds to an AIG or a GM and takes a large ownership position, the federal government appropriately has a voice in management policies, such as the level of executive compensation, just as it is legitimate for ordinary shareholders to expect the managers of ordinary firms to heed their interests.

However, even if owners might expect to have a say in firm operations, general rules of corporate governance often shield management from much control by owners, and there is considerable debate over the justification of this managerial protection from ownership control. Nonetheless, the federal government has exercised remarkable intervention in the management of the firms that it has funded through the TARP and other means. This governmental intrusion has focused on executive compensation with the appointment of a "pay czar" to oversee and revise executive pay plans at these firms. Part of the reason for this intervention in management policies normally left to firms is public outrage at perceived excessive compensation and demand for governmental action.

Of all the passions stirred by the financial crisis, executive compensation at financial firms has excited the greatest public anger. In addition to the loss of savings and the decimation of home owners' equity, the financial crisis brought with it the spectacle of taxpayers being forced to bear enormous losses, while executives at offending firms continued to collect annual paychecks larger than the lifetime earnings of ordinary working Americans.

Beyond the palpable injustice that big paydays at failing firms seem to represent, there is potentially a deeper problem—that the chance for huge paydays induced financial executives and traders to put their firms at risk in order to secure great riches for themselves. These potentially perverse incentives have two major social costs. First, riskier corporate strategies increase the chance not only of gain, but also of loss, and when losses occur they must be borne by someone: executives, shareholders, employees, customers, suppliers, or the public at large. Second, the chance for huge payoffs may raise a potentially enormous problem of moral hazard. If risky financial strategies happen to succeed, the firms and their employees reap the profit. However, if the strategies end in disaster, the public bears the loss. Thus, the problem of moral hazard arises with the privatization of profit and the socialization of loss. This possibility induces corporate decision makers to take great risks, knowing they can capture for themselves any profits that accrue, yet foist upon the public the losses they incur.

Executive compensation is among the most studied problems in corporate governance, and it raises complex issues of financial economics, social welfare, and distributive justice. These issues have been addressed in hundreds of academic studies and scores of serious books, so this brief treatment cannot do full justice to the complexities of the issue. However, this discussion attempts to provide a framework for thinking about the issue of executive compensation, and it focuses particularly on aspects of compensation that appear to have played a role in the financial crisis.

Executive compensation refers to the total reward provided by the firm to the top level of executives in a corporation, such as the top five executives in the firm, led by the chief executive officer. At this level in the firm, total compensation takes many forms and may include salaries, bonuses, incentive payments, deferred compensation plans, stock options, and the direct provision of goods and services. In addition to direct cash payments of salaries, bonuses, and the like, the other forms of compensation can be relatively large, yet less visible. Because top-level executives and traders in financial firms are rewarded through so many avenues, and because a considerable portion of this compensation is equity-based—awards of stock or restricted stock, along with stock options—assessing the true level of pay is difficult. In particular, pay through executive stock options (ESOs) is particularly difficult to value.

Pay at Financial Firms

By virtually any measure, financial firms pay their CEOs and other executives quite well. For 2006, the last year untouched by the financial crisis, table 14.1 shows a conservative estimate of pay for the CEOs at leading financial firms. The table consciously omits certain hard-to-measure elements of compensation, such as changes in the value of pension plans, perquisites, various retirement benefits, and so on. As such, it provides solid estimates of minimum compensation. For these firms, the 2006 compensation of CEOs ranged from a low of $10 million for Fannie Mae to a high above $48 million for Countrywide Financial, with an average compensation level of almost $30 million. (Median annual household income in the United States in 2006 was $48,201, so the average compensation of these executives equaled 618 years of the median income of American households.) As the table shows, most of the compensation was tied in some way to the firm's performance or to the value of the firm's stock. Other executives also had more modest, but similarly structured, pay plans. Further down the ranks, many of the financially skilled workers in all of these companies also had compensation plans tied to various measures of performance. Thus, in almost every instance, these CEOs, executives, and financial experts had strong incentives to make the firm succeed—or at least it would so appear.

But there are at least three major problems with this appearance. First, just how much does compensation vary with performance? If high pay accompanies great success, but similarly high pay accompanies mediocre financial results, what ultimate incentive do these pay plans provide? The second main problem is whether the pay plans reward actual economic performance or merely the simulacrum of such success. After all, if pay is based on the number of deals done, the number of mortgages purchased, or even the quarterly earnings results that the firm publishes, there is a further issue. Do the measures of successful performance reliably represent actual beneficial results—an increase in the firm's enduring economic value? Or might those measures be not only imperfect, but actually pernicious? For example, if one only measures deals done as a basis for compensation, then a deal maker has an incentive to just do deals without regard to their benefits for the firm or the detriments to those on the other side of the deal. Thus there is a third issue of exactly what is being incentivized. If pay is tied to performance, but the measures of performance can be faked, perhaps what is really being incentivized is the faking of performance. Each of these issues has been studied extensively, particularly within the field of executive compensation, and the evidence on each is extremely mixed.

With respect to compensation fluctuating with performance, there is considerable evidence on both sides of the question. It does seem that in many cases poor performance results in adverse wealth consequences for executives and others at financial firms. But that is certainly not always the case, and perhaps it is not even the case in general.

Each year, the Comptroller of the State of New York reports on financial firm bonuses. Figure 14.1 presents some key information from that report from 1985 to 2009. The report shows that the average Wall Street bonus rose from $13,970 to $123,850 over the period. If these bonuses are adjusted to account for inflation, the real bonus, measured in constant dollars, went up more than four times. (The Consumer Price Index almost exactly doubled from 1985 to 2009.) Whether we focus on the nominal or real value of those bonuses, it is clear that they do fluctuate, but that fluctuation is around a very strong upward trend. The largest

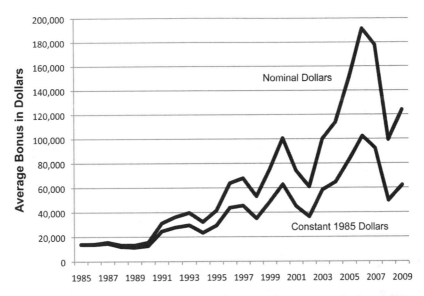

Figure 14.1 Average Wall Street Bonuses, 1985–2009, in Nominal and Constant 1985 Dollars

Source: Office of the State Comptroller of New York, "New York City Securities Industry Bonus Pool," February 23, 2010. Available at: http://www.osc.state.ny.us/ press/releases/feb10/bonus_chart_2009.pdf. Accessed February 25, 2010. Real bonus figures are adjusted by the annual CPI index prepared by the U.S. Bureau of Labor Statistics, available at: http://data.bls.gov/PDQ/servlet/SurveyOutputServlet. Accessed February 25, 2010.

drop was from 2007 to 2008, when the average bonus fell by 44 percent. In 2009, the average bonus rose by 25 percent, perhaps due to the very good profits at these firms, but in the face of continuing public outrage and resentment at high pay. While this one report is hardly definitive, it perhaps does give a reasonable summary picture of bonuses that do fluctuate with results, but it also reveals a pattern of bonuses that seem to steadily increase both in nominal and real terms. Very few categories of workers saw a fourfold increase in their real wages over this period.

Table 14.2 draws on a report by the office of the Attorney General of New York that reported the 2008 bonuses for the nine banks that were the initial recipients of TARP funds. Together, these banks lost more than $81 billion in 2008, yet they had a total bonus pool of more than $32 billion. These nine firms also received $175 billion in TARP funds. In fairness, much banking compensation has a bonus built in as a kind of quasi-salary, yet the banking results for 2008 and employee pay seem

Table 14.1

CEO Compensation at Leading Financial Firms, 2006

	Salary	Cash Bonus[1]	Other Annual Compensation	Restricted Stock	Option Award[2]	All Other	Total
Investment Banks							
Goldman Sachs	600,000	27,243,500	261,906	15,679,642	209,228	82,876	44,077,152
Morgan Stanley	800,000			36,179,980	4,019,945	15,447	41,015,372
Bear Stearns	250,000	17,070,746		14,838,829	35,788	6,154,315	38,349,678
Lehman Brothers	750,000	6,250,000	170,000	10,903,060	700,000	19,585	18,792,645
Merrill Lynch	700,000	18,500,000		26,800,000		2,000,000	48,000,000
Depository Institutions							
JP Morgan Chase	1,000,000	13,000,000		13,000,000			27,000,000
Bank of America	1,500,000	6,500,000		11,698,865	4,966,715	219,969	24,885,549
Citigroup	1,000,000	13,200,000		10,633,333	746,607	258,338	25,838,278
Wells Fargo	995,000	8,500,000			16,826,148	543,521	26,864,669
Washington Mutual	1,000,000	4,074,000		2,251,139	5,148,464	501,572	12,975,175
Countrywide Financial	2,866,667	20,461,473		1,103,745	23,047,104	643,205	48,122,194
Other Firms							
AIG	1,000,000	10,125,000		1,370,657	1916232	6,542,088	20,953,977
Fannie Mae	950,000	3,500,000		4,799,057	962,112	136,072	10,347,241

Source: Proxy Statements (Form DEF 14A) filed with SEC for 2006. Note: In creating this table, every effort was made to avoid overstating actual compensation. For example, the table does not show changes in the value of pension plans, providing of car, driver, planes, apartments, and other perquisites. Therefore, the table somewhat understates the full compensation, and the values reported here may be taken as **minimum** estimates of full compensation.

[1]Includes other non-equity incentive compensation.

[2]For some firms, their 10-K reports show this as securities underlying option award.

Table 14.2

2008 Bonuses for Nine TARP Recipient Firms

Firm	Profit or Loss	Bonus Pool	Number of Employees	Earnings per Employee	Bonus per Employee	TARP Funds	Bonus Distribution		
							Over $3 mil.	Over $2 mil.	Over $1 mil.
	Millions	Millions	Persons	Dollars	Dollars	Millions	Persons	Persons	Persons
Bank of America	4,000	3,300	243,000	16,461	13,580	45,000	28	65	172
Bank of N.Y. Mellon	1,400	945	42,900	32,634	22,028	3,000	12	22	74
Citigroup, Inc.	−27,700	5,330	322,800	−85,812	16,512	45,000	124	176	738
Goldman Sachs Group	2,322	4,823	30,067	77,228	160,420	10,000	212	391	953
J.P. Morgan Chase	5,600	8,693	224,961	24,893	38,642	25,000	>200	0	1,626
Merrill Lynch	−27,600	3,600	59,000	−467,797	61,017	10,000	149	0	696
Morgan Stanley	1,707	4,475	46,964	36,347	95,286	10,000	101	189	428
State Street Corp.	1,811	469	28,475	63,600	16,505	2,000	3	8	44
Wells Fargo & Co.*	−42,933	978	281,000	−152,786	3,479	25,000	7	22	62
Totals	**−81,393**	**32,613**	**1,279,167**			**175,000**	**636**	**873**	**4,793**

*Includes Wachovia's losses.

Source: Adapted with slight modification from Andrew M. Cuomo, "No Rhyme or Reason: The 'Heads I Win, Tails You Lose' Bank Bonus Culture," Attorney General's Office, State of New York, 2009, Appendix A.

incommensurable: for each employee, the average profit was actually a loss equaling -$63,630, while the average bonus was $25,496, and that bonus is averaged across all employees at the firm, from the highest paid to the lowest paid. Thus, when we consider the evidence of figure 14.1 and table 14.2, they certainly seem to sustain the impression that, on Wall Street and at major commercial banks, compensation is much less variable than financial performance.

In theory, much of the incentivizing of compensation works through equity compensation, either through giving stock to executives or by granting executive stock options. As table 14.1 shows, the dollar values in both categories are quite large. A stock grant is fairly easy to understand. In general, the stock that is granted is restricted stock, so the recipient is not permitted to sell it for some period. By contrast, an executive stock option (ESO) is more complex and requires some financial sophistication to comprehend fully.

A typical ESO might be granted to an executive with an initial term to expiration of 10 years.[1] ESOs are nontradable, and the holder can capture the value of these options only through exercising the option or by returning it to the issuing firm in exchange for cash, stock, or more valuable options. ESOs also often carry a vesting requirement of four years, such that an employee who leaves the firm during the vesting period forfeits the option upon departure and receives nothing in exchange. If the holder of a vested option leaves the firm, the exiting employee must exercise the option if it has current cash value or forfeit the option if it has none. (At exercise, the value of an ESO equals either zero or the stock price minus the exercise price of the option, whichever is higher.) This basic description holds for a very large percentage of ESOs, but there are some variations.

While ESOs have long been a feature of the executive compensation landscape, their rise to real prominence dates from 1990 and the publication of an article by Michael Jensen and Kevin Murphy. In this article, the authors decry then recent trends in corporate pay, noting that CEOs in general have little direct financial stake in the fortunes of their firms. Surveying the period from 1974 to 1988, they found that CEO stock holdings as a percentage of corporate value have been declining, and that "a $1,000 change in corporate value corresponds to a change of just 6.7 cents in salary and bonus over two years."[2] They explicitly recommend that "cash compensation should be structured to provide big rewards for outstanding performance and meaningful penalties for poor performance" and that such generous rewards should be coupled with high demands for performance, including making real the "threat of dismissal."[3]

Jensen and Murphy recommend changing the structure of compensation to bring compensation in line with the agency theory of the firm. According to this view of the firm, the CEO is an agent of the shareholders, who are the principals in the firm. The principals contract with their agent to operate the firm on behalf of the principal's interests. Yet there is always a divergence between the interests of the agent and those of the principal. For example, the principal would like the agent to work nonstop, but the agent values personal leisure. Therefore, the agent's employment contract should be designed to mitigate the "incentive incompatibility" between the principal and agent and to strive for "incentive alignment." In other words, the ideal CEO contract should induce the CEO to operate the firm just as the shareholders would if they were at the helm and possessed the CEO's expertise. This understanding of the role of equity-based executive compensation is known as the incentive alignment theory, or the optimal contracting approach. (This theory recognizes that a perfect contract is impossible, so there is always some remaining incentive incompatibility.) Other aspects of the incentive alignment approach stress executive attraction and retention and the use of ESOs to attract the "right" kind of executives (i.e., performance-oriented executives willing to undertake risky projects that are expected to be highly profitable.).

Shareholders presumably want an increasing stock price, so one way of aligning the CEO's incentives with the shareholders is to pay the CEO with an equity stake in the firm. This can be achieved in two main ways: by giving the CEO restricted shares in the firm or by granting ESOs. Because of the inherent leverage of options, paying the CEO with $1 of options rather than $1 of shares makes the CEO's wealth more responsive to the firm's share price for a given compensation cost to the firm. In addition to incentive alignment, paying employees with shares or options can preserve scarce cash, especially in start-up firms. In the technology wave of the 1990s and the ensuing dot-com bubble, firms moved strongly toward the compensation structure advocated by Jensen and Murphy. Equity-based compensation, especially in the form of ESOs, became an extremely important part of executive pay packages. This movement is understood by incentive alignment theorists as a happy outcome, with today's pay packages being granted by boards to executives to make them more effective agents of the shareholders.

There is, however, a competing explanation for the rise of ESOs. The optimal contracting approach requires that the executive's pay package be set in such a way that the CEO behaves as the shareholders wish. But what if the CEO has an important voice in determining his or her own pay? The managerial power approach maintains that this is exactly the case: the CEO and other top executives exercise influence over their own pay packages in a way that results in a markedly suboptimal contract and that has the result of illegitimately transferring wealth from shareholders to executives.

This theory is most strongly associated with Lucian Bebchuk and Jesse Fried in their book and a series of articles.[4] In the Bebchuk and Fried analysis, executives enrich themselves at shareholder expense in a variety of ways. For example, CEOs sometimes even serve on the executive compensation committee of the board, the very group charged with setting CEO pay. Less blatantly, CEOs often have considerable influence over board appointments. Also, according to the Bebchuk and Fried analysis, CEOs and directors form a "club" in which a mutual identification of interests and a kind of mutual "back-scratching" lead to excessive compensation. Bebchuk and Fried do not altogether deny that incentive alignment also occurs, but they maintain that the optimal contracting approach provides merely a part of the story that must be supplemented by their managerial power perspective.

Bebchuk and Fried argue that there are limits to how far this shareholder abuse can go. Pressed too far, grossly excessive CEO pay packages would lead to public and shareholder outrage, and this "outrage cost" provides a limiting factor for executive pay packages. (Public uproar at the bailout costs of the financial crisis certainly seems to have had this outrage effect. As an example, the abstemious head of Goldman Sachs, Lloyd Blankfein, made do with a bonus of "only" $9 million for 2009, in spite of very high profits for his firm. Thus, Blankfein's 2009 bonus was far below the bonus he received for 2007: $67.9 million.)

According to Bebchuk and Fried, the desire to expand executive compensation and to avoid outrage costs leads to efforts to camouflage the magnitude of executive pay. This occurs in several ways, including excessively generous pension and retirement plans. For our purposes, the Bebchuk and Fried account also stresses that one way of camouflaging pay is by using ESOs. The complex features of ESOs make their value less than transparent, and for Bebchuk and Fried, this lack of transparency makes ESOs a powerful vehicle for camouflaging executive pay. There is a vast empirical literature investigating both the incentive alignment theory and the managerial power approach, with extremely mixed results.

Risk-Taking and Executive Compensation in the Financial Crisis

The entire incentive alignment rationale for ESOs in executive compensation is to induce risk-averse CEOs to take more risk on behalf of shareholders. The theory portrays CEOs as shunning risk in their personal lives and being happy to accept a world of quite ample, but not exorbitant, compensation, enjoying a prestigious position and relishing very secure employment. For the incentive alignment model, the problem is to shake up these CEOs and get them to actively accept those risks that maximize the value of their firms.[5] In addition to this risk-incentivizing approach, the pay without performance perspective of Bebchuk and Fried may provide part of the correct understanding of executive pay, while also allowing that incentives encourage risk-taking as the incentive alignment theory insists.

It is at least possible that incentives can be too strong in some cases, encouraging CEOs and their management teams to take too much risk. That is, with pay tied to performance, CEOs may run risks with their firms that have huge potential personal payoffs, thereby accepting risks that are too severe to serve the interest of their principals, the firm's shareholders. Further, with the problem of moral hazard, in which profits can be privatized by managers and shareholders, yet losses can be off-loaded to society at large, high-risk strategies can be especially pernicious. Much of executive compensation is short-term, despite the issuance of long-term ESOs, so there is also the possibility that these incentives encourage CEOs to run great risks, show enormous profits, and collect huge payoffs, all in the short run. The risks that the CEOs accept may never lead to disaster, but if they do, the CEO can gracefully accept dismissal from the firm with boatloads of cash in hand, while leaving huge residual problems to be addressed by future managers.

These problems with CEO and top management incentives are endemic to all industries, but financial institutions, especially those engaged in trading for their own accounts, bring special problems, because not only top executives receive significant performance-based and equity-based compensation. Financial institutions typically compensate successful traders based largely on their annual or quarterly trading profits. A trader who takes positions that report great immediate profits receives large bonuses, but the positions that generated the profits this year may remain on the books of the firm after the bonus is paid. The spectacular financial disasters of the collapse of Barings Bank in 1995 and the $7 billion loss suffered by Société Générale in 2008 were each attributable to the actions of individual identifiable traders who acted alone—Nick Leeson at Barings and Jérôme Kerviel at Société Générale. Each acted contrary to company rules and risk-management policies, but each was lauded and rewarded while racking up big (apparent) profits before the true nature of their trading was uncovered.[6] The rewards to taking risks can be very large indeed and can induce otherwise reasonable people to take extreme risks. The question is to what extent risk-encouraging pay practices helped to create the financial crisis. Examining executive compensation at two prominent financial firms that failed in the crisis, Fannie Mae and Lehman Brothers, helps to provide a perspective on the issues at stake in equity-based executive compensation.

Incentives, Risk-Taking, and Compensation at Fannie Mae

Fannie Mae offers an excellent real-world case for exploring ideas about executive compensation. Before the crisis, Scott Frame and Lawrence White warned of incentives for excessive risk-taking at Fannie Mae and Freddie Mac. For their part, Bebchuk and Fried offered a detailed analysis of compensation in Fannie Mae in 2002–2004 to illustrate their "pay-without performance" thesis and to emphasize the perverse incentives inherent in the firm's pay policies.

Writing in 2004, Frame and White noticed two emerging forces likely to increase competition for Fannie Mae and Freddie Mac— an expanding mortgage purchase role at the Federal Home Loan banks and ". . . the adoption of revised risk-based capital requirements for large U.S. banks (Basel II.)"[7] Frame and White explicitly connected these factors to the likelihood that Fannie and Freddie might be encouraged, through the medium of executive compensation, to take excessive risk. Frame and White concluded that this increased competition: ". . . could result in Fannie Mae and Freddie Mac engaging in riskier behavior, unless restrained by safety-and-soundness regulation."[8] As the public is now painfully aware, they were not restrained and they did engage in riskier behavior.

Almost exactly as Frame and White feared, the GSEs lost market share in 2003–2006, falling from originating almost 60 percent of all mortgages in 2003 to less than 40 percent in 2006, yet they managed to keep the dollar volume of their private label issuances of mortgage-backed securities virtually unchanged in 2004–2006.[9] These facts of over-all greater originations across the entire market, falling market share for Fannie and Freddie, and constant volume for the GSEs in 2004–2006 is exactly consonant with the fears expressed by Frame and White—that the GSEs would take greater risks to maintain profits and would thereby imperil the public.

In their examination of pay at Fannie Mae, Bebchuk and Fried focus on perverse incentives, but they also analyze other issues of pay with-out performance and efforts to camouflage pay levels. The incentive story that Bebchuk and Fried tell about Fannie Mae is compelling. Stating emphatically that they do not know whether the key executives at Fannie Mae operated on the incentives before them, they do explicitly note, under the heading "Perverse Incentives," "Fannie Mae's compen-sation arrangements richly rewarded its executives for reporting higher earnings without requiring them to return the compensation if the earn-ings turned out to be misstated, thus providing incentives to inflate earnings."[10]

In support of this thesis, Bebchuk and Fried rehearse the following facts, after noting that more than half of the earnings for the CEO and CFO depended on reported earnings:

> Seeking to turbo-charge executives' incentives to increase reported earnings, in 2000 Fannie Mae's board adopted a special option grant program, 'Earnings Per Share Challenge Option Grants.' Under its terms, these options would become vested and exercisable in January 2004 if reported earnings per share (EPS) equaled or exceeded $6.46 by December 31, 2003. Raines and Howard [Fannie's CEO and CFO] were awarded 213,000 and 57,000 such options, respectively. Rising to the challenge, Fannie Mae's executives delivered this result—EPS reached $7.91 by the end of 2003—and enjoyed immediate vesting of the options."[11]

For 2003, Raines received almost $20 million in compensation, and he received $13 million in 2000–2003 for meeting the firm's goals on reported earnings.[12]

In 2004, the SEC found that Fannie Mae had violated accounting rules, with the result that earnings had been wildly overstated for the years 2001–2003. The SEC ordered a restatement of earnings for those years that wiped out a large portion of all reported profits.[13] Although Fannie Mae's board forced Raines and Howard out of the firm at the end of 2004, they were allowed to keep all of the compensation they had received, including the portion based on "achieving" Fannie Mae's earnings targets. While Bebchuk and Fried are careful not to assert a direct connection between the earnings incentive and the actions of Raines and Howard, the suggestion is clear. If compensation incentives are strong enough to induce an executive to engage in felonies by misstating earnings, the incentives might also be strong enough to induce an executive to take excessive risk with the firm's money.

In the first decade of the twenty-first century, we know that financial firms took enormous risks that brought nearly all of them into severe financial distress and brought quite a few to ruin. We also know that executive compensation was quite lavish for these firms, as we have seen. The question is whether the leaders of these firms adopted excessively risky strategies in pursuit of enlarging their personal compensation. While it is extremely difficult to say exactly what motivates a certain person to act in a particular way, the connection between high risk and potentially high pay seems too powerful to discount. Fannie Mae certainly seems to fit this model. Even though the incentive effects of executive compensation appear clear, the managerial power view of Bebchuk and Fried also seems to fit the Fannie Mae experience, with Raines and Howard managing to keep a very high level of compensation, even after their supposed performance turned out to be a sham.

After Fannie Mae and Freddie Mac went bankrupt in 2008 and were taken into conservatorship by the federal government, their chief regulator, James Lockhart, said of the two firms: "At the same time, we knew one of our first announcements would be that bonuses would not be paid to senior executives based on 2008 performance."[14] Thus, the U.S. government had figured out that executive bonuses were not absolutely necessary for a pair of firms that had lost $110 billion of taxpayers' money in a single year. However, even if executives were not to receive a reward for their 2008 performance, not all was lost on the bonus front. Less than six months after going into conservatorship, Fannie Mae and Freddie Mac announced new plans to pay a retention bonus totaling $210 million, with more than 200 employees to receive more than $1 million each. But at least there did not appear to be anything underhanded about this plan—it received the support of the firms' new absolute master—the federal government's regulatory official in charge of the two GSEs, who said: "These payments send a signal that we think people are important and we want to keep them."[15]

Executive Compensation at Lehman Brothers

Consider the case of Lehman Brothers and its CEO, Dick Fuld. A month following the Lehman bankruptcy, Fuld was subjected to a humiliating Congressional inquiry in which he was called to testify, and Congressman John Mica informed him: "If you haven't discovered your role, you're the villain today. You've got to act like a villain."[16] For his part, Fuld testified:

> I'm not proud that I lost all that money . . . but my point is, that the [compensation] system worked. . . . I received 85% of my compensation in stock. All the stock that I got, for the last five years, I lost that. Compensation that I received back to '97, '98 and '99, I could have gotten it seven years ago. But I went to the compensation committee and extended it to a 10-year [vesting period]. I lost *all of that*. I got no severance, no golden parachute. I got no contract. I never *asked* for a contract. I never sold my shares, and that's why I had 10 million left. *I believed in this company*. I could have sold that stock. But I *did not*, because I believed we would return to profitability.[17]

Much of Fuld's grilling focused on his compensation, with one congressman referring to his compensation as "unimaginable," pointing out that he got to keep almost $500 million. Fuld attempted to diminish the size of his compensation, putting the figure down closer to $300 million, but still admitting that it was a "large number."[18]

Fuld's defensive perspective receives some support in Andrew Ross Sorkin's *Too Big to Fail*, one of the best selling journalistic accounts of the financial crisis. Sorkin reports there that "Lehman's employees were unique on Wall Street in that they owned a quarter of the company's shares. For all the complaints about Wall Street being short-term oriented, most Lehman employees had a five-year vesting period, which meant huge sums of their own wealth were tied up in the firm without the ability to sell their shares."[19] Sorkin immediately goes on to report that Fuld owned 10.9 million shares, or 1.4 percent of the firm, and had lost $649.2 million from January to September 2008. Sorkin later notes that Fuld's shares that were once worth $1 billion were worth only $65,486.72, and he concludes: "It was a telling paradox in the debate about executive compensation: Fuld was a CEO with most of his wealth directly tied to the firm on a long-term basis, and still he took extraordinary risks."[20]

At another point in the hearing, Fuld said: "Not that anyone on this committee cares about this but I wake up every single night wondering 'what could I have done differently?' In certain conversations, what should I have said? What could I have done? I have searched myself every single night. This is a pain that will stay with me for the rest of my life."[21] Fuld had, in fact, been a lifer at Lehman, starting out as an intern, working for the company for 42 years, and his persona was certainly closely tied to the success of the firm.

So three things about Lehman and Fuld's personal situation seem undeniable: Fuld received hundreds of millions of dollars in compensation at Lehman over the years; he lost hundreds of millions of dollars in Lehman's bankruptcy; and he suffered a terrible humiliation and a crushing personal blow when Lehman collapsed. Yet it also seems that Fuld had Lehman take (in Sorkin's words) "extraordinary risks"—a view that is confirmed by considering Lehman's leverage, as shown in figure 10.1 in chapter 10, along with Lehman's proven vulnerability in the fall of 2008. It also seems clear that Fuld, like many other leaders of financial firms, had strong incentives to take those risks. Yet for any individual viewed from afar, it is impossible to know the actual motivators of their behavior.

In an interesting and valuable study, Lucian A. Bebchuk, Alma Cohen, and Holger Spamann (hereafter BCS) analyze the realized compensation and incentives that faced executives at Bear Stearns and Lehman Brothers.[22] The authors are careful to note that they are not opining on exactly why executives at these firms acted as they did. Instead they examine executives' actual cash flows and the monetary incentives they faced. BCS examine the top five executives at the two firms and focus on their cash flows from bonuses and sales of their own company's stocks in 2000–2008, and they report all dollar figures as inflation-adjusted January 2009 dollars. The CEO was constant for each firm over the period, but the executives in the second to fifth top spots experienced some turnover.

The analysis of BCS shows generally similar stories for Bear and Lehman, and the situation of Dick Fuld can illustrate the general points about incentives, stock holdings, and risk.[23] BCS report that over the period from 2000 to 2008, Fuld received a total of $70,594,415 in bonuses and non-equity based compensation. He also sold 12,422,277 shares of

Lehman for a total of $470,695,782. At the collapse of Lehman, Fuld still held 10,851,540 Lehman shares, which BCS estimate as having zero post-bankruptcy value. Thus, Fuld received $541,290,697 in bonuses and as proceeds from the sale of Lehman stock from 2000–2008, all measured in 2009 dollars. At the end of 2007, a Lehman share was worth $65.44. Assuming for convenience that Fuld held the same number of shares at the beginning of 2008 that BCS report for him at the collapse—10,851,540 shares—the bankruptcy cost him more than $710 million.[24]

Leaving BCS behind for the moment, if we consider someone in Fuld's position (but without making any assertions about Fuld's personal behavior or motivations), it is clear that very strong incentives are in play. A fully unscrupulous executive could consciously undertake a strategy of accepting very high risk in the hope of short-term payoffs, with the realization that the firm might eventually collapse. After all, a personal financial result like the one that Fuld actually realized would be extremely motivating for many people, even if it came with personal disgrace. Alternatively, an executive might be driven to compete with other leaders in his or her industry and might accept a high level of risk in such a pursuit, believing that such a course of management was perfectly reasonable. Yet another person might adopt a high risk strategy in the pursuit of personal gain, never thinking that the firm could collapse. Yet another CEO might believe that firm risk controls were in place, that the management of the firm was in the most capable hands, and that everything was just as it should be, with the firm generating handsome returns for shareholders and rich rewards for a deserving CEO. It is impossible to say whether any of these descriptions applies to Fuld or to another particular CEO of a financial firm that suffered losses in the financial crisis. But it seems that each of these descriptions might apply.

Returning now to BCS, it seems that their key conclusions are very much on the mark: ". . . the cases of Bear Stearns and Lehman if anything provide a basis for concerns about the incentives executives there had, not for dismissing such concerns," that the ". . . design of bonus compensation provides executives with incentives to seek improvements in short-term earnings figures even at the cost of maintaining an excessively high risk of large losses down the road," that ". . . the top executives of those two firms were not financially devastated by their management of the firms during 2000–2008," and finally that ". . . the large paper losses that the executives suffered when their companies collapsed should not provide a basis for dismissing either the possibility that executives' choices have been influenced by excessive risk-taking incentives or the importance of improving compensation structures going forward."[25]

Incentive Conflicts

There can be little doubt that CEOs had strong personal incentives to increase the risks at their firms. As we have seen, however, the great ascendancy of agency theory that began in 1990 and rocked executive compensation in U.S. companies from then to the present explicitly developed pay plans to induce CEOs to increase the risk of their firms in the belief that such policies would benefit shareholders. If CEO incentives were properly aligned with those of shareholders, then the increases in risk that promised personal enrichment for CEOs would serendipitously benefit shareholders as well. In assessing a disaster like the financial crisis, the question might well arise as to whether CEO incentives were poorly aligned with those of shareholders and whether CEOs selfishly took positions for personal benefit, knowing that the likely consequences for shareholders could be very poor indeed.

As an anecdotal account, we have seen that Lehman's CEO, Dick Fuld, made out quite well personally in a purely financial sense, although he also lost a tremendous amount of wealth in 2008 and suffered dramatic career and personal reversals. Other CEOs over the period of the early twenty-first century also reaped large rewards, as shown in a study by Fahlenbrach and Stulz. For example, in the financial industry at least 20 CEOs held equity stakes in their own companies that were valued at more than $100 million at the end of 2006, and on average CEOs at financial firms owned 1.6 percent of their own firm's shares. Further, some stakes held by CEOs at the end of 2006 were extremely large, with the five largest being: Fuld at Lehman, $1,003 million; Cayne at Bear Stearns, $953 million; O'Neal at Merrill Lynch, $359 million; John Mack at Morgan Stanley, $320 million; and Mozilo at Countrywide Financial, $285 million.[26]

The picture that we have seen for Lehman and Fuld is fairly representative and was widely repeated, although often on a much smaller scale, as reported by Fahlenbrach and Stulz. Examining the fates of CEOs at 98 large banks, they find a number of interesting results. Like Fuld, other bank CEOs tended to be quite wealthy and to be heavily invested in their own firms. On average, the CEOs lost $31.5 million in their equity stakes over 2007–2008. Few CEOs cashed out a large portion of their holdings, and more than 75 percent of CEOs did not sell any shares over 2007–2008. This leads Fahlenbrach and Stulz to conclude that ". . . CEOs made large losses on their wealth during the crisis and that most of these losses came from holding on to their shares. Had CEOs seen the crisis coming, they could have avoided most of these losses by selling their shares. They clearly did not do so."[27]

Thus the picture that emerges is not one of CEOs ruthlessly taking risks with their firms merely for their personal enrichment. Instead, the following seems broadly to be the case:

- Well before and through the crisis, CEOs operated with pay plans that were designed to give them personal incentives to take risks, in the belief that such a design would benefit shareholders.
- CEOs actively guided their firms to take large risks generally, and they increased those risk levels as the crisis approached.
- CEOs failed to anticipate the crisis, and they suffered large wealth losses as a result of the crisis.
- Nonetheless, CEOs made out extremely well financially through their stewardship of their respective firms, generally holding many millions of dollars of personal wealth even in the aftermath of the crisis.
- CEOs generally made out much better financially than did rank-and-file employees and shareholders in their firms.

Perhaps the last point is the most galling—the very person who took the biggest risks and caused the most employee hardships and shareholder losses still made out quite well. Of these CEOs, some still possess enormous wealth and continue to command their firms (e.g., Blankfein at Goldman Sachs, Dimon at JPMorgan Chase, Mack at Morgan Stanley), while others skulk away in embarrassment or even disgrace to enjoy their millions (Fuld at Lehman; Cayne at Bear Stearns; Mozilo at Countrywide). In contrast, the shareholders' positions have been decimated or even wiped out, and rank-and-file employees find themselves without jobs and wondering whether they can find new employment— employment they very much need, as their retirement accounts have also largely disappeared.

Corporate Governance in the Financial Crisis

For any corporation, the board of directors has the ultimate responsibility for governing the firm, and this role has many dimensions. Two of the most fundamental aspects of that governance are setting the right risk posture for the firm and establishing compensation plans that provide employees with incentives to serve the firm well. Judged on these two criteria, corporate governance in financial firms before and during the financial crisis failed miserably.

The extreme leverage of financial firms as the crisis approached left them in a terribly vulnerable position, as we have seen. A 4 percent swing in the value of their assets had the potential to wipe out most firms entirely. Such high leverage, if even conceivable as a wise policy, would demand the most exquisitely precise and beautifully calibrated risk management. As we have seen, risk management proved completely inadequate to the job.

Beyond the finance industry, the entire economic landscape from the 1990s well into the first decade of the twenty-first century promoted an environment of risk, especially in the housing sector. We have seen that the federal government actively encouraged expansion of home lending to the less affluent, that the United States was awash in a sea of liquidity for much of this period, and that interest rates were at relatively quite low levels. All of these factors contributed to making the financial environment more risky, especially with respect to the housing industry and market. Thus, the situation demanded particular care in corporate governance.

We have seen that the originate-to-distribute (OTD) system of mortgage production included a chain of incentive conflicts. These incentive conflicts are fairly obvious upon inspection. The system of OTD mortgage origination, with its endemic incentive conflicts, is beyond the control of any single firm, but each firm knew that it was operating in a financial landscape that included the OTD system as an important feature. Faced with this operating environment, good corporate governance at financial firms required particular attention to the compensation plans and their incentives. This was true not only for CEOs, but also down the corporate chain, especially to those involved in the OTD system.

Financial institutions originated mortgages, bought mortgages, securitized mortgages, commissioned ratings for these securities, sold these securities, and invested in mortgages and the securities built upon them. Instead of taking particular care to govern the incentive conflicts that their employees faced, many financial firms festively participated in this potentially corrupted environment. Perhaps no one captured the attitude better than Chuck Prince, the CEO of Citigroup in July 2007, when he said: "When the music stops, in terms of liquidity, things will be complicated. But as long as the music is playing, you've got to get up and dance. We're still dancing."[28]

Good corporate governance in the mortgage arena would have insisted that firms originate solid mortgages to financially credible homebuyers on honest terms. Such mortgages would have made profits for the firm, yet avoided both predatory lending and falling victim to predatory borrowing, thereby promoting the true value of the firm. When a well-governed financial firm purchased mortgages, it would have done true due diligence, rather than hiring a due-diligence firm to perform a kabuki dance creating an illusion of prudence. An honest firm would then have secured a genuine and valid rating of the securities that it created from the mortgages it had purchased. Finally, a well-governed firm would not have sold radically over-valued mortgage securities to others or invested in them for their own portfolios.

Instead of behaving as described, many financial firms acted in much the opposite manner. That they did so must be attributed in large part to the system of incentives that pervaded the management of these banks. And the broad-scale management of firms is exactly the task of corporate governance that failed in setting risk levels, risk management systems, and compensation incentive systems that would operate well for CEOs, other top executives, and throughout the firm.[29]

Consequences of the Financial Crisis and the Future It Leaves Us

The massive federal bailouts, rescues, assisted transactions, and stimulus programs aimed at resolving the financial crisis are among the largest set of expenditures for the U.S. government since World War II, relative to GDP. By early 2010, it seemed clear that financial disaster had been averted, and the economy showed clear signs of at least modest recovery. However, as in most recoveries, productivity improved early, but the unemployment rate remained high well into the recovery. Optimists believe that the high unemployment rate is consistent with its traditional performance as a lagging indicator of recovery. By contrast, other observers fear a permanent economic realignment in the international economy that may lead to persistently high unemployment in the United States. Virtually all observers agree that the economic institutions of our country behaved poorly in this humiliating episode, and there is widespread agreement that the United States needs to act to forestall the recurrence of such a crisis.

Measuring the Damage: A Warning

At this juncture in the recovery from the economic crisis, it is possible to make an initial assessment of the costs of the bailout and to assess the broader and even larger economic consequences of the crisis. In table 8.1 of chapter 8, we saw a *New York Times* estimate from September 2009 that gauged the cost of the federal portion of the financial crisis as a commitment of $12 trillion and expenditures already made of $2 trillion. It now seems apparent that much of the $12 trillion that was committed will never be spent and that much of the $2 trillion that has been disbursed will be returned. However, table 8.1 focuses on just the federal portion of the cost of the financial crisis, and the federal portion is merely that, a portion, and not even the major portion.

Estimates, such as that prepared by the *New York Times* and including the one that follows, are attempts to hit a moving target, and all are likely to be wrong. Because trying to understand the costs of and responsibilities for the financial crisis go to the most fundamental issues of economic, political, and social organization, ideology threatens to enter the analysis at every point. The discussion that follows attempts to pick a way through these thorny issues in a way that is balanced, but that is sure to be open to criticism, and that will certainly require revision as history unfolds.

The Bailout and Its Costs

The federal response to the crisis started in a massive way in 2008 and has been led by the Federal Reserve System and the U.S. Treasury Department. Bailouts were initiated through two key pieces of legislation, the Emergency Economic Stabilization Act (the TARP) and the Housing and Economic Recovery Act of 2008, the second of these being aimed principally at rescuing Fannie Mae and Freddie Mac. The TARP Act made $700 billion (technically $698.8 billion) available, and the second committed $400 billion, for a total of $1.1 trillion.

Table 15.1 summarizes, as of July 2010, some of the actual expenditures in support of various bailout initiatives under the TARP and the Housing and Economic Recovery Act. Some of the $537 billion in outflows has led to inflows, either through revenues or repayments. As of July 2010, revenues totaled $25.12 billion and stem from payments by recipients to the federal government in the form of interest charged, dividends paid, or monies realized from disposing of equity interests (warrants or preferred shares) held by government. In addition, some of the recipients have repaid all or part of the monies they received, and these repayments totaled $150.43 billion by July 2010. This leaves $280

State of the Bailout: Funds Actually Spent, Invested, or Loaned

Recipient	Disbursements ($ billions)	Percent of Total
Financial Institutions	244.90	47.9
Fannie Mae and Freddie Mac	125.90	24.6
AIG	45.30	8.9
Auto Companies	79.70	15.6
Toxic Asset Purchases	15.90	3.1
Foreclosure Relief	.06	0.0
Total	**$511.8**	**100.0**

Source: http://bailout.propublica.org. Accessed March 13, 2010.

billion of the funds summarized in table 15.1 still at risk. As we will see, much of this $280 billion will probably be repaid. However, the ultimate federal stake is much larger than the $537 billion outlay and $280 billion remaining exposure indicate.

The Emergency Economic Stabilization Act spawned a number of programs, each with its own commitments, as table 15.2 shows. Not all of the $700 billion of the TARP has been committed, so there is the possibility that these programs could be enlarged or that new programs could be initiated. Given that the crisis seems to be receding, such expansion seems unlikely. However, there is the likelihood that some of the uncommitted TARP funds will be diverted to other spending, rather than being directed solely to overcoming the financial crisis.

Some of the recipients of the largest amounts from these programs have generated substantial profits for the Treasury already. Table 15.3 shows the current standing of the twelve firms that received $10 billion or more from the bailout programs. In particular, all of the large banks, with the exception of Citigroup, have already repaid the $160 billion they received from the TARP, along with profits to the government of $13.9 billion. For these twelve large recipients, the amount still at risk, as of July 2010, is $279.76 billion. If no more money is ever repaid— contrary to all expectations—the total loss associated with these firms would be $254.6 billion. The largest remaining exposures in Table 15.4 are to Fannie Mae and Freddie Mac ($144.9 billion), the auto industry ($68.5 billion including GMAC, but excluding Chrysler Financial which received $1.5 billion), AIG ($47.5 billion), and Citigroup ($18.8 billion).

Table 15.2

Programs Under TARP

Program	Amount Promised	Proportion of TARP Funds
Capital Purchase Program (CPP)	204.89	29.32
Automotive Industry Financing Program	81.35	11.64
Systemically Significant Failing Institutions (AIG)	69.83	9.99
Making Homes Affordable (Mortgage Modifications)	48.50	6.94
Targeted Investment Program (Citi and BofA)	40.00	5.72
Public-Private Investment Program (PPIP) to purchase toxic assets	30.00	4.29
Small Business Lending Program	30.00	4.29
Term Asset-Back Securities Loan Facility	30.00	4.29
Auto Supplier Support Program	3.50	0.50
Housing Finance Agency Innovation Fund	1.50	0.21
Community Development Capital Initiative	0.78	0.11

Source: http://bailout.propublica.org/programs/index. Accessed March 13, 2010.

To the first half of 2010, repayment experience has been much better than anticipated. Of the figures shown in table 15.3 much of the money disbursed to General Motors, Fannie Mae, and Freddie Mac will probably never return. Funds committed to AIG remain at serious risk, but mid-2010 revealed AIG actively selling some of its valuable divisions to secure funds for repayment.

While $1.1 trillion from these two acts seems to be a large amount, the true federal commitment is actually much larger. Much of this additional commitment is in the form of guarantees made, or lines of credit extended, by the federal government. Table 15.4 summarizes additional commitments not included in the $1.1 trillion covered by the TARP and GSE (government-sponsored enterprises) legislation. The firm figures in table 15.4, when added to the TARP legislation and the GSE bailout, bring the total to just over $1.5 trillion.

As we have seen in chapter 8, starting in November 2008, the Federal Reserve initiated the Term Asset-Backed Securities Loan Facility

Table 15.3

Recipients of $10 Billion or More in TARP Funds

Firm	Received	Returned	Remaining Exposure	Profit to Federal Government
Bank of America	45.00	45.00	0.00	4.30
JPMorgan Chase	25.00	25.00	0.00	1.75
Wells Fargo	25.00	25.00	0.00	1.44
Goldman Sachs	10.00	10.00	0.00	1.42
Morgan Stanley	10.00	10.00	0.00	1.27
Chrysler	10.75	0.28	10.47	−10.41
GMAC	16.29	0.00	16.29	−15.44
Citigroup	45.00	20.00	25.00	−22.22
AIG	45.31	0.00	45.31	−45.31
Freddie Mac	50.70	0.00	50.70	−46.42
General Motors	50.74	1.40	49.35	−48.89
Fannie Mae	75.20	0.00	75.20	−72.73
Totals	408.99	136.68	272.31	−251.25

Source: http://bailout.propublica.org/main/list/index. Accessed March 13, 2010.

(TALF) to support the asset-backed securities market by essentially buying these illiquid assets. More exactly, the Federal Reserve accepted these securities as collateral and lent an amount against them that was supposed to equal the value of the securities, less a "haircut." (The haircut is a small percentage to keep the purchase safe—that is, to ensure that the collateral's value would be sufficient to cover the amount lent.) However, these are nonrecourse loans, so if the loan is not repaid, the Fed merely owns the collateral and cannot seek funds beyond the amount that selling the collateral would yield. This arrangement gave the borrower the choice to redeem the loan and recover the collateral, or to walk away with the loan funds in hand and leave the Fed stuck with the collateral. It now appears that the TALF may even make a small profit.

While $1.5 trillion of fairly visible funds may start to seem like real money, the really big costs and impacts are more obscure and difficult to quantify. Beyond the $400 billion explicitly committed to Fannie and

Table 15.4

Additional Federal Commitments to Specific Firms

Firm	Commitment ($ Billions)	Note
JPMorgan	$30.00	Credit line issued and risk bearing for toxic assets associated with acquisition of Bear Stearns.
AIG	110.17	An initial $85 billion commitment has been expanded in pieces to total $180 billion.
Citigroup	235.00	Beyond the $45 billion Citi received under TARP, the federal government has provided other guarantees to limit losses on toxic assets.
Bank of America	97.20	Beyond the $45 billion BofA received under TARP, which has been repaid, the federal government has committed up to $97.2 billion to limit losses on toxic assets.
Total	**$472.37**	
Fannie Mae & Freddie Mac	Unknown	In December 2009, the Treasury removed any cap on total aid. Essentially, these two firms are 100 percent owned by the federal government, and the government will honor all debts of the two firms.

Source: http://bailout.propublica.org/programs/index. Accessed: March 13, 2010.

Freddie, the federal government now stands behind all of the commitments of these GSEs, which is an enormous potential obligation. In addition, another large and much less visible action by the federal government to support financial markets has been conducted through the Federal Reserve. Beyond the $1.5 trillion discussed so far, the Federal Reserve has been active in purchasing mortgage-backed securities (MBS) and other asset-backed securities (ABS). By March 2010, the Fed was planning to wind down this program, with total purchases of securities amounting to $1.25 trillion in asset-backed securities, plus an additional $175 billion in debt guaranteed by Fannie Mae and Freddie Mac. Thus, this rather obscure commitment of support totaled $1.425 trillion, almost as much as the other figures for the TARP, TALF, GSE bailout, and other measures discussed earlier in this chapter. However, the real cost of this program is not clear. The assets purchased are supposed to be worth the prices paid by the Fed, implying low risk and cost. On the other hand, only the Fed seemed willing to undertake this "business opportunity," suggesting that there may be real costs associated with the endeavor. The ultimate cost of such a program is almost impossible to measure.[1]

Beyond these various bailouts and asset purchases, the government instituted a $700 billion fiscal stimulus to combat the recession that grew out of the financial crisis. Much of that $700 billion has not been disbursed as of mid-2010, yet some have been arguing for a new and additional stimulus package. Taken together, and even with pessimistic estimates of additional TARP repayments, finishing the bailouts of Fannie Mae and Freddie Mac, including the existing stimulus plan, plus the fiscal threat of additional stimulus, the total figures above fall in the $2–3 trillion range. As a rough, conservative, but still risky, estimate, let us put these figures in total in the $2–2.5 trillion range.

From 2006 to 2009: Our Economic World and How It Has Changed

The $2–2.5 trillion costs of the financial crisis discussed so far are somewhat petty in the overall picture. The real changes in our economic circumstances over the crisis period are much grander in scale, even harder to measure, and certainly are due to the crisis in part, but only in part. Comparing the full years of 2006 and 2009 allows us to begin to come to grips with the ultimate costs of the crisis and our altered economic circumstances. Measured in terms of GDP, 2006 was a good year, with real GDP growing 2.67 percent. Taken as a full year, 2009 was a year of recession, with negative real GDP of -2.42 percent, but by mid-2010, it did appear that the recession had technically ended, even though unemployment remained high.

Table 15.5 compares other dimensions of the 2006–2009 period. First, real GDP was essentially unchanged, making 2006–2009 the worst three-year period since 1946–1948, the recession that followed World War II. This represents three lost years of economic growth. In essence, the United States wasted three years of opportunity to improve its productive capacity. In spite of an essentially zero increase in production for the 2006–2009 period, personal consumption grew by almost 2 percent. However, private investment fell by more than 30 percent. This decreasing investment augurs ill for the future productive capacity of the economy. For the 2006–2009 period, expenditures by the federal government increased almost 15 percent in real terms.

Comparing activities of 2006 and 2009, table 15.5 shows that banks charged off $27 billion in bad debts for 2006, but this exploded to $191 billion in 2009, for an increase of 607 percent. No banks failed in 2006, but the FDIC closed 140 in 2009. Further, officials at the FDIC feared that 2010 would bring even higher charge-offs and more bank failures than 2009. Personal and business bankruptcies filed in federal courts accelerated dramatically over the 2006–2009 period, with personal bankruptcies increasing by 136 percent, while business bankruptcies increased by 209 percent.

As the statistics in table 15.5 demonstrate, 2009 was a horrible year economically, and the 2006–2009 period was one of great economic hardship. However, table 15.5 ultimately says little about our economic future, because these unfortunate developments may appear to be completely reversible, as has happened so often throughout U.S. history. But

Table 15.5

Changes in Economic Circumstances from 2006 to 2009

	From 2006 to 2009	
Growth in real GDP	0.11%	
Growth in real U. S. personal consumption	1.79%	
Growth in real gross private domestic investment	−31.42%	
Growth in real federal government expenditures	14.72%	
	2006	**2009**
Bank loan charge-offs, billions of dollars	27.0	191.0
Bank failures	0	140
Personal bankruptcies filed in federal courts	597,965	1,412,838
Business bankruptcies filed in federal courts	19,695	60,837

Source: Macroeconomic data were acquired from:
http://www.bea.gov/national/nipaweb/ Accessed March 14, 2010. Data on bankruptcies were drawn from:
http://www.uscourts.gov/Press_Releases/2010/BankruptcyFilingsDec2009.cfm
Accessed March 10, 2010. Bank failure and charge-off data are from the FDIC.

the situation at the end of 2009 may give cause for deeper and more long-term concern.

Reduced Circumstances: Our Economic Future

Table 15.6 presents some key measures that show how dramatically the economic standing of the United States has been reduced and how real are the economic problems that we face. Further, they suggest that we may now be standing at a precipice of permanently altered economic circumstances, and not merely at the beginning of a boom to follow the Great Recession.

The value of the U.S. housing stock, all plant and equipment, and even land is trivial compared to the value of human capital and its earning capacity. As the first line of table 15.6 shows, the official unemployment rate rose from a low rate of 4.3 percent to end 2009 at 9.7 percent, exceeding 10 percent along the way. The unemployment rate remained at 9.7 percent well into 2010. As the recession recedes, this is bound to improve, but the real question is whether the employment prospects of Americans have changed in some fundamental way. We have already seen that the United States appears to be in a persistent state of importing more than it exports, and currently many fear that the loss of employment suffered in the Great Recession may have permanent effects, leading to reduced employment circumstances for U.S. citizens as a whole. If this materializes as a partial consequence of the financial crisis, the loss of economic value for our country will be boundless and incalculable, beyond any meaningful attempt to place a dollar value on such a calamity.

While the effect on future earnings from employment dwarfs other potential results, other losses in the trillions of dollars are more certain and somewhat easier to measure. At the end of 2006, the value of all stocks on the New York Stock Exchange and NASDAQ stood at $19.29 trillion, as table 15.6 shows. At the end of 2009, the value was $14.82 trillion, for a loss of $4.46 trillion. While some significant portion of this loss must be attributed to the housing bubble and the financial crisis, the overarching point is that this loss of wealth points to reduced economic circumstances in our society.

While the $4.5 trillion fall in the value of stocks is large, the loss in residential real estate value is significantly greater. The Federal Reserve reports the total value of all residential real estate in the United States every quarter, which was $22.94 trillion at the end of 2006, but fell to $16.58 trillion, which is a reduction of $6.36 trillion, or 27.7 percent. The actual performance was somewhat worse than these figures indicate, because the U.S. population grew in 2006–2009, increasing the number of households, and the United States experienced modest inflation over the period, so the real value of the total housing stock fell more than 27.7 percent.

The fall in home prices essentially took the value of the U.S. housing stock back to the situation that obtained in the third quarter of 2004, when the total value of the housing stock was $16.79 trillion. However, there is a real question as to how much of the $6.36 trillion loss was a real loss, in contrast to the correction of an illusion. In the aftermath of the housing price collapse, it seems hard to believe that the prices that prevailed at the peak represented true value. Given how wrong so many of us were about housing values in the boom years, how confident can we be that current prices represent true value? Thus, the figure of a $6.36 trillion loss may overstate the reduction in true value. Alternatively, if housing prices fall further, the actual decrease from the peak in prices to the trough may turn out to be even larger. While it is impossible to gauge precisely the loss of true value in the collapse of the housing bubble, it is certain that trillions of dollars were actually lost.

Table 15.6

Notes on the Economic Future of the United States

At Year End:	2006	2009
Official unemployment rate, percent, not seasonally adjusted	4.3	9.7
U.S. stock market capitalization, trillions of dollars	19.29	14.82
Total Value of U.S. residential real estate, trillions of dollars	22.94	16.58
FDIC Deposit Insurance Fund Balance, billions of dollars	50.2	−20.9
Number of FDIC-insured problem institutions	50	702
Assets of FDIC-insured problem institutions, billions of dollars	8.3	402.8
Debt of U. S. Treasury, trillions of dollars	8.68	12.31
U. S. Treasury Debt as percentage of annual GDP	64.8	86.3

However, there is another huge cost of the housing bubble that is extremely difficult to assess. As we have seen, in the run-up in housing prices, especially from 2000 to 2006, many people literally used their homes as piggy banks that they could raid for consumption. While only a metaphor, it is not too outlandish to say that many people spent their houses on Gucci bags and trips to Hawaii. This is a harsh assessment made in retrospect; at the time, many of those who took out home equity loans to finance personal consumption may have thought they were genuinely richer, with their true wealth increasing as their home equity grew. Now we know that the run-up in home prices was illusory, but the withdrawals of equity resulted in real debt. The equity that was withdrawn and consumed is permanently gone.

Figure 15.1 shows the effect of falling home prices, combined with aggressive borrowing, on the home equity position of Americans. From 2000 to 2009, the equity percentage of home values declined precipitously from about 58 to 38 percent. In other words, Americans as a whole owned 58 percent of the value of their homes in 2000, but now only 38 percent. At the end of 2009, some estimates suggested that as many as one-third of Americans owed more on their homes than those houses were worth. This greater indebtedness for housing for the U.S. economy as a whole certainly implies greatly reduced financial flexibility and capacity for years to come.

While the financial crisis may be over and the Great Recession winding to an end, there are likely to be some lingering and costly

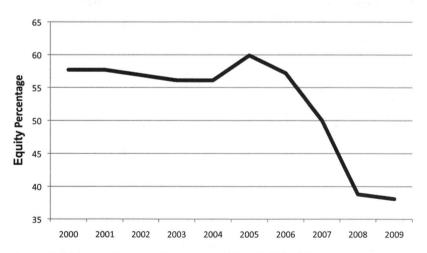

Figure 15.1 Owners' Equity as a Percentage of Household Real Estate

aftereffects from the crisis. From 2006 to 2009, the FDIC Deposit Insurance Fund was depleted by $71.1 billion, taking it from $50.2 billion down to a negative balance of $20.9 billion. This Fund consists of fees paid by depository institutions, but these monies come from bank customers, so they really come from the U.S. public at large. While the Fund is in deficit, and it can garner more monies from additional fees, the Fund will also certainly face more withdrawals. As table 15.6 shows, there were only 50 "problem banks" holding $8.3 billion in assets in 2006, according to the FDIC. At the end of 2009, 702 problem institutions held $402.8 billion in assets. Some of those 702 institutions will certainly fail—in fact, the FDIC estimates that bank failures in 2010 will exceed the 140 failures of 2009. (In the first half of 2010, 86 FDIC-insured banks failed, and in the first quarter of 2010, the number of problem institutions escalated to 775 holding assets of $431 billion.)

At the same time that these looming bank failures, reductions in income producing capacity, stock market losses, and decreases in home equity have devastated our economic landscape, the federal government has been piling on debt, partially in an attempt to combat the recession. Table 15.6 shows the increase in federal debt in 2006–2009. At the end of 2006, U.S. Treasury debt stood at $8.68 trillion, but it grew by 42 percent in three years to reach $12.31 trillion by the end of 2009. This increase in debt of $3.63 trillion also casts a shadow over our economic future, as the size of this debt escalated from 64.8 to 86.3 percent of GDP. Assuming that the United States will honor this debt at some point, this burgeoning obligation imposes further economic constraints on our future.

In early 2010, the Obama administration presented a budget proposal that forecast continuing deficits and growing debt into the indefinite future. The Congressional Budget Office's (CBO) analysis of the budget proposal agreed that the deficits were real, but estimated them to be quite a bit larger than the administration acknowledged. According to the CBO, the proposed budget would generate a deficit of $1.5 trillion for 2010 and $1.3 trillion for 2011, and that deficits would continue into the indefinite future.

Further, in 2010 the United States enacted health care reform that created a vast new entitlement for Americans, extending health insurance coverage to 30 million additional citizens. While the cost of such a plan is a subject of contentious debate, any serious observer knows that the cost over the next several decades will amount to trillions of dollars. Further, other entitlements that are similar in scope and magnitude—Social Security, Medicare, Medicaid—all stand under the shadow of looming insolvency due to persistent failure to pay for the costs associated with these programs as they have been incurred. These existing obligations all impose additional constraints on our economic future.

▬▬▬ Beyond the Merely Economic—American Recessional or American Renewal?

The financial crisis of our time has been an economic event of the first order of magnitude. It is surely the second worst economic disaster of the last century, with only the Great Depression exceeding the Great Recession. Yet the ultimate meaning of our financial crisis may exceed the import of the Great Depression. After the Great Depression, the United States entered its period of greatest geopolitical ascendancy and stood for many decades at the pinnacle of the world's social, economic, and cultural order. The prospects for the United States in the aftermath of the Great Recession hardly seem to promise the same happy outcome.

The relative position of the United States has weakened as other nations have advanced, with many of them emerging from a persistent history of self-imposed poverty and impotence. Today, the name of China is on every person's lips as the emergent counterpoint to the United States, and China, already the world's largest exporter, stands poised to surpass Japan as the world's second-largest economy.

Viewed against this picture of an exhausted imperium confronting a vital contender with a much larger population, the true significance of the financial crisis and the Great Recession may be their contribution to waning American preeminence. Of course, the financial crisis cannot be the sole cause of a loss of position in world power for the United States, for America's weakening certainly antedates the financial crisis. Nonetheless, time may well prove that the financial crisis and the Great Recession accelerated America's loss of primacy. In addition, the financial problems of the early twenty-first century may come to symbolize a fatigue in national character and may serve as a prime example of the weakening of the political and social institutions that formerly sustained a nation's greatness.

There is, of course, a rich literature of imperial and cultural decline, the most notable account of an "arc of empire" being Edward

Gibbon's magisterial *Decline and Fall of the Roman Empire*. Gibbon traces the 300-year arc from the second century of the Christian era, when ". . . the Empire of Rome comprehended the fairest part of the earth and the most civilised portion of mankind" and assays the ". . . circumstances of its decline and fall: a revolution which will ever be remembered, and is still felt by the nations of the earth."[2] This cyclical view of empire and history extends down through Oswald Spengler's *The Decline of the West* to the present day.[3]

Over the last decade, numerous books have addressed America's waning and China's waxing geopolitical prospects. Some include a call for action, while others speak nostalgically of the beneficial role of empire in the world order.[4] Already moving past the possibility of a beneficial exercise of American imperial might, Fareed Zakaria's *The Post-American World* consciously alludes to Spengler's *Decline of the West*, but says his story is one of "the rise of the rest." Yet his title portrays a world in which the contest for supremacy is over, and the United States might, at best, enjoy a twilight interregnum among nations as the *primus inter pares*.

Geopolitical power emerges, of course, from economics, as Cicero encapsulated in his famous aphorism: "Endless money forms the sinews of war." He might have added that it provides the sinews of so much else as well. Thus, financial folly that leads to economic ruin has its own wider consequences, a theme explicitly addressed in several books that explicitly connect the economic weakening of the United States with the growing strength of China and point toward a shift in world power that may result in China's hegemony.[5]

But not all matters turn merely on the exercise of state power and influence through economic power. There is also a battle of ideas and ideology. Financial folly and economic disaster in the seat of democratic capitalism give heart to those who advance the Chinese model of state and business relations, one that Henry Kissinger has characterized as a "market-authoritarian" mode. Amplifying a similar theme, Stefan Halper speaks of "authoritarian capitalism" and elaborates what he sees as the possible consequences of such an economic and ideological shift in *The Beijing Consensus: How China's Authoritarian Model Will Dominate the Twenty-First Century*.

While the crisis surely weakened the economic position of the United States for many years to come, the real question is the extent to which it may have contributed to permanently sapping our economic vitality. In addition, the resources squandered and the economic opportunities lost have increased the probability that the baton of world leadership will pass from the hands of the United States to those of some other nation.

These economic failures are representative of, and at least partially a consequence of, more general endemic institutional failings in the United States. Beyond the economic dimension, other institutional failings have been long in development, such as problems with the educational system in the United States and the general neglect of infrastructure and other public investment. Other failures have been quite surprising, as when we discovered in 2000 that our election system was unable to quickly and accurately count votes—a failing of a simple system, yet one that strikes at the heart of a democracy. Further, we see some of the prime institutions of government subject to a lack of confidence and respect, with Congress currently suffering a 76 percent disapproval rating, its worst in history. President George W. Bush suffered a majority disapproval rating for most of his presidency, but even President Barack Obama, wildly popular at his inauguration, dipped to majority disapproval within 14 months of taking office. To be explicit, these mere suggestions of a general failure of institutions may betoken a cultural lack of confidence or an exhaustion of energy that can lead to major societal problems.

If the era of America's world leadership is really drawing to a close, if our economy has been permanently weakened by the financial crisis and broader economic failings, and if the United States really has suffered a fundamental weakening of key institutions, then our ability to reform our economic institutions and the regulation of our financial system may be gravely impaired. At the very least, the weakening of our economic standing and legitimate concerns over the strength of our civil institutions suggest that we must approach the strengthening of our financial system in a new way and with a heightened seriousness.

Of course, there is no dearth of Cassandras who foretell America's demise. In 1956, Soviet premier Nikita Khrushchev said to the West: "We will bury you." However, the next half-century of history failed to follow his script. The United States has repeatedly surprised the world with its vigor and resiliency. For example, if during the Great Depression, a seer had accurately foretold America's sudden rise to unquestioned primacy after World War II, that visionary probably would have found few believers. Thus, such grand-scale predictions are extremely hazardous. Whether the financial crisis proves to be a signpost on the way to economic ruin and imperial demise will become clearer in the decades ahead.

Just as some clearly predict a world in which China plays a dominant role over the United States, others see the United States entering upon a new full century of greatness. For example, Joel Kotkin's *The Next Hundred Million: America in 2050*, foresees an expanding population, a growing importance of suburbs as vital cultural and social centers, and a period of economic flourishing. Similar in its tone of optimism, *Rebound: Why America Will Emerge Strong from the Financial Crisis*, by labor economist Stephen J. Rose, also sees a bright economic future for the United States, drawing largely from its underlying strengths in education, middle class values, and social institutions that are much stronger than many think.

These contrasting visions of decline and ascendancy, of doom and glory, reveal that the United States does not face a preordained outcome, but that we confront a serious choice. There is no doubt that the United States has suffered a decline in its economic world position and a very severe and self-inflicted economic blow from the financial crisis. However, while there are good reasons for real concern about the position of the United States in the world, a new spirit of seriousness and institutional renewal can revalidate and reestablish the position that the United States has long seen as its natural place in the world order. While this book does not offer grand proposals for re-invigorating our entire economy and culture, it is clear that addressing and confronting the economic structures that permitted the financial crisis will be key to that renewal and that business as usual cannot be expected to be sufficient to solve our problems.

Perfecting the Fatally Flawed Regulatory Regimes of the Past

We have seen that policies, regulations, business rules and practices designed to ensure a safe and sound financial system failed repeatedly. These range from federal support of home ownership, resulting in vast unintended consequences, to an overwhelming failure of prudential regulation to restrain managers of financial institutions from their own impulses. In addition, the OTD model of mortgage production created a system of perverse incentive that ran from the most humble mortgage applicant, through the entire securitization process, to afflict the grandest financial CEOs, and seduce unsophisticated investors around the world.

Already a vast number of prescriptions have been written for restoring integrity to our financial system. As one example, in his book *On the Brink*, former Secretary of the Treasury Henry Paulson set out a number of suggestions for avoiding another crisis. Some of these focus on macro issues, such as reducing global trade imbalances and calling for the United States to reduce its fiscal deficit. Most of his concrete suggestions, however, focus on improving the regulatory system for financial institutions, such as: achieving a global accord to increase bank capital, granting regulators new powers to deal with the failure of systemically important institutions, curtailing the role of the GSEs, improving the regulatory architecture to avoid gaps and redundancy in regulation, and not relying on credit ratings in the regulatory process.[6]

Similarly, Christopher Dodd, chairman of the Senate's Committee on Banking, Housing, and Urban Affairs, introduced legislation in early 2010 to reform the financial regulatory system. In support of the bill, which stood poised for final passage in mid-2010, the Committee published a summary of claims about what the bill would accomplish, including: creating a financial consumer protection agency, ending "too big to fail," streamlining bank supervision, enforcing regulation already on the books, improving corporate governance, and so on.[7] Of course, this proposed legislation had little chance of becoming actual legislation in its original form, with critics immediately denying that the legislation would end "too big to fail" in any case.[8]

Proposals such as Paulson's and Dodd's, and many others being advanced in a similar vein, while well-intentioned and certainly containing elements of a satisfactory solution, miss the essential point. These proposals recommend modest changes in the old model of regulation, such as shifting the regulation of small commercial banks from one existing agency to another. This has already been tried and has already failed. Following the S&L crisis of the 1980s and 1990s, Congress enacted regulatory form of a similar scale and scope, with the idea that another disaster like the S&L crisis—which cost about $150 billion—should never be allowed to happen. Of course, the result was no such thing—instead we have suffered a financial crisis of much greater proportions that resulted in much larger and much more widespread economic damage.

The essential point that such modest proposals seem to miss is a widespread and very serious failure of fundamental institutions in the United States. The basic criticism of proposals such as those advanced by Paulson, Dodd, and many others, is that they merely shift responsibilities among institutions that have already proven their inability to deal with the kinds of problems that confront us. Similarly, we can hardly expect that proposing the creation of this or that new agency on the model of those that have already failed to perform can be adequate to the problems that confront us. In essence, proposals like those advanced by Paulson and by Dodd seek to perfect a regulatory regime that has already proven its inadequacy.

▒▒▒▒ The Financial Crisis, the Great Recession, and Institutional Failures

Within the economic sector, the serious institutional failures we have witnessed fall under three main heads:

1. Disastrous public policies provided malignant incentives and unwisely embraced enormous public commitments.
2. Prudential regulation failed generally and nearly completely to perform its functions, and this failure infected virtually the entire financial system.
3. Corporate governance of firms failed to respond to the needs of society or the legitimate demands of their shareholders.

The decades-long effort to expand home ownership by encouraging financial institutions to lend to the less affluent, combined with a creeping public commitment to stand behind trillions of dollars in mortgages and MBS, played a major role in propelling us to disaster. As we have seen, these long-standing policies incentivized individuals and families to buy homes they could not afford and induced financial institutions to make loans that were economically unsound. While it may be a wonderful thing for government to clear away obstacles that prevent citizens from realizing their own dreams of home ownership, it should also be acknowledged that the federal government has no compelling interest in whether a family chooses to rent a home or own a house. For decades, governmental policies have leaned too heavily toward home ownership through subsidies of mortgage rates and favorable tax treatment of home ownership, while denying comparable benefits to renters. As a result, it can hardly be surprising that those whose family economics require that they should rent, instead decide to buy a home. (Given that renters are generally poorer than home owners, any subsidies should favor renters rather than home owners on grounds of distributive justice in any case.) Favorable tax treatments for home owners, coupled with subsidies to home ownership operating through GSEs such as Fannie Mae and Freddie Mac, create obvious advantages of owning over renting that are sure to create inappropriate incentives, while at the same time burdening the public with enormous implicit obligations that quickly became explicit in the financial crisis.

This commitment to subsidizing home ownership has also had a corrupting influence on the political system. With billions of dollars of subsidies to the GSEs sloshing through the political system, some politicians became both patrons and clients of Fannie Mae and Freddie Mac. Reflecting these relationships, some in Congress vociferously defend the interests of the GSEs, while receiving large political contributions from these same firms. Emblematic of this interweaving of business and politics, a citizen might note that Franklin Raines moved from being vice chairman of Fannie Mae to become White House budget director during the Clinton administration and then returned directly to Fannie Mae as CEO and chairman, only to resign from Fannie Mae in disgrace following the exposure of Fannie Mae's fraudulent accounting in 2004. At every juncture with Fannie Mae, Raines collected many millions in personal compensation.

Prudential financial regulation also exhibited massive failure during the financial crisis. This system, which was supposed to have been improved and repaired following the S&L crisis, once more presided over an even larger disaster in the financial crisis—the present crisis is perhaps 20 times as large as the S&L crisis in explicit costs, and much larger still in its overall economic and social consequence. The regulatory powers already in possession of various federal regulatory agencies—the Federal Reserve, the Comptroller of the Currency, the FDIC, the Treasury Department, the Office of Thrift Supervision, the SEC, and on and on—are actually quite extensive. Many believe that these powers were already adequate to prevent the crisis, but that regulators failed to exercise their existing powers in a responsible manner. For example, depository institutions failed to maintain adequate capital for the risks they were taking, even though their direct supervisors are fully empowered to enforce capital requirements. As we have seen, these failures of regulators to regulate under the powers they already possessed occurred again and again, whether the regulated firm was a depository institution, a GSE, an investment bank, or a credit rating agency.

The problem of regulatory agencies failing to meet their mandates arises with great frequency among financial regulators and also pervades the regulation of many industries. The persistent problem of "regulatory capture," in which regulatory agencies essentially become captives of the industries they are supposed to regulate, threatens every interface between business and government. When captured, the regulatory agency takes on the attributes of an industry lobbying group, and the public finds that the regulatory agencies they fund are failing to serve the public interest. For example, when the SEC designates a few credit rating agencies as "Nationally Recognized Statistical Rating Organizations," it thereby confers upon the lucky designees entry to an oligopoly and effectively paves their way to riches.[9]

This problem of regulatory capture has been well recognized and is a central topic of exploration in "public choice theory," which applies the methods of economics to problems in political science. If we think of governmental regulators as people with their own interests, it is not too surprising to find that those interests sometimes conflict with the strict exercise of their regulatory function in the public interest. While regulators may be agents of the public, they have their own interests as persons, so there is as much of an agency problem for regulators as there is for CEOs.[10]

Problematic aspects of these conflicting interests are the fodder of frequent journalistic reports. For example, regulators routinely come from and return to industry, passing through a revolving door between industry and government. As a striking and controversial example, Henry Paulson moved from being the CEO of Goldman Sachs to secretary of the Treasury, where he faced the financial crisis and was forced to undertake actions with potentially overwhelming consequences for his old firm. This is not to suggest that Paulson acted inappropriately as secretary of the Treasury, but his actions certainly raised suspicions at the time of the crisis, and his dual role provides a powerful illustration of the potential for conflict.

As always with questions of intention, it is extremely difficult to know whether a person acted out of some inappropriate or compromised motivation. However, there can be no doubt that a regulatory system characterized by regulatory capture and fraught with conflict of interests between the public good and the interests of an individual regulator is one that is subject to failure. While it may not be possible to ascribe the failure of prudential regulation to regulatory capture, there certainly was a failure, and one can only expect that merely tinkering with an existing regulatory framework will lead to exactly the same kind of failures we have already suffered.

Not all problems reside at the level of government—there was surely a massive failure of corporate governance of private firms as well. We have seen that the OTD model of mortgage production was fraught with incentive conflicts at virtually every step of the process. This system was not designed by any single party, but rather emerged from a variety of uncoordinated forces, and individual firms found themselves working in an industry dominated by the OTD model. These firms needed to solve the governance problem of managing their business in a system infested with perverse incentives. Against this background, there were two major failures of corporate governance, one in the general operation of the firm, and the other in managing executives and their compensation.

We have seen that firms active in the securitization business sent their line managers into the field to buy mortgages and that they hired due diligence firms to test the quality of mortgages before purchase. However, compensation systems often rewarded the firm's rank-and-file employees based on the principal value of mortgages they succeeded in buying. The incentive conflicts put in place by such an arrangement are palpable and constitute a clear failure of proper management. The goal for the firm was to buy sound mortgages at a good price, but employees were instead rewarded merely for buying mortgages. This failure must be ascribed to the senior management of the firm, for these actors bear principal responsibility for rewarding and managing line employees. To establish such a system of compensation when the potential conflicts were so manifest is a clear failure of managerial performance. It is also similar to the failure to manage traders properly, when they are managed under a reward system that encourages them to take large risks to generate quick profits without regard to the ultimate effect on the overall health of the firm. Again in this instance, management bears responsibility for specifying a sloppy reward system that encourages employees to pursue the simple selfish interests before them, even though those interests are inimical to the well-being of the firm.

At a more senior level, boards of directors bear responsibility for managing the senior leaders of the firm and for establishing their pay and reward structure. Here we see the same fault repeated—financial firms operated with reward systems for CEOs and senior managers that focused on the short run and encouraged aggressive risk-taking. The financial crisis resulted in large from excessive risk-taking by top management of financial firms, a posture toward risk that happened to be in alignment with their own incentive arrangements.

Given that boards of directors give top managers incentives that encourage them to focus on short-term payoffs, it may seem less surprising that they would institute similar compensation arrangements for their supervisees. In fact, one could see the exact advantage of those CEOs providing short-term incentives to their supervisees that would accord all too well with their own narrow interests. A CEO might reason: send employees into the field to buy any mortgage that can be bundled to make any kind of security to pump up earnings this quarter and this year, thereby pumping up my own salary right now. Years later down the road, if mortgagors can't pay and these securities don't perform, we can worry about the problem then—or I might be at another firm by then, anyway.

The history of the financial crisis and an analysis of its causes shows the widespread failure of key economic institutions: large-scale governmental policies and programs, prudential regulation, and corporate governance. These are the institutional failures that played the greatest role in causing the financial crisis and the Great Recession.

Fundamental Reform?

If the United States really has suffered a major weakening of its economic position in the world accompanied by serious impairment to its basic institutions, as I believe it has, the timid reforms suggested by Henry Paulson, Christopher Dodd, and many others will prove inadequate to the challenge. The real problem of reforming our financial system has three dimensions. First, we must preserve for all businesses reasonable freedom of operation to make business-oriented decisions in the pursuit of profit. Abandoning this first principle would be to turn our backs on centuries of accumulated knowledge about how to produce wealth and would be an abnegation of our cultural commitment to personal freedom. Second, because the financial system is so key to the entire economy, and because problems in financial firms can have such disastrous consequences for the real sector, we must act to protect the broader public from management failures at financial institutions, while still allowing these firms to seek profits. Third, we have seen strong evidence that managers can react to incentives that promise them great personal wealth, but that lead them into adopting risky commercial strategies that imperil their shareholders and other stakeholders in their firms. This is the perennial problem of faulty incentive alignment between principals and agents, most notably between shareholders and managers. Addressing these three problems in a serious way would result in financial firms that aggressively pursue profits on behalf of their owners, without endangering public welfare.

While we have seen that the dimensions of failures in the financial system have been manifold, those that affect the broader public can be addressed largely by the satisfactory solution to just two major public policy issues—the problem of financial institutions being "too big to fail" and the general problem of corporate governance.

"Too Big to Fail"

The problem of a financial institution's being "too big to fail" is not a matter of size alone. Rather, the real issue is that some financial institutions become so big and so interconnected with other firms that their difficulties pose a systemic threat to the financial sector and the broader economy. This problem of "systemic threat" is the real issue, and it does arise largely as financial institutions become very large. We have seen that attempts to resolve the financial crisis led to dramatic concentration in the financial sector, along with a tremendous growth in size for the financial firms that were already the largest in the sector before the financial crisis. As a result, we now have two firms with assets in excess of $2 trillion, two firms with assets above $1 trillion, and at least five firms with assets above $750 billion, as table 10.1 of chapter 10 shows.

To some extent, financial firms of larger size are more efficient economically and can confer benefits to the public in the form of lower prices and greater services. Thus, the last decades in the United States have seen the passing of many small financial institutions and much consolidation throughout the industry. There is little systemic risk from the merger of small or even fairly large financial institutions. However, as financial institutions become very large, they not only become too big to fail, but there is good reason to believe that they also become too large to manage. This has long been a charge leveled at Citigroup.[11] Even if increasing size, scope, and interconnectedness at very large firms continues to provide greater economic efficiency, there comes a point at which this same enlargement brings with it social costs in the form of heightened systemic risk. As a matter of public policy, there is a trade-off between capturing the benefits of increasing scale and interconnectedness and avoiding the costs of systemic risk that excessive size and systemic influence bring.

This is the key systemic risk that public policy must address. The problem of financial institutions being "too big to fail" is a staple of economic literature and of regulatory hand wringing. The financial crisis has made it clear that all previous attempts to address this problem have been ineffective, and it is further evident that the many mergers thrown together to address the crisis have made this problem worse. There is absolutely no reason to believe that past and present models of financial regulation can address this problem, so it is time to consider a new approach.

I suggest that the United States consider a policy of prohibiting any financial firm to achieve or maintain a size, scope, and level of interconnectedness that allows it to pose a systemic threat to the financial system or the real economy. This is not merely a matter of size, and the specification of limitations on firm size and activity is a matter that requires careful study to specify correctly. Any such system of constraining financial firms will also require continuing management and judgment to keep size and scope limitations relevant as the financial system evolves. Leaving the present regulatory structure to enforce such limitations offers little promise based on their past performance. To remedy this problem of regulatory failure requires accountability at a higher level than bureaucrats swimming obscurely in the alphabet soup of federal regulatory agencies.

To promote a new spirit of seriousness and to ensure accountability at the highest levels of our government and financial system, I suggest that legislation be enacted to require an annual joint statement by the president of the United States, the secretary of the Treasury, and the chairman of the Federal Reserve Board that would affirm two principles:

> No financial firm operating in the United States has a size, scope, or degree of interconnectedness that poses a systemic threat to the financial system or the real economy; and no financial firm that suffers financial distress will receive federal assistance to continue operations, to support its merger with another firm, or to compensate or support the firm's creditors beyond those depositors explicitly covered by insurance through the Federal Deposit Insurance Corporation.

The enactment of such a proposal might well incur social costs in the form of limiting the economic efficiency of a few financial firms, and this is a serious potential cost that must be evaluated carefully. However, the costs that financial distress at too-big-to-fail firms imposes is also demonstrably large. The intuition behind this proposal is that there exists a "sweet spot" in the size of financial institutions that allows them to be sufficiently large and interconnected to provide all, or at least almost all, the benefits of economic efficiency without imposing threats to the broader economic system. Even if this intuition about efficiency proves false, avoiding the threat of institutions that are too systemically important confers benefits on society that are certainly very large and that may overwhelm any loss in efficiency that results from restrictions imposed on these very large financial institutions.

At the very least, it is time to try a different approach to dealing with the problem of financial institutions being "too big to fail." So far, our efforts to respond by changing the names and acronyms of failed regulators or by re-drawing the organizational charts of regulatory agencies with much of the same personnel in place have proven totally inadequate.[12] It is past time to try a new approach with greater identifiable accountability lodged at a higher level of government.

Corporate Governance, Executive Compensation, and Firms' Risk-Taking

In the financial crisis, the spectacle of financial executives at failing firms receiving huge paydays brought public outrage to a whiter heat than any other aspect of the entire fiasco. But public outrage over high executive compensation antedates the financial crisis and pertains to compensation at firms across many industries. In the financial crisis, this outrage had a particular saliency, because the public was forced to bail out all too many miscreant firms. But even when the public has no particular stake in the operations of a firm or the pay of its executives, high pay still generates a similar outrage. (To some extent this is peculiar, as we do not observe the same indignation at movie stars who command millions for appearing in a single film; nor do we see the same general disgust at sports stars who receive many millions for 16 Sunday afternoon football appearances.)

If we are able to resolve the problem of financial institutions being of a size that threatens the public, such a change will eliminate one ground of public outrage—the concern that the public bears the burden of paying high executive compensation at a financial firm as it fails and imposes great social costs. However, this still leaves a quite legitimate concern over executive compensation, even if there is no broad public interest attached to the operations of any particular firm. There still remains the question of whether the compensation scheme induces executives to adopt risky operating policies that promise them personal enrichment, while threatening the well-being of the firm and its stakeholders.

This perceived gap between shareholder interests and corporate management is one important factor that delegitimizes business in our culture. The resultant lack of public support makes it more difficult for businesses to perform their core social function of increasing societal wealth. As businesses are the key source of wealth generation, their social standing should be a key public concern.

There is an active debate and widespread disagreement over the extent to which shareholders should have more control in the management of the firms they own. If corporate governance became a matter of democratic voting by firm owners, many fear it would lead to an inability of firm managers to follow any coherent commercial strategy, with a resulting tremendous loss in shareholder value. Alternatively, current pay practices give good grounds for wondering whether compensation policies operate in the interest of shareholders. After all, is it really necessary for shareholders to pay many millions per year to bring forth the best efforts of the best managers? Is it really necessary to tolerate huge wealth gaps between executives and workers to have firms managed efficiently? These remain unanswered questions with greatly divided opinion.

Corporate governance is a delicate institutional mechanism that should not be altered lightly. However, I believe that one principle is quite clear, and that is that the firm should be operated to benefit the firm's owners, subject to the restrictions of law and with due attention to social customs and mores.[13] I believe substantial evidence documents a gap between managerial incentives and shareholder interest that requires the firm's owners to enforce their interests more vigorously.

Part of current regulatory reform efforts reflect the belief that pay practices do not conform to legitimate shareholder interests. This has been expressed through "say-on-pay" policies—the idea that shareholders should be allowed an annual nonbinding vote to express their approval or disapproval of the pay plan for the firm's top executives. Say-on-pay principles have been incorporated into various reform proposals and have received the explicit support of the U.S. Treasury in proposed legislation.[14] The Treasury proposal also requires a separate proposal for voting on "golden parachutes"—the special payments that executives often receive when their firm is acquired.

The Treasury Department believes that the expression of outrage expressed by a no vote, as well as just the threat of a no vote, will restrain executive pay packages and encourage a tighter link between compensation design and firm performance. The say-on-pay movement antedates the Treasury proposal. A number of companies have allowed their shareholders to vote on whether to institute such a policy, and it has been accepted at many companies, but shareholders have also rejected the idea at a surprising number of firms.

The corporation has evolved over centuries and has proven to be a remarkably effective form of business organization for increasing societal wealth. Like all such core institutions, the corporation possesses an organic quality that is the outgrowth of much thought, the slow development of custom, and endless adjustment. Therefore, efforts to change the basic structure of corporate governance should proceed with great care and a light touch. Nonetheless, one may reasonably doubt that a non-binding say-on-pay is sufficient shareholder empowerment. On the other hand, the fact that shareholders at quite a few companies have turned down the opportunity to offer their say-on-pay voice may indicate that they find present rules of corporate governance to be satisfactory. Alternatively, these rejections of the say-on-pay prescription may be due to the non-binding nature of the vote and shareholders' perception that it would still leave them without a meaningful voice.

Achieving the optimal linkage between the desire of principals and the incentive of executives is so important that it demands continuing effort. If such a linkage can be achieved, firms can more successfully undertake the right business opportunities with the proper degree of risk. I do not presume to know the exact corporate governance structure that will give shareholders effective control over their firms, yet not destroy the firm's ability to implement a coherent commercial strategy. However, it does seem apparent that we should work carefully to increase the shareholder's voice in corporate governance. Only by visibly making firm management respond to shareholders' interests can we increase the legitimacy of commercial enterprise in the public's perception, and only through increased legitimacy can firms operate with their greatest effectiveness to build wealth for society.

Conclusion: Dopes, Geniuses, Saints, Scoundrels, and Ordinary People

The preface to this book posed the question: "Why would millions of dopes, geniuses, saints, scoundrels, and ordinary people all work together to lose trillions of dollars?" The intervening pages have tried to provide an answer to this question, which now can be summarized in seven sentences:

- The federal government instituted and pursued policies over many decades to support home ownership in the United States with disastrous unintended consequences.
- Trade deficits, world capital flows, and policies to maintain low interest rates promoted excessive investment in homes, resulting in illusory rising prices.
- Buoyed by a false sense of increasing wealth, home buyers and owners failed to save, consumed excessively, and took personal financial risks that led to ruin as home prices fell.
- When it was most needed, regulation of the financial sector failed most miserably.
- Housing finance and mortgage securitization grew into an originate-to-distribute system that provided perverse incentives to everyone who came in contact with the process, from home buyers, to appraisers, to mortgage brokers, to financial institutions, to credit rating agencies, to investors in mortgage-backed securities.
- Large financial firms created and relied on financial innovations and complex risk management systems that they did not fully understand, leading them to take excessive risks that proved disastrous.
- Financial firms, like those in many other industries, operated within a framework of corporate governance that rewarded top executives and other managers for focusing on the short run and taking large risks, paving the way to disaster.

While the exact constellation of causes that led to the financial crisis and Great Recession will never arise again, problems of regulation and corporate governance will persist. The two proposals advanced in the previous section—to simplify, yet strengthen, the general principles of financial regulation and to reduce incentive incompatibilities between shareholders and corporate managers by increasing the shareholders' voice—address some key persistent problems. Improved regulation can help protect the economy from financial disaster, and better corporate governance can improve firm management and risk-taking. However, history suggests that another financial crisis will arise and take us unaware. Yet we must struggle to emerge from our present economic ruins, to learn from our past mistakes, and to prepare ourselves for the next challenge.

The overarching fact of the permanent human condition is to live life knowing that death is inevitable. Perhaps an inescapable part of modern life compels us to struggle to evade the next grand example of human economic folly, conscious that new conditions will arise to fool us or our descendants once again. But studying our recent past can perhaps save us from the humiliation of repeating the same mistakes from which we now struggle to recover.

Adjustable-rate mortgage (ARM)	A mortgage in which the interest rate charged for the mortgage varies over time as interest rates rise or fall; typically, the rate is indexed to an interest rate benchmark, such as the **London Interbank Offered Rate (LIBOR)**
Alt-A	Originally a type of mortgage security (and by extension a type of mortgage) offered to a financially credible borrower who does not quality for a **conforming mortgage**, perhaps due to a reluctance or inability to prove income; in the housing bubble, the quality of these mortgages declined to approximate **subprime mortgages**
Amortization	The repayment of principal on a loan that occurs over time as regular payments on the loan are made
Asset-backed security	A debt security issued with the backing of a specific pool of assets dedicated to serving as collateral; the promised cash flow on the security can be quite different in pattern from the assets that are in the pool of collateral: typical assets in such pools include mortgages, car loans, accounts receivable, etc.

Automated underwriting system (AUS)	A computer program designed to make decisions on mortgage lending automatically as a function of information provided to the program
Basel Accords	Two sets of nonbinding agreements among central bankers from the **G10 countries**, Basel I (1988) and Basel II (2004); these accords provide guidance for central banks regarding "best practices" for national banking regulations
Capital	Solid wealth, usually held in a **liquid** form, that is used to found a business and to provide backing for a firm's financial obligations in times of financial stress
Capital Purchase Program (CPP)	A part of the **Troubled Asset Relief Program (TARP)** under which the U. S. Treasury would purchase senior preferred shares in financial institutions
Collateralized debt obligation (CDO)	A debt security that promises payments derived from the cash inflows of a pool of assets that serve as collateral for the CDO; often such securities are issued with various **tranches**, which can have different payment patterns; see **asset-backed security** and **collateralized mortgage obligation (CMO)**
Collateralized mortgage obligation (CMO)	A type of **collateralized debt obligation (CDO)** in which a pool of mortgages serve as collateral for the security
Conforming mortgage	A residential mortgage with characteristics specified by a **GSE** that makes them eligible for purchase by the **GSE;** these characteristics relate to quality of the property, size of the loan, and borrower documentation, and are subject to change over time
Counterparty	In a financial transaction, a trading partner; if two firms enter a financial contract, each is a counterparty to the other
Credit default swap (CDS)	A **financial derivative** with characteristics similar to an insurance policy, in which the insured event is a default on a financial obligation, such as a bond; the CDS purchaser makes periodic payment to the CDS seller, and the seller is obligated to pay the purchaser if the defined credit event occurs

Credit derivative	A **financial derivative** designed to pay the purchaser of the derivative contract if a specific credit event occurs, such as a payment that becomes due if a particular bond defaults; most prominently a **credit default swap (CDS)**
Credit enhancement	A set of techniques designed to improve the credit rating of a new security issuance
Credit rating agency	A business firm, typically a corporation, that offers opinions on the likelihood that a particular debt security will default, or fail to make all payments in full and at the time promised; the most prominent such firms are Moody's, S&P, and Fitch; see also **nationally recognized statistical rating organization (NRSRO)**
Depository institution	In the United States, a financial institution that is legally empowered to accept monetary deposits; prominent such institutions are commercial banks, savings institutions, and credit unions
Equity tranche	In a **collateralized debt obligation (CDO), the tranche** that stands last in order of priority; owners of the equity tranche receive payments if and only if all other tranche owners have received all payments owed
Eurodollar	A loan in the international market denominated in U.S. dollars; often specifically refers to a dollar-denominated bank deposit held in a bank outside the United States
Excess spread	A technique of **credit enhancement** in which the interest rate promised on a **collateralized debt obligation (CDO)** is less than the interest rate promised by the assets that form the collateral pool
Fannie Mae	Similar to **Freddie Mac**, a principal **GSE;** a previously privately owned firm sponsored by the federal government to transact in the mortgage market in support of the housing industry; now under conservatorship of the federal government
Federal Deposit Insurance Corporation (FDIC)	An agency of the U.S. Treasury that guarantees the safety of deposits at U.S. depository institutions

FICO score	For consumers, the most commonly cited rating of financial capacity; FICO stands for Fair Isaac Corporation, with the score ranging from 350 to 800, with higher values indicating greater quality of credit standing; a **subprime** mortgage is often defined as one offered to a borrower with a low FICO score, such as 650 or lower
Financial derivative	A financial contract in which the payments depend on the behavior of an underlying, or reference, financial instrument; example: the value of a stock option (the financial derivative) is a function of the value of a share of stock (the underlying, or reference, financial instrument)
Fixed-rate mortgage	A mortgage in which the interest rate is constant, or fixed, over the life of the mortgage; contrasts with **adjustable rate mortgage**
Freddie Mac	Similar to **Fannie Mae**, a principal **GSE;** a previously privately owned firm sponsored by the federal government to transact in the mortgage market in support of the housing industry; now under conservatorship of the federal government
G10 countries	A group of ten large industrialized countries that meet and sometimes act together to establish economic and financial policies; the group actually now consists of eleven countries: Belgium, Canada, France, Germany, Italy, Japan, the Netherlands, Sweden, Switzerland, the United Kingdom, and the United States
Government-sponsored enterprise (GSE)	A private firm established by the federal government with a public purpose; the two principal **GSEs** are **Fannie Mae** and **Freddie Mac;** the public purpose of these firms was to increase the robustness of the residential mortgage market in the United States; originally established as private firms, **Fannie Mae** and **Freddie Mac** are now under a conservatorship of the U.S. federal government

Haircut	A percentage deducted from the face value of an asset that serves as collateral; example: a debt security with a face value of $100 might serve as collateral for a loan of $90, reflecting a 10 percent haircut; also, a percentage deducted from the full value of an obligation in settlement of an obligation; example: for a debtor in distress, a creditor might accept $40 in payment of a $50 debt, implying a 20 percent haircut
Hedge fund	An investment fund that is lightly regulated and whose investors are restricted to other investment funds or wealthy individuals; as the name suggests, such funds originally took both long and short positions, so that the risks of one could offset the risks of the others, consistent with their being *hedge* funds; now these funds follow a wide variety of investment policies
Investment bank	A financial institution whose primary business is advising business clients and whose key function is assisting corporations in the raising of capital through the issuance of debt obligations and common stock
Jumbo mortgage	A mortgage with a principal balance that exceeds the level established for a **conforming mortgage**
Junior tranche	In a **collateralized debt obligation (CDO)**, a tranche that receives a lower priority than a **senior tranche**; see also **equity tranche, mezzanine tranche**, and **toxic waste**
Leverage	In finance, the degree to which a firm uses borrowed funds to finance its assets; often measured as the ratio of total assets to total stockholders' capital; example: a firm that starts with $50 of capital, borrows $100, and purchases $150 of assets, would be levered 3:1
Liar's loan	A perjurious term for a mortgage loan granted based on a statement of the borrower's financial circumstances, rather than proof of financial capacity; see also **low-doc loan** and **stated-Income loan**

Liquidity	For an asset, the degree to which it can be converted to cash immediately with no reduction in value
Loan-to-value (LTV) ratio	In mortgage finance, the ratio of the principal owed on a mortgage relative to the value of the underlying home that secures the mortgage loan
London Interbank Offered Rate (LIBOR)	The interest rate at which large international banks lend to each other; the rate varies by the currency and duration of the loan, with the most common type of LIBOR rate pertaining to 90-day loans of U.S. dollars
Low-doc loan	A mortgage loan made without full proof and documentation of the borrower's financial income, wealth, and other obligations; see also **liar's loan** and **stated-income loan**
Mark-to-market accounting	A principle of accounting in which the accounting value of an asset or liability is shown as the "true" current market value of the instrument; contrasts with historical accounting principles in which an asset or liability is kept on the books at a value that reflects its original price
Mezzanine tranche	In a **collateralized debt obligation (CDO)** a kind of **junior tranche** that lies in the middle range of priorities, below the **senior tranche(s)** but above the **equity tranche**
Monoline insuror	An insurance company that specializes in guaranteeing payments on debt issues in the event the original issuer defaults
Moral hazard	The risk that the behavior of one party to a transaction may change its behavior in a manner that is adverse to the other party in the transaction as a result of entering the transaction; example: securing a fire insurance policy might reduce the policyholder's fire mitigation efforts
Mortgage broker	A person or firm that acts as an intermediary between a mortgage borrower and lender and matches borrowers with lenders in exchange for compensation

Mortgage fraud	The acquisition of a mortgage loan based on the material misrepresentation of relevant information, such as the borrower's assets, income, or intentions for using a property
Mortgage-backed security (MBS)	A debt obligation whose promised payments are derived from a pool of underlying mortgages that serve as collateral; see also **asset-backed security, collateralized debt obligation (CDO)**, and **collateralized mortgage obligation (CMO)**
Nationally recognized statistical rating organization (NRSRO)	A firm officially recognized by the Securities Exchange Commission as a **credit rating agency**; dominant example firms are Moody's, S&P, and Fitch
Negative amortization	In a debt obligation, the increase in the principal amount that results when periodic payments are less than the interest accrued for the period; see **amortization**
Off-balance sheet	For a firm, an asset, liability, or operation of the firm that is not reflected in the firm's balance sheet and other financial statements; the purpose of such an accounting practice may be to reflect the actual condition of the firm, or it may be to make the firm's financial position appear stronger than it actually is
Option-ARM	An adjustable rate mortgage that gives the mortgagor the right to skip some monthly payments or to pay less than the normal amount in some periods, with the deficiency in payment leading to an increased principal balance
Over-collateralization	A technique of **credit enhancement** in a **collateralized debt obligation (CDO)**, in which the face value of the pool of assets that serves as collateral exceeds the face value of the obligations issued in the CDO; example: a CDO issue with $100 million of face value that has a pool of assets with $105 million of face value is over-collateralized by $5 million

Pass-through security	A security that gives title to a fractional ownership of an underlying pool of assets; in each period, a pass-through investor receives a fraction of all cash flows from the underlying pool of assets that is proportional to the fraction of pass-throughs the investor owns
Piggyback mortgage	A type of second mortgage that is issued at the same time as a first mortgage on a newly acquired property; the piggyback mortgage is often used to borrow some or all of the down payment required by the first mortgage; example: for a house priced at $100,000, the first mortgage might have a principal amount of $80,000 and the house buyer could acquire a piggyback mortgage for $15,000, giving 95 percent financing for the house purchase
Predatory lending	In mortgage finance, the making of a loan that abuses or disadvantages the borrower, often taking advantage of the borrower's ignorance or lack of financial sophistication
Prime mortgage	Another term for **conforming mortgage**
Regulatory arbitrage	The exploitation of a difference between the regulatory treatment and the true economics of a position or transaction, in which a firm restructures the position or transaction to secure a more favorable regulatory treatment without changing the underlying economic realities
Savings and loan association (S&L)	In the United States, a type of depository institution long associated with mortgage lending and previously distinguished from commercial banks by regulations distinguishing the powers of the two types of institutions; now a depository institution essentially similar to a commercial bank, but holding a charter as an S&L as an artifact of a previous regulatory era
Securitization	A process in which financial assets (e.g., home mortgages or car loans) are collected to form a pool of assets and, based on the cash flows promised from the pool, a new security is issued with payment characteristics different from those assets that form the pool; see **collateralized debt obligation (CDO), collateralized mortgage obligation (CMO), asset-backed security (ABS)**

Securitizer	A financial institution that undertakes a securitization
Senior tranche	In a **collateralized debt obligation (CDO)**, the class of constituent, newly issued securities that has first claim on the cash flows from the underlying pool of assets that serves as collateral
Short sale	A process in which an investor or speculator borrows a financial asset from another party and sells it in the marketplace; key to this transaction is that the short seller does not own the asset that is being sold; example: a stock trader believes that Apple Computer is overvalued, so the trader borrows 1,000 shares from her broker and sells those shares in the market; to conclude the transaction, the trader must buy those shares at some point and return the shares to the broker, with a gain arising from a fall in the price of the shares compared to the original sale price, or a loss resulting from an increase in the price of the shares compared to the original sale price
Special-purpose entity (SPE)	A legal entity (corporation, trust, limited liability company, or partnership) typically formed by, and completely owned by, a financial institution, to undertake the acquisition and financing of particular types of financial instruments; the SPE is often formed as a foreign entity technically outside the purview of the sponsoring financial institution, at least for regulatory purposes; often the entity is held off the financial statements of the sponsoring institution, which makes the financial condition of the sponsor appear stronger; similar to a **special-purpose vehicle (SPV)** or **structured-investment vehicle (SIV)**
Special-purpose vehicle (SPV)	See **special-purpose entity (SPE)**; similar to a Structured-investment vehicle (SIV)
Stated-income loan	A mortgage loan in which the lender grants a loan based on a statement of the borrower's income rather than proof of that income; See also **liar's loan** and **low-doc loan**

Structured-finance	See **collateralized debt obligation (CDO)** and **collateralized mortgage obligation (CMO)**
Structured-investment vehicle (SIV)	See **special-purpose entity (SPE)**; similar to a special-purpose vehicle (SPV)
Subprime	In mortgage finance, a home loan made to a borrower with a poor credit record or limited financial means compared to a borrower with stronger financial credentials; often vaguely defined as a home loan made to a borrower with a **FICO score** in the range of 650 or lower
Swap	A financial transaction in which two parties agree to exchange a sequence of payments over time; example: two parties may contract with one promising to make a series of periodic interest payments at a fixed rate of interest, while the other party promises to make a series of periodic interest payments at a floating rate of interest
TED spread	The interest rate differential between a U.S. Treasury obligation and a **Eurodollar** deposit of the same maturity; the U.S. Treasury will have a lower interest rate, and the interest rate differential indicates the perceived riskiness of large banks engaged in the international money markets
Term-Asset Backed Securities Loan Facility (TALF)	A program of the Federal Reserve initiated during the financial crisis to support the issuance of **asset-backed securities (ABS)**, in an effort to stimulate consumer lending
Too Big to Fail	A regulatory concern that some financial institutions have a size, interconnectedness, and financially systemic importance that prevents regulators from allowing such a firm to go into bankruptcy for a fear of damage to the financial system
Toxic waste	In a structured finance security, the **tranche** that is paid last in the order of priority, and is thus the riskiest **tranche** in a given security offering, but one that offers the highest return if all payments on the underlying financial obligations are honored; see also **equity tranche**

Tranche	In a **structured-finance** security, one of a number of related securities that make up the entire offering; in a typical offering, each **tranche** has different payment characteristics that can be differentiated by priority in the order of payment, in the rate of payment, in the duration of the stream of payments, and so on; see also **collateralized debt obligation (CDO)**, **collateralized mortgage obligation (CMO)**, **senior tranche, mezzanine tranche**, and **junior tranche**
Troubled-Asset Relief Program (TARP)	A program established by the Emergency Stabilization Act of 2008 with an initial capitalization of $700 billion to purchase illiquid assets from financial institutions in response to the financial crisis; these funds were eventually used to purchase equity positions in financial institutions and to form a variety of additional sub-programs; see **capital purchase program (CPP)**
Underwriter	In mortgage finance, an agent or employee of a financial institution that assesses the creditworthiness of a potential borrower and determines whether to grant a loan
Unwind	To terminate an existing financial position or commitment by undertaking further financial transactions to eliminate an economic or financial risk; example: If one owns a stock option, one can unwind the position by selling an identical stock option
Value-at-Risk (VaR)	A quantitative, financial, risk-management technique designed to measure a firm's financial exposure as a function of the probability of exceeding a loss of a certain size over a given period; example: The outcome of a VaR analysis might result in a finding that a firm can be 95 percent confident that the loss on a given portfolio will not exceed 7 percent over the next 10 days

Waterfall   In a **structured-finance** security, the flow of cash that proceeds from fully satisfying the highest-priority **tranche** to fulfilling obligations to subsequent **tranches** of lower priority; as a metaphor, the cash flows from the underlying securities fall first into the coffers of the highest priority **tranche** and upon complete satisfaction of that obligation, the balance flows to the next priority **tranche** and so on, until the cash flow is exhausted

Timeline of the Subprime
Financial Crisis

Sources: This time line draws heavily upon, and is a radical abridgment of, "The Financial Crisis: A Timeline of Events and Policy Actions," of the Federal Reserve Bank of St. Louis, which is available at: http://timeline.stlouisfed.org/pdf/CrisisTimeline.pdf, accessed February 23, 2010. It is supplemented by the author's research.

Second Quarter, 2006: Home Prices Peak according to the S&P/Case-Shiller Index

First Quarter, 2007: Home prices peak according to the index of the Office of Federal Home Enterprises Oversight.

February 27, 2007: The Federal Home Loan Mortgage Corporation (Freddie Mac) announces that it will no longer buy the most risky subprime mortgages and mortgage-related securities.

March 13, 2007: The Mortgage Bankers Association reports that 4.95 percent of all mortgages and 13.3 percent of subprime loans experienced late or missed payments.

June 1, 2007: Standard and Poor's and Moody's Investor Services downgrade over 100 bonds backed by second-lien subprime mortgages.

June 7, 2007: Bear Stearns suspends redemptions from its High-Grade Structured Credit Strategies Enhanced Leverage Fund.

June 12, 2007: Moody's downgrades ratings for $5 billion MBS.

June 12, 2007: Bear Stearns announces problems at two of its hedge funds, due to deterioration in the value of the funds' MBS.

June 22, 2007: Bear Stearns injects capital into its two troubled hedge funds in a bailout attempt.

July 11, 2007: Standard and Poor's places 612 securities backed by subprime residential mortgages on a credit watch.

July 24, 2007: Countrywide Financial Corporation warns of "difficult conditions."

July 31, 2007: Bear Stearns liquidates two hedge funds that invested in various types of mortgage-backed securities.

August 16, 2007: Fitch Ratings downgrades Countrywide Financial Corporation, and Countrywide borrows its entire $11.5 billion credit line from other banks.

August 17, 2007: Fed reduces discount rate from 6.25 percent to 5.75 percent. This is the first of 12 reductions that will take the discount rate down to 0.50 percent.

August 23, 2007: Bank of America injects $2 billion into Countrywide.

September 14, 2007: Northern Rock, the United Kingdom's fifth-largest mortgage lender, experiences England's first bank run in almost 150 years. The Chancellor of the Exchequer authorizes the Bank of England to provide liquidity support.

October 9, 2007: The Dow Jones Industrial Average closes at 14,164.53. This will come to be recognized as the peak of the stock market.

October 15, 2007: Citigroup announces a $6.4 billion write-down of assets.

October 24, 2007: Merrill Lynch & Co announces an $8.4 billion write-down.

November 4, 2007: Citigroup increases its write-down to $11 billion; CEO resigns.

November 7, 2007: Morgan Stanley announces a $3.7 billion write-down.

December 13, 2007: Citigroup Inc. brings $49 billion in distressed assets onto its balance sheet.

January 11, 2008: Bank of America announces that it will purchase Countrywide Financial in an all-stock transaction worth approximately $4 billion.

January 18, 2008: Washington Mutual reports a $1.87 billion loss for fourth quarter 2007.

January 18, 2008: Fitch Ratings downgrades Ambac Financial Group's insurance financial strength rating to AA, Credit Watch Negative. Standard and Poor's place Ambac's AAA rating on CreditWatch Negative.

February 13, 2008: President Bush signs the Economic Stimulus Act of 2008.

February 17, 2008: Northern Rock is taken into state ownership by the Treasury of the United Kingdom.

March 14, 2008: The Federal Reserve Board approves the financing arrangement announced by JPMorgan Chase and Bear Stearns.

June 5, 2008: The Federal Reserve Board approves Bank of America's plan to acquire Countrywide Financial Corporation.

June 5, 2008: Standard and Poor's downgrades monoline bond insurers AMBAC and MBIA from AAA to AA.

July 11, 2008: The Office of Thrift Supervision closes IndyMac Bank, F.S.B.

July 13, 2008: The Federal Reserve Board authorizes the Federal Reserve Bank of New York to lend to the Federal National Mortgage Association (Fannie Mae) and the Federal Home Loan Mortgage Corporation (Freddie Mac), should such lending prove necessary.

July 13, 2008: The U.S. Treasury Department announces a temporary increase in the credit lines of Fannie Mae and Freddie Mac and a temporary authorization for the Treasury to purchase equity in either GSE if needed.

July 30, 2008: President Bush signs into law the Housing and Economic Recovery Act of 2008. This act authorizes the Treasury to purchase GSE obligations and reforms the regulatory supervision of the GSEs under a new Federal Housing Finance Agency.

August 17, 2008: The Federal Open Market Committee announces notes that the "downside risks to growth have increased appreciably."

September 7, 2008: The Federal Housing Finance Agency (FHFA) places Fannie Mae and Freddie Mac in government conservatorship.

September 15, 2008: Bank of America announces its plan to purchase Merrill Lynch for $50 billion.

September 15, 2008: Lehman Brothers Holdings Incorporated files for Chapter 11 bankruptcy protection.

September 16, 2008: The Federal Reserve Board authorizes the Federal Reserve Bank of New York to lend up to $85 billion to the American International Group (AIG).

September 17, 2008: The SEC announces a temporary emergency ban on naked short selling in the stocks of all companies.

September 19, 2008: The SEC announces a temporary emergency ban on the short selling of all 799 companies in the financial sector.

September 21, 2008: The Federal Reserve Board allows investment banking companies Goldman Sachs and Morgan Stanley to become bank holding companies.

September 25, 2008: The Office of Thrift Supervision closes Washington Mutual Bank, and the FDIC facilitates WaMu's assets to JPMorgan Chase.

September 29, 2008: The FDIC announces that Citigroup will purchase the banking operations of Wachovia Corporation. The FDIC agrees to enter into a loss-sharing arrangement with Citigroup on a $312 billion pool of loans, with Citigroup absorbing the first $42 billion of losses and the FDIC absorbing losses beyond that. In return, Citigroup would grant the FDIC $12 billion in preferred stock and warrants.

October 3, 2008: Wells Fargo announces a competing proposal to purchase Wachovia Corporation that does not require assistance from the FDIC.

October 3, 2008: Congress passes and President Bush signs into law the Emergency Economic Stabilization Act of 2008 (Public Law 110-343), which establishes the $700 billion Troubled Asset Relief Program (TARP).

October 7, 2008: The FDIC announces an increase in deposit insurance coverage to $250,000 per depositor as authorized by the Emergency Economic Stabilization Act of 2008.

October 8, 2008: The Federal Reserve Board authorizes the Federal Reserve Bank of New York to borrow up to $37.8 billion in investment-grade, fixed-income securities from American International Group (AIG) in return for cash collateral.

October 10, 2008: The TED spread hits a maximum of 5.76 percent.

October 12, 2008: The Federal Reserve Board announces its approval of an application by Wells Fargo to acquire Wachovia Corporation.

October 14, 2008: U.S. Treasury Department announces the Troubled Asset Relief Program (TARP) that will purchase capital in financial institutions under the authority of the Emergency Economic Stabilization Act of 2008. The U.S. Treasury will make available $250 billion of capital to U.S. financial institutions. This facility will allow banking organizations to apply for a preferred stock investment by the U.S. Treasury. Nine large financial organizations announce their intention to subscribe to the facility in an aggregate amount of $125 billion.

November 10, 2008: The Federal Reserve Board approves the applications of American Express and American Express Travel Related Services to become bank holding companies.

November 10, 2008: The Federal Reserve Board and the U.S. Treasury Department announce a restructuring of the government's financial support of AIG. The Treasury will purchase $40 billion of AIG preferred shares under the TARP program, a portion of which will be used to reduce the Federal Reserve's loan to AIG from $85 billion to $60 billion. The terms of the loan are modified to reduce the interest rate to the three-month LIBOR plus 300 basis points and lengthen the term of the loan from two to five years. The Federal Reserve Board also authorizes the Federal Reserve Bank of New York to establish two new lending facilities for AIG: the Residential Mortgage-Backed Securities Facility will lend up to $22.5 billion to a newly formed limited liability company (LLC) to purchase residential MBS from AIG; the Collateralized Debt Obligations Facility will lend up to $30 billion to a newly formed LLC to purchase CDOs from AIG (Maiden Lane III LLC).

November 17, 2008: Three large U.S. life insurance companies seek TARP funding: Lincoln National, Hartford Financial Services Group, and Genworth Financial announce their intentions to purchase lenders/depositories and thus qualify as savings and loan companies to access TARP funding.

November 18, 2008: Executives of Ford, General Motors, and Chrysler testify before Congress, requesting access to the TARP for federal loans.

November 20, 2008: Fannie Mae and Freddie Mac announce that they will suspend mortgage foreclosures until January 2009.

November 23, 2008: The U.S. Treasury Department, Federal Reserve Board, and FDIC jointly announce an agreement with Citigroup to provide a package of guarantees, liquidity access, and capital. Citigroup will issue preferred shares to the Treasury and FDIC in exchange for protection against losses on a $306 billion pool of commercial and residential securities held by Citigroup. The Federal Reserve will backstop residual risk in the asset pool through a non-recourse loan. In addition, the Treasury will invest an additional $20 billion in Citigroup from the TARP.

November 25, 2008: The Federal Reserve Board announces the creation of the Term Asset-Backed Securities Lending Facility (TALF), under which the Federal Reserve Bank of New York will lend up to $200 billion on a non-recourse basis to holders of AAA-rated asset-backed securities and recently originated consumer and small business loans. The U.S. Treasury will provide $20 billion of TARP money for credit protection.

November 25, 2008: The Federal Reserve Board announces a new program to purchase direct obligations of housing related government-sponsored enterprises (GSEs)—Fannie Mae, Freddie Mac, and Federal

Home Loan Banks—and MBS backed by the GSEs. Purchases of up to $100 billion in GSE direct obligations will be conducted as auctions among Federal Reserve primary dealers. Purchases of up to $500 billion in MBS will be conducted by asset managers.

November 26, 2008: The Federal Reserve Board announces approval of the notice of Bank of America Corporation to acquire Merrill Lynch and Company.

December 10, 2008: The FDIC reiterates the guarantee of federal deposit insurance in the event of a bank failure.

December 11, 2008: The Business Cycle Dating Committee of the National Bureau of Economic Research announces that a peak in U.S. economic activity occurred in December 2007 and that the economy has since been in a recession.

December 16, 2008: Fed reduces discount rate to 0.50 percent. This will prove to be the final of 12 successive discount rate reductions, and this rate will remain in place for more than two years, until February 19, 2010.

December 19, 2008: The U.S. Treasury Department authorizes loans of up to $13.4 billion for General Motors and $4.0 billion for Chrysler from the TARP.

December 19, 2008: The Federal Reserve Board announces revised terms and conditions of the Term Asset-Backed Securities Loan Facility (TALF). Among the revisions are an extension of TALF loans from maturities of one year to three years and an expansion of eligible ABS collateral.

December 22, 2008: The Federal Reserve Board approves the application of CIT Group, an $81 billion financing company, to become a bank holding company. The Board cites "unusual and exigent circumstances affecting the financial markets" for expeditious action on CIT Group's application.

December 24, 2008: The Federal Reserve Board approves the applications of GMAC LLC and IB Finance Holding Company, LLC (IBFHC) to become bank holding companies, on conversion of GMAC Bank, a $33 billion Utah industrial loan company, to a commercial bank. GMAC Bank is a direct subsidiary of IBFHC and an indirect subsidiary of GMAC LLC, a $211 billion company. The Board cites "unusual and exigent circumstances affecting the financial markets" for expeditious action on these applications. As part of the agreement, General Motors will reduce its ownership interest in GMAC to less than 10 percent.

December 29, 2008: The U.S. Treasury Department announces that it will purchase $5 billion in equity from GMAC as part of its program to assist the domestic automotive industry. The Treasury also agrees to lend up to $1 billion to General Motors "so that GM can participate in a rights offering at GMAC in support of GMAC's reorganization as a bank holding company." This commitment is in addition to the support announced on December 19, 2008.

December 30, 2008: The Federal Reserve Board announces that it expects to begin to purchase mortgage-backed securities backed by Fannie Mae, Freddie Mac, and Ginnie Mae under a previously announced program in early January 2009 (see November 25, 2008).

January 5, 2009: The Federal Reserve Bank of New York begins purchasing fixed-rate mortgage-backed securities guaranteed by Fannie Mae, Freddie Mac, and Ginnie Mae under a program first announced on November 25, 2008.

January 8, 2009: Moody's Investor Services issues a report suggesting that the Federal Home Loan Banks are currently facing the potential for significant accounting write-downs on their $76.2 billion private-label MBS securities portfolio. According to Moody's, only four of 12 Banks' capital ratios would remain above regulatory minimums under a worst-case scenario.

January 13, 2009: The Federal Home Loan Bank of Seattle reports that it will likely report a risk-based capital deficiency and suspend its dividend because of a decline in the market value of its mortgage-backed securities portfolio. The move follows a similar announcement on January 8 by the Federal Home Loan Bank of San Francisco.

January 16, 2009: The Treasury, Federal Reserve, and FDIC announce a package of guarantees, liquidity access, and capital for Bank of America. The Treasury and the FDIC will enter a loss-sharing arrangement with Bank of America on a $118 billion portfolio of loans, securities, and other assets in exchange for preferred shares. In addition, and if necessary, the Federal Reserve will provide a non-recourse loan to backstop residual risk in the portfolio. Separately, the Treasury will invest $20 billion in Bank of America from the TARP in exchange for preferred stock.

January 28, 2009: The National Credit Union Administration (NCUA) Board announces that the NCUA will guarantee uninsured shares at all corporate credit unions through February 2009 and establish a voluntary guarantee program for uninsured shares of credit unions through December 2010. The Board also approves a $1 billion capital purchase in

U.S. Central Corporate Federal Credit Union. Corporate credit unions provide financing, check clearing, and other services to retail credit unions.

February 6, 2009: The Federal Reserve Board releases additional terms and conditions of the Term Asset-Backed Securities Loan Facility (TALF). Under the TALF, the Federal Reserve Bank of New York will lend up to $200 billion to eligible owners of certain AAA-rated asset-backed securities backed by newly and recently originated auto loans, credit card loans, student loans, and SBA-guaranteed small business loans.

February 10, 2009: U.S. Treasury Secretary Timothy Geithner announces a Financial Stability Plan involving Treasury purchases of convertible preferred stock in eligible banks, the creation of a Public-Private Investment Fund to acquire troubled loans and other assets from financial institutions, expansion of the Federal Reserve's Term Asset-Backed Securities Loan Facility (TALF), and new initiatives to stem residential mortgage foreclosures and to support small business lending.

February 10, 2009: The Federal Reserve Board announces that is prepared to expand the Term Asset-Backed Securities Loan Facility (TALF) to as much as $1 trillion and broaden the eligible collateral to include AAA-rated commercial mortgage-backed securities, private-label residential mortgage-backed securities, and other asset-backed securities. An expansion of the TALF would be supported by $100 billion from the Troubled Asset Relief Program (TARP). The Federal Reserve Board will announce the date that the TALF will commence operations later this month.

February 17, 2009: The Treasury Department releases its first monthly survey of bank lending by the top 20 recipients of government investment through the Capital Purchase Program. The survey found that banks continued to originate, refinance, and renew loans from the beginning of the program in October through December 2008.

February 17, 2009: President Obama signs into law the "American Recovery and Reinvestment Act of 2009," which includes a variety of spending measures and tax cuts intended to promote economic recovery.

February 18, 2009: President Obama announces the Homeowner Affordability and Stability Plan. The plan includes a program to permit the refinancing of conforming home mortgages owned or guaranteed by Fannie Mae or Freddie Mac that currently exceed 80 percent of the value of the underlying home. The plan also creates a $75 billion Homeowner Stability Initiative to modify the terms of eligible home loans to reduce monthly loan payments. In addition, the Treasury Department will increase its preferred stock purchase agreements with Fannie Mae and Freddie Mac to $200 billion, and increase the limits on the size of Fannie Mae and Freddie Mac's portfolios to $900 billion.

February 23, 2009: The Treasury Department, Federal Deposit Insurance Corporation, Office of the Comptroller of the Currency, Office of Thrift Supervision, and the Federal Reserve Board issue a joint statement that the U.S. government stands firmly behind the banking system, and that the government will ensure that banks have the capital and liquidity they need to provide the credit necessary to restore economic growth. Further, the agencies reiterate their determination to preserve the stability of systemically important financial institutions.

February 25, 2009: The Federal Reserve Board, Federal Deposit Insurance Corporation, Office of the Comptroller of the Currency, and Office of Thrift Supervision announce that they will conduct forward-looking economic assessments or "stress tests" of eligible U.S. bank holding companies with assets exceeding $100 billion. Supervisors will work with the firms to estimate the range of possible future losses and the resources to absorb such losses over a two-year period. The assessment process is expected to be completed by the end of April 2009.

February 26, 2009: The FDIC announces that the number of "problem banks" increased from 171 institutions with $116 billion of assets at the end of the third quarter of 2008, to 252 insured institutions with $159 billion in assets at the end of fourth quarter of 2008. The FDIC also announces that there were 25 bank failures and five assistance transactions in 2008, which was the largest annual number since 1993.

February 26, 2009: Fannie Mae reports a loss of $25.2 billion in the fourth quarter of 2008, and a full-year 2008 loss of $58.7 billion. Fannie Mae also reports that on February 25, 2009, the Federal Housing Finance Agency submitted a request for $15.2 billion from the Treasury Department under the terms of the Senior Preferred Stock Purchase Agreement in order to eliminate Fannie Mae's net worth deficit as of December 31, 2008.

February 27, 2009: The Federal Deposit Insurance Corporation (FDIC) announces changes in its risk-based assessment system and a 20 basis point emergency special assessment on insured depository institutions to be collected on September 30, 2009.

March 2, 2009: The Treasury Department and Federal Reserve Board announce a restructuring of the government's assistance to American International Group (AIG). Under the restructuring, AIG will receive as much as $30 billion of additional capital from the Troubled Asset Relief

Program (TARP). In addition, the Treasury Department will exchange its existing $40 billion cumulative preferred shares in AIG for new preferred shares with revised terms that more closely resemble common equity. Finally, AIG's revolving credit facility with the Federal Reserve Bank of New York will be reduced from $60 billion to no less than $25 billion and the terms will be modified. In exchange, the Federal Reserve will receive preferred interests in two special purpose vehicles created to hold the outstanding common stock of two subsidiaries of AIG: American Life Insurance Company and American International Assurance Company Ltd. Separately, AIG reports a fourth quarter 2008 loss of $61.7 billion, and a loss of $99.3 billion for all of 2008.

March 3, 2009: The Treasury Department and the Federal Reserve Board announce the launch of the Term Asset-Backed Securities Loan Facility (TALF). Under the program, the Federal Reserve Bank of New York will lend up to $200 billion to eligible owners of certain AAA-rated asset-backed securities backed by newly and recently originated auto loans, credit card loans, student loans, and small business loans that are guaranteed by the Small Business Administration. The Federal Reserve and Treasury expect to include asset-backed securities backed by other types of loans in future monthly fundings. Subscriptions for funding in March will be accepted on March 17, 2009. Securitizations will be funded by the program on March 25, 2009. The program will hold monthly fundings through December 2009 or longer if extended by the Federal Reserve Board.

March 4, 2009: The Treasury Department announces guidelines to enable servicers to begin modifications of eligible mortgages under the Homeowner Affordability and Stability Plan.

March 11, 2009: The Federal Reserve Board releases the minutes of its meetings from July 13, 2008, through December 16, 2008 concerning Federal Reserve liquidity facilities and other issues related to the financial turmoil.

March 11, 2009: Freddie Mac announces that it had a net loss of $23.9 billion in the fourth quarter of 2008, and a net loss of $50.1 billion for 2008 as a whole. Further, Freddie Mac announces that its conservator has submitted a request to the U.S. Treasury Department for an additional $30.8 billion in funding for the company under the Senior Preferred Stock Purchase Agreement with the Treasury.

March 17, 2009: The Federal Deposit Insurance Corporation (FDIC) decides to extend the debt guarantee portion of the Temporary Liquidity Guarantee Program (TLGP) from June 30, 2009 through October 31,

2009, and to impose a surcharge on debt issued with a maturity of one year or more, beginning in the second quarter of 2009, to gradually phase out the program.

March 18, 2009: The FOMC votes to maintain the target range for the effective federal funds at 0 to 0.25 percent. In addition, the FOMC decides to increase the size of the Federal Reserve's balance sheet by purchasing up to an additional $750 billion of agency mortgage-backed securities, bringing its total purchases of these securities to up to $1.25 trillion this year, and to increase its purchases of agency debt this year by up to $100 billion to a total of up to $200 billion. The FOMC also decides to purchase up to $300 billion of longer-term Treasury securities over the next six months to help improve conditions in private credit markets. Finally, the FOMC announces that it anticipates expanding the range of eligible collateral for the TALF (Term Asset-Backed Securities Loan Facility).

March 18, 2009: The Federal Reserve Bank of New York releases more information on the Federal Reserve's plan to purchase Treasury securities. The Desk will concentrate its purchases in nominal maturities ranging from 2 to 10 years. The purchases will be conducted with the Federal Reserve's primary dealers through a series of competitive auctions and will occur two to three times a week. The Desk plans to hold the first purchase operation late next week.

March 19, 2009: The U.S. Department of the Treasury announces an Auto Supplier Support Program that will provide up to $5 billion in financing to the automotive industry. The Supplier Support Program will provide selected suppliers with financial protection on monies ("receivables") they are owed by domestic auto companies and the opportunity to access immediate liquidity against those obligations. Receivables created with respect to goods shipped after March 19, 2009, will be eligible for the program. Any domestic auto company is eligible to participate in the program. Any U.S.-based supplier that ships to a participating auto manufacturer on qualifying commercial terms may be eligible to participate in the program.

March 19, 2009: The Federal Reserve Board announces an expansion of the eligible collateral for loans extended by the Term Asset-Backed Securities Loan Facility (TALF) to include asset-backed securities backed by mortgage servicing advances, loans, or leases related to business equipment, leases of vehicle fleets, and floor plan loans. The new categories of collateral will be eligible for the April TALF funding.

March 19, 2009: The Federal Reserve Bank of New York releases the initial results of the first round of loan requests for funding from the

Term Asset-Backed Securities Loan Facility (TALF). The amount of TALF loans requested at the March 17–19 operation was $4.7 billion.

March 19, 2009: The FDIC completes the sale of IndyMac Federal Bank to OneWest Bank. OneWest will assume all deposits of IndyMac, and the 33 branches of IndyMac will reopen as branches of OneWest on March 20, 2009. As of January 31, 2009, IndyMac had total assets of $23.5 billion and total deposits of $6.4 billion. IndyMac reported fourth quarter 2008 losses of $2.6 billion, and the total estimated loss to the Deposit Insurance Fund of the FDIC is $10.7 billion. The FDIC had been named conservator of IndyMac FSB on July 11, 2008.

March 23, 2009: The Federal Reserve and the U.S. Treasury issue a joint statement on the appropriate roles of each during the current financial crisis and into the future, and on the steps necessary to ensure financial and monetary stability. The four points of agreement are: (1) The Treasury and the Federal Reserve will continue to cooperate in improving the functioning of credit markets and fostering financial stability; (2) the Federal Reserve should avoid credit risk and credit allocation, which are the province of fiscal authorities; (3) the need to preserve monetary stability, and that actions by the Federal Reserve in the pursuit of financial stability must not constrain the exercise of monetary policy as needed to foster maximum sustainable employment and price stability; and (4) the need for a comprehensive resolution regime for systemically critical financial institutions. In addition, the Treasury will seek to remove the Maiden Lane facilities from the Federal Reserve's balance sheet.

March 23, 2009: The Treasury Department announces details on the Public-Private Investment Program for Legacy Assets. The program will have two parts: a Legacy Loans Program and a Legacy Securities Program. The Legacy Loans Program will facilitate the creation of individual Public-Private Investment Funds which will purchase distressed loans that are currently held by banks. The Treasury intends to provide 50 percent of the equity capital for each fund. The FDIC will provide oversight for the formation, funding, and operation of these funds, and guarantee the debt issued by the funds. Under the Legacy Securities Program, the Treasury Department will approve up to five asset managers who will have the opportunity to raise private capital to acquire distressed securities currently held by banks. The Treasury will provide 50 percent of the equity capital for each investment fund and will consider requests for loans to each fund. In addition, the investment funds would also be eligible for non-recourse loans from the Term Asset-Backed Securities Facility (TALF).

March 25, 2009: The Treasury Department proposes legislation that would grant the U.S. government authority to put certain financial institutions into conservatorship or receivership to avert systemic risks posed by the potential insolvency of a significant financial firm. The authority is modeled on the resolution authority that the FDIC has with respect to banks and that the Federal Housing Finance Agency has with regard to the GSEs. The authority would apply to nonbank financial institutions that have the potential to pose systemic risks to the economy but that are not currently subject to the resolution authority of the FDIC or the Federal Housing Finance Agency.

March 26, 2009: The Treasury Department outlines a framework for comprehensive regulatory reform that focuses on containing systemic risks in the financial system. The framework calls for assigning responsibility over all systemically important firms and critical payment and settlement systems to single independent regulator. Further, it calls for higher standards on capital and risk management for systemically important firms; for requiring all hedge funds above a certain size to register with a financial regulator; for a comprehensive framework of oversight, protection, and disclosure for the over-the-counter derivatives market; for new requirements for money market funds; and for stronger resolution authority covering all financial institutions that pose systemic risks to the economy.

March 31, 2009: The General Accounting Office (GAO) releases a report on the status of efforts to address transparency and accountability issues for the Troubled Asset Relief Program (TARP). The report provides information about the nature and purpose of TARP funding through March 27, 2009, the performance of the Treasury Department's Office of Financial Stability, and TARP performance indicators.

March 31, 2009: The U.S. Treasury Department announces an extension of its temporary Money Market Funds Guarantee Program through September 18, 2009. This program will continue to provide coverage to shareholders up to the amount held in participating money market funds as of the close of business on September 19, 2008. The Program currently covers over $3 trillion of combined fund assets and was scheduled to end on April 30, 2009.

March 31, 2009: Four bank holding companies announced that they had redeemed all of the preferred shares that they had issued to the U.S. Treasury under the Capital Purchase Program of the Troubled Asset Relief Program (TARP). The four banks are: Bank of Marin Bancorp (Novato, CA), Iberiabank Corporation (Lafayette, LA), Old National Bancorp (Evansville, IN), and Signature Bank (New York, NY).

April 1, 2009: Federal Reserve Chairman Bernanke and Federal Reserve Bank of New York President Dudley respond to questions from the Congressional Oversight Panel about the Term Asset-Backed Loan Facility (TALF), explaining in detail the rationale and operation of the TALF.

April 2, 2009: The Financial Accounting Standards Board approves new guidance to ease the accounting of troubled assets held by banks and other financial companies. In particular, the Board provides new guidance on how to determine the fair value of assets for which there is no active market.

April 6, 2009: The Federal Reserve announces new reciprocal currency agreements (swap lines) with the Bank of England, the European Central Bank, the Bank of Japan and the Swiss National Bank that would enable the provision of foreign currency liquidity by the Federal Reserve to U.S. financial institutions.

April 7, 2009: The Congressional Oversight Panel releases its monthly report on the Troubled Asset Relief Program (TARP). This report, entitled "Assessing Treasury's Strategy: Six Months of TARP," provides information about expenditures and commitments to date of TARP funds, evaluates the Treasury Department's strategy for improving the condition and functioning of financial institutions and markets, and discusses potential policy alternatives.

April 23, 2009: The Federal Reserve publishes the annual financial statements for the combined Federal Reserve Banks, the 12 individual Federal Reserve Banks, the limited liability companies that were created in 2008 to respond to strains in the financial markets, and the Board of Governors for the years ended December 31, 2008 and 2007.

April 24, 2009: The Federal Reserve Board publishes a white paper describing the process and methodologies employed by federal banking supervisory authorities in their forward looking assessment ("stress test") of large U.S. bank holding companies.

May 7, 2009: Fed reports results of stress test of 19 largest bank holding companies. Nine of 19 banks have adequate capital. Ten firms would need to add capital to maintain reserves under adverse scenario.

May 21, 2009: FDIC approves GMAC Financial Services to participate in the Temporary Liquidity Guarantee Program, which allows GMAC to issue up to $7.4 billion in debt guaranteed by the FDIC.

June 1, 2009: General Motors and subsidiaries file for bankruptcy.

June 9, 2009: Treasury announces that ten financial institutions participating in the Capital Purchase Program will be allowed to repay the Treasury.

June 24, 2009: Fed extends variety of liquidity programs to February 1, 2010.

June 26, 2009: Treasury announces that banks that issued warrants to Treasury will be allowed to repurchase them at fair market value.

August 17, 2009: Fed and Treasury announce extension of Term Asset-Backed Securities Loan Facility (TALF) to June 30, 2010.

December 24, 2009: Treasury removes $200 billion caps on the amount of preferred stock it may purchase in Fannie Mae and Freddie Mac.

February 18, 2010: Fed raises discount rate from 0.5 percent to 0.75 percent. First increase since June 29, 2006, when the rate was raised from 6.0 percent to 6.25 percent.

The Original TARP Proposal:
Legislative Proposal for Treasury
Authority To Purchase
Mortgage-Related Assets

Section 1. Short Title.

This Act may be cited as _____.

Sec. 2. Purchases of Mortgage-Related Assets.

(a) Authority to Purchase.—The Secretary is authorized to purchase, and to make and fund commitments to purchase, on such terms and conditions as determined by the Secretary, mortgage-related assets from any financial institution having its headquarters in the United States.

(b) Necessary Actions.—The Secretary is authorized to take such actions as the Secretary deems necessary to carry out the authorities in this Act, including, without limitation:

(1) appointing such employees as may be required to carry out the authorities in this Act and defining their duties;

(2) entering into contracts, including contracts for services authorized by section 3109 of title 5, United States Code, without regard to any other provision of law regarding public contracts;

(3) designating financial institutions as financial agents of the Government, and they shall perform all such reasonable duties related to this Act as financial agents of the Government as may be required of them;

(4) establishing vehicles that are authorized, subject to supervision by the Secretary, to purchase mortgage-related assets and issue obligations; and (5) issuing such regulations and other guidance as may be necessary or appropriate to define terms or carry out the authorities of this Act.

Sec. 3. Considerations.

In exercising the authorities granted in this Act, the Secretary shall take into consideration means for—(1) providing stability or preventing disruption to the financial markets or banking system; and (2) protecting the taxpayer.

Sec. 4. Reports to Congress.

Within three months of the first exercise of the authority granted in section 2(a), and semiannually thereafter, the Secretary shall report to the Committees on the Budget, Financial Services, and Ways and Means of the House of Representatives and the Committees on the Budget, Finance, and Banking, Housing, and Urban Affairs of the Senate with respect to the authorities exercised under this Act and the considerations required by section 3.

Sec. 5. Rights; Management; Sale of Mortgage-Related Assets.

(a) Exercise of Rights.—The Secretary may, at any time, exercise any rights received in connection with mortgage-related assets purchased under this Act.

(b) Management of Mortgage-Related Assets.—The Secretary shall have authority to manage mortgage-related assets purchased under this Act, including revenues and portfolio risks therefrom.

(c) Sale of Mortgage-Related Assets.—The Secretary may, at any time, upon terms and conditions and at prices determined by the Secretary, sell, or enter into securities loans, repurchase transactions or other financial transactions in regard to, any mortgage-related asset purchased under this Act.

(d) Application of Sunset to Mortgage-Related Assets.—The authority of the Secretary to hold any mortgage-related asset purchased under this Act before the termination date in section 9, or to purchase or fund the purchase of a mortgage-related asset under a commitment entered into before the termination date in section 9, is not subject to the provisions of section 9.

Sec. 6. Maximum Amount of Authorized Purchases.

The Secretary's authority to purchase mortgage-related assets under this Act shall be limited to $700,000,000,000 outstanding at any one time.

Sec. 7. Funding.

For the purpose of the authorities granted in this Act, and for the costs of administering those authorities, the Secretary may use the proceeds of the sale of any securities issued under chapter 31 of title 31, United States Code, and the purposes for which securities may be issued under chapter 31 of title 31, United States Code, are extended to include actions authorized by this Act, including the payment of administrative expenses. Any funds expended for actions authorized by this Act, including the payment of administrative expenses, shall be deemed appropriated at the time of such expenditure.

Sec. 8. Review.

Decisions by the Secretary pursuant to the authority of this Act are non-reviewable and committed to agency discretion, and may not be reviewed by any court of law or any administrative agency.

Sec. 9. Termination of Authority.

The authorities under this Act, with the exception of authorities granted in sections 2(b)(5), 5 and 7, shall terminate two years from the date of enactment of this Act.

Sec. 10. Increase in Statutory Limit on the Public Debt.

Subsection (b) of section 3101 of title 31, United States Code, is amended by striking out the dollar limitation contained in such subsection and inserting in lieu thereof 11,315,000,000,000.

Sec. 11. Credit Reform.

The costs of purchases of mortgage-related assets made under section 2(a) of this Act shall be determined as provided under the Federal Credit Reform Act of 1990, as applicable.

Sec. 12. Definitions.

For purposes of this section, the following definitions shall apply:

(1) Mortgage-Related Assets.—The term "mortgage-related assets" means residential or commercial mortgages and any securities, obligations, or other instruments that are based on or related to such mortgages, that in each case was originated or issued on or before September 17, 2008.

(2) Secretary.—The term "Secretary" means the Secretary of the Treasury.

(3) United States.—The term "United States" means the States, territories, and possessions of the United States and the District of Columbia.

Chapter 1

1. My account of the early history of mortgage finance draws primarily on two sources: Richard K. Green and Susan M. Wachter, "The American Mortgage in Historical and International Context," *Journal of Economic Perspectives*, Fall 2005, 19(4): 93–114; and Integrated Financial Engineering, Inc., "Evolution of the U.S. Housing Finance System: A Historical Survey and Lessons for Emerging Mortgage Markets," U.S. Department of Housing and Urban Development, April 2006.

2. Richard K. Green and Susan M. Wachter, "The American Mortgage in Historical and International Context," *Journal of Economic Perspectives*, Fall 2005, 19(4): 94–95.

3. For an overview of the Federal Home Loan Bank System, see Mark J. Flannery and W. Scott Frame, "The Federal Home Loan Bank System: The 'Other" Housing GSE," Federal Reserve Bank of Atlanta, *Economic Review*, Third Quarter 2006, pp. 33–54.

4. Judged in terms of survival and freedom from financial crises, the FHA contrasts with many other federal housing finance programs. The FHA has never had a financial crisis and has generally contributed to the Treasury. While the FHA lost money in the 1980s, those losses were easily covered by the reserves it had amassed from previous years. However, see chapter 15 for a potentially emerging problem with FHA.

5. For FNMA purchases during this period, see Funding Universe, http://www.fundinguniverse.com/company-histories/Fannie-Mae-Company-History.html, accessed April 18, 2009. Richard K. Green and

Susan M. Wachter, "The American Mortgage in Historical and International Context," *Journal of Economic Perspectives*, Fall 2005, 19(4): 96, report 93,000 housing units in 1933.

6. Franklin D. Roosevelt, in *The Public Papers and Addresses of Franklin D. Roosevelt* 2, at 135 (1938).

7. All of these presidential quotations appear in Housing and Urban Development, "Homeownership and Its Benefits," *Urban Policy Brief*, no. 2, August 1995.

8. Housing and Urban Development, "Homeownership and Its Benefits," *Urban Policy Brief*, no. 2, August 1995.

9. My statement that it is optimistic that more Americans lived in homes they owned should not be taken to imply that purchasing a home is a better lifestyle choice than renting. However, because home ownership is associated with greater wealth, expanding home ownership does suggest increasing wealth, which I do presume to be a good thing.

10. For a discussion of the impact of this act, see Marcia Millon Cornett and Hassan Tehranian, "An Examination of the Impact of the Garn-St. Germain Depository Institutions Act of 1982 on Commercial Banks and Savings and Loans," *The Journal of Finance*, March 1990, 45(1): 95–111.

11. FDIC, *History of the Eighties: Lessons for the Future*, volume I: *An Examination of the Banking Crises of the 1980s and Early 1990s*, Washington, DC: FDIC, 1997, chapter 4, "The Savings and Loan Crisis and Its Relationship to Banking," p. 180.

12. Ed Kane has famously likened these S&Ls to zombies—they are dead but have returned from the grave to cause mischief. See Edward J. Kane, "What Lessons Might Crisis Countries in Asia and Latin America Have Learned from the Savings and Loan Mess?," in James R. Barth, Susanne Trimbath, and Glenn Yago, *The Savings and Loan Crisis*, Norwell, MA: Kluwer, 2004, pp. 113–131. See specifically, p. 117.

13. The RTC was supposed to pass out of existence by August 1992, but its job was not done. Accordingly, its life was extended twice, and it finally ceased operations in 1995.

14. For estimates and a discussion of why the range of estimates is so large, see Timothy Curry and Lynn Shibut, "The Cost of the Savings and Loan Crisis: Truth and Consequences," *FDIC Banking Review*, 2000, 13:2, 26–35; and FDIC, *History of the Eighties: Lessons for the Future*, volume I: *An Examination of the Banking Crises of the 1980s and Early 1990s*, Washington, DC: FDIC, 1997, chapter 4, "The Savings and Loan Crisis and Its Relationship to Banking," pp. 167–188.

Chapter 2

1. Ginnie Mae Annual Report, 2008, http://www.ginniemae.gov/about/ann_rep/annual_report08.pdf.

2. Congressional Budget Office, *Controlling the Risks of Government-Sponsored Enterprises*, April 1991, chapter 1, p. 2.

3. Fannie Mae, "An Introduction to Fannie Mae," Washington, DC: Fannie Mae, 2008, p. 6.

4. For an account of the issuance of this first CMO, see Michael Lewis, *Liar's Poker*, New York: Norton, 1995, pp. 136–137.

5. See Gregory J. Parseghian, "Collateralized Mortgage Obligations," in Frank J. Fabozzi, T. Dessa Fabozzi, and Irving M. Pollack, *The Handbook of Fixed Income Securities*, 3rd ed., Homewood, IL: Irwin, 1991, pp. 601–632.

6. Federal Reserve Bank of New York, "Nonprime Mortgage Conditions in the United States," http://www.newyorkfed.org/regional/techappendix_spreadsheets.html, accessed on April 29, 2009.

7. While we focus on MBS, the process described here is much more general and applies to the creation of other asset-backed securities, such as those based on pools of credit card receivables or a pool of car loans. However, there are important institutional differences, such as the nature of the securities' issuers, the degree of government involvement, and the types of financial guarantees that issuers and government agencies provide.

8. Standard & Poor's, "The Basics of Credit Enhancement in Securitizations," June 24, 2008, p. 2. http://www2.standardandpoors.com/spf/pdf/media/subprime_credit_enhance_062408.pdf.

Chapter 3

1. All of these statistics are drawn from Fannie Mae, "Understanding America's Homeownership Gaps: 2003 Fannie Mae National Housing Survey," 2004, http://www.fanniemae.com/global/pdf/media/survey/survey2003.pdf.

2. David Berson, David Lereah, Paul Merski, Frank Nothaft, and David Seiders, "America's Home Forecast: The Next Decade for Housing and Mortgage Finance," Homeownership Alliance, no date, pp. 28–29.

3. Forrest Pafenberg, "The Single-Family Mortgage Industry in the Internet Era: Technology Developments and Market Structure," Office of Federal Housing Enterprise Oversight Research Paper, January 2004.

4. See W. Scott Frame and Lawrence J. White, "Fussing and Fuming over Fannie and Freddie: How Much Smoke, How Much Fire?" *Journal of Economic Perspectives*, Spring 2005, 19(2): 165.

5. Forrest Pafenberg, "The Single-Family Mortgage Industry in the Internet Era: Technology Developments and Market Structure," Office of Federal Housing Enterprise Oversight Research Paper, January 2004, p. 25.

6. For an excellent account of Browning and Arc Systems, see Lynnley Browning, "The Subprime Loan Machine," *New York Times*, March 23, 2007.

7. Lynnley Browning, "The Subprime Loan Machine," *New York Times*, March 23, 2007.

8. Kent W. Colton, "Housing Finance in the United States: The Transformation of the U.S. Housing Finance System," Joint Center for Housing Studies, Harvard University, W02-5, July 2002, p. 18.

9. Angelo R. Mozilo, "The American Dream of Homeownership: From Cliché to Mission," John T. Dunlop Lecture, Joint Center for Housing Studies, Harvard University, February 4, 2003, p. 15.

10. See Christopher L. Foote, Kristopher Gerardi, Lorenz Goette, and Paul S. Willen, "Subprime Facts: What (We Think) We Know about the Subprime Crisis and What We Don't," Federal Reserve Bank of Boston, Public Policy Discussion Paper No. 08-2, 2008. Figure 3.10 uses data from table 1, p. 9.

11. Yet these mortgages have been criticized by the Comptroller of the Currency, who acknowledged their potential benefits, yet likened them to subprime mortgages with potential for predatory lending. See Margaret Chadbourn, "Regulator Says Mortgages Aimed at Elderly May be Risky," http://www.bloomberg.com/apps/news?pid=20601213&sid=awPlC3t65 GTk, accessed June 9, 2009.

12. See Martin Neil Baily, Robert E. Litan, and Mathew S. Johnson, "The Origins of the Financial Crisis," Brookings Institution, Fixing Finance Series—Paper 3, November 2008, figure 3, p. 19.

13. Mortgage Banker, "Housing and Mortgage Markets: An Analysis," MBA Research Monograph Series No. 1, September 6, 2005, chart 41, p. 49.

14. Mortgage Bankers Association, "The Residential Mortgage Market and Its Economic Context," January 30, 2007, p. 24.

15. For a discussion of the different meanings of *subprime,* see Kristopher Gerardi, Andreas Lehnert, Shane Sherlund, and Paul Willen, "Making Sense of the Subprime Crisis," *Brookings Papers on Economic Activity*, September 5, 2008.

16. Kristopher Gerardi, Andreas Lehnert, Shane Sherlund, and Paul Willen, "Making Sense of the Subprime Crisis," *Brookings Papers on Economic Activity*, September 5, 2008.

17. Marsha Courchane, Rajeev Darolia, and Peter Zorn, "From FHA to Subprime and Back?" Working paper, March 2009.

18. Kristopher Gerardi, Andreas Lehnert, Shane Sherlund, and Paul Willen, "Making Sense of the Subprime Crisis," *Brookings Papers on Economic Activity*, September 5, 2008. They find that 12.3–13.7 percent of outstanding mortgages were subprime over 2004–2007 and that 25.7–31.0 percent of mortgage originations in 2005–2006 were subprime. (See their table 2.) Gary Gorton reports about 20 percent of the dollar amount of mortgage originations in 2005–2006 were subprime in "The Subprime Panic," *European Financial Management*, January 2009, 15(1): 10–46. Table 4 of Mortgage Bankers Association "Housing and Mortgage Markets: An Analysis," MBA Research Monograph Series No. 1, September 6, 2005, reports that 10.8 percent of mortgage issuances in 2004 were subprime. Mortgage Bankers Association, "The Residential Mortgage Market and Its Economic Context," January 30, 2007, shows about 12–15 percent of outstanding mortgages as being subprime. Chart 36 of Mortgage Bankers Association, "Housing and Mortgage Markets: An Analysis," shows that, for the second half of 2004, 24 percent of the dollar volume of loans originated and 28 percent of the number of loans originated were subprime.

19. For an explication of this idea, see Gary Gorton, "The Subprime Panic," *European Financial Management*, January 2009, 15(1): 10–46, especially section 2.2.

20. The President's Working Group on Financial Markets, "Policy Statement on Financial Market Developments," March 2008. This passage is quoted in Geetesh Bhardwaj and Rajdeep Sengupta, "Where's the Smoking Gun: A Study of Underwriting Standards for U.S. Subprime Mortgages," Federal Reserve Bank of St. Louis, *Working Paper Series*, October 2008.

21. Souphala Chomsisengphet and Anthony Pennington-Cross, "The Evolution of the Subprime Mortgage Market," Federal Reserve Bank of St Louis, *Review*, January–February 2006: 31–56. See table 6.

Chapter 4

1. James R. Woodwell, "The Perfect Calm," *Mortgage Banking*, January 2007.

2. Fratantoni, Michael, "The Residential Mortgage Market and Its Economic Context in 2007," Mortgage Bankers Association, January 30, 2007, p. 1. Emphasis added.

3. Federal Reserve Bank of St. Louis, "The Financial Crisis: A Timeline of Events and Policy Actions," http://timeline.stlouisfed.org/pdf/CrisisTimeline.pdf, accessed May 23, 2009.

4. Freddie Mac, "Freddie Mac Announces Tougher Subprime Lending Standards to Help Reduce the Risk of Future Borrower Default," http://www.freddiemac.com/news/archives/corporate/2007/20070227_subprimelending.html, accessed June 8, 2009.

5. *New York Times*, "Crisis Deepens for Northern Rock," September 17, 2007, http://www.nytimes.com/2007/09/17/world/europe/17iht-17northern.7535479.html, accessed June 12, 2009. My colleague, George Kaufman, emphasizes that the run on Northern Rock was the first *retail* bank run with the high visibility of people standing in line outside offices to make withdrawals. It was not the first bank run considering all types. When institutional customers flee a bank, they withdraw using electronic means, which are not publicly visible.

6. Michiyo Nakamoto, "Citigroup Chief Stays Bullish on Buy-Outs," *Financial Times*, July 9, 2007, http://www.ft.com/cms/s/0/80e2987a-2e50-11dc-821c-0000779fd2ac.html?nclick_check=1, accessed June 9, 2009.

7. These SPEs and SIVs are discussed more fully in chapter 10.

8. Chapter 10 assesses the importance of mark-to-market accounting policies in the crisis.

9. See the FDIC press release of July 18, 2008, http://www.fdic.gov/news/news/press/2008/pr08056.html, accessed June 10, 2009.

10. FDIC, "Failed Bank List," http://www.fdic.gov/bank/individual/failed/banklist.html, accessed June 10, 2009.

11. "Statement by Secretary Henry M. Paulson, Jr., on Treasury and Federal Housing Finance Agency Action to Protect Financial Markets and

Taxpayers," September 7, 2008, hp-1129, http://www.treas.gov/press/releases/hp1129.htm, accessed June 10, 2009.

12. FDIC, Press Release: "JPMorgan Chase Acquires Banking Operations of Washington Mutual—FDIC Facilitates Transaction That Protects All Depositors and Comes at No Cost to the Deposit Insurance Fund," September 25, 2008, http://www.fdic.gov/news/news/press/2008/pr08085.html, accessed June 10, 2009. See also Eric Dash and Andrew Ross Sorkin, "Government Seizes WaMu and Sells Some Assets," *New York Times*, September 26, 2008, http://www.nytimes.com/2008/09/26/business/26wamu.html, accessed June 10, 2009.

13. FDIC, Press Release: "Citigroup Inc. to Acquire Banking Operations of Wachovia, FDIC, Federal Reserve and Treasury Agree to Provide Open Bank Assistance to Protect Depositors," September 29, 2008, http://www.fdic.gov/news/news/press/2008/pr08088.html, accessed June 10, 2009.

14. Another measure is the spread between LIBOR and the overnight index spread, or OIS. See Rajdeep Sengupta and Yu Man Tam, "The LIBOR-OIS Spread as a Summary Indicator," Federal Reserve Bank of St. Louis, *Economic Synopses*, 2008, no. 25.

15. A Eurodollar deposit is a U.S. dollar–denominated deposit held in a bank outside the United States. Calling such deposits Eurodollar deposits stems from the development of the international market when it was more fully dominated by the United States and the leading nations of western Europe.

Chapter 5

1. Angelo R. Mozilo, "The American Dream of Homeownership: From Cliché to Mission," John T. Dunlop Lecture, Joint Center for Housing Studies, Harvard University, February 4, 2003, p. 4.

2. Christina Crapanzano, "Countrywide is Assailed in Protest of Policies," *New York Times*, October 12, 2007.

3. "SEC Complaint Excerpts: Mozilo on 'Toxic' Loans, Borrowers' Income Lies," *Wall Street Journal*, June 4, 2009.

4. "SEC Complaint Excerpts: Mozilo on 'Toxic' Loans, Borrowers' Income Lies," *Wall Street Journal*, June 4, 2009.

5. This account of Countrywide draws upon Countrywide's financial statements and the following sources: Eric Dash and Gretchen Morgenson, "Bank Agrees to Buy Troubled Loan Giant for $4 Billion," *New York Times*, January 11, 2008; Gretchen Morgenson and Geraldine Fabrikant, "Countrywide's Chief Salesman and Defender," *New York Times*, November 11, 2007; Gretchen Morgenson, "Inside the Countrywide Lending Spree," *New York Times*, August 26, 2007; Gretchen Morgenson "Stock Sales by Chief of Lender Questioned," *New York Times*, October 11, 2007; Gretchen Morgenson, "S.E.C. Accuses Countrywide's Ex-Chief of Fraud," *New York Times*, June 5, 2009; Securities and Exchange Commission, *Plaintiff vs. Angelo Mozilo, David Sambol, and Eric Sieracki, Defendants*, June 4, 2009; and Angelo R. Mozilo, "The American Dream of Homeownership: From Cliché to

Mission," John T. Dunlop Lecture, Joint Center for Housing Studies, Harvard University, February 4, 2003.

6. "A Losing Year at Countrywide, but Not for Chief," *New York Times*, April 25, 2008.

7. Mike Hudson, "IndyMac: What Went Wrong?" Center for Responsible Lending, CRL Report, June 30, 2008.

8. Joanna Chung and Saskia Scholtes, "IndyMac Is Latest Credit Turmoil Casualty," *Financial Times*, July 12, 2008.

9. *New York Times*, "IndyMac Bancorp Quits Making New Loans," July 8, 2008.

10. Mike Hudson, "IndyMac: What Went Wrong?" Center for Responsible Lending, CRL Report, June 30, 2008, p. 2.

11. Mike Hudson, "IndyMac: What Went Wrong?" Center for Responsible Lending, CRL Report, June 30, 2008, p. 3.

12. Mike Hudson, "IndyMac: What Went Wrong?" Center for Responsible Lending, CRL Report, June 30, 2008, p. 8.

13. Mike Hudson, "IndyMac: What Went Wrong?" Center for Responsible Lending, CRL Report, June 30, 2008, p. 1.

14. Mike Hudson, "IndyMac: What Went Wrong?" Center for Responsible Lending, CRL Report, June 30, 2008, p. 4.

15. Vikas Bajaj, "Lax Lending Standards Led to IndyMac's Downfall," *New York Times*, July 20, 2008.

16. For the early history of WaMu see Washington, Mutual, Inc., "WaMu is Becoming Chase, History," https://www.wamu.com/about/corporateprofile/history/default.asp, accessed July 3, 2009; and FundingUniverse.com, "Washington, Mutual, Inc.," http://www.fundinguniverse.com/company-histories/Washington-Mutual-Inc-Company-History.html, accessed July 3, 2009.

17. Peter S. Goodman and Gretchen Morgenson, "By Saying Yes, WaMu Built Empire on Shaky Loans," *New York Times*, December 28, 2008, http://www.nytimes.com/2008/12/28/business/28wamu.html, accessed December 28, 2008.

18. Peter S. Goodman and Gretchen Morgenson, "By Saying Yes, WaMu Built Empire on Shaky Loans," *New York Times*, December 28, 2008, http://www.nytimes.com/2008/12/28/business/28wamu.html, accessed December 28, 2008.

19. Gretchen Morgenson, "Was There a Loan It Didn't Like?" *New York Times*, November 2, 2008.

20. John Gittelsohn, "WaMu Loan Millions to O. C. Home Flippers with Fraud History," *Orange County Register*, September 21, 2008, http://www.ocregister.com/articles/soni-washington-mutual-2163800-sonis-family#, accessed July 3, 2009.

21. Equilar, "Compensation for Kerry K. Killinger at Washington Mutual," http://www.equilar.com/CEO_Compensation/WASHINGTON_MUTUAL_INC_Kerry_K._Killinger.php, accessed July 3, 2009.

22. For the computation of the severance package's value, see *Condé-Nast Magazine*, "Killinger's Eight-Figure Severance Package,"

September 11, 2008, http://www.portfolio.com/views/blogs/daily-brief/2008/09/11/killingers-eight-figure-severance-package, accessed July 3, 2009.

23. Eric Dash, "U.S. to Examine Actions of Washington Mutual," *New York Times*, October 16, 2008, http://query.nytimes.com/gst/fullpage.html?res=980CEFD8173EF935A25753C1A96E9C8B63, accessed June 30, 2009.

24. Eric Dash and Andrew Ross Sorkin, "Government Seizes WaMu and Sells Some Assets," *New York Times*, September 26, 2008, http://www.nytimes.com/2008/09/26/business/26wamu.html?pagewanted=print, accessed July 3, 2009.

25. Quoted in Peter S. Goodman S. and Gretchen Morgenson, "By Saying Yes, WaMu Built Empire on Shaky Loans," *New York Times*, December 28, 2008, http://www.nytimes.com/2008/12/28/business/28wamu.html, accessed December 28, 2008

26. "Wachovia-Golden West: Another Deal from Hell?" *Wall Street Journal*, July 22, 2008, http://blogs.wsj.com/deals/2008/07/22/wachovia-golden-west-another-deal-from-hell/, accessed July 4, 2009.

27. Julie Creswell, "Chief Calls Deal a Dream for Wachovia," *New York Times*, May 9, 2006, http://www.nytimes.com/2006/05/09/business/09bank.html?sq=wachovia%20golden%20west&st=cse&scp=5, accessed March 21, 2009.

28. Julie Creswell, "Chief Calls Deal a Dream for Wachovia," *New York Times*, May 9, 2006, http://www.nytimes.com/2006/05/09/business/09bank.html?sq=wachovia%20golden%20west&st=cse&scp=5, accessed March 21, 2009.

29. Julie Creswell, "Chief Calls Deal a Dream for Wachovia," *New York Times*, May 9, 2006, http://www.nytimes.com/2006/05/09/business/09bank.html?sq=wachovia%20golden%20west&st=cse&scp=5, accessed March 21, 2009.

30. Eric Dash, "Wachovia Reports $23.9 Billion Loss for Third Quarter," *New York Times*, October 22, 2008. http://www.nytimes.com/2008/10/23/business/23wachovia.html?dlbk, accessed March 21, 2009.

31. Eric Dash and Andrew Ross Sorkin, "Citigroup Buys Bank Operations of Wachovia," *New York Times*, September 30, 2008, http://www.nytimes.com/2008/09/30/business/30bank.html?hp=&pagewanted=print, accessed March 21, 2009.

32. David Enrich and Matthew Karnitschnig, "Citi, U.S. Rescue Wachovia," *Wall Street Journal*, September 30, 2008, http://online.wsj.com/article/SB122269141590585467.html, accessed March 21, 2009.

33. Sara Lepro, "Citi Recommits to Wachovia Deal Despite Rescue Plan's Failure," *Washington Post*, October 1, 2008, http://www.washingtonpost.com/wp-yn/content/article/2008/09/30/AR2008093002839_pf.html, accessed on March 21, 2009.

34. Eric Dash and Michael de la Merced, "Wachovia's Acquisition Drags Down Wells Fargo," *The New York Times*, January 29, 2009. Available

at: http://www.nytimes.com/2009/01/29/business/29wells.html?_r=1, accessed July 4, 2009.

35. For perspective on the "too-big-to-fail" problem see: George G. Kaufman, "Are Some Banks Too Large to Fail? Myth and Reality," *Contemporary Economic Policy* 1990, 8(4): 1–14; Maureen O'Hara and Wayne Shaw, "Deposit Insurance and Wealth Effects: The Value of Being "Too Big to Fail,"" *The Journal of Finance*, December 1990, 45(5): 1587–1600; Gary H. Stern and Ron J. Feldman, *Too Big to Fail: The Hazards of Bank Bailouts*, Washington, DC: Brookings Institution Press, 2004; and Frederic S. Mishkin, "How Big a Problem Is Too Big to Fail? A Review of Gary Stern and Ron Feldman's *Too Big to Fail: The Hazards of Bank Bailouts*," *Journal of Economic Literature*, December 2006, 44(4): 988–1004.

Chapter 6

1. Bear Stearns Companies, "2006 Form 10-K," p. 8.

2. Yalman Onaran and Jody Shenn, "Cioffi's Hero-to-Villain Hedge Funds Masked Bears Periods in CDOs," *Bloomberg.com*, July 3, 2007, http://www.bloomberg.com/apps/news?pid=20601103&refer=us&sid=azWrpTVCph08#, accessed July 15, 2009.

3. Julie Creswell and Vikas Bajaj, "$3.2 Billion Move by Bear Stearns to Rescue Fund," *New York Times*, June 23, 2007.

4. *The Economist*, "Bearish Turns," June 21, 2007.

5. Julie Creswell and Vikas Bajaj, "$3.2 Billion Move by Bear Stearns to Rescue Fund," *New York Times*, June 23, 2007.

6. The federal government eventually filed criminal charges of securities, wire, and mail fraud against Cioffi and his associate, Matthew Tannin. Cioffi as also charged with insider trading. However, in November 2009, Cioffi and Tannin were acquitted of all charges.

7. *New York Times*, "Bear Stearns Denies Need to Seek Cash from Outside," October 5, 2007.

8. Kate Kelly, "Cayne to Step Down as Bear Stearns CEO," *New York Times*, January 8, 2008.

9. Bryan Burrough, "Bringing Down Bear Stearns," *Vanity Fair*, August 2008.

10. Kate Kelly, "Diary of a Bear Stearns Executive," *Wall Street Journal*, May 8, 2009.

11. Kate Kelly, "Bear Stearns Neared Collapse Twice in Frenzied Last Days," *Wall Street Journal*, May 29, 2008.

12. Landon Thomas, Jr., and Eric Dash, "Seeking Fast Deal, JPMorgan Quintuples Bear Stearns Bid," *New York Times*, March 25, 2008.

13. SEC's Oversight of Bear Stearns and Related Entities: The CSE Program, Report No. 446-A, September 25, 2008, p. 82.

14. As the $10 price JPMorgan paid for Bear indicates, Bear was not really bankrupt, but was the victim of liquidity problems. For its part, Northern Rock also suffered a run, but it really was insolvent as well as suffering from insufficient liquidity.

15. For details on the presumed bear raid on Bear, see: Bryan Burrough, "Bringing Down Bear Stearns," *Vanity Fair*, August 2008; Kara Scannell, "SEC's Bear Stearns Probe Zeroes in on 'Put' Trades," *Wall Street Journal*, March 20, 2008; and Andrew Ross Sorkin, "What Really Killed Bear Stearns?" *New York Times*, June 30, 2008.

16. Kate Kelly, Greg Ip, and Robin Sidel, "Fed Races to Rescue Bear Stearns in Bid to Steady Financial System," *Wall Street Journal*, March 16, 2008.

17. See *Wall Street Journal*, "From General Store to Titan: A Brief History of Lehman," September 1, 2008.

18. See Devin Leonard, "How Lehman Brothers Got Its Real Estate Fix," *New York Times*, May 3, 2009.

19. Susanne Craig, "Lehman Posts $2.8 Billion Loss," *Wall Street Journal*, June 17, 2008.

20. Louise Story and Ben White, "The Road to Lehman's Failure Was Littered with Lost Chances," *New York Times*, October 6, 2008.

21. Louise Story and Ben White, "The Road to Lehman's Failure Was Littered with Lost Chances," *New York Times*, October 6, 2008.

22. Joe Nocera and Edmund L. Andrews, "Struggling to Keep Up as the Crisis Raced On," *New York Times*, October 23, 2008.

23. *Wall Street Journal*, "Lehman Brothers, Loved and Left—Again," September 9, 2008.

24. Carrick Mollenkamp, Susanne Craig, Serena Ng, and Aaron Lucchetti, "Crisis on Wall Street as Lehman Totters, Merrill Is Sold, AIG Seeks to Raise Cash," *Wall Street Journal*, September 15, 2009.

25. Jenny Anderson and Andrew Ross Sorkin, "Lehman Said to Be Looking for a Buyer as Pressure Builds," *New York Times*, September 11, 2008.

26. *Wall Street Journal*, "Black Holes of Value at Lehman Brothers," September 12, 2008.

27. Carrick Mollenkamp and Jeffrey McCracken, "Lehman Moved Cash Fast," *Wall Street Journal*, September 20, 2008.

28. In March 2010 a court-ordered, 2,200-page report was made public that was extremely critical of Lehman's management. The report charges that Lehman used "materially misleading" accounting practices to hide its extreme leverage and evaluates Lehman's accounting practices as "actionable balance sheet manipulation." While the report does not accuse Fuld of criminal conduct, it does assert that he was "at least grossly negligent." The report also documents how demands for additional collateral by Lehman's trading counterparties, including JP Morgan, helped push Lehman into bankruptcy. The report on the nation's largest bankruptcy in history provides support for those who have already filed civil charges against Lehman, and the report may be laying groundwork that prosecutors might use to bolster potential criminal charges. See: Michael J. de la Merced and Andrew Ross Sorkin, "Report Details How Lehman Hid Its Woes as It Collapsed," *New York Times*, March 11, 2010; Mike Spector, Susanne Craig, and Peter Lattman, "Examiner, Lehman

Torpedoed Lehman," *Wall Street Journal*, March 11, 2010; and David Scheer and Joshua Gallu, "Fuld 'Negligent' as Lehman Hid Leverage, Report Says," Bloomberg.com, March 11, 2010.

29. *New York Times*, "Merrill Lynch & Company, Inc.," http://topics.nytimes.com/top/news/business/companies/merrill_lynch_and_company/index.html?scp=1-spot&sq=merrill%20lynch&st=cse, accessed October 15, 2009.

30. Quoted in Gretchen Morgenson, "How the Thundering Herd Faltered and Fell," *New York Times*, November 9, 2009.

31. Gretchen Morgenson, "How the Thundering Herd Faltered and Fell," *New York Times*, November 9, 2009.

32. David Wighton, "Merrill Lynch Shrugs Off Subprime Woes," *Financial Times*, July 17, 2007.

33. Louise Story, "Stunning Fall for Main Street's Brokerage Firm," *New York Times*, September 15, 2008.

34. Francesco Guerrera, Ben White, and Krishna Guha, "Merrill Lynch Hit by $9.4bn Writedown," *Financial Times*, July 17, 2008.

35. Louise Story, "Stunning Fall for Main Street's Brokerage Firm," *New York Times*, September 15, 2008.

36. Andrew Ross Sorkin, "Bank of America in Talks to Acquire Merrill Lynch," *New York Times*, September 14, 2008.

37. Francesco Guerrera, "BofA to Buy Merrill Lynch for $50bn," *Financial Times*, September 14, 2009.

38. Louise Story, "Stunning Fall for Main Street's Brokerage Firm," *New York Times*, September 15, 2008.

39. Edmund L. Andrews, "Bernanke Defends Role on Merrill," *New York Times*, June 26, 2009.

40. See: Zachary Kouwe, "U.S. Role Questioned On Merrill," *New York Times*, April 24, 2009; Greg Farrell and Alan Rappaport, "Lewis Grilled Over Merrill Deal," *Financial Times*, June 11, 2009; Louise Story and Jo Becker, "Bank Chief Tells of U.S. Pressure to Buy Merrill Lynch," *The New York Times*, June 12, 2009; Tom Braithwaite and Krishna Guha, "Bernanke Defends Fed on Merrill Deal," *Financial Times*, June 25, 2009.

41. Terence Blanchard, "Judge Postpones Ruling over Merrill Lynch Executive Bonuses," *Wall Street Journal*, March 13, 2009; Michael J. de La Merced and Louise Story, "Nearly 700 at Merrill in Million-Dollar Club," *New York Times*, February 12, 2009.

42. Zachery Kouwe, "Judge Rejects Settlement over Merrill Bonuses," *New York Times*, September 15, 2009.

43. Landon Thomas, Jr., "Morgan Stanley Chief Grappling with New Risk," *New York Times*, March 11, 2008.

44. Landon Thomas, Jr., "$9.4 Billion Write-Down at Morgan Stanley," *New York Times*, December 20, 2007.

45. Jenny Anderson and Landon Thomas, Jr., "Goldman Sachs Rakes in Profit in Credit Crisis," *New York Times*, November 19, 2007.

46. Ben White, Eric Dash, and Andrew Ross Sorkin, "As Fear Grows, Wall St. Titans See Shares Fall," *The New York Times*, September 18, 2008.

47. Ben White, Eric Dash, and Andrew Ross Sorkin, "As Fear Grows, Wall St. Titans See Shares Fall," *New York Times*, September 18, 2008.

48. *Wall Street Journal*, "Goldman Sachs, Morgan Stanley To Be Bank Holding Companies," September 21, 2008.

49. Joe Nocera, "Lehman Had to Die so Global Finance Could Live," *New York Times*, September 12, 2009.

50. See: Julie Creswell and Ben White, "The Guys From 'Government Sachs,'" *New York Times*, October 19, 2008; Michael J. de la Merced, "Goldman's Shadow Extends Far Past Wall St.," *New York Times*, November 15, 2007; Gretchen Morgenson and Don Van Natta, Jr., "Paulson's Calls to Goldman Tested Ethics During the Crisis," *New York Times*, August 9, 2009; and Matt Taibbi, "The Great American Bubble Machine," *Rolling Stone*, July 13, 2009.

Chapter 7

1. See, for example, Edward J. Kane, "Dangers of Capital Forbearance: The Case of the FSLIC and "ZOMBIE" S&Ls," *Contemporary Economic Policy*, 2007, 5(1): 77–83.

2. Congressional Budget Office, "Controlling the Risks of Government-Sponsored Enterprises," April 1991, xvii.

3. Congressional Budget Office, "Testimony of June E. O'Neill on Assessing the Public Costs and Benefits of Fannie Mae and Freddie Mac before the Subcommittee on Capital Markets, Securities and Government Sponsored Enterprises, Committee on Banking and Financial Services, U.S. House of Representatives," June 12, 1996, p. 2.

4. James C. Miller III and James E. Pearce, "Revisiting the Net Benefits of Freddie Mac and Fannie Mae," Freddie Mac, November 2006.

5. Hearing before the House Committee on Financial Services, September 10, 2003. The C-Span video is available at: http://www.c-spanvideo.org/program/178110-1, accessed November 19, 2009.

6. W. Scott Frame and Lawrence J. White, "Fussing and Fuming over Fannie and Freddie: How Much Smoke, How Much Fire?" *Journal of Economic Perspectives*, Spring 2005, 19(2): 169, table 2.

7. W. Scott Frame and Lawrence J. White, "Fussing and Fuming over Fannie and Freddie: How Much Smoke, How Much Fire?" *Journal of Economic Perspectives*, Spring 2005, 19(2): 161–162.

8. See Alex Berenson, "Prosecutors Investigating Freddie Mac," *New York Times*, June 12, 2003, and Jonathan D. Glater, "Market Place: Freddie Mac Gets Penalty and Rebuke over Scandal," *New York Times*, December 11, 2003.

9. See Eric Dash and Michael J. de la Merced, "Regulators Denounce Fannie Mae," *New York Times*, May 24, 2006; Stephen Labaton, "S.E.C. Says Fannie Mae Violated Accounting Rules," *New York Times*, December 16, 2004; and Stephen Labaton, "Fannie Mae Crisis Raises Concerns on Leadership," *New York Times*, September 29, 2004.

10. Carol D. Leonnig, "How HUD Mortgage Policy Fed the Crisis: Subprime Loans Labeled 'Affordable,'" *Washington Post*, June 10, 2008.

11. For an early and very critical look at problems in regulating the GSEs, see Peter J. Wallison, *Serving Two Masters, Yet Out of Control: Fannie Mae and Freddie Mac*, Washington, DC: American Enterprise Institute for Public Policy Research, 2001.

12. James B. Lockhart III, "Reforming the Regulation of the Government Sponsored Enterprises," Statement of the Honorable James B. Lockhart III, Director Office of Federal Housing Enterprise Oversight before the Senate Banking, Housing and Urban Affairs Committee, February 7, 2008, p. 8.

13. Damian Paletta, "OFHEO Is Pressured over Mortgages: Regulator Urged to Loosen Limits on Fannie, Freddie by Senators, Trade Groups," *Wall Street Journal*, October 24, 2007.

14. Charles Duhigg, Stephen Labaton, and Andrew Ross Sorkin, "As Crisis Grew, a Few Options Shrank to One," *New York Times*, September 8, 2008.

15. Charles Duhigg, "Mortgage Giants to Buy Fewer Risky Home Loans," *New York Times*, August 9, 2008.

16. Aparajita Saha-Bubna, "Freddie Mac CEO Sees a Stronger Footing in '08," *Wall Street Journal*, June 7, 2008.

17. Stephen Labaton, "Treasury Acts to Shore Up Fannie Mae and Freddie Mac," *New York Times*, July 14, 2008.

18. Charles Duhigg, Stephen Labaton, and Andrew Ross Sorkin, "As Crisis Grew, a Few Options Shrank to One," *New York Times*, September 8, 2008.

19. James Lockhart III, Statement Before the Financial Services Subcommittee on Capital Markets, Insurance, and Government-Sponsored Enterprises, June 3, 2009.

20. For an introduction to swaps, see Robert W. Kolb and James A. Overdahl, *Futures Options and Swaps*, 6th ed., Hoboken, NJ: John Wiley & Sons, 2007, chapters 20–21.

21. For a discussion of credit default swaps, see Steven Todd, "Credit Default Swaps," in Robert W. Kolb and James A. Overdahl, *Financial Derivatives*, Hoboken, NJ: John Wiley & Sons, 2010, chapter 13, pp. 177–198.

22. See David Henry, Matthew Goldstein, and Carol Matlack, "How AIG's Credit Loophole Squeezed Europe's Banks," *Business Week*, October 16, 2008.

23. Quoted in Gretchen Morgenson, "Behind Insurer's Crisis, Blind Eye to a Web of Risk," *New York Times*, September 28, 2008.

24. William K. Sjøstrom Jr., "The AIG Bailout," 66 *Washington and Lee Law Review*, 2009, p. 955.

25. Gretchen Morgenson, "Behind Insurer's Crisis, Blind Eye to a Web of Risk," *New York Times*, September 28, 2008.

26. Carrick Mollenkamp, Serena Ng, Liam Pleven, and Randall Smith, "Behind AIG's Fall, Risk Models Failed to Pass Real-World Test," *Wall Street Journal*, October 31, 2008.

27. Carrick Mollenkamp, Serena Ng, Liam Pleven, and Randall Smith, "Behind AIG's Fall, Risk Models Failed to Pass Real-World Test," *Wall Street Journal*, October 31, 2008.

28. See Gary Gorton, "The Panic of 2007," working paper, August, 25, 2008, p. 66.

29. William K Sjøstrom Jr., "The AIG Bailout," 66 *Washington and Lee Law Review*, 2009, p. 975.

30. Mary Williams Walsh, Edmund L. Andrews, and Jackie Calmes, "A.I.G. Lists Firms to Which It Paid Taxpayer Money," *New York Times*, March 16, 2009.

31. See http://blog.foreignpolicy.com/posts/2009/03/17/whither_the_aig_bailout_funds, accessed November 17, 2009.

32. Office of the Special Inspector General for the Troubled Asset Relief Program, "Factors Affecting Efforts to Limit Payments to AIG Counterparties," SIGTARP-10-003, November 17, 2009, Executive Summary.

33. Citi eventually spun off Travelers Property and Casualty business in 2002.

34. Eric Dash and Julie Creswell, "Citigroup Saw No Red Flags Even as It Made Bolder Bets," *New York Times*, November 23, 2008.

35. Eric Dash and Julie Creswell, "Citigroup Saw No Red Flags Even as It Made Bolder Bets," *New York Times*, November 23, 2008.

36. Eric Dash and Julie Creswell, "Citigroup Saw No Red Flags Even as It Made Bolder Bets," *New York Times*, November 23, 2008.

37. Andrew Martin and Gretchen Morgenson, "Can Citigroup Carry Its Own Weight?," *New York Times*, November 1, 2009.

38. Mary Williams Walsh, Edmund L. Andrews, and Jackie Calmes, "A.I.G. Lists Firms to Which It Paid Taxpayer Money," *New York Times*, March 16, 2009.

Chapter 8

1. See Edmund L. Andrews, "Vast Bailout by U.S. Proposed to Stem Financial Crisis," *New York Times*, September 19, 2008; and David Stout, "Officials Meet to Chart Course Through Credit Crisis," *New York Times*, September 19, 2008.

2. The public debt ceiling was raised further on February 17, 2009, to $12.104 trillion, to $14.3 trillion in February 2010, and by the autumn of 2010 it seemed that further increases were imminent. an additional increase was being pursued in late 2009.

3. Ben S. Bernanke, "Testimony Before the Committee on Banking, Housing, and Urban Affairs, U.S. Senate, September 23, 2008.

4. Quoted in Financial Executives International, "Bernanke Tells Senate: Auction Will Help Facilitate Held-to-Maturity Vs. Fire Sale Price," September 24, 2008, http://financialexecutives.blogspot.com/2008/09/bernanke-tells-senate-auction-will-help.html.

5. Quoted in Financial Executives International, "Bernanke Tells Senate: Auction Will Help Facilitate Held-to-Maturity Vs. Fire Sale Price," September 24, 2008, http://financialexecutives.blogspot.com/2008/09/bernanke-tells-senate-auction-will-help.html.

6. Paul Krugman, "Getting Real—and Letting the Cat Out of the Bag," *New York Times*, September 23, 2008.

7. Douglas A. McIntyre, "Paulson Plan Shows a Weakness: Above Market Pricing, Greater Taxpayer Risk," September 23, 2008, http://247wallst.com/2008/09/23/paulson-plan-sh/.

8. Floyd Norris, "A Pledge to Help That Hurts," *New York Times*, September 26, 2008.

9. David M. Herszenhorn, Carl Hulse, and Sheryl Gay Stolberg, "Talks Implode during a Day of Chaos; Fate of Bailout Plan Remains Unresolved," *New York Times*, September 26, 2008.

10. Peter S. Goodman, "Credit Enters a Lockdown," *New York Times*, September 26, 2008.

11. Peter Baker, "Labeled as a Bailout, Plan Was Hard to Sell to a Skeptical Public," *New York Times*, October 1, 2008.

12. Andrew Ross Sorkin, *Too Big to Fail*, New York: Viking, 2009, p. 525.

13. Specifics of the plan are presented in the term sheet presented to the participating banks, U.S. Treasury, "TARP Capital Purchase Program, Senior Preferred Stocks and Warrants," http://www.ustreas.gov/press/releases/reports/document5hp1207.pdf.

14. Federal Reserve Press Release, November 25, 2008.

15. Liz Rappaport and John Hilsenrath, "Fed Moves to Free Up Credit for Consumers," *Wall Street Journal*, March 4, 2009.

16. Edmund Andrews and Eric Dash, "U.S. Expands Plan to Buy Banks' Troubled Assets," *New York Times*, March 24, 2009.

17. Office of the Special Inspector General for the Troubled Asset Relief Program, "Quarterly Report to Congress," October 21, 2009, pp. 89–90.

18. Office of the Special Inspector General for the Troubled Asset Relief Program, "Quarterly Report to Congress," October 21, 2009, pp. 94–95.

19. Jenny Anderson, "Debt-Market Paralysis Deepens Credit Drought," *New York Times*, October 7, 2009.

Chapter 9

1. Mark Jickling, "Causes of the Financial Crisis," Congressional Research Service, 7-5700, R40173, January 29, 2009.

2. At the end of 2006, which is approximately the peak in housing prices, the total value of real estate held by households was $22.9 trillion dollars. Near the end of 2009, this asset class had fallen in value to $16.5 trillion, a drop of 28 percent. See Board of Governors of the Federal Reserve System, *Flow of Funds Accounts of the United States*, December 10, 2009, Table B.100, p. 104.

3. Ben S. Bernanke, "Financial Reform to Address Systemic Risk," Speech of March 10, 2009, http://www.federalreserve.gov/newsevents/speech/bernanke20090310a.htm.

4. Ben S. Bernanke, "Financial Reform to Address Systemic Risk," Speech of March 10, 2009, http://www.federalreserve.gov/newsevents/ speech/bernanke20090310a.htm.

5. Ben S. Bernanke, "Financial Reform to Address Systemic Risk," Speech of March 10, 2009, http://www.federalreserve.gov/newsevents/ speech/bernanke20090310a.htm.

6. Henry M. Paulson, Jr., "Remarks by Secretary Henry M. Paulson, Jr. on Financial Rescue Package and Economic Update," November 12, 2008. http://www.treas.gov/press/releases/hp1265.htm. Far from blaming the crisis on these global balances alone, Paulson went on to say: "In assessing the financial market crisis, I have repeatedly and consistently targeted the vast majority of my criticism at problems in the United States, particularly our flawed and outdated regulatory structure. . . ."

7. For more on the global imbalances as a cause of the crisis, see the following sources: Maurice Obstfeld and Kenneth Rogoff, "Global Imbalances and the Financial Crisis: Products of Common Causes," Working paper, November 2009, http://elsa.berkeley.edu/~obstfeld/santabarbara. pdf, accessed January 9, 2010; Bank for International Settlements, 79th *Annual Report*, June 29, 2009, especially p. 5; Ashok Deo Bardhan, "Of Subprimes and Subsidies: The Political Economy of the Financial Crisis," Working paper, October 2008; International Monetary Fund, *World Economic Outlook: Crisis and Recovery*," April 2009, especially pp. 34–38; and Philip R. Lane and Gian Maria Milesi-Ferretti, "Europe and Global Imbalances," *Economic Policy*, July 2007, 519–573. The Obstfeld and Rogoff account is particularly thorough.

8. For an analysis of the Federal Reserve's role in stimulating the housing bubble by following a policy of low interest rates, see John B. Taylor, *Getting off Track: How Government Actions and Interventions Caused, Prolonged, and Worsened the Financial Crisis*, Stanford, CA: Hoover Institution Press, 2009. Others charge that the Federal Reserve also kept interest rates too low and that this policy stimulated other asset bubbles. See Marc D. Hayford and A. G. Malliaris, "Monetary Policy and the U.S. Stock Market," *Economic Inquiry*, July 2004, 42(3): 387–401.

9. For the legislative history of HMDA, see Patricia A. McCoy, "The Home Mortgage Disclosure Act: A Synopsis and Recent Legislative History," *Journal of Real Estate Research*, 2007, 29(4): 381–397.

10. Quoted in Patricia A. McCoy, "The Home Mortgage Disclosure Act: A Synopsis and Recent Legislative History," *Journal of Real Estate Research*, 2007, 29(4): 381–397, at p. 381.

11. Patricia A. McCoy "The Home Mortgage Disclosure Act: A Synopsis and Recent Legislative History," *Journal of Real Estate Research*, 2007, 29(4): 381–397, at p. 381.

12. Quoted in AKM Rezaul Hossain, "The Past, Present and Future of Community Reinvestment Act (CRA): A Historical Perspective," Working paper, University of Connecticut working paper, 2004-30, October 2004, p. 2.

13. Quoted in AKM Rezaul Hossain, "The Past, Present and Future of Community Reinvestment Act (CRA): A Historical Perspective,"

Working paper, University of Connecticut working paper, 2004-30, October 2004, p. 2.

14. AKM Rezaul Hossain, "The Past, Present and Future of Community Reinvestment Act (CRA): A Historical Perspective," Working paper, University of Connecticut working paper, 2004-30, October 2004, p. 80.

15. Alicia A. Munnell, Lynne E. Browne, James McEneaney, and Geoffrey M. B. Tootell, "Mortgage Lending in Boston: Interpreting HMDA Data," Federal Reserve Bank of Boston Working Paper, No. 92-7, October 1992, p. 1.

16. Alicia A. Munnell, Lynne E. Browne, James McEneaney, and Geoffrey M. B. Tootell, "Mortgage Lending in Boston: Interpreting HMDA Data," Federal Reserve Bank of Boston Working Paper, No. 92-7, October 1992, p. 2.

17. See Vern McKinley, "Community Reinvestment Act: Ensuring Credit Adequacy or Enforcing Credit Allocation?" *Regulation* 1994, 17(4): 32, www.cato.org/pubs/regulation/regv17n4/vmck4-94.pdf.

18. See Peter J. Wallison, "Cause and Effect: Government Policies and the Financial Crisis," *Financial Services Outlook*, American Enterprise Institute for Public Policy Research, November 2008, p. 3. Also, for more recent changes to the act and its regulations, see Richard Marsico, "The 2004-2005 Amendments to the Community Reinvestment Act Regulations: For Communities, One Step Forward the Three Steps Back," New York Law School Public Law and Legal Theory Research Paper Series -5/06 #25.

19. David Listokin, Elvin K. Wyly, Brian Schmitt, and Ioan Voicu, "The Potential and Limitations of Mortgage Innovation in Fostering Homeownership in the United States," Fannie Mae Foundation, 2002, p. 76.

20. Peter L. Swan, "The Political Economy of the Subprime Crisis: Why Subprime Was So Attractive to Its Creators," December 2008, Working paper, p. 2.

21. For a sample of these criticisms, see: Robert B. Avery, Raphael W. Bostic, and Glenn B. Canner, "The Performance and Profitability of CRA-Related Lending, Federal Reserve Bank of Cleveland, November 2000; Glenn B. Canner, Elizabeth Laderman, Andreas Lehnert, and Wayne Passmore, "Does the Community Reinvestment Act (CRA) Cause Banks to Provide a Subsidy to Some Mortgage Borrowers?" Federal Reserve Board of Governors, Working paper, April 2002; Kevin Dowd, "Moral Hazard and the Financial Crisis," *Cato Journal*, Winter 2009, 29(1); Peter L. Swan, "The Political Economy of the Subprime Crisis: Why Subprime Was So Attractive to Its Creators," December 2008, Working paper; David G. Tarr, "The Political, Regulatory and Market Failures That Caused the U.S. Financial Crisis: What Are the Lessons?" Working paper, January 7, 2009; Peter J. Wallison, "Cause and Effect: Government Policies and the Financial Crisis," *Financial Services Outlook*, American Enterprise Institute for Public Policy Research, November 2008; Lawrence H. White, "How Did We Get into This Financial Mess?" *Briefing Papers*, Cato Institute, no. 110, November 18, 2008; and Todd J. Zywicki and Joseph D. Adamson, "The

Law and Economics of Subprime Lending," George Mason University Law and Economics Research Paper Series, 08-17, 2008.

22. George J. Benston, "The Community Reinvestment Act: Looking for Discrimination That Isn't There," Cato Institute, *Policy Analysis*, no. 354, October 6, 1999.

23. Philip Bond, David K. Musto, Bilg Yilmaz, "Predatory Mortgage Lending," *Journal of Financial Economics*, 2009, 94: 412–427.

24. Kevin Park, "Subprime Lending and the Community Reinvestment Act," Joint Center for Housing Studies, Harvard University, Working paper N08-2, November 2008; Luke Mullins, "Sheila Bair: Stop Blaming the Community Reinvestment Act," *U.S. News and World Report*, December 17, 2008; Randall S. Kroszner, "Risk Management and Basel II," speech at the Federal Reserve Bank of Boston AMA Conference, Boston, Massachusetts, May 14, 2008; Bernanke, Ben S., "The Community Reinvestment Act: Its Evolution and New Challenges," speech at the Community Affairs Research Conference, Washington, D.C., March 20, 2007.

25. Kathleen C. Engel and Patricia A. McCoy, "The CRA Implications of Predatory Lending," 29 *Fordham Urban Law Journal*, 1571, 2002. and Kathleen C. Engel and Patricia A. McCoy, "A Tale of Three Markets: The Law and Economics of Predatory Lending," *Texas Law Review*, May 2002, 80(6): 1255–1367.

26. Richard Marsico, "The 2004-2005 Amendments to the Community Reinvestment Act Regulations: For Communities, One Step Forward the three Steps Back," New York Law School Public Law and Legal Theory Research Paper Series -5/06 #25.

27. Federal Reserve Bank of Boston, "Closing the Gap: A Guide to Equal Opportunity Lending," Boston, April 1993, p. 5.

28. Federal Reserve Bank of Boston, "Closing the Gap: A Guide to Equal Opportunity Lending," Boston, April 1993, p. 6.

29. For evidence that securitization helped reduce screening by lenders, see Benjamin J. Keys, Tanmoy Mukherjee, Amit Seru, and Vikrant Vig, "Did Securitization Lead to Lax Screening? Evidence from Subprime Loans," Working paper, December 2008. In addition, Mian and Sufi conclude that the incentive to screen less was a major factor in leading to the mortgage default crisis. Atif Mian and Amir Sufi, "The Consequences of Mortgage Credit Expansion: Evidence from the 2007 Mortgage Default Crisis," January 2008, Working paper.

30. Kevin Park, "Subprime Lending and the Community Reinvestment Act," Joint Center for Housing Studies, Harvard University, Working paper N08-2, November 2008, pp. 3, 5.

31. Three studies offer trenchant analyses of the combined effects of the CRA and the GSEs on underwriting standards and the consequences that such lending policies entailed. See Stan J. Liebowitz, "Anatomy of a Train Wreck: Causes of the Mortgage Meltdown," *Independent Policy Reports*, October 3, 2008; Steven Malanga, "The Long Road to Slack Lending Standards," http://www.realclearmarkets.com/

printpage/?url=http://www.realclearmarkets.com/articles/2008/10/
the_long_road_to_slack_lending.html, accessed October 1, 2008; and Peter
J. Wallison, "Cause and Effect: Government Policies and the Financial
Crisis," *Financial Services Outlook*, American Enterprise Institute for Public
Policy Research, November 2008.

32. Norris, Carole, "New Rules for Fannie and Freddie," National
Housing Institute, Issue #80, March/April 1995, http://www.nhi.org/
online/issues/80/fanny.html, accessed January 13, 2009, p. 3.

33. Quoted in Steven A. Holmes, "Fannie Mae Eases Credit to Aid
Mortgage Lending," *New York Times*, September 30, 1999,. http://query.
nytimes.com/gst/fullpage.html, accessed October 13, 2008.

34. Steven A. Holmes, "Fannie Mae Eases Credit to Aid Mortgage
Lending," *New York Times*, September 30, 1999, http://query.nytimes.com/
gst/fullpage.html, accessed October 13, 2008.

35. Allen J. Fishbein, "Going Subprime," National Housing Institute,
Issue #125, September–October 2002.

36. See Stuart S. Rosenthal, "Eliminating Credit Barriers to Increase
Homeownership: How Far Can We Go?" Low-Income Homeownership
Work Paper Series, Joint Center for Housing Studies of Harvard University,
LIHO.01-3, August 2001.

37. *Wall Street Journal*, "Fannie Mae's Patron Saint," September 9,
2008.

38. Barney Frank, Opening Statement from Hearing before the House
Financial Services Committee, September 11, 2003.

39. Office of Federal Housing Enterprise Oversight, "Mortgage
Markets and the Enterprise in 2006," June 2007, pp. 24, 25.

40. Office of Federal Housing Enterprise Oversight, "Mortgage
Markets and the Enterprise in 2007," July 2008, p. 15.

41. Office of Federal Housing Enterprise Oversight, "Mortgage
Markets and the Enterprise in 2007," July 2008, p. 1.

42. Office of Federal Housing Enterprise Oversight, "Mortgage
Markets and the Enterprise in 2007," July 2008, pp. 1, 32.

43. James B. Lockhart III, "Reforming the Regulation of the
Government Sponsored Enterprises," Testimony before the Senate
Banking, Housing and Urban Affairs Committee, February 7, 2008.

44. James B. Lockhart III, "The Present Condition and Future Status of
Fannie Mae and Freddie Mac," Testimony before the House Financial
Services Committee, June 3, 2009.

45. Paletta Damian, "OFHEO Is Pressured over Mortgages: Regulator
Urged to Loosen Limits on Fannie, Freddie by Senators, Trade Groups,"
Wall Street Journal, October 24, 2007.

46. Charles Duhigg, "Pressured to Take on Risk, Fannie Hit a Tipping
Point," *New York Times*, October 5, 2008, http://www.nytimes.
com/2008/10/05/business/05fannie.html, accessed October 4, 2008.

47. Charles Duhigg, "Pressured to Take on Risk, Fannie Hit a Tipping
Point," *New York Times*, October 5, 2008, http://www.nytimes.
com/2008/10/05/business/05fannie.html, accessed October 4, 2008.

48. Associated Press, "Freddie Mac Pays Record $3.8 Million Fine," April 18, 2006.

49. James B. Lockhart III, "Reforming the Regulation of the Government Sponsored Enterprises," Testimony before the Senate Banking, Housing and Urban Affairs Committee, February 7, 2008.

50. Gretchen Morgenson and Charles Duhigg, "Mortgage Giant Overstated Size of Capital Base," *New York Times*, September 7, 2008.

Chapter 10

1. For a trenchant analysis of the moral failings of regulators, see Edward J. Kane, "Unmet Duties in Managing Financial Safety Nets," forthcoming in *Business Ethics Quarterly*.

2. This is one important difference between banking regulation in the United States and other countries that prevailed for many decades—other countries generally did not require a divorce of commercial and investment banking.

3. For the history of Glass-Steagall and the market forces that brought it under pressure, see William D. Jackson, "Glass-Steagall Act: Commercial vs. Investment Banking," Congressional Research Service, 1987.

4. Oddly, there are 11 countries in the Group of Ten: Belgium, Canada, France, Germany, Italy, Japan, Netherlands, Sweden, Switzerland, United Kingdom, and the United States. The Basel Committee also includes representatives from Luxembourg and Spain.

5. Allen N. Berger, Richard J. Herring, and Giorgio P. Szegö, "The Role of Capital in Financial Institutions," *Journal of Banking and Finance*, 1995, 3–4: 393–430.

6. Counts of failed banks in 2008 and 2009 differ considerably. These figures are from the FDIC. See: Federal Deposit Insurance Corporation, *Quarterly Banking Profile*, Fourth Quarter 2009, p. 3.

7. George Kaufman and A. G. Malliaris, "The Financial Crisis of 2007–09: Missing Financial Regulation or Absentee Regulators?" forthcoming in Robert W. Kolb, *Lessons from the Financial Crisis: Causes, Consequences, and Our Economic Future*, Hoboken, NJ: John Wiley & Sons, 2010.

8. For various perspectives on the role of Basel II in the crisis, see: Douglas W. Arner, "The Global Credit Crisis of 2008: Causes and Consequences," Working paper, January 2009; Randall S. Kroszner, "Risk Management and Basel II," speech at the Federal Reserve Bank of Boston AMA Conference, Boston, Massachusetts, May 14, 2008; Francesco Cannata and Mario Quagliariello, "The Role of Basel II in the Subprime Financial Crisis: Guilty or Not Guilty?" Working paper, January 2009; Francesco Cannata and Mario Quagliariello, "Basel II Put on Trial: What Role in the Financial Crisis?" in Robert W. Kolb (ed.), *Lessons from the Financial Crisis: Causes, Consequences, and Our Economic Future*, Hoboken, NJ: John Wiley & Sons, 2010, chapter 46; and Michael W. Taylor and Douglas W. Arner, "Global Regulation for Global Markets?" in Robert W. Kolb (ed.), *Lessons from the Financial Crisis: Causes, Consequences, and Our Economic Future*, Hoboken, NJ: John Wiley & Sons, 2010, chapter 48.

9. Binyamin Appelbaum, "FDIC Agrees to Sell IndyMac to Investor Group," *Washington Post*, January 3, 2009. The FDIC estimated the loss to fall in the range of $8.5 to $9.4 billion.

10. For a variety of views on the importance of the decision to let Lehman fail, see: Douglas W. Arner, "The Global Credit Crisis of 2008: Causes and Consequences," Working paper, January 2009; John H. Cochrane and Luigi Zingales, "Lehman and the Financial Crisis," *Wall Street Journal*, September 15, 2009; and *Wall Street Journal*, "Evening Reading: Did Paulson Err by Letting Lehman Fail?," October 23, 2008.

11. See FDIC Law, Regulations, Related Acts, 8000, Miscellaneous Statutes and Regulations, Part 32, Lending Limits, Sec. 32.3, http://www.fdic.gov/regulations/laws/rules/8000-7400.html#fdic8000lending32.3, accessed January 30, 2010.

12. See: http://sec.gov/about/whatwedo.shtml, accessed January 30, 2010.

13. Securities and Exchange Commission, "Final Rule: Alternative Net Capital Requirements for Broker-Dealers That Are Part of Consolidated Supervised Entities," June 8, 2004, p. 1. Available at: http://www.sec.gov/rules/final/34-49830.htm, accessed January 30, 2010.

14. Julie Satow, "Ex-SEC Official Blames Agency for Blow-Up of Broker-Dealers," *New York Sun*, September 18, 2008.

15. There are alternative measures of leverage, and many reported leverage ratios for these five firms are larger than those shown here. To standardize these leverage measures as much as possible, all figures were computed using reports filed with the Securities and Exchange Commission, pertained to the consolidated entity, and used the clearly identifiable categories of "Total Assets" and "Total Stockholders' Equity."

16. Securities and Exchange Commission, "Final Rule: Alternative Net Capital Requirements for Broker-Dealers That Are Part of Consolidated Supervised Entities," June 8, 2004, p. 2, http://www.sec.gov/rules/final/34-49830.htm, accessed January 30, 2010.

17. Stephen Labaton, S.E.C. Concedes Oversight Flaws Fueled Collapse," *New York Times*, September 27, 2008.

18. Gary Gorton and Nicholas S. Souleles, "Special Purpose Vehicles and Securitization," National Bureau of Economic Research, Working Paper 11190, March 2005, http://www.nber.org/papers/w11190, accessed January 30, 2010.

19. Ed Stevens, "Evolution in Banking Supervision," Federal Reserve Bank of Cleveland, March 1, 2000.

20. Gary Gorton and Nicholas S. Souleles, "Special Purpose Vehicles and Securitization," National Bureau of Economic Research, Working paper 11190, March 2005, http://www.nber.org/papers/w11190, accessed January 30, 2010, abstract.

21. Gary Gorton and Nicholas S. Souleles, "Special Purpose Vehicles and Securitization," National Bureau of Economic Research, Working Paper 11190, March 2005, http://www.nber.org/papers/w11190, accessed January 30, 2010, p. 2.

22. The legal and financial theory of SPVs is quite complex. Virtually all attempted rationalizations of their widespread use identify the regulatory arbitrage of capital requirement reduction as a feature, but there are many more aspects to these "robot firms," and some observers believe that the regulatory arbitrage may not even be the prime motivation. For discussion of these entities see: Charles W. Calomiris and Joseph R. Mason, "Credit Card Securitization and Regulatory Arbitrage," *Journal of Financial Services Research*, 2004, 26(1): 5–27; Gary Gorton and Nicholas S. Souleles, "Special Purpose Vehicles and Securitization," National Bureau of Economic Research, Working paper 11190, March 2005, http://www.nber.org/papers/w11190, accessed January 30, 2010; and Ed Stevens, "Evolution in Banking Supervision," Federal Reserve Bank of Cleveland, March 1, 2000.

23. For a history of the development of bond ratings and their importance, see Frank Partnoy, "The Siskel and Ebert of Financial Markets?: Two Thumbs Down for the Credit Rating Agencies," *Washington University Law Quarterly*, 1999, 77(3): 619–712. See especially Part II.B.

24. See Frank Partnoy, "The Siskel and Ebert of Financial Markets?: Two Thumbs Down for the Credit Rating Agencies," *Washington University Law Quarterly*, 1999, 77(3): 647–648.

25. For a discussion of ratings as a public good and the 95 percent revenue figure, see Frank Partnoy, "The Siskel and Ebert of Financial Markets?: Two Thumbs Down for the Credit Rating Agencies," *Washington University Law Quarterly*, 1999, 77(3): 619–712xy3.

26. For an extensive account of credit rating agencies, see Herwig M. Langohr and Patricia T. Langohr, *The Rating Agencies and Their Credit Ratings: What They Are, How They Work and Why They Are Relevant*, Hoboken, NJ: John Wiley and Sons, 2008.

27. Securities and Exchange Commission, "Definition of Nationally Recognized Statistical Rating Organization," April 19, 2005, http://www.sec.gov/rules/proposed/33-8570.pdf, accessed January 31, 2010, p. 5.

28. See Frank Partnoy, "The Siskel and Ebert of Financial Markets?: Two Thumbs Down for the Credit Rating Agencies," *Washington University Law Quarterly*, 1999, 77(3): 619–712; and Frank Partnoy, "How and Why Credit Rating Agencies Are Not Like Other Gatekeepers," in Yasuyuki Fuchita and Robert E. Litan (eds.), *Financial Gatekeepers: Can They Protect Investors?* Washington, DC:, Brookings Institution Press, 2006, chapter 3, pp. 59–102.

29. However, even when regulators designate credit rating agencies, Anno Stolper argues that it is possible for the approval scheme to induce agencies to assign correct ratings. See "Regulation of Credit Rating Agencies," *Journal of Banking and Finance*, 2009, 33: 1266–1273.

30. Frank Partnoy, "How and Why Credit Rating Agencies Are Not Like Other Gatekeepers," in Yasuyuki Fuchita and Robert E. Litan (eds.), *Financial Gatekeepers: Can They Protect Investors?* Washington, DC:, Brookings Institution Press, 2006, chapter 3, pp. 59–102. See p. 60.

31. Financial Accounting Standards Board, "Summary of Statement No. 157: Fair Value Measurements,"http://www.fasb.org/st/summary/stsum157.shtml#, accessed February 4, 2010.

32. Euromoney, "Understanding the Mark-to-Market Meltdown," March 3, 2008.

33. Euromoney, "Understanding the Mark-to-Market Meltdown," March 3, 2008.

34. Floyd Norris, "If Market Prices Are Too Low, Ignore Them," *New York Times*, March 28, 2008.

35. John Poirier and Emily Chasan, "SEC Gives Banks More Leeway on Mark-to-Market," Reuters.com, October 1, 2008, http://www.reuters.com/assets/print?aid=USWAT01020020081001, accessed January 31, 2010.

36. U.S. Securities and Exchange Commission, "SEC Office of the Chief Accountant and FASB Staff Clarifications on Fair Value Accounting," 2008-234, September 30, 2008.

37. CNBC.com, "Former FDIC Chair Blames SEC for Credit Crunch," http://www.cnbc.com/id/27100454/print/1/displaymode/1098/, accessed January 31, 2010.

38. U.S. Securities and Exchange Commission, "Report and Recommendation Pursuant to Section 133 of the Emergency Economic Stabilization Act of 2008: Study on Mark-To-Market Accounting," Office of the Chief Accountant, Division of Corporate Finance, December 30, 2008.

39. Depository Trust and Clearing Corporation, "DTCC Addresses Misconceptions about the Credit Default Swap Market," Press Release, October 11, 2008, http://www.dtcc.com/news/press/releases/2008/tiw.php, accessed February 4, 2010. This is the nominal value of contracts outstanding, not the amount of value at risk. The reported number is not for the number of "sides," which counts each trader's position, but is for the nominal values themselves, consisting of two "sides."

40. Scott M. Polakoff, "American International Group: Examining What Went Wrong, Government Intervention, and Implications for Future Regulation," testimony before the Senate Committee on Banking, Housing, and Urban Affairs, March 5, 2009, p. 10.

41. Scott M. Polakoff, "American International Group: Examining What Went Wrong, Government Intervention, and Implications for Future Regulation," testimony before the Senate Committee on Banking, Housing, and Urban Affairs, March 5, 2009, p. 11.

42. Timothy F. Geithner, "Written Testimony Presented to the House Committee on Oversight and Government Reform," January 27, 2010.

Chapter 11

1. See Richard Bookstaber's excellent book, *A Demon of Our Own Design*, Hoboken, NJ: John Wiley & Sons, 2007. Written and published before the crisis, it is a brilliant analysis of faults in the structure of modern finance.

2. See Richard Thaler and Cass Sunstein, "Human Frailty Caused this Crisis," *Financial Times*, November 11, 2008. Their main point is one from

behavioral economics—bounded rationality and limited self-control led people to make sub-optimal decisions, such as getting into mortgages that they understood only poorly.

3. These data are drawn from various issues of the *American Housing Survey* of the U.S. Census Bureau. Data on size of homes is available at http://www.census.gov/hhes/www/housing/ahs/93dtchrt/tab2-3.html.

4. See Gary Gorton, "The Subprime Panic," *European Financial Management*, January 2009, 15(1): 10–46. Gorton argues that a key structural element of the subprime market was structured to require periodic refinancing, which effectively gave the lender the opportunity to call the loan by refusing to refinance.

5. In the run-up to the housing bubble, borrowers were allowed to obtain their own appraisals, but lenders continued to order most appraisals.

6. One academic study examined a sample of mortgages issued by a large mortgage firm and found that all appraisals equaled or exceeded the transaction price. Further, the study found that appraisals were higher for low-quality borrowers and difficult-to-value properties. See Itzhak Ben-David, "Manipulation of Collateral Values by Borrowers and Intermediaries," Working paper, February 2008.

7. For the initial tightening, see Kathleen C. Engel and Patricia A. McCoy, "A Tale of Three Markets: The Law and Economics of Predatory Lending," *Texas Law Review*, May 2002, 80(6): 1255–1367, at p. 1364; for the relaxation under the National Homeownership Strategy, see David Streitfeld and Gretchen Morgenson, "Building Flawed American Dreams," *New York Times*, October 19, 2008.

8. Federal Reserve Bank of Boston, "Closing the Gap: A Guide to Equal Opportunity Lending," Boston, April 1993, p. 7.

9. Federal Reserve Bank of Boston, "Closing the Gap: A Guide to Equal Opportunity Lending," Boston, April 1993, p. 22.

10. U.S. Department of Housing and Urban Development, "Curbing Predatory Home Mortgage Lending," Office of Policy Development and Research, June 1, 2000.

11. Patrick Barta, "False Appraisals May Inflate Prices," *Chicago Tribune*, August 26, 2001.

12. Josh Rosner, "Housing in the New Millennium: A Home Without Equity Is Just a Rental With Debt," *Housing Trends*, GrahamFisher, June 29, 2001, http://ssrn.com/abstract=1162456, accessed February 7, 2010. See page 11.

13. Paul Muolo and Mathew Padilla, *Chain of Blame: How Wall Street Caused the Mortgage and Credit Crisis*, Hoboken, NJ: John Wiley & Sons, 2008, p. 59.

14. Figures on the size of the mortgage broker industry vary considerably, and it is certain that the number of mortgage brokers has been declining recently. Paul Muolo and Mathew Padilla, *Chain of Blame: How Wall Street Caused the Mortgage and Credit Crisis*, Hoboken, NJ: John Wiley & Sons, 2008, pp. 66–67. Richard Bitner, *Confessions of a Subprime*

Lender, Hoboken, NJ: John Wiley & Sons, 2008, p. 48, reports 250,000 mortgage brokers in 2000. The National Association of Mortgage Brokers reported total employees of 418,700 in 2004. See: http://www.namb.org/namb/Mission.asp?SnID=1149970333, accessed February 1, 2009.

15. National Association of Mortgage Brokers, "Model Disclosure Form," June 22, 1997.

16. For a very expansive list of predatory lending practices, see Association of Community Organizations for Reform Now, "Predatory Lending Practices," http://www.acorn.org/index.php?id=754, accessed September 25, 2008. Whether some of the items on the list are predatory depends entirely on the parties involved and the particulars of the loan. Kathleen C. Engel and Patricia A. McCoy, "A Tale of Three Markets: The Law and Economics of Predatory Lending," *Texas Law Review*, May 2002, 80(6): 1255–1367 provide a more sober list that is conceptually based. See p. 1260. Another study defines a predatory loan merely as "... loans that borrowers should decline." See Philip Bond, David K. Musto, Bilg Yilmaz, "Predatory Mortgage Lending," *Journal of Financial Economics*, 2009, 94: 412–427.

17. U.S. Department of Housing and Urban Development, *Curbing Predatory Home Mortgage Lending*, Office of Policy Development and Research, June 1, 2000. See p. 1.

18. David Faber, *And Then the Roof Caved In: How Wall Street's Greed and Stupidity Brought Capitalism to Its Knees*, Hoboken, NJ: John Wiley & Sons, 2009. See pp. 23–24.

19. The President's Working Group on Financial Markets, "Policy Statement on Financial Market Developments," March 2008, p. 2. Emphasis in original.

20. Some of the studies are: Martin Neil Baily, Robert E. Litan, and Mathew S. Johnson, "The Origins of the Financial Crisis," Brookings Institution, Fixing Finance Series, Paper 3, November 2008; Geetesh Bhardwaj and Rajdeep Sengupta, "Where's the Smoking Gun: A Study of Underwriting Standards for U.S. Subprime Mortgages," Federal Reserve Bank of St. Louis, *Working Paper Series*, October 2008; Michael D. Bordo, "An Historical Perspective on the Crisis of 2007–2008," Working Paper; Michel G. Crouhy, Robert A. Jarrow, and Stuart M. Turnbull, "The Subprime Credit Crisis of 2007," *The Journal of Derivatives*, Fall 2008: 1–30; Yuliya Demyanyk and Otto Van Hemert, "Understanding the Subprime Mortgage Crisis," February 2008, Working paper; Luci Ellis, "The Housing Meltdown: Why Did It Happen in the United States?" Bank for International Settlements, BIS Working Papers no. 259, September 2008; Benjamin J. Keys, Tanmoy Mukherjee, Amit Seru, and Vikrant Vig, "Did Securitization Lead to Lax Screening? Evidence from Subprime Loans," Working paper, December 2008; Christopher Mayer, Karen Pence, and Shane M. Sherlund, "The Rise in Mortgage Defaults," *Journal of Economic Perspectives*, Winter 2009, 23(1): 27–50; Shane M. Sherlund, "The Past, Present, and Future of Subprime Mortgages," Federal Reserve Board, Finance and Economics Discussion Series, 2008; and Ronald D. Utt,

"The Subprime Mortgage Market Collapse: A Primer on the Causes and Possible Solutions," *The Heritage Foundation Backgrounder* 2127, April 2008: 1–22.

21. Angelo R, Mozilo, "The American Dream of Homeownership: From Cliché to Mission," John T. Dunlop Lecture, Joint Center for Housing Studies, Harvard University, February 4, 2003, p. 4.

22. Gretchen Morgenson, "Inside the Countrywide Lending Spree," *New York Times*, August 26, 2007.

23. Gretchen Morgenson, "Inside the Countrywide Lending Spree," *New York Times*, August 26, 2007.

24. See Peter S. Goodman and Gretchen Morgenson, "By Saying Yes, WaMu Built Empire on Shaky Loans," *New York Times*, December 28, 2008, http://www.nytimes.com/2008/12/28/business/28wamu.html, accessed on December 28, 2008.

25. U. S. Securities and Exchange Commission, *Plaintiff vs. Angelo Mozilo, David Sambol, and Eric Sieracki, Defendants*, "Complaint for Violations of the Federal Securities Laws," June 4, 2009, p. 42.

26. Gretchen Morgenson and Geraldine Fabrikant, "Countrywide's Chief Salesman and Defender," *New York Times*, November 11, 2007.

Chapter 12

1. Los Angeles Times, "Sub-Prime Mortgage Watchdogs Kept On Leash," March 17, 2008, http://articles.latimes.com/2008/mar/17/business/fi-subprime17, accessed February 9, 2010.

2. Paul Muolo and Mathew Padilla, *Chain of Blame: How Wall Street Caused the Mortgage and Credit Crisis*, Hoboken, NJ: John Wiley & Sons, 2008, pp. 228, 230. The story of these due diligence firms has been quite underreported, but *Chain of Blame* offers an insightful and sustained discussion of this little-known corner of the subprime basement.

3. Paul Muolo and Mathew Padilla, *Chain of Blame: How Wall Street Caused the Mortgage and Credit Crisis*, Hoboken, NJ: John Wiley & Sons, 2008, p. 197.

4. Paul Muolo and Mathew Padilla, *Chain of Blame: How Wall Street Caused the Mortgage and Credit Crisis*, Hoboken, NJ: John Wiley & Sons, 2008, p. 234.

5. Paul Muolo and Mathew Padilla, *Chain of Blame: How Wall Street Caused the Mortgage and Credit Crisis*, Hoboken, NJ: John Wiley & Sons, 2008, p. 181.

6. Los Angeles Times, "Sub-Prime Mortgage Watchdogs Kept On Leash," March 17, 2008, http://articles.latimes.com/2008/mar/17/business/fi-subprime17, accessed February 9, 2010.

7. Los Angeles Times, "Sub-Prime Mortgage Watchdogs Kept On Leash," March 17, 2008, http://articles.latimes.com/2008/mar/17/business/fi-subprime17, accessed February 9, 2010.

8. See Amir Efrati and Ruth Simon, "Due-Diligence Firm to Aid New York Subprime Probe," *Wall Street Journal*, January 29, 2008; and Jenny

Anderson and Vikas Bajaj, "Loan Reviewer Aiding Inquiry Into Big Banks," *New York Times*, January 27, 2008.

9. The following papers give a good understanding of the process of securitization: Adam B. Ashcraft and Til Schuermann, "Understanding the Securitization of Subprime Mortgage Credit," *Federal Reserve Bank of New York Staff Reports*, no. 318, March 2008; Joshua Coval, Jakub Jurek, and Erik Stafford, "The Economics of Structured Finance," *Journal of Economic Perspectives*, Winter 2009, 23(1): 3–25; Maciej Firla-Cuchra and Tim Jenkinson, "Why Are Securitization Issues Tranched?" Working paper, March 2005; and John D. Martin, "A Primer on the Role of Securitization in the Credit Market Crisis of 2007," Working Paper, January 2009.

10. Moody's Investors Services, "Corporate Default and Recovery Rates, 1920-2008," February 2009, http://www.moodys.com/cust/content/content.ashx?source=StaticContent/Free%20Pages/Credit%20Policy%20Research/documents/current/2007400000578875.pdf, accessed February 13, 2010.

11. Moody's Investors Services, "Default and Loss Rates of Structured Finance Securities: 1993–2008, August 2009, p. 3, Exhibit 3.

12. Note that this is not a perfect measure because it compares defaults in a given year to new ratings issued in that year. The overwhelming proportion of defaulting securities will have been issued in various previous years.

13. Moody's Investors Services, "Default and Loss Rates of Structured Finance Securities: 1993–2008, August 2009. See pp. 3–4.

14. Moody's Investor Services, "Code of Professional Conduct," June 2005, p. 6.

15. U.S. Securities and Exchange Commission, "Summary Report of Issues Identified in the Commission Staff's Examinations of Select Credit Rating Agencies," July 2008. See pp. 7–10.

16. U.S. Securities and Exchange Commission, "Summary Report of Issues Identified in the Commission Staff's Examinations of Select Credit Rating Agencies," July 2008, p. 8. It seems there is also substantial theoretical empirical evidence to support this idea that securitizers would "shop for the highest rating" with the credit rating agencies. See Vasiliki Skreta and Laura Veldkamp, "Ratings Shopping and Asset Complexity: A Theory of Ratings Inflation," Working paper, October 2008; Efraim Benmelech and Jennifer Dlugosz, "The Alchemy of CDO Credit Ratings," Working paper; and Efraim Benmelech and Jennifer Dlugosz, "The Alchemy of CDO Credit Ratings," Working paper.

17. Sam Jones, Gillian Tett, and Paul J. Davies, "Moody's Error Gave Top Ratings to Debt Products," *Financial Times*, May 21, 2008.

18. Vikas Bajaj, "Moody's Says Workers Rated Some Securities Incorrectly," *New York Times*, July 2, 2008.

19. Frank Partnoy, "The Siskel and Ebert of Financial Markets?: Two Thumbs Down for the Credit Rating Agencies," *Washington University Law Quarterly*, 1999, 77(3): 619–712. See pp. 649–650.

20. U.S. Securities and Exchange Commission, "Summary Report of Issues Identified in the Commission Staff's Examinations of Select Credit Rating Agencies," July 2008, p. 1.

21. U.S. Securities and Exchange Commission, "Summary Report of Issues Identified in the Commission Staff's Examinations of Select Credit Rating Agencies," July 2008, p. 12. See also Aaron Lucchetti, "S&P Email: 'We Should Not be Rating It,'" *Wall Street Journal*, August 2, 2008, http://online.wsj.com/article_print/SB121764476728206967.html, accessed August 3, 2008.

22. U.S. Securities and Exchange Commission, "Summary Report of Issues Identified in the Commission Staff's Examinations of Select Credit Rating Agencies," July 2008, pp. 24–25 *passim*.

23. Frank Partnoy, "The Siskel and Ebert of Financial Markets?: Two Thumbs Down for the Credit Rating Agencies," *Washington University Law Quarterly*, 1999, 77(3): 619–712; and Frank Partnoy, "How and Why Credit Rating Agencies Are Not Like Other Gatekeepers," in Yasuyuki Fuchita and Robert E. Litan (eds.), *Financial Gatekeepers: Can They Protect Investors?* Washington, DC: Brookings Institution Press, 2006, chapter 3, 59–102. See also Franklin Strier, "Rating the Raters: Conflicts of Interest in the Credit Rating Firms," *Business and Society Review*, 2008, 1134 533–553.

24. Middleton, Reggie, "Digging Deeper into Lehman," Seeking Alpha website, May 26, 2008, http://seekingalpha.com/article/78846-digging-deeper-into-lehman, accessed February 14, 2010.

25. Faber's telling of the story is his chapter 8, "Narvik and Me," in David Faber, *And Then the Roof Caved In: How Wall Street's Greed and Stupidity Brought Capitalism to Its Knees*, Hoboken, NJ: John Wiley & Sons, 2009. For the House of Cards video, see: http://www.cnbc.com/id/15840232?video=1164596286&play=1. My account of Narvik's difficulties relies entirely on these two sources.

26. This account relies on four sources: Charles Duhigg, and Carter Dougherty, "From Midwest to M.T.A, Pain From Global Gamble," *New York Times*, November 2, 2008; *Milwaukee World*, "New Allegations in Reopened School Districts v. Stifel Case," April 23, 2009; CNNMoney.com, "Wall St. Crisis Snares Main St. Schools," http://cnnmoney.printthis.clickability.com/pt/cpt?action=cpt&title=W. . .%2F01%2F15%2Fnews%2Fwisconsin_loss_harlow%2Findex.htm&partnerID=2200, accessed February 16, 2010. See also the web site School Law Suit Facts, at http://pr.schoollawsuitfacts.com/. This site is sponsored by the five Wisconsin school districts.

Chapter 13

1. For accounts of LTCM and other disasters involving financial derivatives, see John E. Marthinsen, *Risk Takers: Uses and Abuses of Financial Derivatives*, 2nd ed., Boston: Prentice Hall, 2009, and John E. Marthinsen, "Derivative Scandals and Disasters," in Robert W. Kolb and James A. Overdahl (eds.), *Financial Derivatives*, Hoboken, NJ: John Wiley & Sons, 2010, chapter 23, pp. 313–332. Roger Lowenstein offers an excellent

book-length account of LTCM in his *When Genius Failed: The Rise and Fall of Long-Term Capital Management*, New York: Random House, 2001.

2. For an introduction to the technical detail of CDOs, see Steven Todd, "Structured Credit Products," in Robert W. Kolb and James A. Overdahl, *Financial Derivatives*, Hoboken, NJ: John Wiley and Sons, 2010, chapter 14, pp. 199–210; Alexander Crawford, "Collateralized Mortgage Obligations," in Frank J. Fabozzi and Steven V. Mann, *The Handbook of Fixed Income Securities*, 7th ed., New York: McGraw-Hill, 2005, pp. 541–578; Douglas J. Lucas, Laurie S. Goodman, and Frank J. Fabozzi, "Collateralized Debt Obligations and Credit Risk Transfer," Yale ICF Working Paper No. 07-06, 2007; and Joseph R. Mason and Joshua Rosner, "Where Did the Risk Go? How Misapplied Bond Ratings Cause Mortgage Backed Securities and Collateralized Debt Obligation Market Disruptions," Working paper.

3. This phenomenon first came to attention with an excellent account by Gretchen Morgenson, "Guess What Got Lost in the Loan Pool?" *New York Times*, March 1, 2009. Her account draws on Samuel L. Bufford and R. Glen Ayers, "Where's the Note, Who's the Holder: Enforcement of Promissory Note Secured by Real Estate," American Bankruptcy Institute, April 3, 2009, http://livinglies.wordpress.com/2009/02/19/this-is-it-where's-the-note-who's-the-holder-enforcement-of-promissory-note-secured-by-real-estate/, accessed February 18, 2010.

4. Samuel L. Bufford and R. Glen Ayers, "Where's the Note, Who's the Holder: Enforcement of Promissory Note Secured by Real Estate," American Bankruptcy Institute, April 3, 2009, p. 1, http://livinglies.wordpress.com/2009/02/19/this-is-it-where's-the-note-who's-the-holder-enforce-ment-of-promissory-note-secured-by-real-estate/, accessed February 18, 2010.

5. Samuel L. Bufford and R. Glen Ayers, "Where's the Note, Who's the Holder: Enforcement of Promissory Note Secured by Real Estate," American Bankruptcy Institute, April 3, 2009, p. 2, http://livinglies.wordpress.com/2009/02/19/this-is-it-where's-the-note-who's-the-holder-enforce-ment-of-promissory-note-secured-by-real-estate/, accessed February 18, 2010.

6. Gretchen Morgenson, "Guess What Got Lost in the Loan Pool?" *New York Times*, March 1, 2009.

7. Gretchen Morgenson, "Guess What Got Lost in the Loan Pool?" *New York Times*, March 1, 2009.

8. For an introduction to the CDS market and its economics, see: Depository Trust and Clearing Corporation, "DTCC Addresses Misconceptions About the Credit Default Swap Market," Press Release, October 11, 2008, http://www.dtcc.com/news/press/releases/2008/tiw.php, accessed February 4, 2010; and Steven Todd, "Credit Default Swaps," in Robert W. Kolb and James A. Overdahl, *Financial Derivatives*, Hoboken, NJ: John Wiley and Sons, 2010, chapter 13, pp. 177–198. For the role of CDS in the crisis, see René M. Stulz, "Credit Default Swaps and the Credit Crisis," *Journal of Economic Perspectives*, Winter 2010, 24(1): 73–92; and Satyajit Das, "Credit Default Swaps: Problem Child of the Global Financial Crisis, April

13, 2009, http://prudentbear.com/index.php?view=article&id=10214%3A Credit+D . . . +Financial+Crisis&tmpl=component&print=1&page=&option=com_content, accessed May 28, 2009.

9. Quoted in Satyajit Das, "Credit Default Swaps: Problem Child of the Global Financial Crisis," April 13, 2009, http://prudentbear.com/index. php?view=article&id=10214%3ACredit+D . . . +Financial+Crisis&tmpl=component&print=1&page=&option=com_content, accessed May 28, 2009.

10. Satyajit Das, "Credit Default Swaps: Problem Child of the Global Financial Crisis," April 13, 2009, http://prudentbear.com/index.php?view=article&id=10214%3ACredit+D . . . +Financial+Crisis&tmpl=component&print=1&page=&option=com_content, accessed May 28, 2009. For the $6 billion figure, see Depository Trust and Clearing Corporation, "DTCC Addresses Misconceptions About the Credit Default Swap Market," Press Release, October 11, 2008, http://www.dtcc.com/news/press/releases/2008/tiw.php, accessed February 4, 2010.

11. Henry M. Paulson, Jr., *On the Brink*, New York: Hachette Book Group, 2010, pp. 204–205.

12. Quoted in Brady Dennis, "Bernanke Blasts AIG for 'Irresponsible Bets' That Led to Bailouts," *Washington Post*, March 4, 2009.

13. See *Wall Street Journal*, "AIG and Systemic Risk," November 23, 2009.

14. For a comprehensive treatment of enterprise risk management, see John Fraser and Betty J. Simkins (eds.), *Enterprise Risk Management: Today's Leading Research and Best Practices for Tomorrow's Executives*, Hoboken, NJ: John Wiley & Sons, 2010. For the Basel II framework, see especially pp. 341–343. See also Basel Committee on Bank Supervision, *International Convergence of Capital Measurements and Capital Standards: Comprehensive Version*, Basel, Switzerland: Bank for International Settlements, 2006. See also Linda Allen, "The Basel Capital Accords and International Mortgage Markets: A Survey of the Literature," *Financial Markets, Institutions, and Instruments*, May 2004, 13(2): 41–108.

15. Peter L. Bernstein, *Against the Gods: The Remarkable Story of Risk*, Hoboken, NJ: John Wiley & Sons, 1998.

16. For the performance of VaR during the financial crisis, see Michel Crouhy, "Risk Management Failures during the Financial Crisis," in Robert W. Kolb (ed.), *Lessons from the Financial Crisis: Causes, Consequences, and Our Economic Future*, Hoboken, NJ: John Wiley & Sons, 2010, chapter 36, pp. 283–291; and Steven L. Schwarcz, "Secondary-Management Conflicts," in Robert W. Kolb (ed.), *Lessons from the Financial Crisis: Causes, Consequences, and Our Economic Future*, Hoboken, NJ: John Wiley & Sons, 2010, chapter 52, pp. 419–426. See also Joe Nocera, "Risk Mismanagement," *New York Times*, January 4, 2009.

17. Nassim Nicholas Taleb, *The Black Swan: The Impact of the Highly Improbable*, New York: Random House, 2007. "People are often ashamed of losses, so they engage in strategies that produce very little volatility but contain the risk of a large loss—like collecting nickels in front of steamrollers," p. 204.

18. For a journalistic treatment of this issue, see Michael Lewis, "Inside Wall Street's Black Hole," *Condé Nast Portfolio*, March 2008.

19. David X. Li, "On Default Correlation: A Copula Function Approach," *Journal of Fixed Income*, April 2000, 20(2).

20. Quoted in Mark Whitehouse, "How a Formula Ignited Market That Burned Some Big Investors," *The Wall Street Journal*, September 12, 2005. For other accessible accounts of Li's model and its role in the financial crisis, see also: Sam Jones, "The Formula That Felled Wall Street," *Financial Times*, April 24, 2009; Scott Patterson, *The Quants: How a New Breed of Math Whizzes Conquered Wall Street and Nearly Destroyed It*," New York: Crown Business, 2010; and Felix Salmon, "Recipe for Disaster: The Formula That Killed Wall Street," *Wired Magazine*, February 23, 2009, http://www.wired.com/print/techbiz/it/magazine/17-03/wp_quant, accessed June 4, 2009.

21. Sam Jones, "The Formula That Felled Wall Street," *Financial Times*, April 24, 2009.

22. See Christian Plumb and Dan Wilchins, "Citi to Take $49 Billion in SIVs onto Balance Sheet," Reuters, December 13, 2007, http://www.reuters.com/assets/print?aid=USN1326316020071214, accessed February 26, 2010; and Jonathan Weil, "Citigroup SIV Accounting Looks Tough to Defend," Bloomberg, October 24, 2007, http://www.bloomberg.com/apps/news?pid=20670001&sid=a6dgIOAfMIrI, accessed February 26, 2010.

Chapter 14

1. This account of ESOs is partially adapted from Robert W. Kolb "Executive Compensation," in Robert W. Kolb (ed.), *Encyclopedia of Business, Ethics, and Society*, Thousand Oaks: CA, Sage Publications, 2008, Volume 2, pp. 825–830; and Robert W. Kolb, "Executive Stock Options," in Robert W. Kolb and James A. Overdahl (eds.), *Financial Derivatives: Pricing and Risk Management*, Hoboken, NJ: John Wiley & Sons, 2010 pp. 211–220. Until recently, tax laws in the United States provided that an ESO issued with a strike price equal to the current stock price of the firm generated no expense for accounting purposes. Thus, for many years, virtually all ESOs were issued with a strike price equal to the exercise price. (Now current law requires recognition of the value of an options grant as an expense in the period in which it is granted.)

2. Michael C. Jensen and Kevin J. Murphy, "CEO Incentives: It's Not How Much You Pay, But How," *Harvard Business Review*, May–June 1990: 138–149. See p. 139.

3. Michael C. Jensen and Kevin J. Murphy, "CEO Incentives: It's Not How Much You Pay, But How," *Harvard Business Review*, May–June 1990: 138–149. See p. 141, 142.

4. See Lucian A. Bebchuk and Jesse M. Fried: *Pay Without Performance: The Unfulfilled Promise of Executive Compensation*, Cambridge, MA: Harvard University Press, 2006; "Executive Compensation as an Agency Problem," *Journal of Economic Perspectives*, 2003, 17(3): 71–92; "Stealth Compensation via Retirement Benefits," 2004, Working paper; "Executive Compensation at Fannie Mae: A Case Study of Perverse Incentives, Nonperformance Pay,

and Camouflage," *Journal of Corporation Law*, 2005, 30. 807–822; "Pay Without Performance: Overview of the Issues," *Journal of Corporation Law*, Summer 2005: 647–673. See also Lucian A. Bebchuk and Yaniv Grinstein, "The Growth of Executive Pay," *Oxford Review of Economic Policy*, 2005, 2: 283–303.

5. In the light of the risks that so many financial firms willingly took, this framework may seem absurd. As we have seen, financial firms exhibited a hunger for risk rather than a reluctance to accept risk. This perspective has not been lost on those who study incentive compensation, and many scholars are now wondering if the perception of CEOs as preferring the quiet life may be radically wrong.

6. For a very brief account of these two firms, see John E. Marthinsen, "Derivative Scandals and Disasters," in Robert W. Kolb and James A. Overdahl, *Financial Derivatives*, Hoboken, NJ: John Wiley & Sons, 2010, chapter 23, pp. 313–332, but see p. 318 especially. See also John Marthinsen, *Risk Takers: Uses and Abuses of Financial Derivatives*, 2nd ed., Boston: Prentice Hall, 2009. Leeson went to prison in Singapore, but now brags on his web site (nickleeson.com) that he ". . . caused the biggest financial scandal of the 20th century," reports that he is the CEO of a firm in Ireland, and "continues to be one of the world's most in-demand conference and after dinner speakers." While Leeson's "only in America" story seems actually to be possible in Ireland as well, Kerviel still faces trial in France, scheduled for late 2010.

7. W. Scott Frame and Lawrence J. White, "Emerging Competition and Risk-Taking Incentives at Fannie Mae and Freddie Mac," February 2004, Federal Reserve Bank of Atlanta Working Paper No. 2004-4. The quotation appears in the abstract.

8. W. Scott Frame and Lawrence J. White, "Emerging Competition and Risk-Taking Incentives at Fannie Mae and Freddie Mac," February, 2004, Federal Reserve Bank of Atlanta Working Paper No. 2004-4, pp. 22–23.

9. These figures are taken from congressional testimony by the principal regulator of these GSEs. See James B. Lockhart III, "Statement before the Financial Services Subcommittee on Capital Markets, Insurance, and Government-Sponsored Enterprises," June 3, 2009, slides 2 and 4.

10. Lucian A. Bebchuk and Jesse M. Fried, "Executive Compensation at Fannie Mae: A Case Study of Perverse Incentives, Nonperformance Pay, and Camouflage," *Journal of Corporation Law*, 2005, 30: 807–822. See p. 807.

11. Lucian A. Bebchuk and Jesse M. Fried, "Executive Compensation at Fannie Mae: A Case Study of Perverse Incentives, Nonperformance Pay, and Camouflage," *Journal of Corporation Law*, 2005, 30: 807–822. See p. 807.

12. Lucian A. Bebchuk and Jesse M. Fried, "Executive Compensation at Fannie Mae: A Case Study of Perverse Incentives, Nonperformance Pay, and Camouflage," *Journal of Corporation Law*, 2005, 30: 807–822. See p. 810.

13. For contemporaneous accounts of Fannie Mae's compensation and accounting problems see: Riva D. Atlas, "Fannie Mae to Review Pay Packages of Ex-Officials," *New York Times*, December 28, 2004; Stephen Labaton, "Fannie Mae Crisis Raises Concerns on Leadership," *New York*

Times, September 29, 2004; and Stephen Labaton, "S.E.C. Says Fannie Mae Violated Accounting Rules," *New York Times*, December 16, 2004.

14. James B. Lockhart III, "Statement before the Financial Services Subcommittee on Capital Markets, Insurance, and Government-Sponsored Enterprises," June 3, 2009, p. 9.

15. Charles Duhigg, "Big Bonuses at Fannie and Freddie Draw Fire," *New York Times*, April 4, 2009. More generally, for the waning of Fannie and Freddie and the government's stewardship of these two firms, see Peter J. Wallison "Fannie and Freddie by Twilight," *Financial Services Outlook*, American Enterprise Institute for Public Policy Research, August 2008; and Peter J. Wallison and Charles W. Calomiris, "The Last Trillion-Dollar Commitment: The Destruction of Fannie Mae and Freddie Mac," *Financial Services Outlook*, American Enterprise Institute for Public Policy Research, September 2008.

16. Quoted in Andrew Clark and Elana Schor, "Lehman Brothers Chief Executive Grilled by Congress over Compensation," *Manchester Guardian*, http://www.guardian.co.uk/business/2008/oct/06/creditcrunch.lehmanbrothers/print, accessed February 25, 2010. Emphases as reported in source.

17. *Wall Street Journal*, "Congress Grills Lehman Brothers' Dick Fuld: Highlights of the Hearing," October 6, 2008. Emphases as reported in source.

18. Andrew Clark and Elana Schor, "Lehman Brothers Chief Executive Grilled by Congress over Compensation," *Manchester Guardian*, http://www.guardian.co.uk/business/2008/oct/06/creditcrunch.lehmanbrothers/print, accessed February 25, 2010.

19. Andrew Ross Sorkin, *Too Big to Fail*, New York: Viking, 2009, p. 294. Actually, Lehman was not unique in this respect. Employees at Bear probably owned a larger share of their firm than was the case at Lehman.

20. Andrew Ross Sorkin, *Too Big to Fail*, New York: Viking, 2009, p. 596.

21. Quoted in Andrew Clark and Elana Schor, "Lehman Brothers Chief Executive Grilled by Congress over Compensation," *Manchester Guardian*, http://www.guardian.co.uk/business/2008/oct/06/creditcrunch.lehmanbrothers/print, accessed February 25, 2010.

22. Lucian A. Bebchuk, Alma Cohen, and Holger Spamann, "The Wages of Failure: Executive Compensation at Bear Stearns and Lehman 2000–2008," November 22, 2009, working paper.

23. In general, as BCS report, Lehman and Bear had similar results. In both firms, the executives in the second through fifth spots did quite well too in the aggregate, although not nearly as well as the respective CEOs.

24. Note that this is not the calculation of BCS, although it relies on their number of shares. Further, this figure is not inflation-adjusted, and it is not certain how many shares Fuld held through 2008, but this provides a reasonable estimate of his losses on his shares in 2008.

25. Lucian A. Bebchuk, Alma Cohen, and Holger Spamann, "The Wages of Failure: Executive Compensation at Bear Stearns and Lehman 2000–2008," November 22, 2009, Working paper, pp. 25, 26, and 28 *passim*.

26. Rüdiger Fahlenbrach and René Stulz, "Bank CEO Incentives and the Credit Crisis," July 2009, Fisher College of Business WO 2009-03-013, Working paper. See p. 8.

27. Rüdiger Fahlenbrach and René Stulz, "Bank CEO Incentives and the Credit Crisis," July 2009, Fisher College of Business WO 2009-03-013, Working paper. See p. 16.

28. Michiyo Nakamoto and David Wighton, "Citigroup Chief Stays Bullish on Buy-Outs," *Financial Times*, July 9, 2007.

29. There are many aspects of corporate governance and its role in the financial crisis beyond those discussed here. The articles listed below provide a consideration of risk management, incentives in compensation, and many other issues in corporate governance from a variety of perspectives, all with a particular focus on the financial crisis: Renée Adams, "Governance and the Financial Crisis," April 2009, Working paper, http://ssrn.com/abstract_id=1398583.; Brian R. Cheffins, "Did Corporate Governance 'Fail' During the 2008 Stock Market Meltdown? The Case of the S&P 500," Working paper, http://ssrn.com/abstract=1396126; Blanaid Clarke, "Where Was the 'Market for Corporate Control' When We Needed It?" Working paper, http://ssrn.com/abstract=1524785; Counterparty Risk Management Policy Group III, "Containing Systemic Risk: The Road to Reform," August 6, 2008; Grant Kirkpatrick, "The Corporate Governance Lessons from the Financial Crisis," *Financial Market Trends*, 2009(1): 1–30; and Andrew W. Lo, "Regulatory Reform in the Wake of the Financial Crisis of 2007–2008," *Journal of Financial Economic Policy*, 2009, 1(1): 4–43.

Chapter 15

1. Sewell Chan, "Fed Affirms Plan to End Mortgage Intervention," *New York Times*, March 16, 2010.

2. Edward Gibbon, *The Decline and Fall of the Roman Empire*, New York: Random House, no date. Originally published in 1776, chapter 1, first paragraph.

3. Other recent contributions to this literature of decline include Arnold Toynbee's *A Study of History* and Paul Kennedy's *The Rise and Fall of the Great Powers*. Niall Ferguson summarizes this kind of approach and calls it into question in his "Complexity and Collapse: Empires on the Edge of Chaos," *Foreign Affairs* March/April 2010. Ferguson alludes to these approaches, while suggesting that one might think of the American empire as a complex system, subject to a violent effect from an apparently moderate, or even trivial, cause.

4. Niall Ferguson addresses issues of empire in *Empire: The Rise and Demise of the British World Order and the Lessons for Global Power*, which weighs the British Empire and finds it to have done much good. His *Colossus: The Rise and Fall of the American Empire* decries America's refusal to accept its imperial nature and to fulfill its mission as a liberal empire.

5. See, for example, DeLong and Cohen's *The End of Influence: What Happens When Other Countries Have the Money*. Without economic power there can be no political power, and ultimately no military power, and

Eamonn Fingleton's title, *In the Jaws of the Dragon: America's Fate in the Coming Era of Chinese Hegemony*, leaves no room for misunderstanding the roles of those who exercise, and those who suffer, hegemony.

6. See Henry M. Paulson Jr., *On the Brink*, New York: Hachette Book Group, 2010. His suggestions for reform appear in the *Afterword*, and include many more suggestions than those enumerated here.

7. Senate Committee on Banking, Housing, and Urban Affairs, "Summary: Restoring American Financial Stability: Create a Sound Economic Foundation to Grow Jobs, Protect Consumers, Rein in Fall Street, End Too Big to Fail, Prevent Another Financial Crisis," http://banking. senate.gov/public/_files/FinancialReformSummary231510FINAL.pdf, accessed March 19, 2010.

8. Clive Crook, "Dodd Misses the Point of Financial Reform," *National Journal Magazine*, March 20, 2010, http://www.nationaljournal.com/ njmagazine/print_friendly.php?ID=wn_20100320_9861, accessed March 19, 2010.

9. For more on regulatory capture, see: Dieter Helm, "Regulatory Reform, Capture, and the Regulatory Burden," *Oxford Review of Economic Policy*, 2006, 22(2): 169–185; Ernesto Dal Bó, "Regulatory Capture: A Review," *Oxford Review of Economic Policy*, 2006, 22(2): 203–225; and Daniel C. Hardy, "Regulatory Capture in Banking," International Monetary Fund Working Paper, WP/06/34, 2006. Bó shows that regulatory capture is an endemic problem across many regulators and industries, while Hardy argues that the banking industry is particularly susceptible to regulatory capture.

10. For the classic statement of the public choice approach, see James M. Buchanan and Gordon Tullock, *The Calculus of Consent*, Ann Arbor: University of Michigan Press, 1962. Levine and Forrence specifically relate the issue of regulatory capture to a public choice framework: Michael E. Levine and Jennifer L. Forrence, "Regulatory Capture, Public Interest, and the Public Agenda: Toward a Synthesis," *Journal of Law, Economics, and Organization*, Special Issue 1990, 6: 167–198.

11. 2010 saw these problems of the past frankly acknowledged, and Citi was clearly struggling to reduce its size and transform itself into a firm of manageable proportions. See Eric Dash, "Citigroup's Chief Shrinks Company, Eyeing Growth," *New York Times*, April 5, 2010.

12. Thus, in response to the S&L crisis, the failed Federal Home Loan Bank Board was replaced by the Office of Thrift Supervision, so the FHLBB became the OTS. Similarly, the Office of Federal Housing Enterprise Oversight presided over the bankruptcy of its two key regulatees, Fannie Mae and Freddie Mac in 2008, and became the Federal Housing Finance Agency. In this case the OFHEO became the FHFA, but with the same top executive in place.

13. I am well aware that many hold opposite views and that many believe that the firm should be operated in a manner to benefit all or many stakeholders, such as stockholders, employees, customers, and suppliers, while balancing the competing interests of such parties in some way that is

fair to all concerned. This stockholder vs. stakeholder debate continues to rage and shows no sign of resolution. However, it is really not germane to my argument. Even if the stakeholder theory happened to be correct, it would still be the case that corporate governance needs to align the incentives of managers with the interests of stakeholders, so the essential problem of corporate governance and executive compensation must still be faced.

14. See U.S. Treasury Department, "Fact Sheet: Administration's Regulatory Reform Agenda Moves Forward: Say-On-Pay," July 16, 2009, http://www.ustreas.gov/press/releases/tg219.htm, accessed: April 4, 2010.

Adams, Renée, "Governance and the Financial Crisis," April 2009, Working paper, available at: http://ssrn.com/abstract_id=1398583.

Akerlof, George A., and Robert J. Shiller, *Animal Spirits: How Human Psychology Drives the Economy, and Why It Matters for Global Capitalism*, Princeton: Princeton University Press, 2009.

Allen, Linda, "The Basel Capital Accords and International Mortgage Markets: A Survey of the Literature," *Financial Markets, Institutions, and Instruments*, May 2004, 13(2): 41–108.

Anderson, Jenny, "Debt-Market Paralysis Deepens Credit Drought," *New York Times*, October 7, 2009.

Anderson, Jenny, and Vikas Bajaj, "Loan Reviewer Aiding Inquiry into Big Banks," *New York Times*, January 27, 2008.

Anderson, Jenny, and Landon Thomas, Jr., "Goldman Sachs Rakes in Profit in Credit Crisis," *New York Times*, November 19, 2007.

Andrews, Edmund L., "Bernanke Defends Role on Merrill," *New York Times*, June 26, 2009.

Andrews, Edmund L., "Vast Bailout by U.S. Proposed to Stem Financial Crisis," *New York Times*, September 19, 2008.

Andrews, Edmund, and Eric Dash, "U.S. Expands Plan to Buy Banks' Troubled Assets," *New York Times*, March 24, 2009.

Appelbaum, Binyamin, "FDIC Agrees to Sell IndyMac to Investor Group," *Washington Post*, January 3, 2009.

Association of Community Organizations for Reform Now, "Predatory Lending Practices," http://www.acorn.org/index.php?id=754, accessed September 25, 2008.

Arner, Douglas W., "The Global Credit Crisis of 2008: Causes and Consequences," Working paper, January 2009.

Ashcraft, Adam B., and Til Schuermann, "Understanding the Securitization of Subprime Mortgage Credit," *Federal Reserve Bank of New York Staff Reports*, no. 318, March 2008.

Associated Press, "Freddie Mac Pays Record $3.8 Million Fine," April 18, 2006.

Avery, Robert B., Raphael W. Bostic, and Glenn B. Canner, "The Performance and Profitability of CRA-Related Lending," Federal Reserve Bank of Cleveland, November 2000.

Baily, Martin Neil, Robert E. Litan, and Mathew S. Johnson, "The Origins of the Financial Crisis," Brookings Institution, Fixing Finance Series, Paper 3, November 2008.

Bajaj, Vikas, "Lax Lending Standards Led to IndyMac's Downfall," *New York Times*, July 20, 2008.

Bajaj, Vikas, "Moody's Says Workers Rated Some Securities Incorrectly," *New York Times*, July 2, 2008.

Baker, Peter, "Labeled as a Bailout, Plan Was Hard to Sell to a Skeptical Public," *New York Times*, October 1, 2008.

Bank for International Settlements, *79th Annual Report*, June 29, 2009.

Bardhan, Ashok Deo, "Of Subprimes and Subsidies: The Political Economy of the Financial Crisis," Working paper, October 2008.

Barta, Patrick, "False Appraisals May Inflate Prices," *Chicago Tribune*, August 26, 2001.

Barth, James R., Susanne Trimbath, and Glenn Yago, *The Savings and Loan Crisis: Lessons from a Regulatory Failure*, Norwell, MA: Kluwer Academic Publishers, 2004.

Basel Committee on Bank Supervision, *International Convergence of Capital Measurements and Capital Standards: Comprehensive Version*, Basel, Switzerland: Bank for International Settlements, 2006.

Bebchuk, Lucian A., Alma Cohen, and Holger Spamann, "The Wages of Failure: Executive Compensation at Bear Stearns and Lehman 2000-2008," Working paper, November 22, 2009.

Bebchuk, Lucian A., and Jesse M. Fried, "Executive Compensation as an Agency Problem," *Journal of Economic Perspectives*, 2003, 17(3): 71–92.

Bebchuk, Lucian A. and Jesse M. Fried, *Pay Without Performance: The Unfulfilled Promise of Executive Compensation*, Cambridge, MA: Harvard University Press, 2006.

Bebchuk, Lucian A., and Jesse M. Fried, "Stealth Compensation via Retirement Benefits," Working paper, 2004.

Bebchuk, Lucian A., and Jesse M. Fried, "Executive Compensation at Fannie Mae: A Case Study of Perverse Incentives, Nonperformance Pay, and Camouflage," *Journal of Corporation Law*, 2005, 30: 807–822.

Bebchuk, L. A., and Jesse M. Fried, "Pay Without Performance: Overview of the Issues," *Journal of Corporation Law*, Summer 2005: 647–673.

Bebchuk, Lucian A., and Yaniv Grinstein, "The Growth of Executive Pay," *Oxford Review of Economic Policy*, 2005, 2: 283–303.

Ben-David, Itzhak, "Manipulation of Collateral Values by Borrowers and Intermediaries," Working Paper, February 2008.

Benmelech, Efraim and Jennifer Dlugosz, "The Alchemy of CDO Credit Ratings," Working paper.

Benmelech, Efraim, and Jennifer Dlugosz, "The Credit Rating Crisis," Working paper.

Benston, George J., "The Community Reinvestment Act: Looking for Discrimination That Isn't There," Cato Institute, *Policy Analysis*, No. 354, October 6, 1999.

Berger, Allen N., Richard J. Herring, and Giorgio P. Szegö, "The Role of Capital in Financial Institutions," *Journal of Banking and Finance*, 1995, 3–4: 393–430.

Bernanke, Ben S., "The Community Reinvestment Act: Its Evolution and New Challenges," speech at the Community Affairs Research Conference, Washington, DC, March 20, 2007.

Bernanke, Ben S., "The Economic Outlook," Testimony before the Joint Economic Committee, October 20, 2005.

Bernanke, Ben S., "Financial Reform to Address Systemic Risk," Speech of March 10, 2009, available at: http://www.federalreserve.gov/newsevents/speech/bernanke20090310a.htm.

Bernanke, Ben S., "Testimony before the Committee on Banking, Housing, and Urban Affairs, U.S. Senate, September 23, 2008.

Berenson, Alex, "Prosecutors Investigating Freddie Mac," *New York Times*, June 12, 2003.

Berson, David, David Lereah, Paul Merski, Frank Nothaft, and David Seiders, "America's Home Forecast: The Next Decade for Housing and Mortgage Finance," Homeownership Alliance, no date.

Berndt, Antje, and Anurag Gupta, "Moral Hazard and Adverse Selection in the Originate-to-Distribute Model of Bank Credit," Working paper, October 2008.

Bernstein, Peter L., *Against the Gods: The Remarkable Story of Risk*, Hoboken, NJ: John Wiley & Sons, 1998.

Bhardwaj, Geetesh, and Rajdeep Sengupta, "Did Prepayments Sustain the Subprime Market?" Federal Reserve Bank of St. Louis *Working Paper Series*, October 2008.

Bhardwaj, Geetesh and Rajdeep Sengupta, "Where's the Smoking Gun: A Study of Underwriting Standards for U.S. Subprime Mortgages," Federal Reserve Bank of St. Louis, *Working Paper Series*, October 2008.

Bitner, Richard, *Confessions of a Subprime Lender*, Hoboken, NJ: John Wiley & Sons, 2008.

Bó, Ernesto Dal, "Regulatory Capture: A Review," *Oxford Review of Economic Policy*, 2006, 22(2): 203–225.

Board of Governors of the Federal Reserve System, *Flow of Funds Accounts of the United States*, December 10, 2009.

Bond, Philip, David K. Musto, Bilg Yilmaz, "Predatory Mortgage Lending," *Journal of Financial Economics*, 2009, 94: 412–427.

Bookstaber, Richard, *A Demon of Our Own Design*, Hoboken, NJ: John Wiley & Sons, 2007.

Bordo, Michael D., "An Historical Perspective on the Crisis of 2007-2008," Working paper, November 2008.

Braithwaite, Tom, and Krishna Guha, "Bernanke Defends Fed on Merrill Deal," *Financial Times*, June 25, 2009.

Browning, Lynnley, "The Subprime Loan Machine," *New York Times*, March 23, 2007.

Bruner, Robert F., and Sean D. Carr, *The Panic of 1907*, Hoboken, NJ: John Wiley & Sons, 2007.

Buchanan, James M., and Gordon Tullock, *The Calculus of Consent*, Ann Arbor: University of Michigan Press, 1962.

Bufford, Samuel L., and R. Glen Ayers, "Where's the Note, Who's the Holder: Enforcement of Promissory Note Secured by Real Estate," American Bankruptcy Institute, April 3, 2009. Available at: http://livinglies.wordpress.com/2009/02/19/this-is-it-where's-the-note-who's-the-holder-enforcement-of-promissory-note-secured-by-real-estate/. Accessed February 18, 2010.

Burrough, Bryan, "Bringing Down Bear Stearns," *Vanity Fair*, August, 2008.

Calomiris, Charles W., and Joseph R. Mason, "Credit Card Securitization and Regulatory Arbitrage," *Journal of Financial Services Research*, 2004, 26:1, 5–27.

Cannata, Francesco, and Mario Quagliariello, "Basel II Put on Trial: What Role in the Financial Crisis?" in Robert W. Kolb (ed.), *Lessons from the Financial Crisis: Causes, Consequences, and Our Economic Future*, Hoboken, NJ: John Wiley & Sons, 2010, chapter 46.

Cannata, Francesco, and Mario Quagliariello, "The Role of Basel II in the Subprime Financial Crisis: Guilty or Not Guilty?" Working paper, January 2009.

Canner, Glenn B., Elizabeth Laderman, Andreas Lehnert, and Wayne Passmore, "Does the Community Reinvestment Act (CRA) Cause Banks to Provide a Subsidy to Some Mortgage Borrowers?" Federal Reserve Board of Governors, Working paper, April 2002.

Chadbourn, Margaret, "Regulator Says Mortgages Aimed at Elderly May be Risky," http://www.bloomberg.com/apps/news?pid=20601213&sid=awPlC3t65GTk, accessed June 9, 2009.

Chan, Sewell, "Fed Affirms Plan to End Mortgage Intervention," *New York Times*, March 16, 2010.

Cheffins, Brian R., "Did Corporate Governance 'Fail' During the 2008 Stock Market Meltdown? The Case of the S&P 500," Working paper. Available at: http://ssrn.com/abstract=1396126.

Chomsisengphet, Souphala, and Anthony Pennington-Cross, "The Evolution of the Subprime Mortgage Market," Federal Reserve Bank of St. Louis, *Review*, January–February 2006, 31–56.

Chung, Joanna, and Saskia Scholtes, "IndyMac is Latest Credit Turmoil Casualty," *Financial Times*, July 12, 2008.

Clark, Andrew, and Elana Schor, "Lehman Brothers Chief Executive Grilled by Congress over Compensation," *Manchester Guardian*. Available at: http://www.guardian.co.uk/business/2008/oct/06/creditcrunch.lehmanbrothers/print. Accessed February 25, 2010.

CNBC.com, "Former FDIC Chair Blames SEC for Credit Crunch," Available at: http://www.cnbc.com/id/27100454/print/1/display-mode/1098/. Accessed January 31, 2010.

CNNMoney.com, "Wall St. Crisis Snares Main St. Schools," Available at: http://cnnmoney.printthis.clickability.com/pt/cpt?action=cpt&title=W. . .%2F01%2F15%2Fnews%2Fwisconsin_loss_harlow%2Findex.htm&partnerID=2200. Accessed February 16, 2010.

Cochrane, John H., and Luigi Zingales, "Lehman and the Financial Crisis," *Wall Street Journal*, September 15, 2009.

Colton, Kent W., "Housing Finance in the United States: The Transformation of the U.S. Housing Finance System," Joint Center for Housing Studies, Harvard University, W02-5, July 2002.

Committee on Global Financial System, "Ratings in Structured Finance: What Went Wrong and What Can be Done to Address Shortcomings?" Bank for International Settlements, CGFS Papers No. 32, July 2008.

Condé-Nast Magazine, "Killinger's Eight-Figure Severance Package," September 11, 2008. Available at: http://www.portfolio.com/views/blogs/daily-brief/2008/09/11/killingers-eight-figure-severance-package. Accessed July 3, 2009.

Congressional Budget Office, *Controlling the Risks of Government-Sponsored Enterprises*, April 1991.

Congressional Budget Office, "Testimony of June E. O'Neill on Assessing the Public Costs and Benefits of Fannie Mae and Freddie Mac before the Subcommittee on Capital Markets, Securities and Government Sponsored Enterprises, Committee on Banking and Financial Services, U.S. House of Representatives," June 12, 1996.

Cornett, Marcia Millon and Hassan Tehranian, "An Examination of the Impact of the Garn–St. Germain Depository Institutions Act of 1982 on Commercial Banks and Savings and Loans," *The Journal of Finance*, March 1990, 45(1): 95–111.

Counterparty Risk Management Policy Group III, "Containing Systemic Risk: The Road to Reform," August 6, 2008.

Courchane, Marsha, Rajeev Darolia, and Peter Zorn, "From FHA to Subprime and Back?" Working paper, March 2009.

Coval, Joshua, Jakub Jurek, and Erik Stafford, "The Economics of Structured Finance," *Journal of Economic Perspectives*, Winter 2009, 23(1): 3–25.

Craig, Susanne, "Lehman Posts $2.8 Billion Loss," *Wall Street Journal*, June 17, 2008.

Crapanzano, Christina, "Countrywide is Assailed in Protest of Policies," *New York Times*, October 12, 2007.

Crawford, Alexander, "Collateralized Mortgage Obligations," in Frank J. Fabozzi and Steven V. Mann, *The Handbook of Fixed Income Securities*, 7th ed., New York: McGraw-Hill, 2005, pp. 541–578.

Creswell, Julie, "Chief Calls Deal a Dream for Wachovia," *New York Times*, May 9, 2006.

Creswell, Julie, and Ben White, "The Guys From 'Government Sachs,'" *New York Times*, October 19, 2008.

Creswell, Julie, and Vikas Bajaj, "$3.2 Billion Move by Bear Stearns to Rescue Fund," *New York Times*, June 23, 2007.

Crook, Clive, "Dodd Misses the Point of Financial Reform," *National Journal Magazine*, March 20, 2010. Available at: http://www.nationaljournal.com/njmagazine/print_friendly.php?ID=wn_20100320_9861. Accessed March 19, 2010.

Crouhy, Michel, "Risk Management Failures During the Financial Crisis," in Robert W. Kolb (ed.), *Lessons from the Financial Crisis: Causes, Consequences, and Our Economic Future*, Hoboken, NJ: John Wiley & Sons, 2010, chapter 36, pp. 283–291.

Crouhy, Michel G., Robert A. Jarrow, and Stuart M. Turnbull, "The Subprime Credit Crisis of 2007," *The Journal of Derivatives*, Fall 2008: 1–30.

Cuomo, Andrew M., "No Rhyme or Reason: The 'Heads I Win, Tails You Lose' Bank Bonus Culture," Attorney General's Office, State of New York, 2009.

Curry, Timothy, and Lynn Shibut, "The Cost of the Savings and Loan Crisis: Truth and Consequences," *FDIC Banking Review*, 2000, 13(2): 26–35.

Das, Satyajit, "Credit Default Swaps: Problem Child of the Global Financial Crisis," April 13, 2009. Available at: http://prudentbear.com/index.php?view=article&id=10214%3ACredit+D. . .+Financial+Crisis&tmpl=component&print=1&page=&option=com_content. Accessed May 28, 2009.

Dash, Eric, "Citigroup's Chief Shrinks Company, Eyeing Growth," *New York Times*, April 5, 2010.

Dash, Eric, "U.S. to Examine Actions of Washington Mutual," *New York Times*, October 16, 2008. Available at: http://query.nytimes.com/gst/fullpage.html?res=980CEFD8173EF935A25753C1A96E9C8B63. Accessed June 30, 2009.

Dash, Eric, "Wachovia Reports $23.9 Billion Loss for Third Quarter," *New York Times*, October 22, 2008. Available at: http://www.nytimes.com/2008/10/23/business/23wachovia.html?dlbk. Accessed on March 21, 2009.

Dash, Eric, and Julie Creswell, "Citigroup Saw No Red Flags Even as it Made Bolder Bets," *New York Times*, November 23, 2008.

Dash, Eric, and Michael J. De La Merced, "Regulators Denounce Fannie Mae," *New York Times*, May 24, 2006.

Dash, Eric, and Michael de la Merced, "Wachovia's Acquisition Drags Down Wells Fargo," *New York Times*, January 29, 2009. Available at: http://www.nytimes.com/2009/01/29/business/29wells.html?_r=1, accessed on July 4, 2009.

Dash, Eric, and Andrew Ross Sorkin, "Citigroup Buys Bank Operations of Wachovia," *New York Times*, September 30, 2008. Available at: http://www.nytimes.com/2008/09/30/business/30bank. html?hp=&pagewanted=print, accessed on March 21, 2009.

Dash, Eric, and Andrew Ross Sorkin, "Government Seizes WaMu and Sells Some Assets," *New York Times*, September 26, 2008, available at: http://www.nytimes.com/2008/09/26/business/26wamu. html?pagewanted=print. Accessed July 3, 2009.

Dash, Eric, and Gretchen Morgenson, "Bank Agrees to Buy Trouble Loan Giant for $4 Billion," *New York Times*, January 11, 2008.

DeGennaro, Ramon P., "Government Sponsored Entities: Fannie Mae and Freddie Mac," *Journal of Structured Finance* Spring 2008, 14(1): 18–22.

DeLong, J. Bradford, and Stephen S. Cohen, *The End of Influence: What Happens When Other Countries Have the Money*, New York: Basic Books, 2010.

DeMarco, Edward J., "The Future of the Mortgage Market and the Housing Enterprises," Testimony before the U.S. Senate Committee on Banking Housing, and Urban Affairs, October 8, 2009.

Demyanyk, Yuliya, and Otto Van Hemert, "Understanding the Subprime Mortgage Crisis," Working paper, February 2008.

Depository Trust and Clearing Corporation, "DTCC Addresses Misconceptions About the Credit Default Swap Market," Press Release, October 11, 2008. Available at: http://www.dtcc.com/news/press/releases/2008/tiw.php. Accessed February 4, 2010.

Dowd, Kevin, "Moral Hazard and the Financial Crisis," *Cato Journal*, Winter 2009, 29(1).

Duhigg, Charles, "Big Bonuses at Fannie and Freddie Draw Fire," *New York Times*, April 4, 2009.

Duhigg, Charles, and Carter Dougherty, "From Midwest to M.T.A, Pain From Global Gamble," *New York Times*, November 2, 2008.

Duhigg, Charles, "Mortgage Giants to Buy Fewer Risky Home Loans," *New York Times*, August 9, 2008.

Duhigg, Charles, "Pressured to Take on Risk, Fannie Hit a Tipping Point," *New York Times*, October 5, 2008. Available at: http://www.nytimes.com/2008/10/05/business/05fannie.html. Accessed October 4, 2008.

Duhigg, Charles, Stephen Labaton, and Andrew Ross Sorkin, "As Crisis Grew, a Few Options Shrank to One," *New York Times*, September 8, 2008.

The Economist, "Bearish Turns," June 21, 2007.

Efrati, Amir, and Ruth Simon, "Due-Diligence Firm to Aid New York Subprime Probe," *Wall Street Journal*, January 29, 2008.

Ellis, Luci, "The Housing Meltdown: Why Did It Happen in the United States?" Bank for International Settlements, BIS Working Papers No. 259, September 2008.

Engel, Kathleen C., and Patricia A. McCoy, "The CRA Implications of Predatory Lending," 29 *Fordham Urban Law Journal* 1571, 2002.

Engel, Kathleen C., and Patricia A. McCoy, "A Tale of Three Markets: The Law and Economics of Predatory Lending," *Texas Law Review*, May 2002, 80(6): 1255–1367.

Enrich, David, and Matthew Karnitschnig, "Citi, U.S. Rescue Wachovia," *Wall Street Journal*, September 30, 2008. Available at: http://online.wsj.com/article/SB122269141590585467.html. Accessed March 21, 2009.

Equilar, "Compensation for Kerry K. Killinger at Washington Mutual." Available at: http://www.equilar.com/CEO_Compensation/WASHINGTON_MUTUAL_INC_Kerry_K._Killinger.php. Accessed July 3, 2009.

Euromoney, "Understanding the Mark-to-Market Meltdown," March 3, 2008.

Faber, David, *And Then the Roof Caved In: How Wall Street's Greed and Stupidity Brought Capitalism to Its Knees*, Hoboken, NJ: John Wiley & Sons, 2009.

Fabozzi, Frank J., and Steven V. Mann, *The Handbook of Fixed Income Securities*, 7th ed., New York: McGraw-Hill, 2005.

Fahlenbrach, Rüdiger, and René Stulz, Bank CEO Incentives and the Credit Crisis," Fisher College of Business WO 2009-03-013, Working paper, July 2009.

Fannie Mae, "An Introduction to Fannie Mae," Washington, DC: Fannie Mae, 2008.

Fannie Mae, "Understanding America's Homeownership Gaps: 2003 Fannie Mae National Housing Survey," 2004.

Farrell, Greg, and Alan Rappaport, "Lewis Grilled over Merrill Deal," *Financial Times*, June 11, 2009.

FDIC, *History of the Eighties: Lessons for the Future*, Volume I: *An Examination of the Banking Crises of the 1980s and Early 1990s*, 1997, chapter 4, "The Savings and Loan Crisis and Its Relationship to Banking," pp. 167–188.

Federal Reserve Bank of Boston, "Closing the Gap: A Guide to Equal Opportunity Lending," Boston, April 1993.

Federal Reserve Bank of New York, "Nonprime Mortgage Conditions in the United States," http://www.newyorkfed.org/regional/techappendix_spreadsheets.html. Accessed on April 29, 2009.

Federal Reserve Bank of St. Louis, "The Financial Crisis: A Timeline of Events and Policy Actions." Available at: http://timeline.stlouisfed.org/pdf/CrisisTimeline.pdf. Accessed May 23, 2009.

Ferguson, Niall, *Colossus: The Rise and Fall of the American Empire*, New York: Penguin Books, 2004.

Ferguson, Niall, "Complexity and Collapse: Empires on the Edge of Chaos," *Foreign Affairs* March/April 2010.

Ferguson, Niall, *Empire: The Rise and Demise of the British World Order and the Lessons for Global Power*, New York: Basic Books, 2004.

Fingleton, Eamonn, *In the Jaws of the Dragon: America's Fate in the Coming Era of Chinese Hegemony*, New York: St. Martin's Press, 2008.

Financial Accounting Standards Board, "Summary of Statement No. 157: Fair Value Measurements," Available at: http://www.fasb.org/st/summary/stsum157.shtml#. Accessed February 4, 2010.

Financial Executives International, "Bernanke Tells Senate: Auction Will Help Facilitate Held-to-Maturity Vs. Fire Sale Price," September 24, 2008. Available at: http://financialexecutives.blogspot.com/2008/09/bernanke-tells-senate-auction-will-help.html.

Firla-Cuchra, Maciej and Tim Jenkinson, "Why Are Securitization Issues Tranched?" Working paper, March 2005.

Fishbein, Allen J., "Going Subprime," National Housing Institute, Issue #125, September–October 2002.

Flannery, Mark J. and W. Scott Frame, "The Federal Home Loan Bank System: The 'Other" Housing GSE," Federal Reserve Bank of Atlanta, *Economic Review*, Third Quarter 2006, pp. 33–54.

Foote, Christopher L., Kristopher Gerardi, and Paul S. Willen, "Negative Equity and Foreclosure: Theory and Evidence," Federal Reserve Bank of Boston, *Public Policy Discussion Papers*, No. 08–3, June 5, 2008.

Foote, Christopher L., Kristopher Gerardi, Lorenz Goette, and Paul S. Willen, "Subprime Facts: What (We Think) We Know about the Subprime Crisis and What We Don't," Federal Reserve Bank of Boston, Public Policy Discussion Paper No. 08–2, 2008.

Frame, W. Scott, and Lawrence J. White, "Emerging Competition and Risk-Taking Incentives at Fannie Mae and Freddie Mac," February 2004, Federal Reserve Bank of Atlanta Working Paper No. 2004–4.

Frame, W. Scott, and Lawrence J. White, "Fussing and Fuming over Fannie and Freddie: How Much Smoke, How Much Fire?" *Journal of Economic Perspectives*, Spring 2005, 19(2): 159–184.

Frank, Barney, Opening Statement from Hearing before the House Financial Services Committee, September 11, 2003.

Fraser, John, and Betty J. Simkins (eds.), *Enterprise Risk Management: Today's Leading Research and Best Practices for Tomorrow's Executives*, Hoboken, NJ: John Wiley & Sons, 2010.

Fratantoni, Michael, "The Residential Mortgage Market and Its Economic Context in 2007," Mortgage Bankers Association, January 30, 2007.

Freddie Mac, "Freddie Mac Announces Tougher Subprime Lending Standards to Help Reduce the Risk of Future Borrower Default." Available at: http://www.freddiemac.com/news/archives/corporate/2007/20070227_subprimelending.html. Accessed June 8, 2009.

Fuchita, Yasuyuki, and Robert E. Litan (eds.), *Financial Gatekeepers: Can They Protect Investors?* Washington, DC:, Brookings Institution Press, 2006.

FundingUniverse.com, "Washington, Mutual, Inc." Available at: http://www.fundinguniverse.com/company-histories/Washington-Mutual-Inc-Company-History.html. Accessed July 3, 2009.

Geithner, Timothy F., "Written Testimony Presented to the House Committee on Oversight and Government Reform," January 27, 2010.

Gerardi, Kristopher, Andreas Lehnert, Shane Sherlund, and Paul Willen, "Making Sense of the Subprime Crisis," *Brookings Papers on Economic Activity*, September 5, 2008.

Gibbon, Edward, *The Decline and Fall of the Roman Empire*, New York: Random House, no date. Originally published in 1776.

Ginnie Mae Annual Report, 2008. Available at: http://www.ginniemae.gov/about/ann_rep/annual_report08.pdf

Gittelsohn, John, "WaMu Loan Millions to O. C. Home Flippers with Fraud History," *Orange County Register*, September 21, 2008. Available at: http://www.ocregister.com/articles/soni-washington-mutual-2163800-sonis-family#. Accessed July 3, 2009.

Glater, Jonathan D., "Market Place: Freddie Mac Gets Penalty and Rebuke Over Scandal," *New York Times*, December 11, 2003.

Goodman, Peter S., "Credit Enters a Lockdown," *New York Times*, September 26, 2008.

Goodman, Peter S., and Gretchen Morgenson, "By Saying Yes, WaMu Built Empire on Shaky Loans," *New York Times*, December 28, 2008. Available at: http://www.nytimes.com/2008/12/28/business/28wamu.html?_r=1&hp=&pagewanted=print. Accessed December 28, 2008.

Gorton, Gary, "The Panic of 2007," Working paper, August, 25, 2008.

Gorton, Gary, "The Subprime Panic," *European Financial Management*, January 2009, 15(1): 10–46.

Gorton, Gary, and Nicholas S. Souleles, "Special Purpose Vehicles and Securitization," National Bureau of Economic Research, Working Paper 11190, March 2005. Available at: http://www.nber.org/papers/w11190. Accessed January 30, 2010.

Green, Richard K., and Susan M. Wachter, "The American Mortgage in Historical and International Context," *Journal of Economic Perspectives*, Fall 2005, 19(4): 93–114.

Guerrera, Francesco "BofA to Buy Merrill Lynch for $50bn," *Financial Times*, September 14, 2009.

Guerrera, Francesco Ben White, and Krishna Guha, "Merrill Lynch Hit by $9.4bn Writedown," *Financial Times*, July 17, 2008.

Halper, Stefan, *The Beijing Consensus: How China's Authoritarian Model Will Dominate the Twenty-First Century*, New York: Basic Books, 2010.

Hardy, Daniel C., "Regulatory Capture in Banking," International Monetary Fund Working Paper, WP/06/34, 2006.

Hayford, Marc D., and A. G. Malliaris, "Monetary Policy and the U.S. Stock Market," *Economic Inquiry*, July 2004, 42(3): 387–401.

Helm, Dieter, "Regulatory Reform, Capture, and the Regulatory Burden," *Oxford Review of Economic Policy*, 2006, 22(2): 169–185.

Henry, David, Matthew Goldstein, and Carol Matlack, "How AIG's Credit Loophole Squeezed Europe's Banks," *Business Week*, October 16, 2008.

Herszenhorn, David M., Carl Hulse, and Sheryl Gay Stolberg, "Talks Implode During a Day of Chaos; Fate of Bailout Plan Remains Unresolved," *New York Times*, September 26, 2008.

Holmes, Steven A., "Fannie Mae Eases Credit to Aid Mortgage Lending," *New York Times*, September 30, 1999. Available at: http://query.nytimes.com/gst/fullpage.html. Accessed on October 13, 2008.

Hossain, AKM Rezaul, "The Past, Present and Future of Community Reinvestment Act (CRA): A Historical Perspective," Working paper, University of Connecticut, 2004–30, October 2004.

Hudson, Mike, "IndyMac: What Went Wrong?" Center for Responsible Lending, CRL Report, June 30, 2008.

Integrated Financial Engineering, Inc., "Evolution of the U.S. Housing Finance System: A Historical Survey and Lessons for Emerging Mortgage Markets," U.S. Department of Housing and Urban Development, April 2006.

International Monetary Fund, *World Economic Outlook: Crisis and Recovery,"* April 2009.

Jackson, William D., "Glass-Steagall Act: Commercial vs. Investment Banking," Congressional Research Service, 1987.

Jensen, Michael C., and Kevin J. Murphy, "CEO Incentives: It's Not How Much You Pay, But How," *Harvard Business Review*, May–June 1990, 138–149.

Jickling, Mark, "Causes of the Financial Crisis," Congressional Research Service, 7–5700, R40173, January 29, 2009.

Jones, Sam, "The Formula That Felled Wall Street," *Financial Times*, April 24, 2009.

Jones, Sam, Gillian Tett, and Paul J. Davies, "Moody's Error Gave Top Ratings to Debt Products," *Financial Times*, May 21, 2008.

Kane, Edward J., "Dangers of Capital Forbearance: The Case of the FSLIC and "ZOMBIE" S&Ls, Contemporary Economic Policy, 2007, 5:1, 77–83.

Kane, Edward J. "Unmet Duties in Managing Financial Safety Nets," forthcoming in *Business Ethics Quarterly*.

Kaufman, George G., "Are Some Banks Too Large to Fail? Myth and Reality," Contemporary Economic Policy 1990, 8(4): 1–14.

Kaufman, George, and A. G. Malliaris, "The Financial Crisis of 2007–09: Missing Financial Regulation or Absentee Regulators?" in Robert W. Kolb, *Lessons from the Financial Crisis: Causes, Consequences, and Our Economic Future*, Hoboken, NJ: John Wiley & Sons, 2010, pp. 337–343.

Kelly, Kate, "Bear Stearns Neared Collapse Twice in Frenzied Last Days," *Wall Street Journal*, May 29, 2008.

Kelly, Kate, "Cayne to Step Down as Bear Stearns CEO," *New York Times*, January 8, 2008.

Kelly, Kate, Greg Ip, and Robin Sidel, "Fed Races to Rescue Bear Stearns in Bid to Steady Financial System," *The Wall Street Journal*, March 16, 2008.

Keys, Benjamin J., Tanmoy Mukherjee, Amit Seru, and Vikrant Vig, "Did Securitization Lead to Lax Screening? Evidence from Subprime Loans," Working paper, December 2008.

Kirkpatrick, Grant, "The Corporate Governance Lessons from the Financial Crisis," *Financial Market Trends*, 2009(1): 1–30.

Kolb, Robert W., "Executive Compensation," in Robert W. Kolb (ed.), *Encyclopedia of Business, Ethics, and Society*, Thousand Oaks: CA, Sage Publications, 2008, Volume 2, pp. 825–830.

Kolb, Robert W., "Executive Stock Options," in Robert W. Kolb and James A. Overdahl (eds.), *Financial Derivatives: Pricing and Risk Management*, Hoboken, NJ: John Wiley & Sons, 2010, pp. 211–220.

Kolb, Robert W., *Executive Stock Options: Financial, Social, and Ethical Issues*, forthcoming from Hoboken, NJ: John Wiley & Sons, 2011.

Kolb, Robert W., *Lessons from the Financial Crisis: Causes, Consequences, and Our Economic Future*, Hoboken, NJ: John Wiley & Sons, 2010.

Kolb, Robert W., and James A. Overdahl, *Financial Derivatives*, Hoboken, NJ: John Wiley & Sons, Inc., 2010.

Kolb, Robert W., and James A. Overdahl, *Futures Options and Swaps*, 5th ed., Hoboken, NJ: John Wiley & Sons, 2007.

Kotkin, Joel, *The Next Hundred Million: America in 2050*, New York: Penguin Press, 2010.

Kouwe, Zachary, "Judge Rejects Settlement over Merrill Bonuses," *New York Times*, September 15, 2009.

Kouwe, Zachary, "U.S. Role Questioned on Merrill," *New York Times*, April 24, 2009.

Kroszner, Randall S., "Risk Management and Basel II," speech at the Federal Reserve Bank of Boston AMA Conference, Boston, Massachusetts, May 14, 2008.

Krugman, Paul, "Getting Real—and Letting the Cat Out of the Bag," *New York Times*, September 23, 2008.

Labaton, Stephen, "Fannie Mae Crisis Raises Concerns on Leadership," *New York Times*, September 29, 2004.

Labaton, Stephen, "S.E.C. Concedes Oversight Flaws Fueled Collapse," *New York Times*, September 27, 2008.

Labaton, Stephen, "S.E.C. Says Fannie Mae Violated Accounting Rules," *New York Times*, December 16, 2004.

Labaton, Stephen, "Treasury Acts to Shore Up Fannie Mae and Freddie Mac," *New York Times*, July 14, 2008.

Lane, Philip R., and Gian Maria Milesi-Ferretti, "Europe and Global Imbalances," *Economic Policy*, July 2007: 519–573.

Langohr, Herwig M., and Patricia T. Langohr, *The Rating Agencies and Their Credit Ratings: What They Are, How They Work and Why They Are Relevant*, Hoboken, NJ: John Wiley and Sons, 2008.

Leonard, Devin, "How Lehman Brothers Got Its Real Estate Fix," *New York Times*, May 3, 2009.

Leonnig, Carol D., "How HUD Mortgage Policy Fed the Crisis: Subprime Loans Labeled 'Affordable,'" *Washington Post*, June 10, 2008.

Lepro, Sara, "Citi Recommits to Wachovia Deal Despite Rescue Plan's Failure," *Washington Post*, October 1, 2008. Available at: http://www.washingtonpost.com/wp-yn/content/article/2008/09/30/AR2008093002839_pf.html. Accessed on March 21, 2009.

Levine, Michael E., and Jennifer L. Forrence, "Regulatory Capture, Public Interest, and the Public Agenda: Toward a Synthesis," *Journal of Law, Economics, and Organization*, Special Issue 1990, Volume 6: 167–198.

Lewis, Michael, "Inside Wall Street's Black Hole," *Condé Nast Portfolio*, March 2008.

Lewis, Michael, *Liar's Poker*, New York, Norton, 1995.

Li, David X., "On Default Correlation: A Copula Function Approach," *Journal of Fixed Income*, March 2000, 9(4): 43–54.

Liebowitz, Stan J., "Anatomy of a Train Wreck: Causes of the Mortgage Meltdown," *Independent Policy Reports*, October 3, 2008.

Listokin, David, Elvin K. Wyly, Brian Schmitt, and Ioan Voicu, "The Potential and Limitations of Mortgage Innovation in Fostering Homeownership in the United States," Fannie Mae Foundation, 2002.

Listokin, David, Elvin K. Wyly, Brian Schmitt, and Ioan Voicu, "Executive Summary: The Potential and Limitations of Mortgage Innovation in Fostering Homeownership in the United States," Fannie Mae Foundation, 2002.

Lockhart, James B., III, "Reforming the Regulation of the Government Sponsored Enterprises," Statement of the Honorable James B. Lockhart III, Director Office of Federal Housing Enterprise Oversight before the Senate Banking, Housing and Urban Affairs Committee, February 7, 2008.

Lockhart, James B., III, "Statement before the Financial Services Subcommittee on Capital Markets, Insurance, and Government-Sponsored Enterprises," June 3, 2009.

Los Angeles Times, "Sub-Prime Mortgage Watchdogs Kept On Leash," March 17, 2008. Available at: http://articles.latimes.com/2008/mar/17/business/fi-subprime17. Accessed February 9, 2010.

Lowenstein, Roger *When Genius Failed: The Rise and Fall of Long-Term Capital Management*, New York: Random House, 2001.

Lucas, Douglas J., Laurie S. Goodman, and Frank J. Fabozzi, "Collateralized Debt Obligations and Credit Risk Transfer," Yale ICF Working Paper No. 07–06, 2007.

Lucchetti, Aaron, "S&P Email: 'We Should Not be Rating It,'" *The Wall Street Journal*, August 2, 2008. Available at: http://online.wsj.com/article_print/SB121764476728206967.html. Accessed on August 3, 2008.

Malanga, Steven, "The Long Road to Slack Lending Standards," October 1, 2008. Available at: http://www.realclearmarkets.com/printpage/?url=http://www.realclearmarkets.com/articles/2008/10/the_long_road_to_slack_lending.html.

Marsico, Richard, "The 2004–2005 Amendments to the Community Reinvestment Act Regulations: For Communities, One Step Forward and three Steps Back," New York Law School Public Law and Legal Theory Research Paper Series -5/06 #25.

Marthinsen, John E., "Derivative Scandals and Disasters," in Robert W. Kolb, and James A. Overdahl, *Financial Derivatives*, Hoboken, NJ: John Wiley & Sons, 2010, chapter 23, pp. 313–332.

Marthinsen, John, *Risk Takers: Uses and Abuses of Financial Derivatives*, 2nd ed. Boston: Prentice Hall, 2009.

Martin, John D., "A Primer on the Role of Securitization in the Credit Market Crisis of 2007," Working Paper, January 2009.

Martin, Andrew and Gretchen Morgenson, "Can Citigroup Carry Its Own Weight?," *The New York Times*, November 1, 2009.

Mason, Joseph R., and Joshua Rosner, "Where Did the Risk Go? How Misapplied Bond Ratings Cause Mortgage Backed Securities and Collateralized Debt Obligation Market Disruptions," Working paper, May 2007.

Mayer, Christopher, Karen Pence, and Shane M. Sherlund, "The Rise in Mortgage Defaults," *Journal of Economic Perspectives*, Winter 2009, 23(1): 27–50.

McCoy, Patricia A. "The Home Mortgage Disclosure Act: A Synopsis and Recent Legislative History," *Journal of Real Estate Research*, 2007, 29(4): 381–397.

McIntyre, Douglas A., "Paulson Plan Shows a Weakness: Above Market Pricing, Greater Taxpayer Risk," September 23, 2008. Available at: http://247wallst.com/2008/09/23/paulson-plan-sh/.

McKinley, Vern, "Community Reinvestment Act: Ensuring Credit Adequacy or Enforcing Credit Allocation?" *Regulation* 1994, 17(4): 32. Available at: www.cato.org/pubs/regulation/regv17n4/vmck4-94.pdf.

Merced, Michael J. de la, "Goldman's Shadow Extends Far Past Wall St.," *New York Times*, November 15, 2007.

Merced, Michael J. de la, and Andrew Ross Sorkin, "Report Details How Lehman Hid Its Woes as It Collapsed," *New York Times*, March 11, 2010.

Merced, Michael J. de la, and Louise Story, "Nearly 700 at Merrill in Million-Dollar Club," *New York Times*, February 12, 2009.

Mian, Atif, and Amir Sufi, "The Consequences of Mortgage Credit Expansion: Evidence from the 2007 Mortgage Default Crisis," Working paper, January 2008.

Middleton, Reggie, "Digging Deeper into Lehman," Seeking Alpha web site, May 26, 2008. Available at: http://seekingalpha.com/article/78846-digging-deeper-into-lehman. Accessed February 14, 2010.

Miller, James C., III, and James E. Pearce, "Revisiting the Net Benefits of Freddie Mac and Fannie Mae," Freddie Mac, November 2006.

Milwaukee World, "New Allegations in Reopened School Districts v. Stifel Case," April 23, 2009.

Mishkin, Frederic S., "How Big a Problem is Too Big to Fail? A Review of Gary Stern and Ron Feldman's *Too Big to Fail: The Hazards of Bank Bailouts*," *Journal of Economic Literature*, December 2006, 44(4): 988–1004.

Mollenkamp, Carrick, and Jeffrey McCracken, "Lehman Moved Cash Fast," *The Wall Street Journal*, September 20, 2008.

Mollenkamp, Carrick, Serena Ng, Liam Pleven, and Randall Smith, "Behind AIG's Fall, Risk Models Failed to Pass Real-World Test," *Wall Street Journal*, October 31, 2008.

Moody's Investor Services, "Code of Professional Conduct," June 2005.

Moody's Investors Services, "Corporate Default and Recovery Rates, 1920–2008," February 2009. Available at: http://www.moodys.com/cust/content/content.ashx?source=StaticContent/Free%20Pages/Credit%20Policy%20Research/documents/current/2007400000578875.pdf. Accessed February 13, 2010.

Moody's Investors Services, "Default and Loss Rates of Structured Finance Securities: 1993–2008, August 2009.

Morgenson, Gretchen, "Behind Insurer's Crisis, Blind Eye to a Web of Risk," *New York Times*, September 28, 2008.

Morgenson, Gretchen, "Guess What Got Lost in the Loan Pool?" *New York Times*, March 1, 2009.

Morgenson, Gretchen, "S.E.C. Accuses Countrywide's Ex-Chief of Fraud," *New York Times*, June 5, 2009.

Morgenson, Gretchen, "How the Thundering Herd Faltered and Fell," *New York Times*, November 9, 2009.

Morgenson, Gretchen, "Inside the Countrywide Lending Spree," *New York Times*, August 26, 2007.

Morgenson, Gretchen, "Stock Sales by Chief of Lender Questioned," *New York Times*, October 11, 2007.

Morgenson, Gretchen, "Was There a Loan It Didn't Like?" *New York Times*, November 2, 2008.

Morgenson, Gretchen, and Charles Duhigg, "Mortgage Giant Overstated Size of Capital Base," *New York Times*, September 7, 2008.

Morgenson, Gretchen, and Geraldine Fabrikant, "Countrywide's Chief Salesman and Defender," *New York Times*, November 11, 2007.

Morgenson, Gretchen, and Don Van Natta, Jr., "Paulson's Calls to Goldman Tested Ethics During the Crisis," *New York Times*, August 9, 2009.

Mortgage Bankers Association, "Housing and Mortgage Markets: An Analysis," MBA Research Monograph Series No. 1, September 6, 2005.

Mortgage Bankers Association, "The Residential Mortgage Market and Its Economic Context," January 30, 2007.

Mozilo, Angelo R., "The American Dream of Homeownership: From Cliché to Mission," John T. Dunlop Lecture, Joint Center for Housing Studies of Harvard University, February 4, 2003.

Mullins, Luke, "Sheila Bair: Stop Blaming the Community Reinvestment Act," *U.S. News and World Report*, December 17, 2008.

Munnell, Alicia A., Lynne E. Browne, James McEneaney, and Geoffrey M. B. Tootell, "Mortgage Lending in Boston: Interpreting HMDA Data," Federal Reserve Bank of Boston Working Paper, No. 92-7, October 1992.

Muolo, Paul, and Mathew Padilla, *Chain of Blame: How Wall Street Caused the Mortgage and Credit Crisis*, Hoboken, NJ: John Wiley & Sons, 2008.

Nakamoto, Michiyo, and David Wighton, "Citigroup Chief Stays Bullish on Buy-Outs," *Financial Times*, July 9, 2007.

National Association of Mortgage Brokers, "Model Disclosure Form," June 22, 1997.

Negroni, Andrea Lee, and Joya K. Raha, "Mortgage Brokers—What Fiduciary Duties Exist?" *Mortgage Banking*, October 2007: 129–133.

New York Times, "Bear Stearns Denies Need to Seek Cash from Outside," October 5, 2007.

New York Times, "Crisis Deepens for Northern Rock," September 17, 2007. Available at: http://www.nytimes.com/2007/09/17/world/europe/17iht-17northern.7535479.html. Accessed June 12, 2009.

New York Times, "IndyMac Bancorp Quits Making New Loans," July 8, 2008.

New York Times, "A Losing Year at Countrywide, but Not for Chief," April 25, 2008.

New York Times, "Merrill Lynch & Company, Inc." Available at: http://topics.nytimes.com/top/news/business/companies/merrill_lynch_and_company/index.html?scp=1-spot&sq=merrill%20lynch&st=cse. Accessed October 15, 2009.

Nocera, Joe, "Lehman Had to Die so Global Finance Could Live," *New York Times*, September 12, 2009.

Nocera, Joe, "Risk Mismanagement," *New York Times*, January 4, 2009.

Nocera, Joe, and Edmund L. Andrews, "Struggling to Keep Up as the Crisis Raced On," *New York Times*, October 23, 2008.

Norris, Carole, "New Rules for Fannie and Freddie," National Housing Institute, Issue #80, March/April 1995. Available at: http://www.nhi.org/online/issues/80/fanny.html. Accessed January 13, 2009.

Norris, Floyd, "If Market Prices are Too Low, Ignore Them," *New York Times*, March 28, 2008.

Norris, Floyd, "A Pledge to Help That Hurts," *New York Times*, September 26, 2008.

Obstfeld, Maurice, and Kenneth Rogoff, "Global Imbalances and the Financial Crisis: Products of Common Causes," Working paper, November 2009. Available at: http://elsa.berkeley.edu/~obstfeld/santabarbara.pdf. Accessed January 9, 2010.

Office of Federal Housing Enterprise Oversight, "Mortgage Markets and the Enterprise in 2006," June 2007.

Office of Federal Housing Enterprise Oversight, "Mortgage Markets and the Enterprise in 2007," July 2008.

Office of the Special Inspector General for the Troubled Asset Relief Program, "Factors Affecting Efforts to Limit Payments to AIG Counterparties," SIGTARP-10-003, November 17, 2009.

Office of the State Comptroller of New York, "New York City Securities Industry Bonus Pool," February 23, 2010.

O'Hara, Maureen, and Wayne Shaw, "Deposit Insurance and Wealth Effects: The Value of Being "Too Big to Fail,"" *The Journal of Finance*, December 1990, 45(5): 1587–1600.

Onaran, Yalman, and Jody Shenn, "Cioffi's Hero-to-Villain Hedge Funds Masked Bears Periods in CDOs," *Bloomberg.com*, July 3, 2007. Available at: http://www.bloomberg.com/apps/news?pid=20601103&refer=us&sid=azWrpTVCph08#. Accessed July 15, 2009.

Pafenberg, Forrest, "The Single-Family Mortgage Industry in the Internet Era: Technology Developments and Market Structure," Office of Federal Housing Enterprise Oversight Research Paper, January 2004.

Paletta, Damian, "OFHEO Is Pressured Over Mortgages: Regulator Urged to Loosen Limits on Fannie, Freddie by Senators, Trade Groups," *Wall Street Journal*, October 24, 2007.

Park, Kevin, "Subprime Lending and the Community Reinvestment Act," Joint Center for Housing Studies, Harvard University, Working paper N08-2, November 2008.

Parseghian, Gregory J., "Collateralized Mortgage Obligations," in Frank J. Fabozzi, T. Dessa Fabozzi and Irving M. Pollack, *The Handbook of Fixed Income Securities*, 3rd ed., Homewood, IL: Irwin, 1991, pp. 601–632.

Partnoy, Frank, "How and Why Credit Rating Agencies Are Not Like Other Gatekeepers," in Yasuyuki Fuchita and Robert E. Litan (eds.), *Financial Gatekeepers: Can They Protect Investors?* Washington, DC:, Brookings Institution Press, 2006, chapter 3, pp. 59–102.

Partnoy, Frank, "The Siskel and Ebert of Financial Markets?: Two Thumbs Down for the Credit Rating Agencies," *Washington University Law Quarterly*, 1999, 77(3): 619–712.

Patterson, Scott, *The Quants: How a New Breed of Math Whizzes Conquered Wall Street and Nearly Destroyed It*," New York: Crown Business, 2010.

Paulson, Henry M., Jr., *On the Brink*, New York: Hachette Book Group, Inc., 2010.

Paulson, Henry M., Jr., "Remarks by Secretary Henry M. Paulson, Jr. on Financial Rescue Package and Economic Update," November 12, 2008. Available at: http://www.treas.gov/press/releases/hp1265.htm.

Paulson, Jr., Henry M., "Statement by Secretary Henry M. Paulson, Jr. on Treasury and Federal Housing Finance Agency Action to Protect Financial Markets and Taxpayers," September 7, 2008 hp 1129, Available at: http://www.treas.gov/press/releases/hp1129.htm, accessed June 10, 2009.

Plumb, Christian and Dan Wilchins, "Citi to Take $49 Billion in SIVs Onto Balance Sheet," Reuters, December 13, 2007. Available at: http://www.reuters.com/assets/print?aid=USN1326316020071214. Accessed February 26, 2010.

Poirier, John, and Emily Chasan, "SEC Gives Banks More Leeway on Mark-to-Market," Reuters.com, October 1, 2008. Available at: http://www.reuters.com/assets/print?aid=USWAT01020020081001. Accessed January 31, 2010.

Polakoff, Scott M., "American International Group: Examining What Went Wrong, Government Intervention, and Implications for Future Regulation," testimony before the Senate Committee on Banking, Housing, and Urban Affairs, March 5, 2009.

The President's Working Group on Financial Markets, "Policy Statement on Financial Market Developments," March 2008.

Rappaport, Liz, and John Hilsenrath, "Fed Moves to Free Up Credit for Consumers," *Wall Street Journal*, March 4, 2009.

Roosevelt, Franklin D. in *The Public Papers and Addresses of Franklin D. Roosevelt* 2, at 135, 1938.

Rose, Stephen J., *Rebound: Why America Will Emerge Strong from the Financial Crisis*, New York: St. Martin's Press, 2010.

Rosenthal, Stuart S., "Eliminating Credit Barriers to Increase Homeownership: How Far Can We Go?" Low-Income Homeownership Work Paper Series,

Joint Center for Housing Studies, Harvard University, LIHO.01-3, August 2001.

Rosner, Josh, "Housing in the New Millennium: A Home Without Equity Is Just a Rental With Debt," *Housing Trends*, GrahamFisher, June 29, 2001. Available at: http://ssrn.com/abstract=1162456. Accessed February 7, 2010.

Saha-Bubna, Aparajita, "Freddie Mac CEO Sees a Stronger Footing in '08," *Wall Street Journal*, June 7, 2008.

Salmon, Felix, "Recipe for Disaster: The Formula that Killed Wall Street," *Wired Magazine*, February 23, 2009. Available at: http://www.wired.com/print/techbiz/it/magazine/17-03/wp_quant. Accessed June 4, 2009.

Satow, Julie, "Ex-SEC Official Blames Agency for Blow-Up of Broker-Dealers," *New York Sun*, September 18, 2008.

Scannell, Kara, "SEC's Bear Stearns Probe Zeroes in on 'Put" Trades," *Wall Street Journal*, March 20, 2008.

Scheer, David and Joshua Gallu, "Fuld 'Negligent' As Lehman Hid Leverage, Report Says," Bloomberg.com, March 11, 2010.

Schwarcz, Steven L., "Secondary-Management Conflicts," in Robert W. Kolb (ed.), *Lessons from the Financial Crisis: Causes, Consequences, and Our Economic Future*, Hoboken, NJ: John Wiley & Sons, 2010, chapter 52, pp. 419–426.

"SEC Complaint Excerpts: Mozilo on 'Toxic' Loans, Borrowers' Income Lies," *Wall Street Journal*, June 4, 2009.

"SEC's Oversight of Bear Stearns and Related Entities: The CSE Program," Report No. 446-A, September 25, 2008, p. 82.

Sengupta, Rajdeep and Yu Man Tam, "The LIBOR-OIS Spread as a Summary Indicator," Federal Reserve Bank of St. Louis, *Economic Synopses*, 2008, no. 25.

Shiller, Robert J., *The Subprime Solution*, Princeton, NJ: Princeton University Press, 2008.

Sherlund, Shane M., "The Past, Present, and Future of Subprime Mortgages," Federal Reserve Board, Finance and Economics Discussion Series, 2008.

Sjøstrom, William K., Jr., "The AIG Bailout," *Washington and Lee Law Review*, 2009, 66: 943–991.

Skreta, Vasiliki and Laura Veldkamp, "Ratings Shopping and Asset Complexity: A Theory of Ratings Inflation," Working paper, October 2008.

Sorkin, Andrew Ross, "Bank of America in Talks to Acquire Merrill Lynch," *New York Times*, September 14, 2008.

Sorkin, Andrew Ross, *Too Big to Fail*, New York: Viking, 2009.

Sorkin, Andrew Ross, "What Really Killed Bear Stearns?" *New York Times*, June 30, 2008.

Spector, Mike, Susanne Craig, and Peter Lattman, "Examiner, Lehman Torpedoed Lehman," *Wall Street Journal*, March 11, 2010.

Standard & Poor's, "The Basics of Credit Enhancement in Securitizations," June 24, 2008.

Stern, Gary H. and Ron J. Feldman, *Too Big to Fail: The Hazards of Bank Bailouts*, Washington, DC: Brookings Institution Press, 2004.

Stolper, Anno, "Regulation of Credit Rating Agencies," *Journal of Banking and Finance*, 2009, 33: 1266–1273.

Story, Louise "Stunning Fall for Main Street's Brokerage Firm," *New York Times*, September 15, 2008.

Story, Louise, and Ben White, "The Road to Lehman's Failure Was Littered with Lost Chances," *New York Times*, October 6, 2008.

Story, Louise, and Jo Becker, "Bank Chief Tells of U.S. Pressure to Buy Merrill Lynch," *New York Times*, June 12, 2009.

Stout, David, "Officials Meet to Chart Course Through Credit Crisis," *New York Times*, September 19, 2008.

Streitfeld, David, and Gretchen Morgenson, "Building Flawed American Dreams," *New York Times*, October 19, 2008.

Strier, Franklin, "Rating the Raters: Conflicts of Interest in the Credit Rating Firms," *Business and Society Review*, 2008, 113(4): 533–553.

Stulz, René M., "Credit Default Swaps and the Credit Crisis," *Journal of Economic Perspectives*, Winter 2010, 24(1): 73–92.

Swan, Peter L., "The Political Economy of the Subprime Crisis: Why Subprime Was So Attractive to Its Creators," December 2008, Working Paper.

Taibbi, Matt, "The Great American Bubble Machine," *Rolling Stone*, July 13, 2009.

Taleb, Nassim Nicholas, *The Black Swan: The Impact of the Highly Improbable*, New York: Random House, 2007.

Tarr, David G., "The Political, Regulatory and Market Failures that Caused the U.S. Financial Crisis: What Are The Lessons?" Working paper, January 7, 2009.

Taylor, John B., *Getting off Track: How Government Actions and Interventions Caused, Prolonged, and Worsened the Financial Crisis*, Stanford, CA: Hoover Institution Press, 2009.

Taylor, Michael W., and Douglas W. Arner, "Global Regulation for Global Markets?" in Robert W. Kolb (ed.), *Lessons from the Financial Crisis: Causes, Consequences, and Our Economic Future*, Hoboken, NJ: John Wiley & Sons, 2010, chapter 48.

Thaler, Richard, and Cass Sunstein, "Human Frailty Caused this Crisis," *Financial Times*, November 11, 2008.

Thomas, Landon, Jr., "$9.4 Billion Write-Down at Morgan Stanley," *New York Times*, December 20, 2007.

Thomas, Landon, Jr., "Morgan Stanley Chief Grappling With New Risk," *New York Times*, March 11, 2008.

Thomas, Landon, Jr., and Eric Dash, "Seeking Fast Deal, JP Morgan Quintuples Bear Stearns Bid," *New York Times*, March 25, 2008.

Thornton, Daniel, L., "What the Libor-OIS Spread Says," Federal Reserve Bank of St. Louis, *Economic Synopses*, 2008, no. 24.

Todd, Steven, "Credit Default Swaps," in Robert W. Kolb and James A. Overdahl, *Financial Derivatives*, Hoboken, NJ: John Wiley & Sons, 2010, chapter 13, pp. 177–198.

Todd, Steven, "Structured Credit Products," in Robert W. Kolb and James A. Overdahl, *Financial Derivatives*, Hoboken, NJ: John Wiley and Sons, 2009, chapter 14, pp. 199–210.

U. S. Census Bureau, Housing Vacancies and Homeownership, http://www.census.gov/hhes/www/housing/hvs/historic/index.html

U.S. Department of Housing and Urban Development, *Curbing Predatory Home Mortgage Lending*, Office of Policy Development and Research, June 1, 2000.

U.S. Department of Housing and Urban Development, "Homeownership and Its Benefits," Urban Policy Brief, Number 2, August 1995.

U.S. Securities and Exchange Commission, "Definition of Nationally Recognized Statistical Rating Organization," April 19, 2005. Available at: http://www.sec.gov/rules/proposed/33-8570.pdf. Accessed January 31, 2010.

U. S. Securities and Exchange Commission, "Final Rule: Alternative Net Capital Requirements for Broker-Dealers That Are Par of Consolidated Supervised Entities," June 8, 2004. Available at: http://www.sec.gov/rules/final/34-49830.htm. Accessed January 30, 2010.

U. S. Securities and Exchange Commission, *Plaintiff vs. Angelo Mozilo, David Sambol, and Eric Sieracki, Defendants*, "Complaint for Violations of the Federal Securities Laws," June 4, 2009.

U.S. Securities and Exchange Commission, "Report and Recommendation Pursuant to Section 133 of the Emergency Economic Stabilization Act of 2008: Study on Mark-To-Market Accounting," Office of the Chief Accountant, Division of Corporate Finance, December 30, 2008.

U.S. Securities and Exchange Commission, "SEC Office of the Chief Accountant and FASB Staff Clarifications on Fair Value Accounting," 2008-234, September 30, 2008.

U.S. Securities and Exchange Commission, "Summary Report of Issues Identified in the Commission Staff's Examinations of Select Credit Rating Agencies," July 2008.

U.S. Treasury Department, "Fact Sheet: Administration's Regulatory Reform Agenda Moves Forward: Say-On-Pay," July 16, 2009. Available at: http://www.ustreas.gov/press/releases/tg219.htm. Accessed: April 4, 2010.

U.S. Treasury Department, "TARP Capital Purchase Program, Senior Preferred Stocks and Warrants." Available at: http://www.ustreas.gov/press/releases/reports/document5hp1207.pdf.

Utt, Ronald D., "The Subprime Mortgage Market Collapse: A Primer on the Causes and Possible Solutions," *The Heritage Foundation Backgrounder* 2127, April 2008: 1–22.

Wall Street Journal, "AIG and Systemic Risk," November 23, 2009.

Wall Street Journal, "Bernanke Goes Off Script to Address Fire-Sale Risks," September 23, 2008.

Wall Street Journal, "Black Holes of Value at Lehman Brothers," September 12, 2008.

Wall Street Journal, "Congress Grills Lehman Brothers' Dick Fuld: Highlights of the Hearing," October 6, 2008.

Wall Street Journal, "Evening Reading: Did Paulson Err by Letting Lehman Fail?," October 23, 2008.

Wall Street Journal, "Fannie Mae's Patron Saint," September 9, 2008.

Wall Street Journal, "From General Store to Titan: A Brief History of Lehman," September 1, 2008.

Wall Street Journal, "Goldman Sachs, Morgan Stanley To Be Bank Holding Companies," September 21, 2008.

Wall Street Journal, "Lehman Brothers, Loved and Left—Again," September 9, 2008.

Wall Street Journal, "Wachovia-Golden West: Another Deal from Hell?" July 22, 2008. Available at: http://blogs.wsj.com/deals/2008/07/22/wachovia-golden-west-another-deal-from-hell/. Accessed on July 4, 2009.

Wallison, Peter J., "Cause and Effect: Government Policies and the Financial Crisis," *Financial Services Outlook*, American Enterprise Institute for Public Policy Research, November 2008.

Wallison, Peter J., "Fannie and Freddie by Twilight," *Financial Services Outlook*, American Enterprise Institute for Public Policy Research, August 2008.

Wallison, Peter J., *Serving Two Masters, Yet Out of Control: Fannie Mae and Freddie Mac*, Washington, DC: American Enterprise Institute for Public Policy Research, 2001.

Wallison, Peter J., and Charles W. Calomiris, "The Last Trillion-Dollar Commitment: The Destruction of Fannie Mae and Freddie Mac," *Financial Services Outlook*, American Enterprise Institute for Public Policy Research, September 2008.

Walsh, Mary Williams, Edmund L. Andrews, and Jackie Calmes, "A.I.G. Lists Firms to Which It Paid Taxpayer Money," *New York Times*, March 16, 2009.

Washington, Mutual, Inc., "WaMu is Becoming Chase, History." Available at https://www.wamu.com/about/corporateprofile/history/default.asp. Accessed July 3, 2009.

Weil, Jonathan, "Citigroup SIV Accounting Looks Tough to Defend," Bloomberg, October 24, 2007. Available at: http://www.bloomberg.com/apps/news?pid=20670001&sid=a6dgIOAfMIrI. Accessed February 26, 2010.

White, Ben, Eric Dash, and Andrew Ross Sorkin, "As Fear Grows, Wall St. Titans See Shares Fall," *New York Times*, September 18, 2008.

White, Lawrence H., "How Did We Get Into This Financial Mess?" *Briefing Papers*, Cato Institute, no. 110, November 18, 2008.

Whitehouse, Mark, "How a Formula Ignited Market That Burned Some Big Investors," *Wall Street Journal*, September 12, 2005.

Wighton, David, "Merrill Lynch Shrugs Off Subprime Woes," *Financial Times*, July 17, 2007.

Woodwell, James R., "The Perfect Calm," *Mortgage Banking*, January 2007.

Zakaria, Fareed, *The Post-American World*, New York: W. W. Norton, 2008.

Zandi, Mark, *Financial Shock: A 360° Look at the Subprime Mortgage Implosion and How to Avoid the Next Financial Crisis*, Upper Saddle River, NJ: FT Press, 2009.

Zywicki, Todd J., and Joseph D. Adamson, "The Law and Economics of Subprime Lending," George Mason University Law and Economics Research Paper Series, 08–17, 2008.

Commodity Futures Trading
Commission, 160
Community Reinvestment Act
(CRA), 150–51, 336–37,
338n.24
compensation
equity-based, 247
executive, 239–41, 249–50,
284–86
executive stock option (ESO),
241, 246–48
Fannie Mae, 250–53
financial firms, 241–49
risk taking and, 249–50, 284–86
shareholders, 247
Washington Mutual Bank
(WaMu), 81
competition, savings and loan
association (S&Ls), 12–13
Comptroller of State of New York,
bonuses, 242
concentration of risk, restrictions
on, 169–70
conforming mortgages, 22, 110,
290
Congressional Budget Office
(CBO), 322n.2
analysis of budget proposal, 271
Fannie Mae and Freddie Mac,
111
government-sponsored entity
(GSE), 21
unemployment rate, 140
Congressional Research Service,
143
Consumer Price Index, 242
Cooper, Keysha, Washington
Mutual Bank (WaMu), 80
corporate governance
compensation and risk-taking,
284–86
financial crisis, 257–59, 277,
354n.29

financial firms, 240
stockholder vs. stakeholder,
285, 355–56n.13
Corrigan, Gerald, 229–30
Corzine, Jon, 103
cost assessment, financial crisis,
140–42
counterparty, 92, 290
Countrywide Financial
Corporation, 67, 74, 164, 170
Bank of America, 63, 167, 168
CEO Mozilo, 256–57
crisis response, 184–85
crisis timeline, 302–3
difficulties, 71
executive compensation, 241,
244
financial statements,
326–27n.5
loans, 206
mortgage operation, 43, 204–7
mortgage originator, 221
subprime crisis, 75–77
"too big to fail," 84–85
underwriting methodology,
43–44
Cox, Christopher, Securities and
Exchange Commission, 95,
129, 172
Cramer, Jim, 103
credit default swap (CDS),
333n.21, 350n.10, 350n.9
AIG, 117–20, 166
definition, 290
Depository Trust and Clearing
Corporation (DTCC),
349–50n.8
financial instrument, 227,
229–32
securitizer, 35, 226
credit derivatives
capital regulation and, 166
definition, 291